KU-689-668

THE HISTORY OF
THE RUSSIAN
REVOLUTION

"Represents an astonishing combination of dramatic narrative and searching analysis. The union of man and action of literary stylist, as well perhaps as a certain flamboyance of temperament and cocksureness in prediction, suggest the comparison with Winston Churchill . . . It is good to have this historical classic once more in print in its English dress."—*Times Literary Supplement.*

"The problem of writing about events of one's own lifetime stands by itself. It was brilliantly solved by Trotsky in his *History of the Russian Revolution* . . . It's a splendid book; the best first-hand evidence we shall ever get."—Kingsley Martin—*New Statesman.*

"I choose Leon Trotsky's *History of the Russian Revolution* as my book of the year . . . It has a Churchillian grandeur, being the work of a master who not only made history himself but could interpret it as it unfolded in universal terms. Like Churchill, Trotsky was a military strategist as well as a politician. Perhaps it was this that enabled him to express the Marxist dialectic in human language. Evil has never been so dazzlingly presented." —*Sunday Telegraph.*

A hard-cover edition of this book complete in one volume
is available from Victor Gollancz Ltd., London, W.C.2

Also by Leon Trotsky and available in Sphere Books

VOLUMES ONE AND TWO

The History of the Russian Revolution by Leon Trotsky

VOLUME THREE

Translated from the Russian
by Max Eastman

SPHERE BOOKS LIMITED LONDON

First published in England in three volumes 1932-33,
by Victor Gollancz Ltd., London, W.C.2
First published in England in single volume edition
1934, by Victor Gollancz Ltd., London, W.C.2
Reissued 1965
Second impression October 1965
First Sphere Books edition in three volumes 1967

A hard-cover edition of this book complete in one
volume is available from Victor Gollancz Ltd.,
London, W.C.2

Canadian agent:	Thomas Nelson and Sons (Canada) Limited, 81 Curlew Drive, Don Mills, Ontario.
Australian agent:	Thomas Nelson (Australia) Ltd, 597 Little Collins Street, Melbourne, Australia.
New Zealand agent:	Hodder & Stoughton Limited, 52 Cook Street, Auckland C.1, New Zealand.
South African agent:	Thomas Nelson & Sons (South Africa) (Pty) Ltd, Lewis and Marks Building, 65 President Street, Johannesburg, South Africa.
East African agent:	Thomas Nelson & Sons Ltd, P.O. Box 25012, Nairobi, Kenya.
West African agent:	Thomas Nelson & Sons Ltd, P.O. Box 336, Apapa, Nigeria.
Israel agent:	Steimatzky's Agency Ltd, Citrus House, P.O. Box 628, Tel-Aviv, Israel.

TRADE MARK

Printed in Great Britain by
Hazell Watson & Viney Ltd
Aylesbury, Bucks

VOL III

THE TRIUMPH OF THE SOVIETS

CONTENTS

Chapter I

The Peasantry Before October

Civilisation has made the peasantry its pack animal. The bourgeoisie in the long run only changed the form of the pack. Barely tolerated on the threshold of the national life, the peasant stands essentially outside the threshold of science. The historian is ordinarily as little interested in him as the dramatic critic is in those grey figures who shift the scenery, carrying the heavens and earth on their backs, and scrub the dressing-rooms of the actors. The part played by the peasantry in past revolutions remains hardly cleared up to this day.

"The French bourgeoisie began by liberating the peasantry," wrote Marx in 1848. "With the help of the peasantry they conquered Europe. The Prussian bourgeoisie was so blinded by its own narrow and close-by interests that it lost even this ally, and turned it into a weapon in the hands of the feudal counter-revolution." In this contrast what relates to the German bourgeoisie is true; but the assertion that "the French bourgeoisie began by liberating the peasantry" is an echo of that official French legend which exercised an influence in its day even upon Marx. In reality the bourgeoisie, in the proper sense of the term, opposed the peasant revolution with all the power it had. Even from the rural instructions of 1789 the local readers of the Third Estate threw out, under the guise of editing, the keenest and most bold demands. The famous decision of August 4, adopted by the National Assembly amid the glow of rural conflagrations, long remained a pathetic formula without content. The peasants who would not reconcile themselves to this deceit were adjured by the Constituent Assembly to "return to the fulfilment of their duties and have the proper respect for [feudal!] property." The civil guard tried more than once to put down the peasantry in the country. But the city workers, taking the side of those in revolt, met the bourgeois punitive expeditions with stones and broken tile.

Throughout five years the French peasantry rose at every critical moment of the revolution, preventing a deal between the feudal and bourgeois property-holders. The Parisian Sans-culottes, pouring out their blood for the republic, liberated the peasant from his feudal chains. The French republic of 1792 marked a new social régime—in contradistinction to the German republic of 1918, or the Spanish republic of 1931, which mean only the old régime minus the dynasty. At the bottom of this difference it is not hard to find the agrarian question.

The French peasant did not think directly of a republic: he wanted to throw off the landlord. The Parisian republicans ordinarily forgot all about the country. But it was only the peasant pressure upon the landlord which guaranteed the creation of a republic, clearing the feudal rubbish out of its road. A republic with a nobility is not a republic. This was excellently understood by the old man Machiavelli, who in his Florentine exile 400 years before the presidency of Ebert, between hunting thrushes and playing at tric-trac with the butcher, generalised the experience of democratic revolutions. "Whoever wants to found a republic in a country where there are many nobles, can only do this if to begin with he exterminates them all. The Russian Muzhiks were essentially of the same opinion, and they revealed this openly without any "Machiavellianism."

While Petrograd and Moscow played the main rôle in the movement of the workers and soldiers, the first place in the peasant movement must be accorded to the backward Great Russian agricultural centre, and the middle region of the Volga. Here the relics of serfdom had especially deep roots; the nobles' proprietorship in the land was most parasitic in character; the differentiation of the peasantry was far behind and the poverty of the village thus more nakedly revealed. Bursting out in this region as early as March, the movement had been immediately adorned with acts of terror. Through the efforts of the dominant parties it was soon switched, however, into the channel of compromise politics.

In the industrially backward Ukraine, agriculture, carried on for export, had acquired a far more progressive and consequently more capitalistic character. Here the stratification of the peasantry had gone considerably farther than in Great Russia. The struggle for national liberation moreover inevitably delayed, at least for the time being, other forms of social struggle. But the variation in regional, and even national, conditions expressed itself in the long run only in a difference of dates. By autumn the territory of the peasant struggle had become almost the whole country. Out of the 624 counties constituting old Russia, 482, or 77 per cent., were involved in the movement. And omitting the borderlands, distinguished by special agrarian conditions—the northern district, the Transcaucasus, the region of the steppes, and Siberia—out of 481 counties, 439, or 91 per cent., were drawn into the peasant revolt.

The methods of struggle differ according to whether it is a question of ploughed land, forest, pasture, of rentals or of hired labour. The struggle changed its forms and methods, too, at various stages of the revolution. But in general the movement of the villages passed, with inevitable delay, through the same two great stages as the movement of the cities. In the first stage the peasants were still accommodating themselves to the new régime, and trying to solve their problems by means of the new institutions. Even here, however, it was more a matter of form than substance. The Moscow liberal newspaper—tinted before the revolution with a Narodnik hue—expressed with admirable directness the state of mind of the landlord circles in the summer of 1917. "The muzhik is glancing round, he is not doing anything yet, but look in his eyes—his eyes will tell you that all the land lying around him is his land." A perfect key to this "peaceful" policy of the peasantry, is a telegram sent in April by one of the Tombov villages to the Provisional Government: "We desire to keep the peace in the interests of the freedom won. But for this reason, forbid the sale of the landlords' land until the Constituent Assembly. Otherwise we will shed blood, but we will not let anyone else plough the land."

The muzhik found it easy to maintain a tone of respectful threat, because in bringing his pressure to bear against historic rights, he hardly had to come into direct conflict with the state at all. Organs of the governmental power were lacking in the localities. The village committees controlled the militia, the courts were disorganised, the local commissars were powerless. "We elected you," the peasants would shout at them, "and we will kick you out."

During the summer the peasants, developing the struggle of the preceding months, came nearer and nearer to civil war, and their left wing even stepped over its threshold. According to a report of the landed proprietors of the Taganrog district, the peasants on their own initiative seized the hay crop, took possession of the land, hindered the ploughing, named arbitrary rental prices, and removed proprietors and overseers. According to a report of the Nizhegorod commissar, violent activities and seizures of land and forest in his province were multiplying. The county commissars were afraid of seeming to the peasants like defenders of the big landlords. The rural militia were not to be relied on. "There have been cases when officers of the militia took part in violence together with the mob." In Schlüsselburg county a local committee prevented the landlords from cutting their own forest. The thought of the peasants was simple: No Constituent Assembly can resurrect the trees that are cut down. The commissar of the Ministry of the Court complains of the seizure of hay: We have had to buy hay for the court horses! In Kursk province the peasants divided among themselves the fertilised fallow land of Tereshchenko. The proprietor was Minister of Foreign Affairs. The peasants declared to Schneider, a horse breeder of Orlov province, that they would not only cut the clover on his estate, but him too they might "send into the army." The village committee directed the overseer of Rodzianko's estate to surrender the hay to the peasants: 'If you don't listen to this land committee, you'll get treated differently, you'll get arrested. . . ." Signed and sealed.

From all corners of the country complaints and wails poured in—from victims, from local authorities, from noble-minded observers. The telegrams of the landowners constitute a most brilliant refutation of the crude theory of class struggle. These titled nobles, lords of the latifundia, spiritual and temporal rulers, are worrying exclusively about the public weal. Their enemy is not the peasants, but the Bolsheviks—sometimes the anarchists. Their own property engages the landlord's interest solely from the point of view of the welfare of the fatherland. 300 members of the Kadet Party in Chernigov province declare that the peasants, incited by Bolsheviks, are removing the war prisoners from work and themselves independently reaping the harvest. As a result, they cry, we are threatened with "inability to pay the taxes." The very meaning of existence for these liberal landlords lay in supporting the national treasury! The Podolsk branch of the State Bank complains of the arbitrary actions of village committees, "whose presidents are often Austrian prisoners." Here it is injured patriotism that speaks. In Vladimir province, in the manor of a registrar of deeds, Odintsov, the peasants took away building materials that had been "made ready for philanthropic institutions." Public officials live only for the love of mankind! A bishop from Podolsk reports the arbitrary seizure of a forest belonging to the house of the Archbishop. The procurator complains of the seizure of meadowlands from the Alexandro-Nevsky Monastery. The Mother Superior of the Kizliarsk Convent calls down thunder and lightning upon the members of the local committee. They are interfering in the affairs of the convent, confiscating rentals for their own use, "inciting the nuns against their superiors." In all these cases the spiritual needs of the church are directly affected. Count Tolstoi, one of the sons of Leo Tolstoi, reports in the name of the League of Agriculturists of Ufimsk province that the transfer of land to the local committees "without waiting for a decision of the Constituent Assembly . . . is causing an outburst of dissatisfaction . . . among the peasant proprietors, of whom there are more than 200,000 in the province" The hereditary lord is troubled exclusively about his lesser brothers. Senator Belgardt, a proprietor of Tver province, is ready to reconcile himself to cuttings in the forest, but is grieved and offended that the peasants "will not submit to the bourgeois government." A Tombov landlord, Veliaminop, demands the rescue of two estates which "are serving the needs of the army." By accident these two estates happened to belong to him. For the philosophy of idealism these landlord telegrams of 1917 are verily a treasure. A materialist will rather see in them a display of the various models of cynicism. He will add perhaps that great revolutions deprive the property-holders even of the privilege of dignified hypocrisy.

The appeals of the victims to the county and provincial authorities, to the Minister of the Interior, to the President of the Council of Ministers, brought as a general rule no result. From whom then shall we ask aid? From Rodzianko, president of the State Duma! Between the July Days and the Kornilov insurrection. the Lord Chamberlain again felt himself an influential figure: much was done at a ring from his telephone.

The functionaries of the Ministry of the Interior send out circulars to the localities about bringing the guilty to trial. The brusque landlords of Samara telegraph in answer: "Circulars without the signature of the socialist minister have no force." The function of socialism is thus revealed. Tseretelli is compelled to overcome his bashfulness. On the 18th of July he sends out a wordy instruction about taking "swift and decisive measures." Like the landlords themselves, Tseretelli worries solely about the army and the state. It seems to the peasants, however, that Tseretelli is protecting the landlords.

There came a sudden change in the government's method of

pacifying the peasants. Up to July the prevailing method had been talking them out of it. If military detachments were also sent into the localities, it was only in the capacity of a guard for the government orator. After the victory over the Petrograd workers and soldiers, however, cavalry troops—now without vocal persuaders—put themselves directly at the disposal of the landlords. In Kazan province, one of the most tumultuous, they succeeded—to quote the young historian, Yugov—"only by means of arrests, by bringing armed troops into the villages, and even by reviving the custom of flogging . . . in reducing the peasants to submission." In other places, too, these measures of repression were not without effect. The number of damaged landlord properties fell somewhat in July: from 516 to 503. In August the government achieved still further successes: the number of unsatisfactory counties fell from 325 to 288—that is, 11 per cent; the number of properties involved in the movement was even reduced 33 per cent.

Certain districts, heretofore the most restless, now quiet down or retire to second place. On the other hand, districts which were reliable yesterday now come into the struggle. Only a month ago the Penza commissar was painting a consoling picture: "The country is busy reaping the harvest. . . . Preparations are under way for the elections to the village zemstvos. The period of governmental crisis passed quietly. The formation of the new government was greeted with great satisfaction." In August there is not a trace left of this idyll. "Mass depredations upon orchards and the cutting down of forests. . . . To quell the disorders, we have had to resort to armed force."

In its general character the summer movement still belongs to the "peaceful" period. However, unmistakable, although indeed weak, symptoms of radicalisation are already to be observed. Whereas in the first four months cases of direct attack upon the landlords' manors decreased, from July on they begin to increase. Investigators have established in general the following classification of the July conflicts, arranged in a diminishing order starting with the most numerous: Seizure of meadows, of crops, of food-stuffs and fodder, of ploughed fields, of implements; conflict over the conditions of employment; destruction of manors. In August the order is as follows: Seizure of crops, of reserve provisions and fodder, of meadows and hay, of land and forest; agrarian terror.

At the beginning of September Kerensky, in his capacity of

commander-in-chief, issued a special order repeating the recent arguments and threats of his predecessor, Kornilov, against "violent activities" on the part of the peasants. A few days later Lenin wrote: "Either . . . all the land to the peasants immediately . . . or the landlords and capitalists . . . will bring things to the point of an endlessly ferocious peasant revolt." During the months following this became a fact.

The number of properties affected by agrarian conflicts in September rose 30 per cent. over that in August; in October, 43 per cent. over that in September. In September and the first three weeks of October there occurred over a third as many agrarian conflicts as all those recorded since March. Their resoluteness rose, however, incomparably faster than their number. During the first months even direct seizures of various appurtenances wore the aspect of bargains mitigated and camouflaged by the compromisist institutions. Now the legal mask falls away. Every branch of the movement assumes a more audacious character. From various forms and degrees of pressure, the peasants are now passing over to violent seizures of the various parts of the landlord's business, to the extermination of the nests of the gentility, the burning of manors, even the murder of proprietors and overseers.

The struggle for a change in the conditions of rent, which in June exceeded in number of cases the destructive movement, falls in October to $\frac{1}{40}$ the number. Moreover the rent movement itself changes its character, becoming merely another way of driving out the landlord. The veto on buying and selling land and forest gives place to direct seizure. The mass wood-cuttings and mass grazings acquire the character of a deliberate destruction of the landlord's goods. In September 279 cases of open destruction of property are recorded; they now constitute more than one eighth of all the conflicts. Over 42 per cent. of all the cases of destruction recorded by the militia between the February and the October revolution occurred in the month of October.

The struggle for the forests was especially bitter. Whole villages were frequently burned to the ground. The timber was strongly guarded and selling at a high price; the muzhik was starving for timber; moreover the time had come to lay up firewood for the winter. Complaints came in from Moscow, Nizhegorod, Petrograd, Orel, and Volyn provinces—from all corners of the country—about the destruction of forests and the seizure of the reserves of corded wood. "The peasants are arbitrarily and ruthlessly cutting down the forest. Two hundred dessiatins of the landlard's forest have been burned by the peasants." "The peasants of Klimovichevsky and Cherikovsky counties are destroying the forests and laying waste the winter-wheat. . . ." The forests guards are in flight; the landlord's forests are groaning; the chips are flying throughout the whole country. All that autumn the muzhik's axe was feverishly beating time for the revolution.

In the districts which imported grain the food situation in the villages deteriorated at a faster pace than in the city. Not only food was lacking, but seed. In the exporting regions, in consequence of a redoubled pumping out of food resources, the situation was but little better. The raising of the fixed price of grain hit the poor. In a number of provinces there occurred hunger riots, plundering of granaries, assaults on the institutions of the Food Administration. The population resorted to substitutes for bread. Reports came in of cases of scurvy and typhus, of suicides from despair. Hunger and its advancing shadow made the neighbourhood of opulence and luxury especially intolerable. The more destitute strata of the villages moved into the front ranks of the fight.

These waves of bitter feeling raised up no little slime from the bottom. In Kostroma province "a Black Hundred and anti-Jew agitation is observed. Criminality is on the increase. . . . A waning of interest in the political life of the country is noticeable." This latter phrase in the report of the commissar means: The educated classes are turning their back on the revolution. The voice of Black Hundred monarchism suddenly rings out from Podolsk province: The committee of the village of Demidovka does not recognise the Provisional Government and considers the Czar Nikolai Alexandrovich "the most loyal leader of the Russian people. If the Provisional Government does not retire, we will join the Germans." Such bold acknowledgments, however, are unique. The monarchists among the peasants have long ago changed colour, following the example of the landlords. In places—for instance, in that same Podolsk province—military detachments in company with the peasants invade the wine cellars. The commissar reports anarchy. "The villages and the people are perishing; the revolution is perishing." No, the revolution is far from perishing. It is digging itself a deeper channel The raging waters are nearing their mouth.

On a night about the 8th of September, the peasants of the village Sychevka in Tombov province, going from door to door armed with clubs and pitchforks, called out everybody, small and great, to raid the landlord, Romanov. At a village meeting one group proposed that they take the estate in an orderly fashion, divide the property among the population, and keep the buildings for cultural purposes. The poor demanded that they burn the estate, leaving not one stone upon another. The poor were in the majority. On that same night an ocean of fire swallowed up the estates of the whole township. Everything inflammable was burned, even the experimental fields. The breeding cattle were slaughtered. "They were drunk to madness." The flames jumped over from township to township. The rustic warriors were now no longer content with the patriarchal scythe and pitchfork. A provincial commissar telegraphed: "Peasants and unknown persons armed with revolvers and hand grenades are raiding the manors in Ranenburg ad Riazhsky counties." It was the war that introduced this high technique into the peasant revolt. The League of Landowners reported that 24 estates were burned in three days. "The local authorities were powerless to restore order." After some delay troops arrived, sent by the district commander. Martial law was declared, meetings forbidden, the instigators arrested. Ravines were filled with the landlord's possession and much of the booty was sunk in the river.

A Penza peasant, Begishev, relates: "In September all rode out to raid Logvin (he was raided in 1905, too). A troop of teams and wagons streamed out to his estate and back, hundreds of muzhiks and wenches began to drive and carry off his cattle, grain, etc." A detachment called out by the land administration tried to get back some of the booty, but the muzhiks and wenches assembled 500 strong in the village, and the detachment dispersed. The soldiers were evidently not at all eager to restore the trampled rights of the landlord. In Tauride province, beginning with the last seven days of September, according to the recollections of the peasant, Gaponenko, "the peasants began to raid the buildings, drive out the overseers, take the work animals, the machinery, the grain from the granaries. . . . They even tore off the blinds from the windows, the doors from their frames, the floors from the rooms, and the zinc roofs, and carried them away. . . ." "At first they only came on foot, took what they could and lugged it off," relates Grunko, a peasant from Minsk, "but afterwards they hitched up the horses, whoever had any, and carried things away in whole wagon-loads. There was no room to pass. They just dragged and carried things off, beginning at twelve o'clock noon, for two days and two nights without a stop. In those forty-eight hours they cleaned out everything." The seizure of property, according to a Moscow peasant, Kuzmichev, was justified as follows: "The landlord was ours, we worked for him, and the property he had ought to belong to us alone." Once upon a time the landlords used to say to the serfs: "You are mine and what is yours is mine." Now the peasants were giving their answer: "He was our lord and all his goods are ours."

"In several localities they began to knock up the landlords in the night," remembers another Minsk peasant, Novikov. "Oftener and oftener they would burn the landlord's manor." It came the turn of the estate of the Grand Duke Nikolai Nikolaivich, former commander-in-chief. "When they had taken away all they could get, they began breaking up the stoves, removing the flue-plates, ripping up the floors and planks, and dragging it all home. . . ."

Behind these destructive activities stood the century-old, thousand-year-old strategy of all peasant wars: to raze to the ground the fortified position of the enemy. Leave him no place to cover his head. "The more reasonable ones," remembers a Kursk peasant, Tzygankov, "would say 'We must not burn up the buildings—they will be of use to us for schools and hospitals,' but the majority were the kind that shout out 'We must destroy everything so that in case anything happens our enemy will have no place to hide.'" "The peasants seized all the landlords' property," relates an Orel peasant, Savchenko, "drove the landlords out of the estates, smashed the windows, doors, ceilings and floors of the landlords' houses. . . . The soldiers said 'If you destroy the wolves' nests, you must strangle the wolves too.' Through such threats the biggest and most important landlords hid out, and for that reason there was no murder of landlords."

In the village of Zalessye, in Vitebsk province, they burned barns full of grain and hay in the estate belonging to a Frenchman, Barnard, The muzhiks were the less inclined to investigate questions of nationality, since many of the landlords had transferred their land in a hurry to privileged foreigners. "The French embassy requests that measures be taken. . . ." In the front region in the middle of October it was difficult to take "measures," even in behalf of the French embassy.

The destruction of the great estates near Riazan continued

four days. "Even children took part in the looting." The League of Landed Proprietors brought to the attention of the ministers that if measures were not taken "lynch-law, famine and civil war would break out." It is difficult to understand why the landlords were still speaking of civil war in the future tense. At a congress of the Co-operatives at the beginning of September, Berkenheim, one of the leaders of the strong trading peasantry, said: "I am convinced that not yet all Russia has become a madhouse, that as yet for the most part only the population of the big cities has gone mad." This self-complacent voice of the solid and conservative part of the peasantry was hopelessly behind the times. It was during that very month that the villages totally broke loose from all the nooses of reason, and the ferocity of their struggle left the "madhouse" of the cities far behind.

In April Lenin had still considered it possible that the patriotic Co-operators and the kulaks would drag the main mass of the peasantry after them along the road of compromise with the bourgeoisie and the landlord. For this reason he so tirelessly insisted upon the creation of special soviets of farm hands' deputies, and upon independent organisations of the poorest peasantry. Month by month it became clear, however, that this part of the Bolshevik policy would not take root. Except in the Baltic state there were no soviets of farm hands. The peasant poor also failed to find independent forms of organisation. To explain this merely by the backwardness of the farm hands and the poorest strata of the villages, would be to miss the essence of the thing. The chief cause lay in the substance of the historic task itself—a democratic agrarian revolution.

Upon the two principal questions, rent and hired labour, it becomes convincingly clear how the general interests of a struggle against the relics of serfdom cut off the road to an independent policy not only for the poor peasants, but for the hired hands. The peasants rented from the landlords in European Russia 27 million dessiatins—about 60 per cent. of all the privately owned land—and they paid a yearly rental tribute of 400 million roubles. The struggle against peonage conditions of rent became after the February revolution the chief element of the peasant movement. A smaller, but still very important, place was occupied by the struggle of the rural wage-workers, which brought them in opposition not only to the landlord, but also to the peasant exploiters. The tenant was struggling for an alleviation of the conditions of rent, the worker for an improvement in the conditions of labour. Both of them, each in his own way, started out by recognising the landlord as property-holder and boss. But as soon as the possibility opened of carrying the thing through to the end—that is, of taking the land and occupying it themselves—the poor peasants ceased to be interested in questions of rent, and the trade union began to lose its attraction for the hired hand. It was these rural workers and poor tenants who by joining the general movement gave its ultimate determination to the peasant war and made it irrevocable.

But the campaign against the landlord did not draw in quite so completely the opposite pole of the village. So long as it did not come to open revolt, the upper circles of the peasantry played a prominent rôle in the movement, at times a leading rôle. In the autumn period, however, the well-to-do muzhiks looked with continually increasing distrust at the spread of the peasant war. They did not know how this would end; they had something to lose; they stood aside. But they did not succeed in holding off entirely: the village would not permit it.

More reserved and hostile than "our own" communal kulaks, were the small landowners standing outside the commune. In the whole country there were 600,000 homesteads of peasants owning plots up to 50 dessiatins. In many localities they constituted the backbone of the Co-operatives, and gravitated, especially in the south, towards the conservative Peasant Union which had already become a bridge towards the Kadets. "The Secessionists[1] and rich peasants," according to Gullis, a Minsk peasant, "supported the landlords and tried to appease the peasantry with arguments." In some places, under the influence of local conditions, the strugle within the peasantry assumed a furious character even before the October revolution. The Secessionists suffered most cruelly in this struggle. "Almost all their farm buildings were burnt," says Kuzmichev, a Nizhegorod peasant. "Their property was partly annihilated and partly seized by the peasants." The Secessionist was "the landlord's servant entrusted with several of the landlord's forest tracts; he was a favourite of the police, the gendarmerie and the rulers." The richest peasants and merchants of several villages of Nizhegorod county disappeared in the autumn and returned to their neighbourhoods only after two or three years.

1. Peasants who had left the commune and taken private land under Stolypin's law of November 9, 1906. [Trans.]

But in most sections of the country the inner relations among the peasantry were far from reaching such bitterness. The kulaks conducted themselves diplomatically, put on the breaks and resisted, but tried not to set themselves too sharply against the "mir."[1] The rank-and-file villager, on his part, jealously watched the kulaks and would not let them unite with the landlords. The struggle between the nobles and the peasantry for influence upon the kulak continued throughout the whole year 1917 in various different forms, from "friendly" pressure to ferocious terrorism.

While the lords of the latifundia were ingratiatingly throwing open to the peasant proprietors the main entrances to the assemblies of the nobility, the small landowners were demonstratively drawing apart from the nobility in order not to perish with them. In politics this found expression in the fact that the landlords, who had belonged before the revolution to the extreme right party, redecorated themselves now in the tints of liberalism, adopting them from memory as a protective colouration, whereas the peasant proprietors, who had often supported the Kadets in the past, now shifted to the left.

A congress of petty proprietors of Perm province, held in September, emphatically distinguished itself from the Moscow Congress of Landed Proprietors at the head of whom stood "counts, dukes and barons." An owner of 50 dessiatins said: "The Kadets never wore *armyaki and lapti*[2] and therefore will never defend our interests." Pushing away from the liberals, the labouring proprietor would look around for such "socialists" as would stand for property rights. One of the delegates came out for the social democracy. "The worker?" he said. "Give him land and he will come to the village and stop spitting blood. The social democrats will not take the land away from us." He was speaking, of course of the Mensheviks. "We will not give away our land to anybody. Those will easily part with it who easily got it, as for example, the landlord, but the peasant had a hard time getting the land."

In that autumn period the villages were struggling with the kulaks, not throwing them off, but compelling them to adhere to the general movement and defend it against blows from the right. There were even cases where a refusal to participate in

1. This word, applied to the village as a commune, literally means "the world"—that is, everybody. [Trans.]

2. *Armyak* is a home-made woollen coat, *lapti* are shoes made out of woven strips of bark. [Trans.]

a raid was punished by the death of the culprit. The kulak manœuvred while he could, but at the last moment, scratching the back of his head once more, hitched the well-fed horses to the iron-rimmed wagon and went out for his share. It was often the lion's share. "The well-to-do got the most out of it," says the Penza peasant, Begishev, "those who had horses and free men." Savchenko from Orel expressed himself in almost the same words: "The kulaks mostly got the best of it, being well-fed and with something to draw the wood in."

According to the calculations of Vermenichev, to 4,954 agrarian conflicts with landlords between February and October, there were 324 conflicts with the peasant bourgeoisie. An extraordinarily clear correlation! It alone firmly establishes the fact that the peasant movement of 1917 was directed in its social foundations not against capitalism, but against the relics of serfdom. The struggle against kulakism developed only later, in 1918, after the conclusive liquidation of the landlord.

This purely democratic character of the peasant movement, which should, it would seem, have given the official democracy an unconquerable power, did in fact completely reveal its rottenness. If you look at the thing from above, the peasants were wholly led by the Social Revolutionaries, elected them, followed them, almost blended with them. At the May congress of peasant soviets, in the elections to the executive committee, Chernov received 810 votes, Kerensky 804, whereas Lenin got only 20 votes all in all. It was not for nothing that Chernov dubbed himself Rural Minister! But it was not for nothing, either, that the strategy of the villages brusquely parted company with Chernov's strategy. Their industrial isolation makes the peasants, so determined in struggle with a concrete landlord, impotent before the general landlord incarnate in the state. Hence the organic need of the muzhiks to rely upon some legendary state as against the real one. In olden times they created pretenders, they united round an imagined Golden Edict of the czar, or around the legend of a righteous world. After the February revolution they united round the Social Revolutionary banner "Land and Freedom," seeking help in it against the liberal landlord who had become a governmental commissar. The Narodnik programme bore the same relation to the real government of Kerensky, as the imagined edict of the czar to the real autocrat.

In the programme of the Social Revolutionaries there was

always much that was Utopian. They hoped to create socialism on the basis of a petty trade economy. But the foundation of their programme was democratically revolutionary: to take the land from the landlord. When confronted with the necessity of carrying out its programme, the party got tangled up in a coalition. Not only the landlords rose against the confiscation of the land, but also the Kadet bankers. The banks had loaned against real estate no less than four billion roubles. Intending to dicker with the landlords at the Constituent Assembly regarding prices but end things in a friendly manner, the Social Revolutionaries zealously kept the muzhik away from the land. They went to pieces, therefore, not on the Utopian character of their socialism, but on their democratic inconsistency. It might have taken years to test out their Utopianism. Their betrayal of agrarian democracy became clear in a few months. Under a government of Social Revolutionaries the peasants had to take the road of insurrection in order to carry out the Social Revolutionary programme.

In July, when the government was coming down on the villages with measures of repression, the peasants in hot haste ran for defence to those same Social Revolutionaries. From Pontius the young they appealed for protection to Pilate the old. The month of the greatest weakening of the Bolsheviks in the cities was the month of the greatest expansion of the Social Revolutionaries in the country. As usually happens, especially in a revolutionary epoch, the maximum of organisational scope coincided with the beginning of a political decline. Hiding behind Social Revolutionaries from the blows of a Social Revolutionary government, the peasants steadily lost confidence both in the government and the party. Thus the swelling out of the Social Revolutionary organisations in the villages became fatal to this universal party, which was rebelling at the bottom but restoring order at the top.

In Moscow at a meeting of the Military Organisation on the 30th of July, a delegate from the front, himself a Social Revolutionary, said: Although the peasants still think themselves Social Revolutionaries, a rift has formed between them and the party. The soldiers confirmed this: Under the influence of Social Revolutionary agitation the peasants are still hostile to the Bolsheviks, but in practice they decide the questions of land and power in a Bolshevik manner. The Bolshevik, Povolzhsky, who worked in the Volga region, testifies that the most respected Social Revolutionaries, those who had taken part in the movement of 1905, were more and more feeling themselves pushed aside: "The muzhiks called them 'old men,' treating them with external deference, but voting in their own way." It was the workers and soldiers who had taught the villages to vote and take action "in their own way." It is impossible to weigh the influence of the revolutionary workers upon the peasantry. It was continuous, molecular, penetrating everywhere, and therefore not capable of calculation. A mutual penetration was made easier by the fact that a considerable number of the industrial plants were situated in rural districts. But even the workers of Petrograd, the most European of cities, kept up a close connection with their native villages. Unemployment, increasing during the summer months, and the lockout of the employers, threw back many thousand of workers into the villages. A majority of them became agitators and leaders.

From May to June there were created in Petrograd back-home clubs corresponding to different provinces, counties and even villages. Whole columns in the workers' press were devoted to announcements of back-home club meetings, where reports about journeys to the villages would be heard, instructions drawn up for delegates, and money collected for agitation. Not long before the uprising, these clubs united round a special central bureau under the leadership of the Bolsheviks. This back-home club movement soon spread to Moscow, Tver, and probably to a number of other industrial cities.

However, in the matter of direct influence upon the village the soldiers were still more important. It was only in the artificial conditions of the front or in the city barrack that the young peasants, overcoming to a certain degree their isolation, would come face to face with problems of nation-wide scope. Here too, however, their political dependence made itself felt. While continually falling under the leadership of patriotic and conservative intellectuals and then striving to get free of them, the peasants tried to organise in the army separately from other social groups. The authorities looked unfavourably upon these inclinations, the War Ministry opposed them, the Social Revolutionaries did not welcome them. The soviets of peasants' deputies took but weak root in the army. Even under the most favourable conditions the peasant is unable to convert his overwhelming quantity into a political quality! Only in the big revolutionary centres under the direct influence of the workers did the soviets of peasant soldiers succeed in developing any important work. Thus between April 1917 and January 1, 1918, the peasant soviet in Petrograd sent 1,395 agitators into the villages with special mandates; and about the same number without mandates. These delegates covered 65 provinces. In Kronstadt back-home clubs were formed among the sailors and soldiers, following the example of the workers, and they supplied their delegates with credentials giving them the "right" to free passage on railroads and steamboats. The private lines accepted these papers without a murmur. Conflicts arose on the government lines.

These official delegates of organisations were after all, however, mere drops in the peasant ocean. An infinitely greater work was accomplished by those hundreds of thousands and millions of soldiers who quit the front and the rear garrisons of their own accord with the strong slogans of mass-meeting speeches ringing in their ears. Those who had sat silent at the front became garrulous at home in the villages. They found no lack of greedy listeners. "Among the peasantry surrounding Moscow," says Muralov, one of the Moscow Bolsheviks, "there was a tremendous swing to the left. . . . The villages and towns of Moscow province were swarming with deserters from the front. They were visited also by city proletarians who had not yet cut off their connections with the country." The dreamy and backward villages of Kaluga province, according to the peasant Naumchenkov—"were waked up by soldiers coming home from the front for various reasons during June and July." The Nizhegorod commissar reports that "all the lawbreaking and lawlessness is connected with the appearance within the boundaries of the province of deserters, soldiers on furlough, or delegates from the regimental committees." The overseer of the properties of Princess Bariatinsky of Zolotonoshzky county complains in August of the arbitrary acts of the land committee whose president is a Kronstadt sailor, Gatran. "Soldiers and sailors on furlough," reports the commissar of Bugulminsk county, "are carrying on an agitation with a view to creating anarchy and a pogrom state of mind." "In Mglinsk county, in the village of Bielogosh, an arriving sailor on his own authority forbade the preparation and export of firewood and railroad ties from the forest." And when it was not the soldiers who began the struggle, it was they who finished it. In Nizhegorod county the muzhiks harried a convent, cut the meadow grass, broke down the fences, and bothered the nuns. The mother superior refused to give in, and the militia would carry off the muzhiks and punish them. "So the thing dragged along," writes the peasant Arbekov, "until the soldiers arrived. The buddies immediately took the bull by the horns. . . ." The convent was cleaned out. In Moghiliev province, according to the peasant Bobkov, "the soldiers home from the front were the first leaders in the committee, and directed the expulsion of the landlords."

The men from the front introduced into the business the heavy determination of people accustomed to handle their fellowmen with rifle and bayonet. Even the soldiers' wives caught this fighting mood from their husbands. Says the Penza peasant, Begishev: "In September there was a strong movement of soldiers' wives who spoke at meetings in favour of the raids." The same thing was observed in other provinces. In the cities, too, the soldiers' wives were often the leaven in the lump.

Those cases in which soldiers took the lead in peasant disorders constituted in March, according to Vermenichev's calculations, 1 per cent., in April, 8 per cent., in September, 12 per cent., and in October, 17 per cent. These figures cannot pretend to be accurate, but they show the general tendency unmistakably. The dying leadership of the Social Revolutionary teachers, town-clerks and functionaries, was giving place to the leadership of soldiers who would stop at nothing.

Parvus, a German Marxian writer prominent in his day, who succeeded in acauiring wealth and losing both his principles and his penetration during the war, has compared the Russian soldiers with the mercenary troopers, robbers and hold-up men of mediæval times. For this it is necessary to shut one's eyes to the fact that in all their lawlessness the Russian soldiers remained merely the executive organ of the greatest agrarian revolution in history.

So long as the movement had not broken completely with legality, the sending of troops into the villages preserved a symbolic character. In practice it was almost the Cossacks alone who could be used as punitive troops. "Four hundred Cossacks were sent into Serdobsky county . . . this measure had a tranquilising effect; the peasants declared that they would await the Constituent Assembly," says the liberal paper, *Russkoe Selo*, on the 11th of October. Four hundred Cossacks is certainly an argument in favour of the Constituent Assembly. But there were not enough Cossacks, and moreover they too were uncertain. Meantime the government was oftener and oftener being compelled to "take decisive measures." During the first four months of the revolution Vermenichev counts 17 cases in which armed forces were sent against the peasants; in July and August, 39 cases; in September and October, 105 cases.

To put down the peasantry by armed force was only to pour oil on the fire. In a majority of cases the soldiers went over to the peasants. A county commissar of Podolsk province reports: "The army organisations and even individual units are deciding social and economic questions, are forcing (?) the peasants to carry out seizures and cut the forest, and at times, in certain localities, they themselves take part in the looting. . . . The local military units refuse to join in putting down acts of violence. . . ." Thus the rural revolt loosened the last bolts of the army. There was not the slightest possibility that in the circumstances of a peasant war headed by the workers, the army would permit itself to be thrown against the insurrection in the cities.

From the workers and soldiers the peasants first learned something new—something older than what the Social Revolutionaries had told them—about the Bolsheviks. The slogans of Lenin, and his name, penetrated the village. The steadily increasing complaints against Bolsheviks were, however, in many cases invented or exaggerated. The landlords hoped in this way to make more sure of getting help. "In Ostrovsky county complete anarchy reigns, a consequence of Bolshevik propaganda." From Ufa province comes the news: "A member of a village committee, Vassiliev, is distributing the programme of the Bolsheviks and openly declaring that the landlords are to be hanged." In seeking "protection from robbery" the Novgorod landlord, Polonnik, does not forget to add: "The Executive Committees are brimful of Bolsheviks." That means that they are unfavourable to the landlord. "In August," remembers a Simbirsk peasant, Zumorin, "workers began to make the rounds of the villages, agitating for the Bolshevik Party and telling about its programme." An investigator of Sebezh county tells about the arrival from Petrograd of a weaver Tatiana Mikhailova, 26 years old, who "called on the people of her village to overthrow the Provisional Government, and praised the tactics of Lenin." In Smalensk province towards the end of August, according to the peasant Kotov, "We began to interest ourselves in Lenin, began to listen to the voice of Lenin. . . ." In the village zemstvo, however, they were still electing an immense majority of Social Revolutionaries.

The Bolshevik Party was trying to get closer to the peasant. On the 10th of September Nevsky demanded that the Petrograd committee undertake the publication of a peasant newspaper:

"We must fix things so that we shall not have the experience of the French Commune, where the peasantry did not understand Paris and Paris did not understand the peasantry." The newspaper, *Byednotá*, soon came out. But even so, the purely party work among the peasants remained insignificant. The strength of the Bolshevik Party lay not in technical resources, not in machinery, but in a correct policy. As air currents carry seeds, the whirlwinds of the revolution scattered the ideas of Lenin.

By September," remembers a Tver peasant, Vorobiev, "not only the soldiers, but the poor peasants themselves were oftener and more boldly beginning to come out at meetings in defence of the Bolsheviks. . . ." This is confirmed by the Simbirsk peasant, Zumorin: "Among the poor and some of the middle peasants the name of Lenin was on everybody's lips; the talk was only of Lenin." A Novgorod peasant, Grigoriev, tells how a Social Revolutionary in the village called the Bolsheviks "usurpers" and "traitors" and how the muzhiks thundered: "Down with the dog! Pound him with rock! Don't tell us any more fairy stories. Where is the land? That's enough from you! Give us the Bolsheviks!" It is possible, by the way, that this episode—and there were many like it—derives from the post-October period. Facts stand strong in a peasant's memory but his chronology is weak.

The soldier Chinenov, who came back to his home in Orel province with a trunkful of Bolshevik literature, had not been welcomed by the home village. It's probably German gold, they said. But in October "the village nucleus has 700 members and many rifles, and always comes out in defence of the Soviet power." The Bolshevik Vrachev tells how the peasants of the purely agricultural province of Voronezh "woke up from the effects of the Social Revolutionary fumes, and began to take an interest in our party. Thanks to which we already had a number of village and township locals and subscribers to our papers, and received many good fellows in the tiny headquarters of our committee." In Smolensk province, according to the recollections of Ivanov, "Bolsheviks were very rare in the villages. There were very few of them in the counties. There were no Bolshevik papers. Leaflets were very rarely given out. . . . And nevertheless the nearer it came to October, the more the villages swung over to the Bolsheviks."

"In those counties where there was a Bolshevik influence in the Soviet before October," writes Ivanov again, "the element of raids upon landlords' estates either did not appear, or appeared only to a small extent." In this respect, however, it was not the same everywhere. "The Bolshevik demand for the transfer of land to the peasants," says, for example, Tadeush, "was taken up with extraordinary rapidity by the mass of the peasants of Moghiliev county, who laid waste the estates, in some cases burning them, and seized the harvests and the forest." In essence there is no contradiction between the two testimonies. The general agitation of the Bolsheviks undoubtedly nourished the civil war in the country. But wherever the Bolsheviks had succeeded in putting down firm roots, they naturally tried, without weakening the assault of the peasants, to regulate its forms and decrease the amount of destruction.

The land question did not stand alone. The peasant suffered especially during the last period of the war, both as seller and buyer. Grain was taken from him at a fixed price, and the products of industry were becoming more and more unattainable. The problem of economic correlation between the country and the city, destined subsequently under the name of the "scissors" to become the central problem of Soviet economy, was already showing its threatening face. The Bolsheviks were saying to the peasants: The soviets must seize the power, give you the land, end the war, demobilise industry, establish workers' control of production, and regulate the price relations between industrial and agricultural products. However summary this answer may have been, it did indicate the road. "The partition wall between us and the peasantry," said Trotsky on the 10th of October at a conference of factory committees, "is the little counsellors of Avksentiev. We must break through this wall. We must explain to the village that all the attempts of the worker to help the peasant by supplying the village with agricultural implements will give no result until workers' control of organised production is established." The conference issued a manifesto to the peasants in this sense.

The Petrograd workers created at the factories in those days special commissions which would assemble metals, damaged parts and fragments for the use of a special centre called "Worker to Peasant." This scrap-iron was used for making the simplest agricultural implements and reserve parts. That first planned entry of the workers into the process of production—still tiny in scope and with agitational aims prevailing over economics—nevertheless opened out a prospect for the near future. Frightened at this entrance of the Bolsheviks into the forbidden sphere of the village, the peasant Executive Committee made an attempt to get hold of the new enterprise. But the decrepit Compromisers were no longer in any condition to compete with the Bolsheviks on the city arena when the ground was already slipping from under their feet in the villages.

The echoes of the Bolshevik agitation "so aroused the peasant poor," writes Vorobiev, the Tver peasant, "that we may definitely say: If October had not come in October it would have come in November." This colourful description of the political strength of Bolshevism does not contradict the fact of its organisational weakness. Only through such striking disproportions does a revolution make its way. It is for this very reason, to tell the truth, that its movement cannot be forced into the framework of formal democracy. To accomplish the agrarian revolution, whether in October or November, the peasantry had no other course but to make use of the unravelling web of that same Social Revolutionary Party. Its left elements were hastily and unsystematically forming a group under the pressure of the peasant revolt—following the Bolsheviks and competing with them. During the coming months the political shift of the peasantry will take place chiefly under the glossy banner of the Left Social Revolutionaries. This ephemeral party will become a reflected and unstable form of rural Bolshevism, a temporary bridge from the peasant war to the proletarian revolution.

The agrarian revolution had to have its own local institutions. How did they look? There existed several types of organisation in the village: state institutions such as the executive committee of the township, the land and food committees; social institutions like the soviets; purely political institutions like the parties; and finally organs of self-government exemplified in the town zemstvos. The peasant soviets had as yet developed only on a province, or to some extent a county scale. There were few town soviets. The town zemstvos had been slow to take root. The land and executive committees, on the other hand, although state organs in design, became—strange as it may seem at a first glance—the organs of the peasant revolution.

The head land committee, consisting of governmental functionaries, landlords, professors, scientific agriculturists, Social Revolutionary politicians and an admixture of dubious peasants, became in essence the main brake of the agrarian revolution. The province committees never ceased to be the conducting wires of the governmental policy. The county committees oscillated between the peasants and the men higher up. The town committees, however—elected by the peasants and working right there before the eyes of the village—became the instruments of the agrarian movement. The circumstance that the members of these committees usually registered as Social Revolutionaries made no difference. They kept step with the peasant's hut and not the lord's manor. The peasants especially treasured the state character of their land committees, seeing in this a sort of patent-right to civil war.

"The peasants say that they recognise nothing but the town committee," complains one of the chiefs of militia in Saransky county as early as May. "All the county and city committees, they say, work for the landlords." According to a Nizhegorod commissar, "the attempts of certain town committees to oppose the independent action of the peasants almost always ends in failure and brings about a change of membership of the committee." According to Denissov, a peasant from Pskov, "the committees were always on the side of the peasants' movement against the landlord because the most revolutionary part of the peasantry and soldiers from the front were elected to them."

The county, and more especially the province committees were led by the functionary "intelligentsia," which was trying to keep up peaceful relations with the landlord. "The peasants saw," writes the Moscow peasant, Yurkov, "that this was the same coat only inside out, the same power but with another name." "An effort is under way," reports the Kurksk commissar, ". . . to get new elections to the county committees, which are invariably carrying out the directions of the Provisional Government." It was very hard, however, for the peasants to get into the county committees. The Social Revolutionaries kept hold of the political ties between the villages and townships, and the peasants were thus compelled to act through a party whose chief mission consisted of turning the old coat inside out.

The coolness of the peasantry toward the March soviets, astonishing at first glance, had as a matter of fact very deep causes. The soviet was not a special organisation like the land committee, but a universal organ of the revolution. Now in the sphere of general politics the peasant cannot take a step without leadership. The only question is, where is it to come from. The provincial and county peasant soviets were created on the initiative, and to a considerable extent at the expense, of the

Co-operatives, not as organs of a peasant revolution but as organs of a conservative guardianship over the peasants. The villagers tolerated these Right Social Revolutionary soviets standing above them as a shield against the authorities. But at home, among themselves, they preferred the land committees.

In order to prevent the village from shutting itself up in a circle of "purely peasant interests," the government made haste to create democratic zemstvos. That alone was enough to put the muzhik on his guard. It was frequently necessary to enforce the elections. "There were cases of lawlessness," reports the Penza commissar, "resulting in a break-up of the elections." In Minsk province the peasants arrested the president of the electoral commission of the town, Prince Drutskoi-Liubetskoi, accusing him of tampering with the lists. It was not easy for the muzhiks to come to an agreement with him about the democratic solution of their age-old quarrel. The county commissar of Bugulminsk reported: "The elections to the town zemstvos throughout the county have not gone quite according to plan. . . . The members of the electorate are exclusively peasants. There is a noticeable estrangement from the local intelligentsia, especially from the landowners." In this form the zemstvo was but little different from the committee. "The attitude of the peasant masses toward the intelligentsia, and especially the landowners," complains the Minsk county commissar, "is adverse." We read in a Moghiliev newspaper of September 23: "Cultural work in the country is accompanied with a certain risk, unless one categorically promises to co-operate toward the immediate transfer of all the land to the peasants." Where agreement and even intercourse between the fundamental classes of the population becomes impossible, the ground for democratic institutions disappears. The still-birth of the town zemstvos unmistakably foretold the collapse of the Constituent Assembly.

"The local peasantry," reports the Nizhegorod commissar, "have got a fixed opinion that all civil laws have lost their force, and that all legal relations ought now to be regulated by peasant organisations." Getting control of the militia in certain localities, the town committees would issue local laws, establish rents, regulate wages, put their own overseers on estates, take over the land, the crops, the woods, the forests, the tools, take the machinery away from the landlords, and carry out searches and arrests. The voice of centuries and the fresh experience of the revolution both said to the muzhik that the question of land is a question of power. The agrarian revolution needed the organs of a peasant dictatorship. The muzhik did not yet know this Latin word, but the muzhik knew what he wanted. That "anarchy" of which the landlords, liberal commissars, and compromise politicians complained, was in reality the first stage of the revolutionary dictatorship in the village.

The necessity of creating special, purely peasant organs of land revolution in the localities had been defended by Lenin during the events of 1905–6. "The peasant revolutionary committees," he argued at the party congress in Stockholm, "present the sole road along which the peasant movement can travel." The muzhiks had not read Lenin, but Lenin knew how to read the minds of the muzhiks.

The villages changed their attitude to the soviets only in the fall, when the soviets themselves changed their political course. The Bolshevik and Left Social Revolutionary soviets in the county or provincial city now no longer held back the peasants, but on the contrary pushed them forward. Whereas during the first months the villages had looked to the compromisist soviets for a legal covering, only to come later into hostile conflict with them, now they first began to find in the revolutionary soviets a real leadership. The Saratov peasants wrote in September: "The power throughout all Russia ought to go . . . to the Soviets of Workers, Peasants and Soldiers' Deputies. That will be safer." Only in the fall did the peasantry begin to join their land programme to the slogan of Power to the Soviets. But here, too, they did not know by whom or how these soviets were to be led.

Agrarian disturbances in Russia had their great tradition, their simple but clear programme, their local martyrs and heroes. The colossal experience of 1905 had not passed without leaving its trace in the villages. And to this we must add the work of the sectarian ideas which had taken hold of millions of peasants. "I knew many peasants," writes a well-informed author, "who accepted . . . the October revolution as the direct realisation of their religious hopes." Of all the peasant revolts known to history the movement of the Russian peasantry in 1917 was undoubtedly in the highest degree fertilised by political ideas. If nevertheless it proved incapable of creating an independent leadership and taking the power in its own hands, the causes of this are to be found in the organic nature of an isolated, petty and routine industry. While sucking all the juice out of the muzhik, his economic position did not give him in return the ability to generalise.

The political freedom of a peasant means in practice the ability to choose between different city parishes. But even this choice is not made *a priori*. The peasantry pushed the Bolsheviks toward power with their revolt. But only after conquering the power could the Bolsheviks win over the peasantry, converting their agrarian revolution into the laws of a workers' state.

A group of investigators under the guidance of Yakovlev have made an extremely valuable classification of material, characterising the evolution of the agrarian movement from February to October. Designating the number of disorganised actions in each month as 100, these investigators have estimated that there were in April, 33 organised conflicts; in June, 86; in July, 120. July was the moment of highest success of the Social Revolutionary organisations in the country. In August for one hundred disorganised conflicts there were only 62 organised, and in October, 14. From these figures—wonderfully instructive, although of qualified significance—Yakovlev draws a totally unexpected conclusion. "Whereas up to August," he says, "the movement had grown steadily more organised; in the fall it acquired a more and more 'spontaneous' [1] character." Another investigator, Vermenichev, arrives at the same formula: "The lowering of the figure of organised movements in the period of the pre-October waves, testifies to the spontaneousness of the movements of those months." If the spontaneous is contrasted to the conscious, as blindness to eyesight —and this is the only scientific contrast—then we must come to the conclusion that the consciousness of the peasant movement increased up to August, and then began to fall rapidly enough to disappear completely at the moment of the October insurrection. But this our investigators obviously did not wish to say. Taking a somewhat reflective attitude to the question, it is not difficult to understand, for example, that the peasant elections to the Constituent Assembly, in spite of their externally "organised" character, were incomparably more "spontaneous"—that is, thoughtless, sheeplike, blind—than

1. The Russian word translated "spontaneous" means literally *elemental*, and is commonly contrasted in revolutionary literature to class-conscious movements led by an organisation with a theory and programme. [Trans.]

the "disorganised" peasant campaigns against the landlord, where each peasant knew quite well what he wanted.

In the autumn crisis the peasants did not abandon conscious action of spontaneousness, but abandoned compromisist leadership for the civil war. The decline in organisation was really a superficial feature: the compromisist organisation fell away, but what it left was by no means a vacant space. The peasants came out on the new road under the direct leadership of the most revolutionary elements, the soldiers, sailors and workers. In entering upon decisive activities the peasants would quite often call a mass-meeting, and even take pains that the resolution adopted should be signed by all those living in the same village. "In the autumn period of the peasant movement with its raiding forms," writes a third investigator, Shestakov, "what oftenest appears upon the scene is the 'old peasant assembly. . . .' By means of the assembly the peasants divide the appropriated goods, through the assembly they conduct negotiations with the landlord and overseers, with the county commissars and with punitive expeditions of all kinds."

The question why the town committees, which have led the peasants right up to the civil war, now disappear from the scene, finds no direct answer in these materials. But the explanation comes of itself. A revolution very quickly wears out its organs and implements. Owing to the mere fact that the land committees had been conducting semi-peaceful activities, they were bound to seem of little use for direct assaults. And this general cause is supplemented by particular ones no less weighty. In taking the road of open war with the landlord, the peasants knew too well what awaited them in case of defeat. A number of the land committees even without that were under Kerensky's lock and key. To scatter the responsibility became a tactical need. The "mir" offered the most expedient form for this. The customary mutual mistrust of the peasants undoubtedly worked in the same direction. It was a question now of the direct seizure and division of the landlords' goods; each wanted to take part in this himself, not entrusting his rights to anybody. Thus the highest tension of the struggle led to a temporary retirement of the representative organs in favour of primitive peasant democracy in the form of the assembly and the communal decree.

This crude mistake in defining the character of the peasant movement may seem especially surprising from the pen of Bolshevik investigators. But we must not forget that these are

Bosheviks of the new mould. The bureaucratisation of thought has inevitably led to an overvaluing of those forms of organisation which were imposed upon the peasants from above, an under-valuing of those which the peasants themselves assumed. The educated functionary, following the liberal professor, looks upon social processes from the point of view of administration. In his position as People's Commissar of Agriculture, Yakovlev subsequently showed the same summary bureaucratic mode of approach to the peasantry, but in an infinitely broader and more responsible sphere—that namely of introducing "complete collectivisation." Theoretic superficiality takes a cruel revenge when it comes to a practical action on a large scale!

But we are still a good thirteen years before the mistakes of complete collectivisation. It is now only a question of the expropriation of the landed estates. 134,000 landlords are still trembling for their 18 million dessiatins. Most threatened is the situation of those on the summit, the 30,000 lords of old Russia who own 70 million dessiatins—2,000 on the average per person. A lord, Boborykin, writes to the Chamberlain, Rodzianko: "I am a landlord, and somehow it won't fit into my head that I am to be deprived of my land, and that, too, for a most improbable purpose—for an experimental test of socialistic teachings." But it is the task of revolution to accomplish just those things which will not fit into the heads of the ruling class.

The more far-sighted landlords cannot help realising, however, that they will not be able to keep their estates. They are no longer even trying to. The sooner we get rid of our land, they are saying, the better. The Constituent Assembly presents itself to them primarily as a vast clearing-house where the state will recompense them not only for the land, but also for their anxieties.

The peasant land-owners adhered to this programme of theirs on the left. They were not unwilling to have an end of the parasitical nobility, but they were afraid of unsettling the conception of landed property. The state is rich enough, they declared at their meetings, to pay the landlords something like 12 billion roubles. In their quality of "peasants" they were counting on being able to make use of these noble estates, once they had been paid for by the people, on favourable terms.

The proprietors understood that the extent of the indemnity was a political magnitude to be determined by the correlation of forces at the moment of payment. Up to the end of August there remained a hope that the Constituent Assembly, convoked *à la* Kornilov, would follow a line of agrarian reform midway between Rodzianko and Miliukov. The collapse of Kornilov meant that the possessing classes had lost the game.

During September and October the possessing classes were awaiting the outcome as a hopelessly sick man awaits death. Autumn with muzhiks is the time for politics. The fields are mowed, illusions are scattered, patience is exhausted. Time to finish things up! The movement now overflows its banks, invades all districts, wipes out local peculiarities, draws in all the strata of the villages, washes away all considerations of law and prudence, becomes aggressive, fierce, furious, a raging thing, arms itself with steel and fire, revolvers and hand-grenades, demolishes and burns up the manorial dwellings, drives out the landlords, cleanses the earth and in some places waters it with blood.

Gone are the nests of the gentility celebrated by Pushkin, Turgeniev and Tolstoi. The old Russia has gone up in smoke. The liberal press is a collection of groans and outcries about the destruction of English gardens, of paintings from the brushes of serfs, of patrimonial libraries, the parthenons of Tombov, the riding horses, the ancient engravings, the breeding bulls. Bourgeois historians have tried to put the responsibility upon the Bolsheviks for the "vandalism" of the peasant's mode of settling accounts with the "culture" of his lords. In reality the Russian muzhik was completing a business entered upon many centuries before the Bolsheviks appeared in the world. He was fulfilling his progressive historic task with the only means at his disposal. With revolutionary barbarism he was wiping out the barbarism of the middle ages. Moreover, neither he himself, nor his grandfather, nor his great grandfather before him ever saw any mercy or indulgence!

When the feudal landlords got the best of the Jacquerie four and a half centuries before the liberation of the French peasants, a pious monk wrote in his chronicle: "They did so much evil to the country that there was no need of the coming of the English to destroy the kingdom; these never could have done what was done by the nobles of France." Only the bourgeoisie—in May 1871—proved able to exceed the French nobles in ferocity. The Russian peasants—thanks to the leadership of the workers, and the Russian workers—thanks to the support of the peasants, avoided learning this twofold lesson from the defenders of culture and humanity.

The inter-relations between the fundamental classes of Russia at large were reproduced in the village. Just as the workers and soldiers went into a fight with the monarchy contrary to the plans of the bourgeoisie, so the peasant poor rose boldest of all against the landlord, not heeding the warnings of the kulak. Just as the Compromisers believed that the revolution would stand firmly on its feet only from the moment it was recognised by Miliukov, so the middle peasants, glancing round to right and left, imagined that the signature of the kulak would legitimise the seizures. And finally, somewhat as the bourgeoisie, although hostile to the revolution, did not hesitate to appropriate the power, so the kulaks, after resisting the raids, did not refuse to enjoy their fruits. The power did not remain long in the hands of the bourgeoisie, nor the landlord's chattels in the hands of the kulaks—for like reasons.

The strength of the agrarian-democratic and essentially bourgeois revolution was manifested in the fact that it overcame for a time the class contradictions of the village: the farm hand helped the kulak in raiding the landlord. The 17th, 18th and 19th centuries of Russian history climbed up on the shoulders of the 20th, and bent it to the ground. The weakness of this belated bourgeois revolution was manifested in the fact that the peasant war did not urge the bourgeois revolutionists forward, but threw them back conclusively into the camp of reaction. Tseretelli, the hard-labour convict of yesterday, defended the estates of the landlords against anarchy! The peasant revolution, thus rejected by the bourgeoisie, joined hands with the industrial proletariat. In this way the 20th century not only got free of those past centuries hanging upon it, but climbed up on their shoulders to a new historic level. In order that the peasant might clear and fence his land, the worker had to stand at the head of the state: that is the simplest formula for the October revolution.

Chapter II

The Problem of Nationalities

Language is the most important instrument of human communication, and consequently of industry. It becomes national together with the triumph of commodity exchange which integrates nations. Upon this foundation the national state is erected as the most convenient, profitable and normal arena for the play of capitalist relations. In Western Europe the epoch of the formation of bourgeois nations, if you leave out the struggle of the Netherlands for independence and the fate of the island country, England, began with the great French revolution, and was essentially completed approximately one hundred years later with the formation of the German Empire.

But during that period when in Europe the national state could no longer contain the productive forces and was overgrown into the imperialist state, in the East—in Persia, the Balkans, China, India—the era of national democratic revolutions, taking its impetus from the Russian revolution of 1905, was only just beginning. The Balkan war of 1912 marked the completion of the forming of national states in south-eastern Europe. The subsequent imperialist war completed incidentally the unfinished work of the national revolutions in Europe leading as it did to the dismemberment of Austria-Hungary, the establishment of an independent Poland, and of independent border states cut from the empire of the czars.

Russia was formed not as a national state, but as a state made up of nationalities. This corresponded to its belated character. On a foundation of extensive agriculture and home industry commercial capital developed not deeply, not by transforming production, but broadly, by increasing the radius of its operation. The trader, the landlord and the government official advanced from the centre toward the periphery, following the peasant settlers who, in search of fresh lands and freedom from imposts, were penetrating new territory inhabited by still more backward tribes. The expansion of the state was in its foundation an expansion of agriculture, which with all its primitiveness showed a certain superiority to that of the nomads in the south and east. The bureaucratic-caste state which formed itself upon this enormous and continually broadening basis, became sufficiently strong to subjugate certain nations in the west, possessed of a higher culture but unable because of their small numbers or condition of inner crisis to defend their independence (Poland, Lithuania, the Baltic states, Finland).

To the seventy million Great Russians constituting the main mass of the country, there were gradually added about ninety million "outlanders" sharply divided into two groups: the western peoples excelling Russia in their culture, and the eastern standing on a lower level. Thus was created an empire of whose population the ruling nationality constituted only 43 per cent. The remaining 57 per cent. were nationalities of various degrees of culture and subjection, including Ukrainians 17 per cent., Poles 6 per cent., White Russians 4½ per cent.

The greedy demands of the state and the meagreness of the peasant foundation under the ruling classes gave rise to the most bitter forms of exploitation. National oppression in Russia was incomparably rougher than in the neighbouring states not only on its western but even on its eastern borders. The vast numbers of these nationalities deprived of rights, and the sharpness of their deprivation, gave to the national problem in czarist Russia a gigantic explosive force.

Whereas in nationality homogeneous states the bourgeois revolutions developed powerful centripetal tendencies, rallying to the idea of overcoming particularism, as in France, or overcoming national disunion, as in Italy and Germany—in nationally heterogeneous states on the contrary, such as Turkey, Russia, Austria-Hungary, the belated bourgeois revolution released centrifugal forces. In spite of the apparent contrariness of these processes when expressed in mechanical terms, their historic function was the same. In both cases it was a question of using the national unity as a fundamental industrial reservoir. Germany had for this purpose to be united, Austria-Hungary to be divided.

Lenin early learned the inevitability of this development of centrifugal national movements in Russia, and for many years stubbornly fought—most particularly against Rosa Luxemburg—for that famous paragraph 9 of the old party programme which formulated the right of nations to self-determination—that is, to complete separation as states. In this the Bolshevik Party did not by any means undertake an evangel of separation. It merely assumed an obligation to struggle implacably against every form of national oppression, including the forcible retention of this or that nationality within the boundaries of the general state. Only in this way could the Russian proletariat gradually win the confidence of the oppressed nationalities.

But that was only one side of the matter. The policy of Bolshevism in the national sphere had also another side, apparently contradictory to the first but in reality supplementing it. Within the framework of the party, and of the workers' organisations in general, Bolshevism insisted upon a rigid centralism, implacably warring against every taint of nationalism which might set the workers one against the other or disunite them. While flatly refusing to the bourgeois states the right to impose compulsory citizenship, or even a state language, upon a national minority, Bolshevism at the same time made it a verily sacred task to unite as closely as possible, by means of voluntary class discipline, the workers of different nationalities. Thus it flatly rejected the national-federation principle in building the party. A revolutionary organisation is not the prototype of the future state, but merely the instrument for its creation. An instrument ought to be adapted to fashioning the product; it ought not to include the product. Thus a centralised organisation can guarantee the success of revolutionary struggle—even where the task is to destroy the centralised oppression of nationalities.

For the oppressed nations of Russia the overthrow of the monarchy inevitably meant also their own national revolution. In this matter, however, we observe the same thing as in all other departments of the February régime: the official democracy, held in leash by its political dependence upon an imperialist bourgeoisie, was totally incapable of breaking the old fetters. Holding inviolable its right to settle the fate of all other nations, it continued jealously to guard those sources of wealth, power and influence which had given the Great Russian bourgeoisie its dominant position. The compromisist democracy merely translated traditions of the czarist national policy into the language of libertarian rhetoric: it was now a question of defending the unity of the revolution. But the ruling coalition had also another more pointed argument: wartime expediency. This meant that the aspirations of individual nationalities toward freedom must be portrayed as the work of the Austro-German General Staff. Here too the Kadets played first violin and the Compromisers second.

The new government could not, of course, leave absolutely untouched that disgusting legal tangle, the complicated mediæval mockeries of the outlanders. But it did hope and endeavour to stop at a mere annulment of the exceptional laws against individual nations—that is, to establish a bare equality of all parts of the population before the Great Russian state bureaucracy.

This formal equality gave most of all to the Jews, for the laws limiting their rights had reached the number of 650. Moreover, being city dwellers and the most scattered of all the nationalities, the Jews could make no claim either to state independence or even territorial autonomy. As to the project of a so-called "national-cultural autonomy" which should unite the Jews throughout the whole country around schools and other institutions, this reactionary Utopia, borrowed by various Jewish groups from the Austrian theoretician, Otto Bauer, melted in those first days of freedom like wax under the sun's rays.

But a revolution is a revolution for the very reason that it is not satisfied either with doles or deferred payments. The abolition of the more shameful national limitations established a formal equality of citizens regardless of their nationality, but this revealed only the more sharply the unequal position of the nationalities as such, leaving the major part of them in the position of step-children or foster-children of the Great Russian state.

The proclamation of equal rights meant nothing to the Finns especially, for they did not desire equality with the Russians but independence of Russia. It gave nothing to the Ukrainians, for their rights had been equal before, they having been forcibly proclaimed to be Russian. It changed nothing in the situation of the Letts and Esthonians, oppressed by the German landlord's manor and the Russo-German city. It did not lighten in the least the fate of the backward peoples and tribes of Central Asia, who had been held down to the rock bottom not by juridical limitations, but by economic and cultural ball and chain. All these questions the Liberal-Compromisist coalition refused even to bring up. The democratic state remained the same old state of the Great Russian functionary, who did not intend to yield his place to anybody.

The deeper the revolution sank among the masses in the borderlands, the more clear it became that the Russian state language was there the language of the possessing classes. The régime of formal democracy, with its freedom of press and assemblage, made the backward and oppressed nationalities only the more painfully aware to what extent they were deprived of the most elementary means of cultural development: their own schools, their own courts, their own officials. References to a future Constituent Assembly only irritated them. They knew well enough that the same party would dominate that assembly which had created the Provisional Government, and was continuing to defend the tradition of Russification, making clear with its jealous greed that line beyond which the ruling classes would not go.

Finland became from the first a thorn in the flesh of the February régime. Thanks to the bitterness of the agrarian problem, in Finland a problem of "torpars"—that is, small enslaved tenants—the industrial workers, although comprising only 14 per cent. of the population, carried the rural population with them. The Finnish Seim was the only parliament in the world where the social-democrats got a majority: 103 seats out of 200. Having by their law of June 5 declared the Seim a sovereign power except on questions of war and foreign policy, the Finnish social-democrats appealed for support "to the comrade party of Russia." But their appeal, as it turned out, was sent quite to the wrong address. The Provisional Government stepped aside at first, permitting the "comrade party" to act. An advisory delegation headed by Cheidze went to Helsingfors and returned empty-handed. Then the socialist ministers of Petrograd—Kerensky, Chenov, Skobelev, Tseretelli—decided to dissolve by force the socialist government at Helsingfors. The chief of the headquarters staff, the monarchist Lukomsky, gave warning to the civil authorities and the population of Finland that in case of any action against the Russian army "their cities, and Helsingfors, first of all, would be laid waste." After this preparation, the Government issued a solemn manifesto—a plagiarism from the monarchy even in its literary style—dissolving the Seim. And on the first day of the offensive they placed Russian soldiers withdrawn from the front at the doors of the Finnish parliament. Thus the revolutionary masses of Russia—making their way to October—got a good lesson on the qualified place occupied by the principles of democracy in a struggle of class forces.

Confronted by this unbridled nationalism of the ruling classes, the revolutionary troops in Finland adopted a worthy attitude. A regional congress of the soviets held in Helsingfors early in September announced: "If the Finnish democracy finds it advisable to renew the sessions of the Seim, any attempt to hinder this will be regarded by the Soviet congress as a counter-revolutionary act." That was a direct offer of military help. But the Finnish democracy, in which compromisist tendencies predominated, was not ready to take the road of insurrection. New elections, held under the threat of a new dissolution, gave a majority of 180 out of 200 to those bourgeois parties in agreement with whom the government had dissolved the Seim.

But here domestic questions come to the front, questions which in this Switzerland of the North, a land of granite mountains and greedy proprietors, would lead inexorably to civil war. The Finnish bourgeoisie was half openly preparing its military cadres. Secret nuclei of the Red Guard were forming at the same time. The bourgeoisie turned to Sweden and Germany for weapons and instructors. The workers found support in the Russian troops. Meanwhile in bourgeois circles—yesterday still inclined to agreement with Petrograd—a movement was developing for complete separation from Russia. Their leading newspaper, *Khuvudstatsbladet*, wrote: "The Russian people are possessed by an anarchist frenzy. . . . Ought we not in these circumstances . . . to separate ourselves as far as possible from that chaos?" The Provisional Government found itself obliged to make concessions without awaiting the Constituent Assembly. On the 23rd of October a decree was adopted recognising "in principle" the independence of Finland except in military and foreign affairs. But "independence" given by the hand of Kerensky was not worth much: it was now only two days before his fall.

A second and far more gigantic thorn in the flesh was the Ukraine. Early in June, Kerensky forbade the holding of a Ukrainian soldier-congress convoked by the Rada. The Ukrainians did not submit. In order to save the face of his government Kerensky legalised the congress *ex post facto*, sending a declamatory telegram which the assembled deputies greeted with disrespectful laughter. This bitter lesson did not prevent Kerensky from forbidding three weeks later a military congress of the Mussulmans in Moscow. The democratic government seemed anxious to make it plain to the discontented nations: you will get only what you grab.

In its first "universal" issued on June 10th, the Rada, accusing Petrograd of opposing national independence, declared: "Henceforth we will build our own life." The Kadets denounced the Ukrainian leaders as German agents; the Compromisers addressed them with sentimental admonitions; the Provisional Government sent a delegation to Kiev. In the heated atmosphere of the Ukraine, Kerensky, Tseretelli and Tereschenko felt obliged to take a few steps to meet the Rada. But after the July raids on workers and soldiers, the Government veered right on the Ukrainian question also. On August 5, the Rada by an overwhelming majority accused the government, "imbued with the imperialist tendencies of the Russian bourgeoisie," of having broken the agreement of July 3rd. "When the time came for the government to redeem its pledge," declared the head of the Ukrainian government, Vinnichenko, "it turned out that the Provisional Government . . . is a petty cheat, who hopes to get rid of a great historic problem by swindling." This unequivocal language conveys an adequate idea of the authority of the government even in those circles which ought politically to be rather close to it. For in the long run the Ukrainian Compromiser, Vinnichenko, was distinguished from Kerensky only as a mediocre novelist from a mediocre lawyer.

It is true that in September the government did finally issue a decree recognising for all the nationalities of Russia—within limits to be designated by the Constituent Assembly—the "right of self-determination." But this wholly unguaranteed and inwardly contradictory promise for the future—extremely vague in everything but its limitations—inspired no confidence in anybody. The doings of the Provisional Government were already crying out too loudly against it.

On September 2 the Senate—that same body which refused to admit new members without the old uniform—decided to deny publication to the instructions issued to the Ukrainian General Secretariat—that is, to the Ministerial Cabinet in Kiev—and confirmed by the Government. Justification: no law provides for this Secretariat, and it is impossible to issue instructions to an illegal institution. The lofty jurists did not conceal the fact, either, that the very agreement entered into between the government and the Rada was a usurpation of the rights of the Constituent Assembly—these czarist senators having now become the most inflexible partisans of pure democracy. In this show of courage the oppositionists from the Right were risking nothing at all: they knew that their opposition was quite after the heart of the ruling classes. Although the Russian bourgeoisie had swallowed a certain amount of independence for Finland—united to Russia as she was by weak economic ties—it could not possibly agree to an "autonomy" of Ukrainian grain, Donetz coal, and the ores of Krivorog.

On October 19, Kerensky sent a telegraphic order to the General Secretary of the Ukraine "to come promptly to Petrograd for personal explanations" in regard to a criminal agitation started there in favour of a Ukrainian Constituent Assembly. At the same time the District Attorney of Kiev was directed to begin an investigation of the Rada. But these threats gave as little fright to the Ukraine as the acts of grace had given joy to Finland.

The Ukrainian Compromisers were at this time feeling infinitely more secure than their elder cousins in Petrograd. Aside from the auspicious atmosphere surrounding their struggle for national rights, the comparative stability of the petty bourgeois parties in the Ukraine—as also in a number of other oppressed nations—had economic and social roots describable in one word, *backwardness.* In spite of the swift industrial development of the Donetz and Krivorog Basins, the Ukraine as a whole continued to lag behind Great Russia. The Ukrainian proletariat was less homogeneous, less tempered. The Bolshevik Party was weak both in numbers and quality, had been slow in breaking away from the Mensheviks, and was poorly vested in the political, and especially the national situation. Even in the industrial eastern parts of the Ukraine, a regional conference of the soviets as late as the middle of October showed a slight compromisist majority!

The Ukrainian bourgeoisie was comparatively still weaker. One of the causes of the social instability of the Russian bourgeoisie taken as a whole lay, we remember, in the fact that its more powerful section consisted of foreigners not even dwelling in Russia. In the borderlands this fact was supplemented by another no less significant: their own domestic bourgeoisie did not belong to the same nation as the principal mass of the people.

The population of the cities in these borderlands was completely different in its national ingredients from the population of the country. In the Ukraine and White Russia the landlord, capitalist, lawyer, journalist, was a Great Russian, a Pole, a Jew, a foreigner; the rural population was wholly Ukrainian and White Russian. In the Baltic states the cities were havens of the German, Russian and Jewish bourgeoisie; the country was altogether Lettish and Esthonian. In the cities of Georgia, a Russian and Armenian population predominated, as also in Turkish Azerbaidjan, being separated from the fundamental mass of the people not only by their level of life and culture, but also by language, as are the English in India. Being indebted for the protection of their possessions and income to the bureaucratic machine, and being closely bound up with the ruling classes of all other countries, the landlords, industrialists and merchants in these borderlands grouped around themselves a narrow circle of Russian functionaries, clerks, teachers, physicians, lawyers, journalists, and to some extent workers also, converting the cities into centres of Russification and colonisation.

It was possible to ignore the villages so long as they remained silent. When they began, however, more and more impatiently to lift their voices, the city resisted and stubbornly continued to resist, defending its privileged position. The functionary, the merchant, the lawyer, soon learned to disguise his struggle to retain the commanding heights of industry and culture under the form of a top-lofty condemnation of an increasing "chauvinism." The desire of a ruling nation to maintain the *status quo* frequently dresses up as a superiority to "nationalism," just as the desire of a victorious nation to hang on to its booty easily takes the form of pacifism. Thus MacDonald in the face of Gandhi feels as though he were an internationalist. Thus, too, the gravitation of the Austrians toward Germany appears to Poincaré an offence against French pacifism.

"People living in the cities of the Ukraine"—so wrote a delegation of the Rada to the Provisional Government in May—"see before them the Russified streets of these cities . . . and completely forget that these cities are only little islets in the sea of the whole Ukrainian people." When Rosa Luxemburg, in her posthumous polemic against the programme of the October revolution, asserted that Ukrainian nationalism, having been formerly a mere "amusement" of the commonplace petty bourgeois intelligentsia, had been artificially raised up by the yeast of the Bolshevik formula of self-determination, she fell, notwithstanding her luminous mind, into a very serious historic error. The Ukrainian peasantry had not made national demands in the past for the reason that the Ukrainian peasantry had not in general risen to the height of political being. The chief service of the February revolution—perhaps its only service, but one amply sufficient—lay exactly in this, that it gave the oppressed classes and nations of Russia at last an opportunity to speak out. This political awakening of the peasantry could not have taken place otherwise, however, than through their own native language—with all the consequences ensuing in regard to schools, courts, self-administration. To oppose this would have been to try to drive the peasants back into non-existence.

The difference in nationality between the cities and the villages was painfully felt also in the soviets, they being predominantly city organisations. Under the leadership of the compromise parties the soviets would frequently ignore the national interests of the basic population. This was one cause of the weakness of the soviets in the Ukraine. The soviets of Riga and Reval forgot about the interests of the Letts and the Esthonians. The compromisist soviet in Baku scorned the interests of the basic Turcoman population. Under a false banner of internationalism the soviets would frequently wage a struggle against the defensive nationalism of the Ukrainians or Mussulmans, supplying a screen for the oppressive Russifying movement of the cities. A little time after, under the rule of the Bolsheviks, the soviets of these borderlands began to speak the language of the villages.

Their general economic and cultural primitiveness did not permit the Siberian outlanders—kept down as they were both by nature and exploitation—to rise even to that level where national aspirations begin. Vodka, taxes and compulsory orthodoxy were here from time immemorial the principal instruments of statehood. That disease which the Italians called the French evil, and the French, the Neapolitan, was called "Russian" by the Siberian peoples. That shows from what sources came the seeds of civilisation. The February revolution did not reach that far. The hunters and reindeer breeders of the polar wastes must still wait long for their dawn.

The peoples and tribes along the Volga, in the northern Caucasus, in Central Asia—awakened for the first time out of their pre-historic existence by the February revolution—had as yet neither national bourgeoisie nor national proletariat. Above the peasant or shepherd mass a thin layer had detached itself from among their upper strata, constituting an intelligentsia. Not yet rising to a programme of national self-administration, the struggle here was about matters like having their own alphabet, their own teachers—even at times their own priests. In these ways the most oppressed were being compelled to learn in bitter experience that the educated masters of the state would not voluntarily permit them to rise in the world. The most backward of the backward were thus compelled to seek the most revolutionary class as an ally. Through the left elements of their young intelligentsia the Votiaks, the Chuvashes, the Zyrians, the tribes of Daghestan and Turkestan, began to find their way toward the Bolsheviks.

The fate of the colonial possessions, especially in central

Asia, would change together with the industrial evolution of the centre, passing from direct and open robbery, including trade robbery, to those more disguised methods which converted the Asiatic peasants into suppliers of industrial raw material, chiefly cotton. Hierarchically organised exploitation, combining the barbarity of capitalism with the barbarity of patriarchal life, successfully held down the Asiatic peoples in extreme national abasement. And here the February régime left everything as it was.

The best lands, seized under czarism from the Bashkirs, Buriats, Kirghiz, and other nomadic tribes, had continued in the possession of the landlords and wealthy Russian peasants scattered about in colonising oases among the native population. The awakening of a national spirit of independence here meant first of all a struggle against these colonisers, who had created an artificial strip system of land-ownership and condemned the nomads to hunger and gradual extinction. The colonisers, on their side, furiously defended the unity of Russia—that is, the sanctity of their grabbings—against the "separatism" of the Asiatics. The hatred of the colonisers for the native movements assumed zoological forms in the Transbaikal. Pogroms of the Buriats were in full swing under the leadership of March Social Revolutionaries recruited from village clerks and non-commissioned officers returning from the front.

In their anxiety to preserve the old order as long as possible, all the exploiters and violaters in the colonised regions appealed henceforth to the sovereign rights of the Constituent Assembly. This phraseology was supplied them by the Provisional Government, which had found here its surest bulwark. On the other hand, the privileged upper circles of the oppressed peoples were also calling more and more often on the name of the Constituent Assembly. Even the Mussulman clergy who would lift above the awakening mountain peoples and the tribes of the northern Caucasus, the green banner of the Shariat whenever a pressure from below made their position difficult, were now postponing the question "until the Constituent Assembly." This became the slogan of conservatism, of reaction, of special interest and privilege all over the country. To appeal to the Constituent Assembly meant to postpone and gain time. Postponement meant: assemble your forces and strangle the revolution.

The leadership fell into the hands of the clergy or feudal gentry, however, only at first, only among the backward peoples —almost only among the Mussulmans. In general, the national movement in the villages was headed as a matter of course by rural teachers, village clerks, functionaries and officers of low rank, and, to some extent, merchants. Alongside the Russian or Russianised intelligentsia, composed of the more respectable and well provided elements, there was formed in the borderland cities another layer, a younger layer, closely bound up with its village origin and lacking access to the banquet of capital, and this layer naturally took upon itself the task of representing politically the national, and in part also the social interests of the basic peasant mass.

Although hostilely disposed to the Russian Compromisers along the line of this national aspiration, these borderland Compromisers belonged to the same fundamental type, and even for the most part went by the same name. The Ukrainian Social Revolutionaries and social democrats, the Georgian and Lettish Mensheviks, the Lithuanian "Trudoviks," tried like their Great Russian namesakes to confine the revolution within the framework of the bourgeois régime. But the extreme weakness of the native bourgeoisie here compelled the Mensheviks and Social Revolutionaries, instead of entering a coalition, to take the state power into their own hands. Compelled to go farther on agrarian and labour questions than the central government, these borderland Compromisers had also the great advantage of being able to appear before the army and the country as opponents of the coalitional Provisional Government. All this was sufficient, if not to create different destinies for the Russian Compromisers and those of the borderlands, at least to give a different tempo to their rise and fall.

The Georgian social democrats not only led after them the pauper peasantry of Little Georgia, but also laid claim—and that not without success—to lead the movement of the "revolutionary democracy" for all Russia. During the first months of the revolution the heads of the Georgian intelligentsia regarded Georgia not as a national fatherland, but as a Gironde—a blessed southern province called to provide leaders for the whole country. At the Moscow State Conference one of the prominent Georgian Mensheviks, Chenkeli, boasted that the Georgians had always said even under czarism, in fair weather and foul: "A single fatherland, Russia." "What shall we say of the Georgian nation?" cried this same Chenkeli a month later at the Democratic Conference. "It is wholly at the service of the Great Russian revolution." And it is quite true that the Georgian Compromisers, like the Jewish, were always "at the service" of the great Russian bureaucracy when it was necessary to moderate, or put brakes on the national claims of individual regions.

This continued only so long, however, as the Georgian social democrats still hoped to confine their volution within the framework of bourgeois democracy. In proportion as the danger appeared of a victory of the masses led by Bolshevism, the Georgian social democrats relaxed their ties with the Russian Compromisers and united closely with the reactionary elements of Georgia itself. The moment the soviets were victorious, these Georgian partisans of a single Russia became the trumpeters of separation, and showed to the other peoples of Transcaucasia the yellow fangs of their chauvinism.

This inevitable national disguise of social contradictions—less developed in the borderlands, anyway, as a general rule—adequately explains why the October revolution was destined to meet more opposition in most of the oppressed nations than in Central Russia. But, on the other hand, the conflict of nationalities by its very nature cruelly shook the February régime and created sufficient favourable surroundings for the revolution in the centre.

In these circumstances the national antagonisms whenever they coincided with class contradictions became especially hot. The age-old hostility between the Lettish peasants and the German barons impelled many thousands of labouring Letts to volunteer at the outbreak of the war. The sharp-shooting regiments of Lettish farm hands and peasants were among the best troops at the front. As early as May, however, they had already come out for a Soviet government. Their nationalism was only the outer shell of an immature Bolshevism. A like process took place in Esthonia.

In White Russia, with its Polish or Polised landlords, its Jewish population in the cities and small towns, and its Russian officials, the twice and thrice oppressed peasantry had some time before October, under the influence of the nearby front, poured its national and social indignation into the channel of Bolshevism. In the elections for the Constituent Assembly the overwhelming mass of White Russians would cast its vote for the Bolsheviks.

All these processes in which an awakened national dignity was linked up with social indignation, now holding it back, now pushing it forward, found an extremely sharp expression in the army. Here there was a veritable fever for creating national regiments, and these were at one time patronised, at another tolerated, at still another persecuted by the central government, according to their attitude to the war and the Bolsheviks. But in general they kept growing more and more hostile to Petrograd.

Lenin kept a firm hand on the "national" pulse of the revolution. In a famous article, "The Crisis is Ripe," written toward the end of September, he insistently pointed out that the National curia of the Democratic Conference "had stood second in the matter of radicalism yielding only to the trade unions, and standing higher than the Soviet curia in its percentage of votes against the Coalition (40 out of 55)." This meant that the oppressed people were no longer hoping for any benefit from the Great Russian bourgeoisie. They were more and more trying to get their rights by independent action, a bite at a time and in the form of revolutionary seizures.

In an October congress of the Buriats in far off Verkhneyudinsk, a speaker declared that "the February revolution introduced nothing new" in the position of the outlander. His summing up of the situation made it seem necessary, if not yet to take the side of the Bolsheviks, at least to observe an attitude of more and more friendly neutrality toward them.

An all-Ukrainian soldier-congress which met during the very days of the Petrograd insurrection, adopted a resolution to struggle against the transfer of power to the Ukrainian Soviet, but at the same time refused to regard the insurrection of the Great Russian Bolsheviks as an "anti-democratic action," and promised to take all measures to prevent the soldiers being sent to put down the insurrection. This equivocation which perfectly characterises the petty bourgeois stage of the national struggle, facilitated that revolution of the proletariat which intended to put an end to all equivocations.

On the other hand the bourgeois circles in the borderlands, which had heretofore invariably and always gravitated toward the central power, now launched into a separatism which in many cases no longer had a shred of national foundation. The Baltic bourgeoisie, which only yesterday had been following in a state of hurrah-patriotism the German barons, the first bulwark of the Romanovs, took its stand in the struggle against Bolshevik Russia and its own masses, under the banner of separatism. Still more curious phenomena appeared along this road. On the 20th of October the foundations were laid for a new state formation, "The South-eastern Union of the Cossack Troops, Caucasian Mountaineers and Free Peoples of the

Steppes." Here the leaders of the Don, Kuban, Tyer and Astrakhan Cossacks, the chief bulwark of imperial centralism, were transformed in the course of a few months into passionate defenders of the federal principle, and united on this ground with the leaders of the Mussulman mountaineers and steppe-dwellers. The boundaries of the federative structure were to serve as a barrier against the Bolshevik danger coming from the north. However, before creating the principal drill ground for the civil war against the Bolsheviks, this counter-revolutionary separatism went directly against the ruling coalition, demoralising and weakening it.

Thus the national problem, along with all others, showed the Provisional Government a Medusa's head on which every hair of the March and April hopes had changed into a snake of hate and indignation.

A Further Note on the Problem of Nationalities

The Bolshevik Party did not by any means immediately after the February revolution adopt that attitude on the national question which in the long run guaranteed its victory. This was true not only in the borderlands, with their weak and inexperienced party organisations, but also in the Petrograd centre. During the war the party had so weakened, the theoretical and political level of its cadres had become so lowered, that on the national question too its official leaders took an extremely confused and half-way position until the arrival of Lenin.

To be sure, following their tradition, the Bolsheviks defended the right of a nation to self-determination. But the Mensheviks also subscribed to this formula in words. The text of the two programmes remained identical. It was the question of power which was decisive. And the temporary leaders of the party proved wholly incapable of understanding the irreconcilable antagonism between the Bolshevik slogans on the national, as well as the agrarian, question, and the preservation of a bourgeois-imperialistic régime, even though disguised in democratic forms.

The democratic position found its most crass expression from the pen of Stalin. On March 25, in an article dealing with a government degree on the abolition of national limitations, Stalin tried to formulate the national question on a historic scale. "The social basis of national oppression," he writes, "the power inspiring it, is a decaying land aristocracy." The fact that national oppression developed unprecedentedly during the epoch of capitalism, and found its most barbaric expression in colonial policies, seems to be beyond the ken of the democratic author. "In England," he continues, "where the landed aristocracy shares the power with the bourgeoisie, where the unlimited power of this aristocracy long ago ceased to exist, national oppression is milder, less inhumane—leaving out of account, of course, the circumstance that during the course of the war, when the power had gone over into the hands of the landlords (!), national oppression was considerably strengthened (persecution of Ireland and India)." Those guilty of oppressing Ireland and India are the landlords, who—evidently in the person of Lloyd George—have seized the power thanks to the war. ". . . In Switzerland and North America," continues Stalin, "where there is no landlordism and never has been (!), where the power is undivided in the hands of the bourgeoisie, nationalities have developed freely. National oppression, generally speaking, finds no place. . . ." The author completely forgets the Negro, Indian, immigrant and colonial problems in the United States.

From this hopelessly provincial analysis, which comes only to a confused contrasting of feudalism with democracy, purely liberal political inferences are drawn. "To remove the feudal aristocracy from the political scene, to snatch the power from it—that is exactly the same thing as to put an end to national oppression, to create the actual conditions necessary for national freedom." "Insofar as the Russian revolution has conquered," writes Stalin, "it has actually created these conditions. . . ." We have here perhaps a more principled apology for the imperialistic "democracy" than all that has been written on this theme by the Mensheviks. Just as in foreign policy Stalin, along with Kamenev, hoped to achieve a democratic peace by means of a division of labour with the Provisional Government, so in domestic policy he found in the democracy of Prince Lvov the "actual conditions" of national freedom.

As a matter of fact the fall of the monarchy first fully exposed the fact that not only the reactionary landlords, but also the whole liberal bourgeoisie, and following after it the whole petty bourgeois democracy, along with the patriotic upper crust of the working class, was implacably hostile to a genuine equality of national rights—that is to say, an abolition of the privileges of the dominant nation. Their whole programme came down to a business of mitigation, of cultural sugar-coating, of democratic concealment of the Great Russian ascendancy.

At the April conference, in defending Lenin's resolution on the national question, Stalin formally starts from the thesis that "national oppression is that system . . . those measures which are adopted by the imperialistic circles." But he straightway and inevitably gets off the track and goes back to his March position. "The more democratic a country, the weaker its national oppression and vice versa." Such is the speaker's own summary, and not the one he borrowed from Lenin. The fact that democratic England is oppressing feudal and caste-ridden India escapes, as before, from his limited field of vision. In distinction from Russia, where "an old land aristocracy" has dominated—continues Stalin—"in England and Austria-Hungary the national oppression has never taken the form of pogroms." As though a land aristocracy "never" dominated in England, and as though it does not dominate to this day in Hungary! The combined character of historic development which unites "democracy" with the strangling of weak nations, had remained for Stalin a sealed book.

That Russia took form as a state made up of nationalities, is the result of her historic belatedness. But belatedness is a complex conception inevitably contradictory. The backward country does not follow in the tracks of the advanced, keeping the same distance. In an epoch of world-wide economy the backward nations, becoming involved under pressure from the advanced in the general chain of development, skip over whole series of intermediate stages. Moreover the absence of firmly established social forms and traditions makes the backward country—at least within certain limits extremely hospitable to the last word in international technique and international thought. Backwardness does not, however, for this reason cease to be backwardness. The whole development gets a contradictory and combined character. A predominance of historic extremes is proper to the social structure of a belated nation—predominance of the backward peasants and the advanced proletarians over the intermediate formations of the bourgeoisie. The tasks of one class are shouldered off upon another. In the national sphere also, the uprooting of mediæval remnants falls to the lot of the proletariat.

Nothing so clearly characterises the historic belatedness of Russia when considered as a European country, as the fact that in the twentieth century she had to liquidate compulsory land rent and the pale—those twin barbarisms, serfdom and the Ghetto. But in performing these tasks Russia, exactly because of her belated development, made use of new and utterly modern classes, parties, programmes. To make an end of the idea and methods of Rasputin, she required the ideas and methods of Marx.

Political practice remained, of course, far more primitive than political theory. For things are harder to change than ideas. But theory nevertheless only carried the demands of practical action clear through. In order to achieve liberation and a cultural lift, the oppressed nationalities were compelled to link their fate with that of the working class. And for this they had to free themselves from the leadership of their own bourgeois and petty bourgeois parties—they had to make a long spurt forward, that is, on the road of historic development.

This subordination of the national movements to the fundamental process of the revolution, the struggle of the proletariat for power, was not accomplished at once, but in several stages—and moreover differently in different regions. The Ukrainian, White Russian and Tartar workers, peasants, and soldiers who were hostile to Kerensky, the war and the Russification, became thereby, in spite of their compromisist leadership, allies of the proletarian insurrection. From being an objective support of the Bolsheviks, they became obliged at a further stage to go over consciously also to the Bolshevik road. In Finland, Latvia and Esthonia, and more weakly in the Ukraine, the stratification of the national movement had taken such sharp forms by October, that only the interference of foreign troops could prevent the success of the proletarian revolution. In the Asiatic East, where the national awakening was taking place in more primitive forms, it could only by degrees and with a considerable lag come under the leadership of the proletariat—only, indeed, after the proletariat had conquered the power. If you take this complicated and contradictory process as a whole the conclusion is obvious: the national current, like the agrarian, was pouring into the channel of the October revolution.

The irrevocable and irresistible going over of the masses from the most rudimentary tasks of political, agrarian and national emancipation and abolition of serfdom to the slogan of proletarian rulership, resulted not from "demagogic" agitation, not from preconceived schemes, not from the theory of Permanent Revolution as the Liberals and Compromisers thought, but from the social structure of Russia and the conditions of the world-wide situation. The theory of Permanent Revolution only formulated the combined process of this development.

It is a question here not of Russia alone. This subordination of belated national revolutions to the revolution of the proletariat follows a law which is valid throughout the world. Whereas in the nineteenth century the fundamental problem of wars and revolutions was still to guarantee a national market to the productive forces, the problem of our century is to free the productive forces from the national boundaries which have become iron fetters upon them. In the broad historic sense the national revolutions of the East are only stages of the world revolution of the proletariat, just as the national movements of Russia became stepping stones to the Soviet dictatorship.

Lenin appraised with admirable profundity the revolutionary force inherent in the development of the oppressed nationalities, both in czarist Russia and throughout the world. That hypocritical "pacifism," which "condemns" in the same way the war of Japan against China aiming at her enslavement, and the war of China against Japan in the cause of her liberation, got nothing but scorn from Lenin. For him a war of national liberation, in contrast to wars of imperialistic oppression, was merely another form of the national revolution which in its turn enters as a necessary link in the liberating struggle of the international working class.

This appraisal of national wars and revolutions does not by any means imply, however, that the bourgeoisie of the colonial and semi-colonial nations have a revolutionary mission. On the contrary, this bourgeoisie of backward countries from the days of its milk teeth grows up as agentry of foreign capital, and notwithstanding its envious hatred of foreign capital, always does and always will in every decisive situation turn up in the same camp with it. Chinese compradorism is the classic form of the colonial bourgeoisie, and the Kuomintang is the classic party of compradorism. The upper circles of the petty bourgeoisie, including the intelligentsia, may take an active and occasionally a very noisy part in the national struggles, but they are totally incapable of playing an independent rôle. Only the working class standing at the head of the nation can carry either a national or an agrarian revolution clear through.

The fatal mistake of the Epigones, and above all Stalin, lies in this, that from Lenin's teaching about the progressive historic significance of the struggle of oppressed nations they have inferred a revolutionary mission of the bourgeoisie of the colonial countries. A failure to understand the permanent character of revolution in an imperialist epoch; a pedantic schematisation of the course of development; a chopping up of the living and combined process into dead stages imagined to be necessarily separated in time—all these errors have brought Stalin to a vulgar idealisation of democracy or a "democratic dictatorship," a thing which can be nothing in reality but either an imperialist dictatorship or a dictatorship of the proletariat. Step by step Stalin's groups have proceeded along this road to a complete break with the position of Lenin on the national question, and to their catastrophic policy in China.

In August 1927, in conflict with the Opposition (Trotsky, Rakovsky, and others) Stalin said at a plenary session of the Central Committee of the Bolsheviks: "A revolution in imperialist countries is one thing; there the bourgeoisie . . . is counter-revolutionary at all stages of the revolution. . . . A revolution in colonial and dependent countries is something else . . .; there the national bourgeoisie can at a given stage and a given date support the revolutionary movement of their country against imperialism."

With side remarks and softenings due only to his lack of confidence in himself, Stalin here transfers to the colonial bourgeoisie those same traits with which he was adorning the Russian bourgeoisie in March. Obedient to its deeply organic nature Stalin's opportunism finds its way as though impelled by some law of gravitation, through whatever channels always in the same direction. The choice of theoretic arguments becomes here a purely accidental matter.

From this transfer of his March appraisal of the Provisional Government to the "national" government of China resulted Stalin's three-year co-operation with the Kuomintang, a policy which led up to one of the most shocking facts of modern history. In the capacity of loyal armour-bearer, the Bolshevism of the

Epigones accompanied the Chinese bourgeoisie right up to April 11, 1927, the day of its bloody massacre of the Shanghai proletariat. "The fundamental mistake of the Opposition"—thus Stalin tried to justify his comradeship in arms with Chang Kai Shek—"lies in the fact that it identifies the revolution of 1905 in Russia—in an imperialist country oppressing other peoples, with the revolution in China, an oppressed country. . . ." It is astonishing even in Stalin that he has never thought of viewing the revolution in Russia, not from the standpoint of the nation "oppressing other peoples," but from the standpoint of the experience of these same "other peoples" of Russia who have suffered no less oppression than the Chinese.

In that gigantic field of experience represented by Russia in the course of her three revolutions, you can find every variant of national and class struggle except one: that in which the bourgeoisie of any oppressed nation played a liberating rôle in relation to its own people. At every stage of its development every borderland bourgeoisie, no matter in what colours it might dance, was invariably dependent upon the central banks, trusts, and commercial institutions which were in essence the agents of all Russian capital. They subjected the bourgeoisie to the Russifying movement, and subjected to the bourgeoisie broad circles of the liberal and democratic intelligentsia. The more "mature" a borderland bourgeoisie might be, the more closely was it bound up with the general state machine. Taken as a whole, the bourgeoisie of the oppressed nation played the same rôle in relation to the ruling bourgeoisie that the latter played in relation to international finance capital. The complex hierarchy of antagonisms and dependencies did not remove for one single day the fundamental solidarity of the three in the struggle against the insurrectionary masses.

In the period of counter-revolution (1907–1917), when the leadership of the national movements was in the hands of the native bourgeoisie, they were even more candid than the Russian liberals in seeking a working agreement with the Russian monarchy. The Polish, Baltic, Tartar, Ukrainian, Jewish bourgeois vied with each other in the display of imperialist patriotism. After the February revolution they hid behind the backs of the Kadets—or, like the Kadets, behind the backs of their own national Compromisers. The bourgeoisie of the border nations entered the road of separatism in the autumn of 1917, not in a struggle against national oppression, but in a struggle against the advancing proletarian revolution. In the sum total the bourgeoisie of the oppressed nations manifested no less hostility to the revolution than the Great Russian bourgeoisie.

This gigantic historic lesson of three revolutions has left not a trace, however, in the minds of many of those who took part in the events—notably in the mind of Stalin. The compromisist—that is, petty bourgeois—conception of the correlation of classes within colonial nations, that conception which killed the Chinese revolution of 1925–1927, has even been introduced by the Epigones into the programme of the Communist International, converting this programme in that section into a mere trap for the oppressed peoples of the East.

In order to understand the real character of Lenin's policy on the national question, it is a good idea—following the method of contrasts—to compare it with the policy of the Austrian social democrats. Bolshevism based itself upon the assumption of an outbreak of national revolutions continuing for decades to come, and instructed the advanced workers in this spirit. The Austrian social democracy, on the contrary, submissively accommodated itself to the policy of the ruling classes; it defended the compulsory co-citizenship of ten nations in the Austro-Hungarian monarchy, and at the same time, being absolutely incapable of achieving a revolutionary union of the workers of these different nationalities, fenced them off in the party and in the trade unions with vertical partitions. Karl Renner, an educated Hapsburg functionary, was never tired of probing the inkwells of Austro-Marxism in search of some means of rejuvenating the rule of the Hapsburgs—until one day he found himself the bereaved theoretician of the Austro-Hungarian monarchy. When the Central Empires were crushed, the Hapsburg dynasty again tried to raise the banner of a federation of autonomous nations under its sceptre. The official programme of the Austrian social democracy, based as it was upon the assumption of a peaceful development within the framework of the monarchy, now became in one second the programme of the monarchy itself, covered with the bloody filth of its four years of war. But that rusty hoop which had bound ten nations together flew to pieces. Austria-Hungary fell apart as a result of internal centrifugal tendencies reinforced by the surgery of Versailles. New states were formed, and the old ones reconstructed. The Austrian Germans hung over an abyss. Their problem was no longer to preserve their dominance over other nations, but to avoid falling themselves under a foreign yoke. And Otto Bauer, representing the "left" wing of the Austrian social democracy, considered this a suitable moment to bring forward the formula of national self-determination. That programme which during the preceding decades should have inspired the struggle of the proletariat against the Hapsburgs and the ruling bourgeoisie, was now brought in as an instrument of self-preservation for the nation which had dominated yesterday, but to-day was in danger from the side of the liberated Slavic peoples. Just as the reformist programme of the Austrian social democracy had become in the wink of an eye the straw at which a drowning monarchy tried to grab, so the formula of self-determination, emasculated by these Austro-Marxists, was now to become the anchor of salvation for the German bourgeoisie.

On October 3, 1918, when the matter no longer depended on them in the slightest degree, the social democratic deputies of the reichsrath magnanimously "recognised" the right of the peoples of the former empire to self-determination. On October 4th, the bourgeois parties also adopted the programme of self-determination. Having thus out-stripped the Austro-German imperialists by one day, the social democrats immediately resumed their waiting policy, it being still uncertain what turn things would take and what Wilson was going to say. Only on the 13th of October, when the conclusive collapse of the army and the monarchy had created—in the words of Otto Bauer—"the revolutionary situation for which our national programme was designed," did the Austro-Marxists raise the question of self-determination in a practical form. In very truth they had now nothing to lose. "With the collapse of its rulership over other nations," explains Bauer quite frankly, "the German national bourgeoisie considered at an end that historic mission in whose cause it had voluntarily suffered a separation from the German fatherland." Thus the new programme was put in circulation not because it was needful to the oppressed, but because it had ceased to be dangerous to the oppressors. The possessing classes, driven into a tight place historically, had found themselves obliged to recognise the national revolution juridically, and Austro-Marxism found this an appropriate moment to legitimise it theoretically. This was a mature revolution, they said, timely, historically prepared—it is all over anyway. The spirit of the social democracy is here before us as though in the palm of the hand!

It was quite otherwise with the social revolution, which could not hope for any recognition from the possessing classes. This had to be postponed, compromised, robbed of glory. Since the empire had split up along the weakest, that is the national, seams, Otto Bauer drew the following conclusion as to the character of the revolution: "It was by no means a social, but a national revolution." In reality the movement had had from the very beginning a deep social-revolutionary content. Its "purely national" character is fairly well illustrated by the fact that the possessing classes of Austria openly invited the Entente to take prisoner the whole army. The German bourgeoisie beseeched the Italian general to seize Vienna with Italian troops!

This vulgar and pedantic separation of national form from social content in the revolutionary process, as though they constituted two independent historic stages—we see here how closely Otto Bauer approaches Stalin!—had an extremely utilitarian destination. Its purpose was to justify the collaboration of the social democracy with the bourgeoisie in its struggle against the danger of social revolution.

If you adopt the formula of Marx that revolution is the locomotive of history, then Austro-Marxism occupies the position of the brake. Even after the actual collapse of the monarchy, the social democracy, called to participate in the government, was still unable to make up its mind to a rupture with the old Hapsburg ministry. The "national" revolution limited itself to reinforcing the old ministers with state secretaries. Only after October 9th, when the German revolution had thrown out the Hohenzollerns, did the Austrian social democrats propose to the State Council that they proclaim a republic, frightening their bourgeois partners into it with the movement of the masses at which they were already themselves quaking to the marrow of their bones. "The Christian Socialists," says Otto Bauer with imprudent irony, "who on the 9th and 10th of November were still on the side of the monarchy, decided on November 11 to cease their resistance. . . ." For two whole days the social democrats were in advance of this party of the Black Hundred Monarchy! All the heroic legends of humanity grow pale before this revolutionary audacity.

Against its will the Austrian social democracy took its place automatically from the beginning of the revolution at the head of the nation, just as had the Russian Mensheviks and Social Revolutionaries. Like them too it feared above all things its own power. In the coalition government the social democrats tried to occupy just as small a place as possible. Otto Bauer explains this as follows: "The fact that the social democrats at first demanded only a modest participation in the government corresponded primarily to the purely national character of the revolution." The question of power was decided by those people not on a basis of the real correlation of forces, the might of the revolutionary movement, the bankruptcy of the ruling classes, the political influence of the party, but by a pedantic little label "purely national revolution" pasted by some wiseacre classifiers upon the actual course of events.

Karl Renner waited out the storm in the position of head secretary of the State Council. The other social democratic leaders converted themselves into assistants of the bourgeois ministers. In other words, the social democrats hid under the office tables. The masses, however, were not satisfied to feed on the national shell of that nut whose social meat the Austro-Marxists were saving up for the bourgeoisie. The workers and soldiers shoved out the bourgeois ministers and compelled the social democrats to come out of hiding. The irreplaceable theoretician, Otto Bauer, explains this also: "Only the events of the following days, driving the national revolution over to the side of social revolution, increased our weight in the government." To translate this into intelligible language: under the assault of the masses, the social democrats were compelled to crawl out from under the tables.

But this did not change their function for a moment. They took the power, but only to start a war against romanticism and adventurism, with which titles these sycophants now designated that same social revolution which had "increased their weight in the government." If these Austro-Marxists successfully fulfilled in 1918 their historic mission as guardian angels protecting the Vienna Kreditanstalt from the revolutionary romanticism of the proletariat, it is only because they met no obstacle from the side of a genuine revolutionary party.

The two states composed of nationalities, Russian and Austria-Hungary, have with their most recent fate set a seal upon the difference between Bolshevism and Austro-Marxism. Throughout a decade and a half Lenin, in implacable conflict with all shades of Great Russian chauvinism, preached the right of all oppressed nations to cut away from the empire of the czars. The Bolsheviks were accused of aspiring toward the dismemberment of Russia, but this bold revolutionary formulation of the national problem won for the Bolshevik party the indestructible confidence of the small and oppressed peoples of czarist Russia. In April 1917 Lenin said: "If the Ukranians see that we have a Soviet republic they will not cut away, but if we have a Miliukov republic they will." In this he proved right. History has provided an incomparable checkup of the two policies on the national question. Whereas Austria-Hungary, whose proletariat was educated in the spirit of a cowardly halfway policy, went all to pieces under a formidable shake-up, and moreover the initiative in this process was taken in the main by the national sections of the social democratic party, in Russia on the ruins of czarism a new state composed of nationalities has been formed, and has been closely welded together both economically and politically by the Bolshevik Party.

Whatever may be the further destiny of the Soviet Union—and it is still far from a quiet haven—the national policy of Lenin will find its place among the eternal treasures of mankind.

Chapter III

Withdrawal from the Pre-Parliament and Struggle for the Soviet Congress

Every additional day of war was disintegrating the front, weakening the government, damaging the international position of the country. At the beginning of October the German fleets, both naval and air, developed active operations in the Gulf of Finland. The Baltic sailors fought courageously trying to protect the road to Petrograd. But they, more clearly and profoundly than any other unit of the front, understood the deep contradiction in their position as vanguards of a revolution and involuntary participants in an imperialist war, and through the radio stations on their ships they sent out a cry to the four corners of the horizon for international revolutionary help. "Attacked by superior German forces our fleet will go down in unequal battle. Not one of our ships will decline the fight. The slandered and maligned fleet will do its duty . . . but not at the command of a miserable Russian Bonaparte, ruling by the long-suffering patience of the revolution . . . not in the name of the treaties of our rulers with the Allies, binding in chains the hands of Russian freedom. . . ." No, but in the name of the defence of the approaches to the hearth-fire of the revolution, Petrograd. "In the hour when the waves of the Baltic are stained with the blood of our brothers, while the waters are closing over their bodies, we raise our voice: . . . Oppressed people of the whole world! Lift the banner of revolt!"

These words about battles and victims were not empty. The squadron had lost the ship *Slava* and retired after fighting. The Germans had captured the Moon-sund Archipelago. One more black page in the book of the war had been turned. The government decided to use this new military blow as a pretext for moving the capital. This old idea swam out at every suitable opportunity. It was not that the ruling circles had any particular affection for Moscow, but they hated Petrograd. The monarchist reaction, the liberals, the democracy—all strove in turn to denote the capital, to bring it to its knees, to beat it down. The most extreme patriots were now hating Petrograd with a far more bitter hatred than they felt for Berlin.

The question of evacuating the capital was taken up as a thing to be accomplished in extraordinary haste. Only two weeks were allotted for the transfer of the government together with the Pre-Parliament. It was also decided to evacuate in the briefest possible time the factories working for the defence. The Central Executive Committee as a "private institution" would have to look out for itself.

The Kadet instigators of the plan understood that a mere transfer of the government would not settle their problem, but they counted on afterward capturing the seat of revolutionary infection with hunger, disease and exhaustion. An internal blockade of Petrograd was already in full swing. The factories were being deprived of orders; the supply of fuel had been cut down three-quarters; the Ministry of Provisions was holding up cattle on their way to the capital; freight movements on the Mariinsky Railroad System had been stopped.

The warlike Rodzianko, president of that state Duma which the government had at last dissolved at the beginning of October, spoke quite frankly in the liberal Moscow newspaper *Utro Rossii* about the military danger threatening the capital. "I say to myself, God help her, God help Petrograd. . . . A fear was expressed in Petrograd lest the central institutions (that is the soviets, etc.) will be destroyed. To this I answered that I would be very glad if those institutions were destroyed, for they have brought nothing whatever but evil to Russia." To be sure, with the capture of Petrograd the Baltic fleet also would have been destroyed, but against that too Rodzianko had no complaint: "The ships there are completely depraved." Thanks to the fact that the Lord Chamberlain could not keep his tongue behind his teeth, the people had this chance to find out the most intimate thoughts of noble and bourgeois Russia.

The Russian chargé d'affaires reported from London that the British naval headquarters, in spite of all urgings, did not consider it possible to relieve the situation of its Ally in the Baltic. It was not the Bolsheviks alone who interpreted this answer to mean that the Allies, in common with the patriotic upper circles of Russia herself, looked only for benefits to the common cause from a German blow at Petrograd. The workers and soldiers had no doubt—especially after Rodzianko's confession—that the government was consciously getting ready to send them to school to Ludendorff and Hoffmann.

On the 6th of October the soldiers' section adopted with a unanimity hitherto unknown the resolution introduced by Trotsky: "If the Provisional Government is incapable of defending Petrograd, it must either make peace or give place to another government." The workers were no less irreconcilable. They considered Petrograd their fortress. Their revolutionary hopes were bound up with her. They did not intend to surrender Petrograd. Frightened by the military danger, the evacuation, the indignation of the soldiers and workers, the excitement of the whole population, the Compromisers, on their side, sounded an alarm: We must not abandon Petrograd to the caprice of fate. Convinced that an attempted evacuation would meet resistance from all sides, the government began to draw back: We were not troubled so much, you know, about our own safety as about the question of a meeting-place for the future Constituent Assembly. But this position, too, they could not maintain. In less than a week the government was compelled to announce that it not only intended to remain in the Winter Palace itself, but proposed as before to convoke the Constituent Assembly in the Tauride Palace. This announcement changed nothing in the military and political situation. But it revealed once more the political power of Petrograd, which considered itself called to put an end to the government of Kerensky, and would not let that government escape from its walls. It was only the Bolsheviks who subsequently dared transfer the capital to Moscow. They carried this out without the slightest difficulty because for them it was really a strategic move. They could not have any political reason for flying from Petrograd.

That contrite declaration about the defence of the capital was made by the government upon the demand of the compromisist majority of a commission of the Council of the Russian Republic or "Pre-Parliament." This wonderful institution had at last succeeded in getting born. Plekhanov, who loved jokes and knew how to make them, disrespectfully named this impotent and ephemeral Council of the Republic "the little house on chicken's feet." Politically this definition is not at all inaccurate. It is only necessary to add that for a little house the Pre-Parliament put up a pretty good front: the magnificent Mariinsky Palace, which had formerly sheltered the State Council of Ministers, was placed at its disposal. The contrast between this elegant palace and Smolny Institute, run-down and saturated with soldier smells, made a great impression upon Sukhanov: "Amid all this magnificence," he confesses, "one wanted to rest, to forget about labour and struggle, about hunger and war, about ruin and anarchy, about the country and the revolution." But there was very little time left for rest and forgetfulness.

The so-called "democratic" majority of the Pre-Parliament consisted of 308 men: 120 Social Revolutionaries, among them about 20 Lefts, 60 Mensheviks of various shades, 66 Bolsheviks; after that came the Co-operators, the delegates of the peasant executive committee, etc. The possessing classes were accorded 156 seats, of which the Kadets occupied almost half. Together with the Co-operators, the Cossacks, and the rather conservative members of Kerensky's Executive Committee, the Right Wing on a number of questions came near being a majority. The distribution of seats in that comfortable little house on chicken's feet was thus in flagrant contradiction to all decisive expressions of the will of the people that had been made either in city or country. Moreover, in opposition to the dull grey representation to be found in the soviets and elsewhere, the Mariinsky Palace assembled within its walls the "flower of the nation." Inasmuch as the members of the Pre-Parliament did not depend upon the accidents of elective competition, upon local influences and provincial preferences, each social group and each party sent its most eminent leaders. The personnel was, to quote Sukhanov, "extraordinarily brilliant." When the Pre-Parliament assembled for its first session, a weight was lifted, says Miliuko, from the hearts of many sceptics: "It will be fine if the Constituent Assembly is no worse than this." The flower of the nation looked upon itself in the palace mirrors with great satisfaction and neglected to notice that it was incapable of bearing fruit.

In opening this Council of the Republic on October 7, Kerensky did not forgo the opportunity to remark that although the government possessed "all the fullness of power," it was nevertheless ready to listen to "any genuinely valuable suggestion." Although absolute, that is to say, the government had not ceased to be cultivated. In the præsidium, which consisted of five members with Avksentiev as president, one place was offered to the Bolsheviks: it remained unoccupied. The directors of this pitiful and unhappy comedy felt sick at heart. The entire interest of its grey opening on a rainy day was centred upon the forthcoming action of the Bolsheviks. In the couloirs of the Mariinsky Palace, according to Sukhanov, a "sensational rumour" was in the air: "Trotsky has won by a majority of two or three votes . . . and the Bolsheviks are going to withdraw at once from the Pre-Parliament." In reality the decision to withdraw demonstratively from the Mariinsky Palace was adopted on the 5th at a meeting of the Bolshevik faction by all votes except one. So great had been the shift leftward during the preceding two weeks! Only Kamenev remained true to his original position—or rather he alone dared defend it. In a special declaration addressed to the Central Committee, Kamenev candidly described the course adopted as "very dangerous for the party." The doubt about the intentions of the Bolsheviks caused a certain anxiety in the Pre-Parliament. It was not so much a breakdown of the régime that they feared, as a "scandal" before the eyes of the Allied diplomats, whom the majority had just greeted with an appropriate volley of patriotic applause. Sukhanov relates how they despatched an official personage—Avksentiev himself—to the Bolsheviks to inquire in advance: What is going to happen? "A mere nothing," answered Trotsky, "a mere nothing, a little shot from a pistol." After the opening of the session, upon the basis of rules of order taken over from the state Duma, Trotsky was offered ten minutes for a special announcement in the name of the Bolshevik faction. A tense silence reigned in the hall. The declaration began by stating that the government was at present just as irresponsible as it had been before the Democratic Conference, which was supposed to have been convoked for the curbing of Kerensky, and that the representatives of the possessing classes were present in this provisional council in numbers to which they had not the slightest right. If the bourgeois were really preparing for a Constituent Assembly to meet in a month and a half, their leaders would have no reason to defend so fiercely at the present time the irresponsibility of the government even to this doctored representation. "The essence of it all is that the bourgeois classes have decided to quash the Constituent Assembly." The blow was well aimed, and the Right Wing protested the more noisily. Without departing from the text of the declaration the speaker denounced the industrial, agrarian food policy. It would be impossible to adopt any other policy, even if you set yourself the conscious aim of impelling the masses to insurrection. "The idea of surrendering the revolutionary capital to the German troops . . . we accept as a natural link in a general policy designed to promote . . . a counter-revolutionary conspiracy." The protest here turned into a storm. Cries about Berlin, about German gold, about the sealed train—and on this general background, like pieces of broken bottle in the mud, foul-mouthed abuse. Nothing like it was ever heard during the most passionate conflicts in Smolny, dirty and rundown and spat all over by soldiers as it was. "We only have to get into the good society of Mariinsky Palace," writes Sukhanov, "in order to revive at once that atmosphere of the low-class saloon which prevailed in the state Duma with its restricted franchise."

Picking his way through these explosions of hatred alternating with moments of hush, the speaker concluded: "No, the Bolshevik faction announce that with this government of treason to the people and with this Council of counter-revolutionary connivance we have nothing whatever in common. . . . In withdrawing from the provisional council we summon the workers, soldiers and peasants of all Russia to be on their guard, and to be courageous. Petrograd is in danger! The revolution is in danger! The people are in danger! . . . We address ourselves to the people. All power to the soviets!" As the orator descended from the tribune the few score of Bolsheviks left the hall accompanied by curses. After their moment of alarm the majority heaved a happy sigh of relief. Only the Bolsheviks went out. The flower of the nation remained at their posts. The Left Wing of the Compromisers bent a little under a blow not directed, it seemed, at themselves. "We, the nearest neighbours of the Bolsheviks," confesses Sukhanov, "sat there completely appalled by all that had happened." These immaculate Knights of the word were sensing the fact that the time for words had passed.

The Minister of Foreign Affairs, Tereshchenko, informed the Russian ambassadors about the opening of the Pre-Parliament in a secret telegram: "The first session passed off uneventfully with the exception of a scandal created by the Bolsheviks." The historic break between the proletariat and the state mechanism of the bourgeoisie was conceived by those people as a mere "scandal." The bourgeois press did not miss the opportunity to goad the government by references to the resoluteness of the Bolsheviks: The honourable ministers will only then lead the country out of anarchy when they "acquire as much resolution and will to action as is to be found in Comrade Trotsky." As though it were a question of resolution and the will of individual people and not of the historic destiny of classes! and as though the sorting out of people and characters goes on independently of historic tasks. "They spoke and acted," wrote Miliukov on the subject of the Bolshevik withdrawal from the Pre-Parliament, "like people feeling a power behind them, knowing that the morrow belonged to them."

The loss of the Moon-sund Islands, the growing danger to Petrograd, and the withdrawal of the Bolsheviks from the Pre-Parliament into the street, compelled the Compromisers to take thought for the further development of the war. After a three-day discussion participated in by the Minister of War and Navy, and the commissars and delegates of the army organisations, the Central Executive Committee came at last to a saving decision: "To insist that representatives of the Russian democracy be admitted to the Paris Conference of the Allies." After renewed efforts they named Skobelev as delegate. Detailed instructions were drawn up: Peace without annexations or indemnities; neutralisation of straits and canals, including the Suez and Panama Canals—the Compromisers had a wider outlook geographically than politically; abolition of secret diplomacy; gradual disarmament. The Central Executive Committee explained that the aim of its delegate in the Paris Conference was "to bring pressure to bear upon the Allies." Pressure of Skobelev upon France, Great Britain and the United States! The Kadet paper put a poisonous question! "What will Skobelev do if the Allies unceremoniously reject his conditions? Will he threaten them with another appeal to the people of the whole world?" The Compromisers, alas, had long been blushing for that old appeal of theirs.

While intending to force upon the United States the neutralisation of the Panama Canal, the Central Executive Committee proved incapable in actual fact of bringing pressure to bear even upon the Winter Palace. On the 12th, Kerensky sent Lloyd George a voluminous letter full of gentle reproaches, sorrowful complaints, and fervent promises. The front, he said, is "in better condition than it was last spring." Of course the defeatist propaganda—thus the Russian premier complains to a Britisher against the Russian Bolsheviks—has hindered the carrying out of all the plans indicated. But there can be no talk of peace. The government knows only one question: "How to continue the war!" It goes without saying that as an earnest of his patriotism Kerensky begged for credits.

Having got rid of the Bolsheviks, the Pre-Parliament also lost no time in taking up the war. On the 10th the debate opened on improving the fighting capacity of the army. The dialogue, which occupied three weary sessions, developed according to one invariable scheme. We must convince the army that it is fighting for peace and democracy, said the Left. We must not convince but compel, answered the Right. You have nothing to compel with; in order to compel you must first at least partially convince, answered the Compromisers. In the matter of convincing the Bolsheviks are stronger than you, answered the Kadets. Both sides were right. But a drowning man is also right when he lets out a yell before going down.

On the 18th came that decisive hour which in the nature of things nothing in the world could alter. The formula of the Social Revolutionaries got 95 votes against 127, with 50 abstaining. The formula of the Right got 135 votes against 139. Astonishing! There was no majority! Throughout the hall, according to the newspaper accounts, there was general movement and confusion. In spite of its unity of aim, the flower of the nation proved incapable of adopting even a platonic decision upon the most urgent question of the national life. This was no accident. The same thing was being repeated day by day in the commissions and in the plenary sessions upon all other questions. The fragments of opinion could not be put together. All the groups were living on illusive shadings of political thought: thought itself was absent. Maybe it had gone out into the street with the Bolsheviks? . . . The blind alley of the Pre-Parliament was the blind alley of the whole régime.

To reconvince the army was difficult, but to compel it was also impossible. To a new shout from Kerensky at the Baltic fleet, which had just been through a battle and lost victims, a congress of the sailors addressed to the Central Executive Committee a demand that they remove from the staff of the Provisional Government "a person who is disgracing and destroying the great revolution with his shameless political chantage." It was the first time Kerensky had heard such language from the sailors. The Regional Committee of the Army, Fleet and Russian Workers in Finland, functioning as a sovereign power, held up the government freight. Kerensky threatened the Soviet commissars with arrest. The answer was: The Regional Committee tranquilly accepts the challenge of the Provisional Government. Kerensky made no reply. In essence the Baltic fleet was already in a state of insurrection. On the land front, things had not yet gone so far, but they were travelling in the same direction. The food situation was rapidly deteriorating throughout October. The commander-in-chief of the Northern front reported that hunger "is the chief cause of the moral disintegration of the army." At the same time that the compromisist upper circles on the front were continuing to assert—to be sure, now only behind the backs of the soldiers—that the fighting capacity of the army was improving, the lower ranks, regiment after regiment, were putting forth demands for a publication of the secret treaties and an immediate offer of peace. The commissar of the Western front, Zhdanov, reported during the first days of October: "The mood is extremely alarming, taken in connection with the nearness of cold weather and the deterioration of the food . . . The Bolsheviks are scoring a definite success.

The governmental institutions at the front were hanging in the air. The commissar of the 2nd Army reported that the military courts could not function because the soldier-witnesses refused to appear and testify. "The mutual relations between the commanding staff and the soldiers is embittered. The officers are blamed for dragging out the war. The hostility of the soldiers to the government and the commanding staff had long ago been transferred also to the army committees, which had not been renewed since the beginning of the revolution. Over the heads of the committees the regiments were sending delegates to Petrograd, to the Soviet, to complain of the intolerable situation in the trenches, where they lived without bread, without clothing, without faith in the war. On the Roumanian front, where the Bolsheviks were very weak, whole regiments were refusing to shoot. "In two or three weeks the soldiers themselves will declare an armistice and lay down their arms." The delegates from one of the divisions reported: "With the coming of the first snow the soldiers have decided to go home." The delegates of the 133rd Army Corps made this threat at a plenary session of the Petrograd Soviet: "If there is not a real struggle for peace, the soldiers themselves will take the power and declare an armistice." The commissar of the 2nd Army reported to the War Minister: "There is no little talk to the effect that with the arrival of cold weather they will abandon their position."

Fraternising, which had almost stopped since the July days, began again and grew rapidly. Instances not only of the arrest of officers by the soldiers, but of the murder of the more hateful began to multiply. These things were done almost publicly, before the eyes of the soldiers. Nobody interfered: the majority did not want to, the small minority did not dare. The murderer always succeeded in hiding: he was drowned and lost in the soldier mass. One of the generals wrote: "We convulsively grasp at this or that, we pray for some sort of miracle, but the majority of us understand that there is already no hope of salvation."

Mixing cunning with stupidity, the patriotic papers continued to write about a continuation of the war, about an offensive and about victory. The generals shook their heads; some of them equivocally joined in. "Only completely crazy people," wrote Baron Budberg, the commander of a corps near Dvinsk, on the 7th of October, "could dream about an offensive at the present time." The very next day he was compelled to write in the same diary: "Startled and appalled to receive orders for an offensive not later than October 20th." Headquarters, believing in nothing and shrugging its shoulders at everything, was drawing up plans for a new operation. There were not a few generals who saw the last hope of salvation in a repetition on a grand scale of Kornilov's experiment with Riga: Drag the army into battle and try to bring down a defeat on the head of the revolution.

On the initiative of War Minister Verkhovsky it was decided to transfer the oldest classes into the reserve. The railroad groaned under the burden of these returning soldiers. In the overloaded cars the springs broke and the floors fell through. This did not improve the mood of those left behind. "The trenches are breaking down," writes Budberg. "The communication trenches are flooded; there is refuse and excrement everywhere. . . . The soldiers flatly refuse to work at cleaning up the trenches. . . . It is dreadful to think where this will lead when spring comes and all this begins to rot and decompose." In a state of embittered inaction the soldiers refused in droves even to undergo preventive inoculation. This too became a form of struggle against the war.

After vain efforts to raise the fighting capacity of the army by decreasing its numbers, Verkhovsky suddenly came to the conclusion that only peace could save the country. At a private conference with the Kadet leaders, whom this young and naïve minister imagined he could bring over to his side, Verkhovsky drew a picture of the material and spiritual collapse of the army: "Any attempt to prolong the war can only bring on a catastrophe." The Kadets could not understand this. But while the others remained silent Miliukov scornfully shrugged his shoulders: "The honour of Russia," "loyalty to the Allies." . . . Not believing in one of these words, the leader of the bourgeoisie was stubbornly striving to bury the revolution under the ruins and piles of corpses that would be left by the war. Verkhovsky revealed a certain amount of political audacity.

Without informing or warning the government, he appeared on the 20th before the commission of the Pre-Parliament and announced the necessity of an immediate peace with or without the consent of the Allies. He was furiously attacked by all those who agreed with him in private conversations. The patriotic press wrote that the war minister "had jumped on the footboard of Comrade Trotsky's chariot." Burtsev hinted at the presence of German gold. Verkhovsky was sent away on a vacation. In heart to heart conversations the patriots were saying: In essence he is right. Budberg had to speak cautiously even in his diary: "From the point of view of keeping our word," he wrote, "the proposal, of course, is tricky. But from the standpoint of the egoistic interests of Russia, it is perhaps the only one which offers hope of a saving way out." Incidentally the baron confessed his envy of the German generals to whom "fate has given the good luck to be the authors of victories." He did not foresee that the turn of the German generals would come next. Those people never foresaw anything, even the cleverest of them. The Bolsheviks foresaw much and that was their strength.

The withdrawal from the Pre-Parliament in the eyes of the people burned the last bridges uniting the party of insurrection with official society. With renewed energy—for the nearness of the goal redoubles one's strength—the Bolsheviks carried on their agitation, an agitation called demagogism by the enemy because it brought out into the public square what they themselves were hiding in the chancelleries and private offices. The convincingness of this tireless evangel grew out of the fact that the Bolsheviks understood the course of the objective development, subjected their policy to it, were not afraid of the masses, and unconquerably believed in their own truth and their victory. The people never tired of hearing them. The masses felt a need to stand close together. Each wanted to test himself through others, and all tensely and attentively kept observing how one and the same thought would develop in their various minds with its different shades and features. Unnumbered crowds of people stood about the circuses and other big buildings where the more popular Bolsheviks would address them with the last arguments and the last appeals.

The number of leading agitators had greatly decreased by October. First of all Lenin was lacking—both as an agitator and still more as an immediate day-to-day inspiration. His simple and deep generalisations which could so lastingly insert themselves into the consciousness of the masses, his clear sayings caught up from the people and handed back to them, were sadly missed. The first-class agitator Zinoviev was lacking. Having hidden from prosecution under an indictment for "insurrection" in July, he decisively turned against the October insurrection, and thus for the whole critical period withdrew from the field of action. Kamenev, the irreplacable propagandist, the experienced political instructor of the party, condemned the policy of insurrection, did not believe in the victory, saw catastrophes ahead and gloomily retired into the shadows. Sverdlov, by nature an organiser rather than an agitator, appeared often at mass meeting and his even, powerful and tireless bass voice inspired tranquil confidence. Stalin was neither agitator nor orator. He never appeared as a spokesman at party conferences. But did he appear so much as once in the mass meetings of the revolution? In the documents and memoirs no record of it has been preserved.

A brilliant agitation was conducted by Volodarsky, Lashevich, Kollontai, Chudnovsky, and after them by scores of agitators of lesser calibre. People listened with interest and sympathy—and the mature also with a certain condescension—to Lunacharsky, a skilled orator who knew how to present fact and generalisation and pathos and joke, but who did not pretend to lead anybody. He himself needed to be led. In proportion as the revolution approached, Lunacharsky faded rapidly and lost his colourful effects.

Sukhanov says of the president of the Petrograd Soviet[1]: "Tearing himself from the work in revolutionary headquarters he would fly from the Obukhovsky factory to the Trubocheny, from the Putilov to the Baltic shipyards, from the Riding Academy to the barracks, and seemed to be speaking simultaneously in all places. Every Petrograd worker and soldier knew him and heard him personally. His influence—both in the masses and in headquarters—was overwhelming. He was the central figure of those days, and the chief hero of this remarkable page of history."

But incomparably more effective in that last period before the insurrection was the molecular agitation carried on by nameless workers, sailors, soldiers, winning converts one by one, breaking down the last doubts, overcoming the last hesitations. Those months of feverish political life had created innumerable cadres in the lower ranks, had educated hundreds and thousands of rough diamonds, who were accustomed to look

1. Trotsky. [Trans.]

on politics from below and not above, and for that very reason estimated facts and people with a keenness not always accessible to orators of the academic type. The Petrograd workers stood in the front rank—hereditary proletarians who had produced a race of agitators and organisers of extraordinary revolutionary temper and high political culture, independent in thought, word and action. Carpenters, fitters, blacksmiths, teachers of the unions and factories, each already had around him his school, his pupils, the future builders of the Republic of Soviets. The Baltic sailors, close comrades in arms of the Petrograd workers —to a considerable extent issued from their midst—put forward a brigade of agitators who took by storm the backward regiments, the county towns, the villages of the muzhiks. A generalising formula tossed out in the *Cirque Moderne* by one of the revolutionary leaders would take flesh and blood in hundreds of thinking heads, and so make the rounds of the whole country.

From the Baltic states, from Poland and Lithuania, thousands of revolutionary workers and soldiers had been evacuated during the retreat of the Russian armies, coming with the industrial enterprises or one by one. All these became agitators against the war and those guilty of it. The Lettish Bolsheviks, torn away from their home soil and wholeheartedly standing on the soil of the revolution, convinced, stubborn, resolute, were carrying on day by day and all day long a mining operation in all parts of the country. Their angular faces, harsh accent, and often their broken Russian phrases, gave special expressiveness to an unceasing summons to insurrection.

The mass would no longer endure in its midst the wavering, the dubious, the neutral. It was striving to get hold of everybody, to attract, to convince, to conquer. The factories joined with the regiments in sending delegates to the front. The trenches got into connection with the workers and peasants near by in the rear. In the towns along the front there was an endless series of meetings, conferences, consultations in which the soldiers and sailors would bring their activity into accord with that of the workers and peasants. It was in this manner that the backward White Russian front was won over to Bolshevism.

In places where the local party leadership was irresolute and disposed to wait, as for example in Kiev, Voronezh, and many other points, the masses not infrequently fell into a passive condition. To justify their policy, the leaders would point to this mood of depression which they themselves had created. On the other hand: "The more resolute and bold was his summons to insurrection," writes Povolzhsky, one of the Kazan agitators, "the more trustful and hearty would be the attitude of the soldier mass toward the speaker."

The factories and regiments of Petrograd and Moscow were now more insistently knocking at the wooden gates of the villages. The workers would join together in sending delegates into their native provinces. The regiments would pass resolutions summoning the peasants to support the Bolsheviks. The workers in factories within the cities would make pilgrimages to the surrounding villages, distributing newspapers and laying the foundations of Bolshevik nuclei. From these rounds they would come back bringing in the pupil of their eyes a reflection from the flames of the peasant war.

Bolshevism took possession of the country. The Bolsheviks became an unconquerable power. The people were with them. The city dumas of Kronstadt, Czaritsyn, Kostroma, Shuia, elected on a universal franchise, were wholly in the hands of the Bolsheviks. The Bolsheviks received 52 per cent of the votes at an election to the district dumas of Moscow. In far-off and tranquil Tomsk, as also in the wholly non-industrial Samara, the Bolsheviks dominated in the duma. Out of four members of the Schlüsselberg county zemstvo, three were Bolsheviks. In the Ligovsky county zemstvo, the Bolsheviks got 50 per cent. of the votes. It was not so favourable everywhere, but everywhere it was changing in the same direction. The relative weight of the Bolshevik Party was on the rapid rise.

The Bolshevisation of the masses revealed itself far more clearly, however, in the class organisations. The trade unions in the capital comprised over a half million workers. The Mensheviks themselves, who still had the administration of certain unions, felt that they were a relic of past days. No matter what parts of the proletariat might form an organisation, and no matter what its immediate aim might be, it would inevitably arrive at Bolshevik conclusions. And this was no accident: The trade unions, the factory committees, the economic and cultural assemblies of the working class, both permanent and transitory, were compelled by the whole situation, upon every private problem which might arise, to raise one and the same question: Who is the master of the house?

The workers of the artillery factories, being called together in conference to regulate their relations with the administration, decided that they could best regulate them through a Soviet government. This was no longer a mere formula, but a programme of economic salvation. As they approached the power the workers also approached more and more concretely the problems of industry. The artillery conference even established a special centre for the study of methods of transition from munition factories to peaceful production.

The Moscow conference of factory and shop committees declared that the local Soviet should in the future decide all strike conflicts by decree, on its own authority open the plants shut down by the lockouts, and by sending its own delegates to Siberia and the Donetz Basin guarantee coal and grain to the factories. The Petrograd conference of factory and shop committees devoted its attention to the agrarian question, and upon a report by Trotsky drew up a manifesto to the peasants: The proletariat feels itself to be not only a special class, but also the leader of the people.

The All-Russian conference of factory and shop committees, meeting during the second half of October, raised the question of workers' control to the position of a national problem: "The workers are more interested than the owners in the correct and uninterrupted operation of the plants." Workers' control "is in the interest of the whole country and ought to be supported by the revolutionary peasantry and the revolutionary army." This resolution, opening the door to a new economic order, was adopted by the representatives of all the industrial enterprises of Russia with only five votes opposing and nine abstaining from the vote. The few individual abstainers were old Mensheviks no longer able to follow their own party, but still lacking courage to raise their hands openly for the Bolshevik revolution. To-morrow they will do it.

The democratic municipal governments, only recently created, were dying away along with the organs of the governmental power. The most important tasks, such as guaranteeing water, light, fuel and food to the cities, were all falling more and more upon the soviets and other workers' organisations. The factory committee of the lighting station of Petrograd was rushing about the city and the surroundings hunting up at one time coal, at another grease for the turbines, and getting them both through committees of other plants acting in opposition to their owners and the administration.

No, the government of the soviets was not a chimera, an arbitrary construction, an invention of party theoreticians. It grew up irresistibly from below, from the breakdown of industry, the impotence of the possessors, the needs of the masses.

The soviets had in actual fact become a government. For the workers, soldiers and peasants there remained no other road. No time left to argue and speculate about a Soviet government: it had to be realised.

At the first congress of the soviets, in June, it had been decided to call the congress every three months. The Central Executive Committee, however, had not only failed to call the second conference on time, but had shown a disposition not to call it at all, in order to avoid confronting a hostile majority. The chief task of the Democratic Conference had been to crowd out the soviets, replacing them with organs of the "democracy." But that had not been so easy. The soviets did not intend to make way for anybody.

On September 21, at the close of the Democratic Conference, the Petrograd Soviet raised its voice for the prompt calling of a congress of the soviets. A resolution in this sense was adopted upon the report of Trotsky and a guest from Moscow, Bukharin, formally based on the necessity of getting ready for "a new wave of counter-revolution." Their plan for a defensive which should lay down the road to the coming offensive relied upon the soviets as the sole organisations capable of making the struggle. The resolution demanded that the soviets strengthen their position among the masses. Where the *de facto* power is already in their hands, they are in no case to let it slip. The revolutionary committees created in the Kornilov days must remain ready for action. "In order to unite and co-ordinate the action of all the soviets in their struggle with the advancing danger, and in order to decide problems of organisation of the revolutionary power, the immediate calling of a congress of the soviets is necessary." Thus a resolution on self-defence brings us right up to the necessity of overthrowing the government. The agitation will be conducted on this political key-note from now straight on to the moment of insurrection.

The delegates from the soviets to the Democratic Conference raised the question of a Soviet Congress before the central Executive Committee the next day. The Bolsheviks demanded that the Congress be called within two weeks, and proposed, or rather threatened, to create for this purpose a special body resting on the Petrograd and Moscow Soviets. In reality they preferred to have the Congress called by the old Central Executive Committee. This would obviate quarrels about the juridical rights of the congress, and make it possible to overthrow the Compromisers with their own co-operation. The semi-camouflaged threat of the Bolsheviks was effective. Not yet risking a break with Soviet legality, the leaders of the Central Executive Committee declared that they would entrust to nobody the fulfilment of their duties. The Congress was called for October 20—within less than a month.

The provincial delegates had no more than departed, however, when the leaders of the Central Executive Committee suddenly opened their eyes to the fact that the Congress would be untimely—it would withdraw local party workers from the electoral campaign, and thus do harm to the Constituent Assembly. Their real fear was that the Congress would prove a mighty pretender to the power, but about this they kept a diplomatic silence. On the 26th of September Dan made haste to introduce into the bureau of the Central Executive Committee, without bothering about the necessary preparation, a proposal to postpone the Congress.

With the elementary principles of democracy these patent medicine democrats were least of all concerned. They had just got through quashing the resolution of a Democratic conference, which they themselves had summoned, rejecting a coalition with the Kadets. And now they revealed their sovereign contempt for the soviets, beginning with the Petrograd Soviet upon whose shoulders they had been lifted into their seats. After all, how could they, without abandoning their league with the bourgeoisie, pay any attention to the hopes and demands of those tens of millions of workers, soldiers and peasants who stood for the soviets?

Trotsky answered the proposal of Dan by stating that the Congress would be called just the same, if not constitutionally, then by revolutionary means. The usually so submissive bureau refused this time to follow along the road of a Soviet *coup d'état*. But this little defeat was far from compelling the conspirators to lay down their arms. On the contrary it seemed to egg them on. Dan found an influential support in the military section of the Central Executive Committee, which decided to "query" the organisations of the front as to whether they should carry out a decision twice adopted by the highest Soviet body. In the interval the compromise press opened a campaign against the Congress. In this the Social Revolutionaries were particularly furious. "Shall a congress be summoned or not?" wrote *Dyelo Naroda*. "It can have nothing to say in solution of the question of power. . . . The government of Kerensky will not submit in any case." To what will it not submit? asked Lenin. "To the power of the soviets, to the power of the workers and peasants, which *Dyelo Nardao*, in order to keep up with the pogrom-makers and anti-semites, the monarchists and Kadets, calls the power of Trotsky and Lenin."

The peasant Executive Committee, in its turn, declared this calling of the Congress "dangerous and undesirable." A confusion of ill-will thus prevailed in the Soviet upper-circles. Delegates of the compromise parties travelling over the country mobilised the local organisations against a congress which had been officially called by the supreme Soviet body. The official organ of the Central Executive Committee printed from day to day resolutions against the Congress adopted at the bidding of the leading Compromisers, inspired entirely by the old March ghosts—wearing, to be sure, very imposing names. *Izvestia* buried the soviets in a leading article, declaring them temporary barricades which should be removed as soon as the Constituent Assembly crowns the "edifice of the new structure."

The Bolsheviks least of all were caught napping by this agitation against the Congress. On the 24th of September the Central Committee of the party, without banking upon any action by the Central Executive Committee, had decided to set in motion from below, through the local soviets and organisations of the front, a campaign for the Congress. The Bolsheviks delegated Sverdlov to sit in the Central Executive Committee's official commission on the calling—or rather the sabotage—of the Congress. Under his leadership the local organisations of the party were mobilised, and through them also the soviets. On the 27th all the revolutionary institutions of Reval demanded that the Pre-Parliament be immediately dissolved, and a conference of the soviets for the formation of a government immediately called; they moreover solemnly promised to support it "with all the forces and instrumentalities to be found in the fortress." Many local soviets, beginning with the districts of Moscow, proposed that the function of summoning the Congress be withdrawn from the hands of the disloyal Central Executive Committee. Against the resolutions of the army committees opposing the Congress demands for its convocation flowed in from battalions, regiments, corps and local garrisons. "The Congress of Soviets must seize the power and stop at nothing," says a mass meeting of soldiers in Kyshtin in the Urals. The soldiers of Novgorod province summoned the peasants to take part in the Congress, and pay no attention to the resolution of the peasants' Executive Committee. Provincial soviets, county soviets—these, too, in the farthest corners of the country—factories, mines, regiments, dreadnoughts, destroyers, war hospitals, meetings, an automobile detachment in Petrograd, an ambulance squad in Moscow—all were demanding the removal of the government and the transfer of power to the soviets.

Not content with this agitational campaign, the Bolsheviks created an important organisational base by calling a congress of the soviets of the northern region consisting of 150 delegates from 23 points. That was a well-calculated blow! The Central Executive Committee under the leadership of its great masters in small affairs declared this northern congress a private conference. The handful of Menshevik delegates refused to take part in the work of the Congress, remaining only "for purposes of information." As though that could diminish by a tittle the significance of a congress in which were represented the soviets of Petrograd and its suburbs, Moscow, Kronstadt, Helsingfors, and Reval—that is to say, both capitals, the naval fortresses, the Baltic fleet and the garrisons surrounding Petrograd. The Congress, opened by Antonov—to whom a military tint was being intentionally given—took place under the presidency of Ensign Krylenko, the best agitator of the party at the front, the future Bolshevik commander-in-chief. At the centre of the political report, made by Trotsky, stood the question of the new attempt of the government to remove the revolutionary regiments from Petrograd: The Congress will not permit "the disarming of Petrograd and strangling the Soviet." The question of the Petrograd garrison is an element in the fundamental problem of power. "The whole people is voting for the Bolsheviks; the people are trusting us and authorising us to seize the power." The resolution proposed by Trotsky read: "The hour has come when the question of the central government . . . can be decided only by a resolute and unanimous coming-out of all the soviets." This almost undisguised summons to insurrection was adopted by all votes with three abstaining.

Lashevich urged the other soviets to follow Petrograd's example and get control of the local garrisons. The Lettish delegate, Peterson, promised forty thousand Lettish sharp-shooters for the defence of the Congress of Soviets. This announcement of Peterson, rapturously greeted, was no empty phrase. Only a few days later the Soviet of the Lettish regiments announced: "Only a popular insurrection . . . will make possible the transfer of power to the soviets." On the 13th the radio stations of the warships broadcast throughout the whole country the summons of the Northern Congress to prepare for an All-Russian Congress of Soviets. "Soldiers, sailors, peasants, workers! It is your duty to overcome all obstacles . . ."

The Central Committee of the party suggested to the Bolshevik delegates of the Northern Congress that in view of the approaching Congress of the Soviets they should not leave Petrograd. Individual delegates, at the direction of a bureau elected by the Congress, went to the army organisations and the local soviets to make reports—in other words, to prepare the province for insurrection. The Central Executive Committee saw a powerful apparatus grown up beside itself, resting upon Petrograd and Moscow, conversing with the country through the radio stations on the dreadnoughts, and ready at any moment to replace the decrepit supreme Soviet organ in the matter of summoning the Congress. Petty organisational tricks could be of no help to the Compromisers here.

The struggle for and against the Congress gave the last impulse in the localities to the Bolshevisation of the soviets. In a number of backward provinces, Smolensk for example, the Bolsheviks, either alone or together with the Left Social Revolutionaries, got their first majority only during this campaign for the Congress or during the election of delegates to it. Even in the Siberian congress of the soviets the Bolsheviks succeeded in the middle of October in creating with the Left Social Revolutionaries a permanent majority which easily placed its imprint upon the local soviets. On the 15th the Soviet of Kiev, by 159 votes against 28, with 3 abstaining, recognised the coming Congress of Soviets as "the sovereign organ of power." On the 16th the Congress of Soviets of the north-western region at Minsk—that is, in the centre of the Western front—declared the calling of the Congress unpostponable. On the 18th the Petrograd Soviet held elections for the coming Congress; 443 votes were cast for the Bolshevik list (Trotsky, Kamenev, Volodarsky, Yurenev and Lashevich); for the Social Revolutionaries, 162—these all Left Social Revolutionaries, tending toward the Bolsheviks; for the Mensheviks 44. Under the presidency of Krestinsky a congress of the soviets of the Urals, where 80 out of the 110 delegates were Bolsheviks, demanded in the name of 223,900 organised workers and soldiers that the Congress of Soviets be called at the appointed date. On the same day, the 19th, an All-Russian conference of factory and shop committees, the most direct and indubitable representation of the proletariat in the whole country, came out for an immediate transfer of power to the soviets. On the 20th Ivanovo-Voznesensk declared all the soviets of the provinces to be "in a state of open and ruthless struggle against the Provisional Government," and summoned them to solve independently the industrial and administrative problems of their localities. Against this resolution, which meant the overthrow of local governmental authorities, only one voice was raised, with one abstaining. On the 22nd, the Bolshevik press published a new list of 56 organisations demanding a transfer of power to the soviets. These were all composed of the authentic masses of the people, and to a considerable degree armed masses.

This all-powerful muster-roll of the detachments of the coming revolution did not prevent Dan from reporting to the bureau of the Central Executive Committee that out of 917 existing Soviet organisations, only 50 had responded with an agreement to send delegates, and these had done so "without any enthusiasm." It is easy enough to understand that those few soviets who still considered it necessary to report their feelings to the Central Executive Committee regarded the Congress without enthusiasm. An overwhelming majority of the local soviets and the army committees had simply ignored the Central Executive Committee altogether.

Although they had exposed and compromised themselves with these efforts to sabotage the Congress, the Compromisers did not dare carry the work through to the end. When it became utterly obvious that they could not avoid a congress, they made an abrupt about-face and summoned all the local organisations to elect delegates to the Congress in order not to give the Bolsheviks a majority. Having waked up to the situation too late, however, the Central Executive Committee found itself obliged only two or three days before the appointed date to postpone the Congress to October 25.

Thanks to this last manœuvre of the Compromisers, the February régime, and bourgeois society along with it, received an unexpected period of grace—from which, however, it was no longer capable of deriving any substantial benefits. The Bolsheviks, moreover, employed these five supplementary days to great advantage. The enemy acknowledged this later on. "The postponement of the coming-out," says Miliukov, "was made use of by the Bolsheviks, first of all to reinforce their position among the Petrograd workers and soldiers. Trotsky appeared at meetings in the various units of the Petrograd garrison. The mood created by him is exemplified in the fact that in the

Semenovsky regiment the members of the Executive Committee appearing after him, Skobelev and Gotz, were not allowed to speak."

This turning of the Semenovsky regiment, whose name had been written in letters of ill omen in the history of the revolution, had a kind of symbolic significance. In December 1905, it was the Semenovtsi who did the chief work of crushing the insurrection in Moscow. The commander of the regiment, General Min, gave the order: "Take no prisoners." On the Moscow-Golutvino railroad section the Semenovtsi shot 150 workers and clerks. General Min, flattered by the czar for his heroic deed, was killed in the autumn of 1906 by a Social Revolutionary woman, Konopliannikova. Tangled up in these old traditions the Semenovsky regiment had held its ground longer than the majority of the units of the guard. Its reputation for "reliability" was so strong, that in spite of the doleful failure of Skobelev and Gotz, the government stubbornly continued to count upon the Semenovtsi right up to the day of the insurrection and even after it.

The question of the Congress of the Soviets remained the central political question throughout the five weeks dividing the Democratic Conference from the October insurrection. At the Conference itself the declaration of the Bolsheviks had proclaimed the coming Congress of the Soviets the sovereign organ of the country. "Only such decisions and proposals of the present Conference . . . can find their way to realisation as are ratified by the All-Russian Congress of Workers', Peasants', and Soldiers' Deputies." The resolution favouring a boycott of the Pre-Parliament, supported by one-half of the members of the Central Committee against the other half, declared: "We place the question of our parties' participation in the Pre-Parliament in direct dependence upon those measures which the All-Russian Congress of Soviets shall take to create a revolutionary government." This appeal to the Congress of Soviets runs through all the Bolshevik documents of this period almost without exception.

With the peasant war kindling, the national movements growing bitter, the breakdown going deeper, the front disintegrating, the government unravelling, the soviets were becoming the sole support of the creative forces. Every question turned into a question about the power, and the problem of power led straight to the Congress of Soviets. This Congress must give the answer to all questions, among them the question of the Constituent Assembly.

Not one party had yet withdrawn the slogan of the Constituent Assembly, and this included the Bolsheviks. But almost unnoticeably in the course of the events of the revolution, this chief democratic slogan, which had for a decade and a half tinged with its colour the heroic struggle of the masses, had grown pale and faded out, had somehow been ground between millstones, had become an empty shell, a form naked of content, a tradition and not a prospect. There was nothing mysterious in this process. The development of the revolution had reached the point of a direct battle for power between the two basic classes of society, the bourgeoisie and the proletariat. A Constituent Assembly could give nothing either to the one or the other. The petty bourgeoisie of the town and country could play only an auxiliary and secondary rôle in this conflict. They were in any case incapable of seizing the power themselves. If the preceding months had proved anything, they had proved that. Nevertheless in a Constituent Assembly the petty bourgeoisie might still win—and they actually did win as it turned out—a majority. And to what end? Only to the end of not knowing what to do with it. This reveals the bankruptcy of formal democracy in a deep historic crisis. It reveals the strength of tradition, however, that even on the eve of the last battle neither camp had yet renounced the name of the Constituent Assembly. But as a matter of fact the bourgeoisie had appealed from the Constituent Assembly to Kornilov, and the Bolshevisks to the Congress of Soviets.

It may be confidently assumed that rather wide sections of the people, and even certain small strata of the Bolshevik Party, nourished certain constitutional illusions of their own in regard to the Congress of Soviets—that is, they associated with it the idea of an automatic and painless transfer of power from the hands of the Coalition to the hands of the Soviet. In reality it would be necessary to take the power by force; it was impossible to do this by voting. Only an armed insurrection could decide the question.

However, of all the illusions which accompany as an inevitable premise every great popular movement, even the most realistic, this illusion of a Soviet "parliamentarism" was in all the combined circumstances the least dangerous. The soviets were in reality struggling for the power; they were continually more and more relying upon armed force; they were becoming governments in the localities; they were winning their own congress in a fight. Thus there remained but little place for constitutional illusions, and what few survived were washed away in the process of the struggle.

In co-ordinating the revolutionary efforts of the workers and soldiers of the whole country, giving them a single goal, giving them unity of aim and a single date for action, the slogan of the Soviet Congress, at the same time made it possible to screen the semi-conspirative, semi-public preparation of an insurrection with continual appeals to the legal representation of the workers, soldiers and peasants. Having thus promoted the assembling of forces for the revolution, the Congress of Soviets was afterward to sanction its results and give the new government a form irreproachable in the eyes of the people.

Chapter IV

The Military-Revolutionary Committee

In spite of the change of mood beginning toward the end of July, the Social Revolutionaries and Mensheviks dominated the reorganised Petrograd garrison all through August. The proletariat was disarmed; the Red Guard had kept only a few thousand rifles. In those circumstances, notwithstanding the fact that the masses were again coming over to the Bolsheviks, an insurrection might end in cruel defeat.

The situation steadily changed, however, through September. After the revolt of the generals the Compromisers swiftly lost their following in the garrison. Distrust of the Bolshevik was replaced by sympathy, or at the worst by a watchful neutrality. But the sympathy was not active. The garrison remained in a political sense extremely shaky and—as muzhiks are—suspicious. Aren't the Bolsheviks going to deceive us? Will they really give us peace and land? The majority of the soldiers still had no idea of fighting for these aims under the banner of the Bolsheviks. And since there remained in the garrison an almost completely unabsorbed minority hostile to the Bolsheviks—five or six thousand junkers, three Cossack regiments, a bicycle battalion and an armoured car division—the outcome of a conflict in September seemed doubtful. To help things along, however, the course of events brought one more object lesson in which the fate of the Petrograd soldiers was shown to be inseparably bound up with the fate of the revolution and the Bolsheviks.

The right to control bodies of armed men is a fundamental right of the state power. The first Provisional Government, wished upon the people by the Executive Committee, gave an obligation not to disarm and not to remove from Petrograd those military units which had taken part in the February overturn. This was the formal beginning of a military dualism inseparable in essence from the double sovereignty. The major political disturbances of the succeeding months—the April demonstration, the July days, the preparation of the Kornilov insurrection and its liquidation—each one inevitably ran into the question of the subordination of the Petrograd garrison. But conflicts between the government and the Compromisers upon this theme were, after all, a family matter, and ended amicably. With the Bolshevisation of the garrison things took a different turn. The soldiers themselves now began to recall that obligation given by the government to the Executive Committee in March and treacherously broken by them. On September 8 the soldiers' section of the Soviet put forward a demand that the regiments transferred to the front in connection with the July events be returned to Petrograd. This while the members of the Coalition were tearing their hair about how to get rid of the remaining regiments.

In a number of provincial cities things stood about the same way as in the capital. During July and August the local garrison underwent a patriotic reconstruction; during August and September the reconstructed garrisons underwent a process of Bolshevisation. It was then necessary to begin over from the beginning—that is, once more undertake transfers and reconstructions. In preparing its blow against Petrograd the government began with the provinces. Its political motives were carefully concealed under pretexts of strategy. On September 27 a joint session of the soviets of Reval—that of the city and the fortress—adopted on the question of transfers the following resolution: To consider a re-grouping of forces admissible only when agreed to in advance by the corresponding soviets. The leaders of the Vladimir Soviet inquired of Moscow whether they should obey an order of Kerensky transferring the whole garrison. The Moscow regional bureau of the Bolsheviks observed that "orders of this kind are becoming systematic in relation to the revolutionary-minded garrisons." Before surrendering all its rights, the Provisional Government was trying to get hold of the fundamental right of every government —the right to dispose of armed bodies of men.

The reorganisation of the Petrograd garrison was becoming all the more urgent because the coming Congress of Soviets was destined to carry to a decision one way or other the struggle for power. The bourgeois press, led by the Kadet organ *Rech*, was asserting every morning that we must not "let the Bolsheviks choose the moment for a declaration of civil war." That meant: We must strike a timely blow at the Bolsheviks. The attempt at a preliminary change of the correlation of forces in the garrison flowed inevitably from this premise. Arguments from strategic considerations looked sufficiently impressive after the fall of Riga and the loss of the Moon-sund Islands. District headquarters issued an order for the reorganisation of the Petrograd units in preparation for an offensive. At the same time, upon the initiative of the Compromisers, the matter was brought up in the soldiers' section of the Soviet. Here the plan of the enemy was not bad: presenting a peremptory strategic demand to the Soviet, to snatch their military support from under the feet of the Bolsheviks, or in case the Soviet resisted, to provoke a sharp conflict between the Petrograd garrison and the front, which was in need of supplementary forces and replacements.

The leaders of the Soviet, quite well aware of the trap which had been set for them, made up their minds to feel out the ground carefully before taking any irrevocable step. A flat refusal to fulfil the order was possible only if they were sure that the motives of the refusal would be correctly understood by the front. Otherwise it might be more advantageous to carry out, by agreement with the trenches, a replacement of certain units of the garrison with revolutionary units from the front which were in need of rest. It was in this latter sense, as we have shown above, that the Reval Soviet had already spoken.

The soldiers approached the question more brusquely. Take the offensive at the front now, in the middle of autumn? Reconcile themselves to a new winter campaign? No, they simply had no room in their heads for that idea. The patriotic press immediately opened fire on the garrison: the Petrograd regiments, grown fat in idleness, are betraying the front. The workers took the side of the soldiers. The Putilov men were the first to protest against the transfer of the regiments. From that time on the question was never absent from the order of the day either in barrack or factory. This drew together the two sections of the Soviet. The regiments began to support most heartily the demand that the workers be armed.

Attempting to kindle the patriotism of the masses by threatening the loss of Petrograd, the Compromisers introduced into the Soviet on October 9 a motion to create a "Committee of Revolutionary Defence," whose task should be to take part in the defence of the capital with the active co-operation of the workers. While refusing to assume responsibility for "the so-called strategy of the Provisional Government and in particular the removal of troops from Petrograd," the Soviet nevertheless had made no haste to express itself upon the substance of the order removing the soldiers, but had decided to test its motives and the facts upon which it was based. The Mensheviks had raised a protest: It is not permissible to interfere in the operative orders of the commanding staff. But it was only a month and a half since they had talked the same way about the conspiratorial orders of Kornilov, and they were reminded of this. In order to test the question whether the removal of the troops was dictated by military or political considerations, a competent body was needed. To the extreme surprise of the Compromisers the Bolsheviks accepted the idea of a "Committee of Defence." This committee should be the one to gather all data relating to the defence of the capital. That was an important step. Having snatched this dangerous weapon from the hands of the enemy, the Soviet remained in a position to turn the decision about removing the troops this way or that according to circumstances—but in any case against the government and the Compromisers.

The Bolsheviks quite naturally seized upon this Menshevik project of a military committee, for there had been conversations often enough in their own ranks about the necessity of creating in good season an authoritative Soviet committee to lead the coming insurrection. In the Military Organisation of the party they had even drawn up plans for such a body. The one difficulty they had not yet got over was that of reconciling an instrument of insurrection with an elective and openly functioning Soviet, upon whose benches, moreover, sat representatives of the hostile parties. The patriotic proposal of the Mensheviks, therefore, came up most appropriately, and came up just in time to assist in the creation of a revolutionary headquarters—a body soon to be renamed "Military Revolutionary Committee" and to become the chief lever of the revolution.

Two years after the events described above, the author of this book wrote in an article dedicated to the October revolution: "As soon as the order for the removal of the troops was communicated by Headquarters to the Executive Committee of the Petrograd Soviet . . . it became clear that this question in its further development would have decisive political significance." The idea of an insurrection began to take form from that moment. It was no longer necessary to invent a Soviet body. The real aim of the future committee was unequivocably brought out when in the same session Trotsky concluded his report on the withdrawal of the Bolsheviks from the Pre-Parliament with the exclamation: "Long live the direct and open struggle for a revolutionary power throughout the country!" That was a translation into the language of soviet legality of the slogan: "Long live the armed insurrection!"

On the very next day, the 10th, the Central Committee of the Bolsheviks, adopted in secret session the resolution of Lenin presenting armed insurrection as the practical task of the coming days. From that moment the party assumed a clear and imperative fighting formation. The Committee of Defence was included in its plans for a direct struggle for power.

The government and its allies surrounded the garrison with concentric circles. On the 11th the commander of the Northern front, General Cheremissov, reported to the War Minister a demand of the army committees that the tired-out front units be replaced by Petrograd units from the rear. In this instance Headquarters was merely a transmitting mechanism between the Compromisers in the army committees and their Petrograd leaders, who were striving to create a broad cover for the plans of Kerensky. The Coalition press accompanied this encircling operation with a symphony of patriotic ravings. Daily meetings of the regiments and factories demonstrated, however, that this music of the ruling spheres was not making the slightest impression upon the lower ranks. On the 12th, a mass meeting of the workers of one of the most revolutionary factories of the capital (the Old Parviainen) made the following answer to the attacks of the bourgeoisie: "We declare that we will go into the street when we deem it advisable. We are not afraid of the approaching struggle, and we confidently believe that we will come off victorious."

In creating a commission to draw up regulations for the "Committee of Defence,' the Executive Committee of the Petrograd Soviet designated for the future military body such tasks as the following: To get in touch with the Northern front and with the headquarters of the Petrograd district, with Centrobalt and the regional soviet of Finland, in order to ascertain the military situation and take the necessary measures: to take a census of the personal composition of the garrison of Petrograd and its environs, also of the ammunition and military supplies; to take measures for the preservation of discipline in the soldier and worker masses. The formulæ were all-inclusive and at the same time ambiguous: they almost all balanced on a fine line between defence of the capital and armed insurrection. However, these two tasks, heretofore mutually exclusive, were now in actual fact growing into one. Having seized the power, the Soviet would be compelled to undertake the military defence of Petrograd. The element of defence-camouflage was not, therefore, violently dragged in, but flowed to some extent from the conditions preceding the insurrection.

With this same purpose of camouflage a Social Revolutionary and not a Bolshevik was placed at the head of the commission on the "Committee of Defence." This was a young and modest intendant, Lazimir, one of those Left Social Revolutionaries who were already travelling with the Bolsheviks before the insurrection—although, to be sure, not always foreseeing wither the course would lead. Lazimir's preliminary rough draft was edited by Trotsky in two directions: the practical plans relating to the conquest of the garrison were more sharply defined, the general revolutionary goal was still more glozed over. As ratified by the Executive Committee against the protest of two Mensheviks, the draft included in the staff of the Military Revolutionary Committee the præsidiums of the Soviet and of the soldiers' section, representatives of the fleet, of the regional committee of Finland, of the railroad unions, of the factory committees, the trade unions, the party military organisations, the Red Guard, etc. The organisational basis was the same as in many other cases, but the personal composition of the committee was determined by its new tasks. It was assumed that the organisations would send representatives familiar with military affairs or standing near to the garrison. The character of an organ should be conditioned by its function.

Another new formation of this period was no less important. Under the direction of the Military Revolutionary Committee there was created a Permanent Conference of the Garrison. The soldiers' section represented the garrison politically, the deputies being elected under the party symbols. The Garrison Conference, however, was to consist of the regimental committees which guided the daily lives of their units and thus constituted a more immediate practical "guild" representation. The analogy between the regimental and the factory committees is obvious. Through the mediation of the workers' section of the Soviet the Bolsheviks were able upon big political questions to rely confidently upon the workers. But in order to become masters in the factories it had been necessary to carry the factory and shop committees. The composition of the soldiers' section guaranteed to the Bolsheviks the political sympathy of the majority of the garrison. But in order to get the practical disposal of the military units it was necessary to rely directly on the regimental committees. This explains why in the period preceding the insurrection the Garrison Conference naturally crowded out the soldiers' section and moved to the centre of the stage. The more prominent deputies in the section were also, by the way, members of the Conference.

In an article written not long before these days—"The Crisis is Ripe"—Lenin had reproachfully asked: "What has the party done in the matter of ascertaining the attitude of the troops, etc. . . . ?" Notwithstanding the devoted work of the Military Organisation, Lenin's reproach was just. A strictly military examination of the forces and materials was difficult for the party to achieve: the habit of mind was lacking and the approach. This situation changed the moment the Garrison Conference came on the scene. Henceforth a living panorama of the garrison—not only of the capital but also of the military ring surrounding it—passed before the eyes of the leaders.

On the 12th the Executive Committee took up the regulations drafted by Lazimir's commission. In spite of the session's being secret the debate was carried on to a certain extent in equivocal language. "Here they said one thing and meant another," writes Sukhanov not unjustly. The regulations provided for the establishment under the Committee of departments of defence, supplies, communications, intelligence, etc.: this was a headquarters or counter-quarters. They declared it to be the aim of the Conference to raise the fighting capacity of the garrison: that was entirely true, but a fighting capacity may be applied in different ways. The Mensheviks observed with helpless indignation that an idea advanced by them for patriotic purposes was being converted into a screen for the preparation of an insurrection. The camouflage was by no means impenetrable—everybody understood what the talk was about—but at the same time it could not be broken through. Had not the Compromisers themselves behaved in exactly the same way in the past, grouping the garrison around themselves at critical moments and creating sovereign bodies parallel with those of the government? The Bolsheviks were merely following the traditions, so to speak, of the dual power. But they were bringing a new content into these old forms. What had formerly served the purpose of compromise was now leading to civil war. The Mensheviks demanded that it be placed in the record that they were against the undertaking as a whole. This platonic request was granted.

On the next day the question of the Military Revolutionary Committee and the Garrison Conference was taken up by the soldiers' section, which only a little while before had constituted the lifeguard of the Compromisers. The chief place in this very significant session was rightly occupied by the president of the Centrobalt, the sailor Dybenko, a black-bearded giant, a man who never had to look in his pocket for a word. The speech of this Helsingfors guest crashed into the stagnant atmosphere of the garrison like a keen and fresh sea wind. Dybenko told about the final break of the fleet with the government and their new attitudes to the command. Before the latest naval operations began, he said, the admiral addressed a question to the Congress of Sailors then sitting: Will they carry out military orders? We answered: "We will—under supervision from our side. But . . . if we see that the fleet is threatened with destruction, the commanding staff will be the first to hang from the mast-head." To the Petrograd garrison this was a new language. Even in the fleet it had come into use only in the last few days. It was the language of insurrection. The little group of Mensheviks grumbled distractedly in a corner. The præsidium looked out with some alarm upon that compact mass of grey soldier coats. Not one protesting voice from their ranks! Eyes burned like coals in their excited faces. A spirit of daring was in the air.

In conclusion, stimulated by the universal sympathy, Dybenko confidently exclaimed: "They talk about the need of bringing out the Petrograd garrison for the defence of the approaches to Petrograd and of Reval in particular. Don't believe a word of it. We will defend Reval ourselves. Stay here and defend the interests of the revolution. . . . When we need your support we will say so ourselves, and I am confident that you will support us." This challenge, which exactly matched the mood of the soldiers, called out a veritable whirlwind of sincere enthusiasm in which the protests of a few individual Mensheviks were completely drowned. The question of removing the regiments was settled from that moment.

The regulations proposed by Lazimir were adopted by a majority of 283 votes against 1, with 23 abstaining. These figures, unexpected even to the Bolsheviks, gave a measure of the pressure of the revolutionary masses. The vote meant that the soldiers' section had openly and officially transferred the administration of the garrison from headquarters to the Military Revolutionary Committee. The coming days would show that this was no mere gesture.

On that same day the Executive Committee of the Petrograd Soviet made public the creation under its supervision of a special department of the Red Guard. The matter of arming the workers, neglected under the Compromisers and even obstructed by them, had become one of the most important tasks of the Bolshevik Soviet. The suspicious attitude of the soldiers toward the Red Guard was already far in the past. On the contrary, almost all the resolutions of the regiments contained a demand for the arming of the workers. From now on the Red Guard and the garrison stand side by side. Soon they will be still more closely united by a common submission to the Military Revolutionary Committee.

The government was worried. On the morning of the 14th, a conference of the ministers in Kerensky's office ratified the measures undertaken by headquarters against the "coming out" under preparation. The rulers were guessing: Will it stop this time at an armed demonstration or will it go to the point of insurrection? The commander of the district said to the representatives of the press: "In any case we are ready." Those doomed to death not infrequently experience an afflux of life force just before the end.

At a joint session of the Executive Committees, Dan, imitating the June intonations of Tseretelli, who had now taken refuge in the Caucasus, demanded of the Bolsheviks an answer to the question: Do they intend to come out, and if they do, when? From the answer of Riazanov, the Menshevik Bogdanov drew the not unjustified conclusion that the Bolsheviks were preparing an insurrection and would stand at the head of it. The Menshevik paper wrote: "And the Bolsheviks are evidently relying in their plans for a coming 'seizure of power' on the garrison's staying here." But in this remark the phrase "seizure of power" was in quotation marks. The Compromisers still did not seriously believe in the danger. They did not fear the victory of the Bolsheviks so much as the triumph of the counter-revolution in consequence of new civil war conflicts.

Having undertaken to arm the workers, the Soviet had to find its way to the weapons. This did not happen all at once. Here too each practical step forward was suggested by the masses. It was only necessary to listen attentively to their suggestions. Four years after the event, Trotsky, in an evening devoted to recollections of the October revolution, told the following story: "When a delegation from the workers came to me and said they needed weapons, I answered: 'But the arsenals, you see, are not in our hands.' They answered: 'We have been to the Sestroretsk Arms Factory.' 'Well, and what about it?' 'They said that if the Soviet ordered they would deliver.' I gave an order for five thousand rifles, and they got them the same day. That was the first experiment." The hostile press immediately raised a cry against this delivery of weapons by a government factory upon the order of a person indicted for state treason, and only released from prison on bail. The government kept still, but the highest organ of the democracy came forward with a strict command. Weapons were to be given to nobody without its strict permission—the permission of the Central Executive Committee of the Soviets. It might seem that on the question of delivering weapons Dan and Gotz were as little in a position to forbid, as Trotsky to permit or give orders. The factories and arsenals were supposed to be under government administration. But ignoring the official authorities at all serious moments had become a tradition with the Central Executive Committee, and had permanently entered into the customs of the government itself, corresponding as it did to the nature of things. The violation of tradition and custom came, however, from another direction. Having ceased to distinguish the thunderings of the Central Executive Committee from the lightnings of Kerensky, the workers and soldiers ignored them both.

It was more convenient to demand the transfer of the Petrograd regiments in the name of the front than in the name of the chancelleries at the rear. For these reasons Kerensky placed the Petrograd garrison under the commander-in-chief of the Northern front, Cheremissov. While excluding the capital in its military aspect from his own administration as the head of the government, Kerensky took comfort in the thought that he would subject it to himself as commander-in-chief of the army. In his turn General Cheremissov, who was going to have a very hard nut to crack, sought help from the commissars and committee-men. With their common labours a plan of future activities was drawn up. On the 7th the headquarters at the front, together with the army organisations, was to summon representatives of the Petrograd Soviet to Pskov in order in the presence of the trenches to present them with a brusque demand.

There was nothing for the Petrograd Soviet to do but accept the challenge. The delegation of a score or so appointed at the session of the 16th—about half members of the Soviet and half representatives of the regiments—was headed by the president of the Workers' Section, Feodorov, and leaders of the Soldiers' Section and the Military Organisation of the Bolsheviks—

Lashevich, Sadovsky, Mekhonoshin, Dashkevich and others. A few left Social Revolutionaries and Menshevik-Internationalists, included in the delegation, promised to defend the policy of the Soviet. At a conference of the delegates held before their departure the draft of a declaration proposed by Sverdlov was adopted.

The same session of the Soviet took up the regulations of the Military Revolutionary Committee. This institution had barely come into existence when it assumed in the eyes of the enemy an aspect growing every day more hateful. "The Bolsheviks make no answer," cried an orator of the oppositoin, "to the direct question: Are they preparing an attack? This is either cowardice or lack of confidence in their forces." The meeting greeted this remark with hearty laughter: the representative of the government party was demanding that the party of insurrection open the secrets of its heart to him. The new committee, continued the orator, is nothing else but "a revolutionary headquarters for the seizure of power." They, the Mensheviks would not enter it. "How many are there of you?" cried a voice from the benches: there were indeed only a few Mensheviks in the Soviet, fifty altogether. But nevertheless it seemed authoritatively known to them that "the masses are not in favour of coming out." In his reply Trotsky did not deny that the Bolsheviks were preparing for a seizure of power: "We make no secret of that." But at present, he said, that is not the question. The government has demanded the removal of the revolutionary troops from Petrograd and to that "we have to answer yes or no." The regulations drafted by Lazimir were adopted by an overwhelming majority. The president proposed to the Military Revolutionary Committee to begin work on the following day. Thus one more forward step was taken.

The commander of the district, Polkovnikov, had that day once more reported to the government that an action was under preparation by the Bolsheviks. The report was couched in bold language: the garrison as a whole is on the side of the government; the officers' schools have received an order to be ready. In an appeal to the population Polkovnikov promised in case of necessity to adopt "the most extreme measures." The burgomaster, Schreider, a Social Revolutionary, added a prayer on his part that "no disorders shall be instigated so that we may avoid actual famine in the capital." Threatening and adjuring, making bold and making timid, the press meanwhile was rising to a higher and higher note.

To impress the imagination of delegates from the Petrograd Soviet, a military-theatrical setting was arranged for the reception in Pskov. In the office of headquarters around tables covered with imposing maps stood notable generals, high commissars, with Voitinsky at their head, and representatives of the army committees. The chiefs of the departments read reports of the military situation on land and sea. All the reports came to one and the same conclusion: It is necessary to call out the Petrograd garrison immediately for the defence of the approaches to the capital. The commissars and committee-men indignantly refuted all suspicions in regard to hidden political motives: the whole operation, they declared, has been dictated by strategic necessity. The delegates had no direct proofs to the contrary: in this kind of business evidence does not grow on every bush. But the whole situation was a refutation. The front had no lack of men. What it lacked was willingness to fight. The mood of the Petrograd garrison was by no means such as to reinforce a front so shaken. Moreover the lessons of the Kornilov days were still in the memories of all. Thoroughly convinced of their correctness, the delegation easily resisted the assault of headquarters, and returned to Petrograd more unanimous than when they had left.

Those direct proofs which the participants at that time lacked are now at the disposal of the historian. The secret military correspondence proves that it was not the front which had demanded the Petrograd regiments, but that Kerensky had imposed them upon the front. To a telegram from his War Minister, the commander-in-chief of the Northern front answered on the direct wire: "Secret. 17. X. The initiative for sending the troops of the Petrograd garrison to the front was yours and not mine. . . . When it became clear that the troops of the Petrograd garrison did not want to go to the front, that is, that they are not capable of fighting, I then in a private conversation with your officer-representative said that . . . we have already plenty of such troops at the front; but in view of the desire expressed by you to send them to the front, I did not refuse them and I do not refuse them now, if you, as before, consider their transfer from Petrograd necessary." The semi-bellicose tone of this telegram is explained by the fact that Cheremissov, a general with a taste for high politics, having been considered "Red" while in the czar's army, and having afterward become, according to Miliukov's expression, "the favourite of the revolutionary democracy," had evidently come to the conclusion that it would be better to draw apart in good season from the government and its conflict with the Bolsheviks. The conduct of Cheremissov during the days of the revolution wholly confirms this assumption.

The struggle about the garrison interwove with the struggle about the Soviet Congress. Only four or five days remained before the date originally designated. The "coming-out" was expected in connection with the Congress. It was assumed that as in the July Days the movement would develop on the type of an armed mass demonstration with street fighting. The right Menshevik Potressov, obviously relying upon data supplied by the Intelligence Service, or by the French War Mission—always bold in the manufacture of forged documents—expounded in the bourgeois press the plan of a Bolshevik action which was to take place on the night of October 17. The ingenious authors of the plan did not forget to foretell that at one of the gates of the city the Bolsheviks were to pick up the "dark elements." The soldiers of the Guard regiments were as good at laughing as the gods of Homer. The white pillars and chandeliers of Smolny shook with uproarious volleys when Potressov's article was read at a meeting of the Soviet. But the all-wise government, unable as ever to see what was taking place before its eyes, took serious fright at this awkward forgery, and hastily assembled at two o'clock in the morning in order to hold off these "dark elements." After renewed conferences between Kerensky and the military authorities the necessary measures were taken. The guards of the Winter Palace and the State Bank were reinforced; two training schools were called in from Oranienbaum, and even an armoured train from the Rumanian front. "At the last moment," writes Miliukov, "the Bolsheviks revoked their preparations. Why they did this is not clear." Even several years after the event the learned historian still prefers to believe an invention which contained its own refutation.

The authorities directed the militia to investigate the environs of the city to see if they could find signs of any preparation for a coming out. The reports of the militia were a combination of live observations with police stupidity. In the Alexandro-Nevsky section, which contains a number of big factories, the investigators found complete tranquillity. In the Vyborg district the necessity of overthrowing the government was being openly preached, but "externally" all was quiet. In the Vassilie-Ostrov district the mood was high, but here too "external" signs of an action were not to be observed. On the Narva side a redoubled agitation in favour of action was going on, but it was impossible to get an answer from anybody to the question, just when. Either the day and hour were being kept strictly secret, or they were really unknown to anybody. Decision: to reinforce the patrols in the suburbs and have the commissars of the militia inspect the sentry posts more frequently.

Certain correspondence in the Moscow liberal press is not a bad supplement to the reports of the militia: "In the suburbs, at the Petersburg factories, Nevsky, Obukhovsky and Putilov, Bolshevik agitation in favour of a coming out is in progress everywhere. The workers are in a state to start moving at any moment. During recent days there has been observed in Petrograd an unheard of influx of deserters. . . . At the Warsaw station you can't get through because of the soldiers with their suspicious looks, their burning eyes in excited faces. . . . There is information of the presence in Petrograd of whole gangs of thieves who have caught the smell of their prey. The dark forces are being organised, and the dens and lunch-rooms are brim full of them. . . ." Philistine fright and police rumour here interweave with certain amount of austere fact. In approaching its climax the revolutionary cries stirred up the social deeps to the very bottom. Deserters and robber-gangs and the dens of iniquity did actually all rise at the rumble of the approaching earthquake. The leaders of society gazed with physical horror at the unleashed forces of their own régime, at its ulcers and vices. The revolution had not created but only uncovered them.

At the headquarters of a corps in Dvinsk in those days, Baron Budberg, a man already known to us, a bilious reactionary, but not wanting a gift of observation and his own kind of penetration, wrote: "The Kadets, the Kadetoids, the Octobrists, and the many-coloured revolutionists of the ancient and of the March formation, feel their end approaching and chirp and chatter on all sides, reminding one of the Mussulman who tried to stop an eclipse of the moon with a rattle."

The Garrison Conference was first called together on the 18th. The telephonogram sent to the military units told them to refrain from actions on their own initiative, and fulfil only those orders of headquarters which should be countersigned by the Soldiers' Sections. In this the Soviet was making a decisive and open attempt to take control of the garrison. The telephonogram was in essence nothing else than a summons to overthrow the existing authorities. But it could be interpreted if one wished, as a peaceful act of replacing the Compromisers with Bolsheviks in the mechanic of the dual power. Practically this came to the same thing, but the more flexible interpretation left room for illusions. The præsidium of the Central Executive Committee, considering itself the master of Smolny, made an attempt to stop the despatch of the telephonogram. It only compromised itself once more. The assembly of representatives of the regimental and company committees of Petrograd and the environs occurred at the designated hour, and turned out to be extraordinarily large.

Thanks to the atmosphere created by the enemy, the reports of the participants in this Garrison Conference automatically concentrated upon the question of the prospective "coming-out." There occurred a significant muster-roll, upon which the leaders would scarcely have ventured upon their own initiative. Those against the action were the military school in Peterhof and the Ninth Cavalry Regiment. The squadrons of the cavalry of the Guard were inclined to neutrality. The military School in Oranienbaum would submit only to the commands of the Central Executive Committee. That exhausted the hostile or neutral voices. Those declaring their readiness to come out at a word from the Petrograd Soviet were the following: the Egersky, the Moscow, the Volynsky, the Pavolvsky, the Keksgolmsky, the Semenovsky, the Izmailovsky, the first sharpshooters and the third reserve regiments, the second Baltic crew, the electro-technical battalion and the artillery division of the Guard; the grenadier regiment would come out only at the summons of the Congress of Soviets. That was enough. The less important units followed the lead of the majority. The representatives of the Central Executive Committee, who had not long ago justly considered the Petrograd garrison the source of their power, were now almost unanimously denied the floor. In a state of impotent exasperation they left the "unauthorised" assembly, which immediately thereafter at the suggestion of the president declared: No orders are valid without the countersign of the Soviet.

That which had been preparing in the minds of the garrison during the last months, and especially weeks was now crystallising, The government turned out more insignificant than it had been possible to think. While the town was buzzing with rumours of a coming-out and of bloody battles, the Conference of Regimental Committees, showing an overwhelming predominance of Bolsheviks, made both demonstrations and mass battles essentially unnecessary. The garrison was confidently advancing to the revolution, seeing it not as an insurrection, but as a realisation of the irrefutable right of the Soviet to decide the fate of the country. This movement had incomparable power, but at the same time a certain heaviness. The party was obliged to attune its activity with some skill to the political stride of the regiments, a majority of whom were awaiting a summons from the Petersburg Soviet, but some from the Congress of Soviets.

In order to ward off the danger of even a temporary interference with the development of the offensive, it was necessary to answer one question which was disturbing not only enemies but friends: Will not an insurrection spontaneously break out almost any day? In the tramways, on the streets, in the stores, there was no talk but of an expected coming-out. On the Palace Square, in front of the Winter Palace and the General Staff, long queues of officers were offering the government their services and receiving revolvers in exchange: in the hours of danger neither the revolvers nor their owners will put in one second's appearance. The leading editorials in all the current papers were devoted to the question of the insurrection. Gorky demanded of the Bolsheviks that unless they were the "helpless playthings of the enraged multitude," they should refute these rumours. This alarm of uncertainty penetrated even the workers' sections, and still more the regiments. To them, too, it began to seem as though a coming-out were being prepared without them. And by whom? Why was Smolny silent? The self-contradictory situation of the Soviet as a public parliament and at the same time a revolutionary headquarters, created great difficulties in those last moments. It became impossible to remain longer silent.

"During the last days," declared Trotsky at the end of an evening's session of the Soviet, "the press has been full of communications, rumours, articles about an impeding action. . . . The decisions of the Petrograd Soviet are published and made known to everybody. The Soviet is an elective institution, and . . . cannot have a decision which would not be known to the workers and soldiers. . . . I declare in the name of the Soviet that no armed actions have been settled upon by us, but if the Soviet in the course of events should be obliged to set the date for a coming-out, the workers and soldiers would come out to the last man at its summons. They say that I signed an order for five thousand rifles. . . . Yes, I signed it. . . . The Soviet will continue to organise and arm the workers' guard." The delegates understood: the battle was near, but without them and over their heads the signal would not be given.

However, besides a reassuring explanation, the masses had to have a clear revolutionary prospective. For this purpose the speaker united the two questions—removal of the garrison and coming Congress of Soviets. "We are in conflict with the government upon a question which may become extremely sharp. . . . We will not permit them . . . to strip Petrograd of its revolutionary garrison." This conflict is in its turn subordinate to another that approaches. "It is known to the bourgeoisie that the Petrograd Soviet is going to propose to the Congress of Soviets that they seize the power. . . . And foreseeing an inevitable battle, the bourgeois classes are trying to disarm Petrograd." The political set-up of the revolution was first given in this speech with complete definition: We expect to seize the power, we need the garrison, and we will not give it up. "At the first attempt of the counter-revolution to break up the Congress, we will answer with a counter-attack which will be ruthless, and which we will carry through to the end." Here, too, the announcement of a decisive political offensive was made under the formulæ of military defence.

Sukhanov, who turned up at this meeting with a hopeless plan to draw the Soviet into a celebration of Gorky's fiftieth anniversary, subsequently made an apt comment on the revolutionary knot which was tied there. For Smolny, he said, the question of the garrison is a question of insurrection; for the soldiers it is a question of their own fate. "It would be difficult to imagine a more fortunate starting point for the policy of those days." This did not prevent Sukhanov from considering the policy of the Bolsheviks as a whole ruinous. Along with Gorky and thousands of radical intellectuals he feared above all things that so-called "enraged multitude" which was with admirable deliberation developing its offensive from day to day.

The Soviet was sufficiently powerful to announce openly its programme of state revolution and even set the date. At the same time—right up to the date set by itself for the complete victory—the Soviet was powerless in thousands of great and small questions. Kerensky, politically already reduced to a zero, was still giving out decrees in the Winter Palace. Lenin, the inspirer of this incomparable movement of the masses, was hiding underground, and the Minister of Justice, Miliantovich, had renewed in those days his instructions to the district attorney to bring about Lenin's arrest. Even in Smolny, on its own territory, the all-powerful Petrograd Soviet seemed to be living only by grace of the authorities. The administration of the building, of the cashbox, of the despatching room, the automobiles, the telephones—all was still in the hands of the Central Executive Committee which itself only hung on by the mere thread of an abstract right of succession.

Sukhanov tells how after the meeting he came out in the thick of night on Smolny Square, in black darkness with rain coming down in sheets. The whole crowd of delegates were hopelessly milling around a couple of smoking and stinking automobiles which had been assigned to the Bolshevik Soviet from the opulent garages of the Central Executive Committee. "The president, Trotsky, was also about to approach the automobile," relates this omnipresent observer. "But after stopping and looking on for a minute he chuckled and, splashing through the puddles, disappeared in the darkness." On the platform of the tramcar, Sukhanov ran into some unknown small-sized fellow of modest appearance with a black goatee. The unknown tried to console Sukhanov in all the discomforts of the long journey. "Who is that?" asked Sukhanov of his Bolshevik companion. "An old party worker, Sverdlov." In less than two weeks this small man with a little black goatee will be president of the Central Executive Committee, the supreme governing power of the Soviet Republic. It may be that Sverdlov consoled his travelling companion out of a feeling of gratitude: Eight days before that in the apartment of Sukhanov—to be sure, without his knowledge—had occurred that meeting of the Bolshevik Central Committee which placed the armed insurrection on the order of the day.

The next morning the Central Executive Committee made an attempt to turn back the wheel of events. The præsidium convoked a "lawful" assembly of the garrison, drawing into it also those backward committees which should long ago have been re-elected, and which had not been present the day before. This supplementary test of the garrison, while also giving something new, still more clearly confirmed yesterday's picture. This time those opposed to the coming-out were a majority of the committees of the troops quartered in the Peter and Paul fortress, and the committees of the armoured car division. They both announced their submission to the Central Executive Committee. This information was not to be ignored.

Situated on an island washed by the Neva and its canal, between the centre of the city and two outlying districts, this fortress dominates the near-by bridges, and protects—or, if you will, lays bare—from the side of the river the approaches to the Winter Palace where the government had its seat. Although deprived of military significance in large scale operations, the fortress can speak a weighty word in a street fight. Moreover—and this, perhaps, is more important—the well-stocked Kronverksky arsenal adjoins the fortress. The workers were in need of rifles—yes, and the more revolutionary regiments, too, were almost disarmed. The importance of armoured cars in a street battle needs no explanation. On the side of the government they might cause many fruitless sacrifices; on the side of the insurrection they would shorten the road to victory. In the approaching days the Bolsheviks would have to give special attention to the fortress and the armoured car division. For the rest, the correlation of forces at this new conference turned out to be the same as on the preceding day.The attempt of the Central Executive Committee to carry its own very cautious resolution was coldly repulsed by an overwhelming majority. Not having been summoned by the Petrograd Soviet, it was noted, the conference does not consider itself empowered to adopt decisions. The Compromise leaders had themselves begged for this supplementary slap in the face.

Finding the approach to the regiments barricaded below, the Central Executive Committee tried to get hold of the garrison from above. By agreement with the staff, they appointed Captain Malevsky, a Social Revolutionary, chief commissar for the whole district, and announced their willingness to recognise the commissars of the Soviet on condition that they submit to the chief commissar. This attempt to get astride of the Bolshevik garrison through the instrumentality of a captain unknown to anybody was obviously hopeless. Having rejected it, the Soviet broke off the negotiations.

The insurrection laid bare by Potressov had not occurred. The enemy now confidently named another date, the 20th of October. On that day, as we know, the Congress of Soviets was originally to have opened, and the insurrection followed that Congress like its own shadow. To be sure, the Congress had already postponed its opening five days. Never mind: the object had moved, but the shadow remained. This time, too, all necessary measures were taken by the government to prevent a "coming-out." Reinforced sentry guards were placed in the suburbs; Cossack patrols rode through the workers' districts all night long; cavalry reserves were concealed at various points throughout the city; the militia was made ready for action, and half of its members did continual duty in the commissariats. Armoured cars, light artillery and machine-guns were set up near the Winter Palace. The approaches to the Palace were guarded by patrols.

Once more the insurrection which no one was preparing, and for which no one had issued a call, did not take place. The day went by more peacefully than many others; work in the shops and factories never ceased. *Izvestia*, edited by Dan, crowed about this victory over the Bolsheviks: "Their adventuring with armed demonstrations in Petrograd is about over." The Bolsheviks have been crushed by the mere indignation of the united democracy: "They are already surrendering." One might literally think that the enemy had lost their heads and were deliberately trying with untimely frights and still less timely trumpetings of victory to lead "public opinion" astray, and conceal the actual plans of the Bolsheviks.

The decision to create a Military Revolutionary Committee, first introduced on the 9th, was passed at a plenary session of the Soviet only a week later. The Soviet is not a party; its machinery is heavy. Four days more were required to form the Committee. Those ten days, however, did not go for nothing: the conquest of the garrison was in full swing, the Conference of Regimental Committees had demonstrated its viability, the arming of the workers was going forward. And thus the Military Revolutionary Committee, although it went to work only on the 20th, five days before the insurrection, found ready to its hands a sufficiently well organised dominion. Being boycotted by the Compromisers, the staff of the Committee contained only Bolsheviks and Left Social Revolutionaries: that eased and simplified the task. Of the Social Revolutionaries only Lazimir did any work, and he was even placed at the head of the bureau in order to emphasise the fact that the Committee was a Soviet and not a party institution. In essence, however, the Committee, whose president was Trotsky, and its chief workers Podvoisky, Antonov-Ovseënko, Lashevich, Sadovsky, and Mekhonoshin, relied exclusively upon Bolsheviks. The committee hardly met once in plenary session with delegates present from all the institutions listed in its regulations. The work was carried on through the bureau under the guidance of the president, with Sverdlov brought in upon all important matters. And that was the general staff of the insurrection.

The bulletin of the Committee thus modestly registers its first step: commissars were appointed in the combatant units of the garrison and in certain institutions and store houses "for observation and leadership." This meant that, having won the garrison politically, the Soviet was now getting organisational control of it. The dominant rôle in selecting these commissars was played by the Military Organisation of the Bolsheviks. Among its Petrograd members, approximately a thousand, there was no small number of resolute soldiers and young officers utterly devoted to the revolution, and who had since the July Days been tempered in the prisons of Kerensky. The commissars recruited from its midst found in the troops of the garrison a soil well prepared. The garrison considered them its own and submitted to their orders with complete willingness.

The initiative in getting possession of institutions came in most cases from below. The workers and clerical employees of the arsenal adjoining the Peter and Paul fortress themselves raised the question of the necessity of establishing control over the giving out of arms. A commissar sent there succeeded in stopping a supplemental arming of the junkers, held back 10,000 rifles on their way to the Don region, and smaller assignments to a number of suspicious organisations and persons. This control was soon extended to other arsenals and even to private dealers in weapons. It was only necessary to appeal to the committee of the soldiers, workers or clerical employees of the given institution or store, and the resistance of the administration would be immediately broken. Weapons were given out henceforth only upon the order of the commissars.

The typographical workers, through their union, called the attention of the Committee to an increase of Black Hundred leaflets and brochures. It was decided that in all suspicious cases the printers' union should come for instructions to the Military Revolutionary Committee. This control through the typographical workers was the most effective of all possible forms of control over the printed agitation of the counter-revolution.

Not satisfied with its formal denial of the rumour of an insurrection, the Soviet openly designated Sunday the 22nd as the day for a peaceful review of its forces—not, however, in the form of street processions, but of meetings in the factories, barracks, and all the major institutions of Petrograd. With the obvious aim of provoking bloody interference, some mysterious worshippers set the same day for a church procession through the streets of the capital. Their summons, issued in the name of some unknown Cossacks, invited the citizens to take part in a religious procession "in memory of the delivery of Moscow from the enemy in 1812." This historical pretext was none too genuine, but over and above this the organisations proposed to the Almighty to hand down a blessing upon the Cossack arms "standing guard against the enemies of the Russian land," a proposal which clearly related to the year 1917.

There was no reason to fear a serious counter-revolutionary manifestation. The clergy had no power among the Petrograd masses; they could raise up against the Soviet under church banners only pitiful remnants of the Black Hundred gangs. But with the co-operation of the experienced provocateurs of the Intelligence Service and of Cossack officers, bloody encounters were not impossible. As a measure of prevention the Military Revolutionary Committee undertook in the first place to strengthen its influence upon the Cossack regiments; a stricter régime was also introduced in the building occupied by the revolutionary staff. "It was no longer easy to get into Smolny," writes John Reed. "The pass system was changed every few hours; for spies continually sneaked through." At a meeting of the Garrison Conference on the 21st devoted to a discussion of the "Soviet Day" to follow, the spokesman proposed a series of measures for the prevention of possible street clashes. The fourth Cossack regiment, which stood farthest to the Left, announced through its delegates that it would not take part in the religious procession. The fourteenth Cossack regiment announced that it would struggle with all its power against the attempts of the counter-revolution, but at the same time that it considered a coming-out for the seizure of power "untimely." Of the three Cossack regiments only one was absent—the Uralsky—the most backward regiment, one brought into Petrograd in July for the crushing of the Bolsheviks.

Upon the proposal of Trotsky, the Conference adopted three short resolutions: (1) "The garrison of Petrograd and its environs promises the Military Revolutionary Committee full support in all its steps . . ."; (2) October 22nd is to be a day devoted to a peaceful review of forces. . . . The garrison appeals to the Cossacks: . . . "We invite you to our meeting to-morrow. You are welcome, brother Cossacks!"; (3) "The All-Russian

Congress of Soviets must take the power in its hands and guarantee to the people peace, land and bread." The garrison solemnly promises to place all its forces at the disposal of the Soviet Congress. "Rely upon us, authorised representatives of the soldiers, workers and peasants. We are all at our posts ready to conquer or die." Hundreds of hands were raised for this resolution which sealed the programme of the insurrection. Fifty-seven men abstained. These were the "neutrals"—that is, the wavering enemy. Not one hand was raised against the resolution. The noose around the neck of the February régime was being drawn in a reliable knot.

In the course of the day it became known that the mysterious instigators of the religious procession had given up their demonstration "at the suggestion of the commander-in-chief of the district." This serious moral success, an excellent measure of the social pressure of the Garrison Conference, permitted a confident prediction that on the following day the enemy, generally speaking, would not venture to poke their heads into the street.

The Military Revolutionary Committee appointed three commissars to the district headquarters—Sadovsky, Mekhonishin and Lazimir. Orders of the commander were to become effective only when countersigned by one of these three. At a telephone call from Smolny the staff sent an automobile for the delegation—the customs of the dual power were still in effect—but contrary to expectations this extreme politeness of the staff did not imply a readiness to make concessions.

After listening to the declaration of Sadovsky, Polkovnikov stated that he did not recognise any commissars and had no need of any guardianship. To a hint from the delegation that along that road headquarters might meet with resistance from the side of the troops, Polkovnikov dryly answered that the garrison was in his hands and its submission was assured. "His assurance was sincere," writes Mekhonoshin in his memoirs. "We felt no affectation in it." For the return trip to Smolny the delegates did not receive an official automobile.

A special session of the Conference, to which Trotsky and Sverdlov were summoned, adopted a decision: To consider the break with headquarters an accomplished fact, and make it the starting point for a further offensive. The first condition of success: The districts must be kept in touch with all stages and episodes of the struggle. The enemy must not be allowed to catch the masses unaware. Through the district soviets and committees of the party the information was sent into all parts of the town. The regiments were immediately informed of what had happened. The instructions were confirmed: Carry out only those orders which are countersigned by the commissars. It was also suggested that they send out only the most reliable soldiers for patrol duty.

But headquarters also decided to take measures. Spurred on evidently by his compromisist allies, Polkovnikov called together at one o'clock in the afternoon his own conference of the garrison, with representatives of the Central Executive Committee present. Anticipating this move of the enemy, the Military Revolutionary Committee called an emergency conference of the regimental committees at eleven o'clock, and here it was decided to formulate the break with headquarters. The appeal to the troops of Petrograd and the environs drawn up at this meeting speaks the language of a declaration of war. "Having broken with the organised garrison of the capital, headquarters is a direct instrument of the counter-revolutionary forces." The Military Revolutionary Committee disclaims all responsibility for the activities of headquarters, and standing at the head of the garrison takes upon itself "the defence of revolutionary order against counter-revolutionary attempts."

That was a decisive step on the road to insurrection. Or was it perhaps only the next conflict in the mechanics of that dual power which is so full of conflicts? Headquarters, at any rate, tried for its own consolation so to interpret it—after conferring with the representatives of those units which had not received in good season the summons of the Military Revolutionary Committee. A delegate sent from Smolny under the leadership of the Bolshevik ensign, Dashkevich, briefly made known to headquarters the resolution of the Garrison Conference. The few representatives of the troops present reaffirmed their loyalty to the Soviet, but refused to make a decision and dispersed. "After a prolonged exchange of opinions"—the press so quoted the words of headquarters—"no definite decision was adopted; it was thought necessary to await a solution of the conflict between the Central Executive Committee and the Petrograd Soviet." Headquarters thus conceived its downfall as a quarrel between two soviet institutions as to which one should control its activities. That policy of voluntary blindness had this advantage, that it relieved them of the necessity of declaring war on Smolny, for which act the rulers lacked adequate forces. Thus the revolutionary conflict, already on the point of breaking out, was once more with the help of the governmental organs, confined within the legal framework of the dual power. Fearing to look reality in the face, headquarters the more loyally co-operated in camouflaging the insurrection. But was not this light-minded conduct of the powers only a camouflage for their own actual purpose? Did not headquarters intend, under cover of this bureaucratic naïveté, to deal an unexpected blow at the Military Revolutionary Committee? Such an attempt upon the part of the distraught and demoralised organs of the Provisional Government was considered highly improbable in Smolny. The Military Revolutionary Committee, however, took the most simple measures of precaution: in the nearby barracks companies were kept under arms night and day, ready at the first signal of alarm to come to the aid of Smolny.

In spite of the calling-off of the religious procession, the bourgeois press foretold bloodshed on Sunday. The compromisist paper announced in its morning edition: "To-day the authorities expect a coming-out with better probability than on the 20th." Thus for the third time in one week—the 17th, the 20th, the 22nd—this naughty boy had deceived the people with a false cry of "wolf!" The fourth time, if we can believe the old fable, the boy will fall into the wolf's jaws. The Bolshevik press, in summoning the masses to attend meetings, spoke of a peaceful appraisal of revolutionary forces on the eve of the Congress of Soviets. This fully answered the plan of the Military Revolutionary Committee: to carry out a gigantic review without clashes, without employing weapons, even without showing them. They wanted to show the masses their own numbers, their strength, their resolution. They wanted with unanimous numbers to compel the enemy to hide, to keep out of sight, to stay indoors. By exposing the impotence of the bourgeoisie beside their own masses, they wanted to erase from the consciousness of the workers and soldiers the last hindering recollections of the July Days—to bring it about that having seen themselves the masses should say: Nothing and nobody can any longer oppose us.

"The frightened population," wrote Miliukov five years later, "remained at home or stood aside." It was the bourgeoisie that remained at home, and they really had been frightened by their own press. All the rest of the population thronged out to meetings from early morning to night—young and old, men and women, boys and girls, mothers with children in their arms. No meetings like this had been seen before throughout the revolution. All Petrograd, with the exception of its upper strata, was one solid meeting. In those auditoriums, continually packed to the doors, the audiences would be entirely renewed in the course of a few hours. Fresh and ever fresh waves of workers, soldiers and sailors would roll up to the buildings and flood them full. The petty bourgeoisie of the town bestirred themselves, too, aroused by these waves and by those warnings which were supposed to frighten them. Tens of thousands brimmed that immense building known as the House of the People. They filled all the theatres, filled the auditoriums of the theatres, their smoke-rooms, buffets, and foyers—filled them with a solid and excited and at the same time disciplined mass. From iron columns and upstairs windows human heads, legs and arms were hanging in garlands and clusters. There was that electric tension in the air which forebodes a coming discharge. Down with Kerensky! Down with the war! Power to the Soviets! None of the Compromisers any longer dared appear before these red hot crowds with arguments or warnings. The Bolsheviks had the floor. All the oratorical forces of the party, including delegates to the Congress who were beginning to arrive from the provinces, were brought into action. Occasionally Left Social Revolutionaries spoke—in some places anarchists—but they both tried as little as possible to distinguish themselves from Bolsheviks.

The people of the slums, of the attics and basements, stood still by the hour in threadbare coat or grey uniform, with caps or heavy shawls still on their heads, the mud of the streets soaked through their shoes, an autumn cough catching at their throats. They stood there packed shoulder to shoulder, and crowding even closer to make room for more, to make room for all, listening tirelessly, hungrily, passionately, demandingly, fearing lest they miss a word of what it is so necessary to understand, to assimilate, and to do. It had seemed as though during the months past, the weeks—at least during the very last days—all the words had been spoken. But no! To-day at least those words have a different sound. The masses are experiencing them in a new way, not as a gospel but as an obligation to act. The experience of the revolution, the war, the heavy struggle of a whole bitter lifetime, rose from the deeps of memory in each of those poverty-driven men and women, expressing itself in simple and imperious thoughts: This way we can go no farther, we must break a road into the future.

Everyone who took part in the events here described has subsequently turned his eyes back to that simple and wonderful day so clearly shining out against the background of the revolution —vivid enough even without that. The image of that inspired human flood—inspired, and yet in its unconquerable power restrained—is chiselled for ever in the memory of those who saw it. "The day of the Petrograd Soviet," writes the Left Social Revolutionary, Mstislavsky," was celebrated at innumerable meetings with enormous enthusiasm." The Bolshevik, Testkovsky, who spoke at two factories of the Vassilie-Ostrov district, says: "We spoke frankly to the masses of the coming seizure of power by us, and heard but words of encouragement." "Around me," says Sukhanov, describing a meeting in the House of the People, "there was a mood very near to ecstasy . . . Trotsky had formulated some brief general resolution. . . . Those in favour . . . Thousands and thousands raised their hands as one man. I looked at the lifted hands and burning eyes of men, women, boys, workers, soldiers, peasants, and of typically petty bourgeois characters too. . . . Trotsky continued to speak. The multitude continued to hold their hands in the air. Trotsky chiselled out each word: Let this vote of yours be your oath. . . . The multitude held their hands high. They agreed. They took the oath." The Bolshevik Popov tells of a rapturous oath sworn by the masses: "To rush out at the first word from the Soviet." Mstislavsky tells of an electrified crowd taking an oath of loyalty to the soviets. The same scene was to be observed on a smaller scale in all parts of the city from centre to suburbs. Hundreds of thousands of people, at one and the same hour, lifted their hands and took a vow to carry the struggle through to the end. The daily meetings of the Soviet, the soldiers' section, the Garrison Conference, the factory and shop committees, had given inner solidarity to a big group of leaders; separate mass meetings had united the factories and regiments; but that day, the 22nd of October, welded in one gigantic cauldron and under high temperature the authentic popular masses. The masses saw themselves and their leaders; the leaders saw and listened to the masses. Each side was satisfied with the other. The leaders were convinced: We can postpone no longer! The masses said to themselves: This time the thing will be done!

The success of this Sunday's review of forces by the Bolsheviks shattered the self-confidence of Polkovnikov and his high command. By agreement with the government and the Central Executive Committee, headquarters made an attempt to come to terms with Smolny. Why not after all re-establish the good old friendly customs of contact and compromise? The Military Revolutionary Committee did not refuse to send emissaries for an exchange of opinion: A better opportunity for reconnoitring could hardly be wished. "The negotiations were brief," remembers Sadovsky. "The representatives of headquarters agreed in advance to all the conditions put forth by the Soviet . . . in exchange for which the order of the Military Revolutionary Committee for October 22 was to be annulled." This referred to the document declaring headquarters an instrument of the counter-revolutionary forces. The very same emissaries whom Polkovnikov had so discourteously sent home two days ago now demanded, and received in their hands for the purpose of their report to Smolny, the rough draft of an agreement signed by headquarters. On Saturday these conditions of semi-honourable capitulation would have been accepted. To-day, on Monday, they were already too late. Headquarters awaited an answer which never came.

The Military Revolutionary Committee addressed to the population of Petrograd a proclamation explaining the appointment of commissars in the military units and the most important points of the captial and its environs. "The commissars as representatives of the Soviet are inviolable. Opposition to the commissars is opposition to the Soviet of Workers' and Soldiers' Deputies." The citizens were invited in case of disturbances to appeal to the nearest commissar to call out armed forces. That was the language of sovereignty. But still the Committee did not give the signal for open insurrection. Sukhanov asks: "Is Smolny acting stupidly, or is it playing with the Winter Palace like a cat with a mouse, trying to provoke an attack?" Neither the one nor the other. The Committee is crowding out the government with the pressure of the masses, with the weight of the garrison. It is taking all that it can without a battle. It is advancing its positions without firing, integrating and reinforcing its army on the march. It is measuring with its own pressure the resisting power of the enemy, not taking its eyes off him for a second. Each new step forward changes the disposition of forces to the advantage of Smolny. The workers and the garrison are growing up to the insurrection. Who is to be first to issue the call to arms, will become known in the course of this offensive, this crowding out. It is now only a question of hours. If at the last moment the government finds the courage, or the despair, to give the signal for battle, responsibility for this will lie upon the Winter Palace. But the initiative just the same will have been taken by Smolny. Its declaration of October 23 had meant the overthrow of the power before the government itself was overthrown. The Military Revolutionary Committee was tying up the arms and legs of the enemy régime before striking him on the head. It was possible to apply this tactic of "peaceful penetration," to break the bones of the enemy legally and hypnotically paralyse the remnants of his will, only because of the indubitable superiority of forces on the side of the Committee and because they were increasing hour by hour.

The Committee had been studying from day to day the map of the garrison wide open before it. It knew the temperature of each regiment, and followed every shift in the views and sympathies of the barracks. A surprise from that side was impossible. There remained, however, some dark shadows on the map. An attempt must be made to eradicate, or at least decrease, them. It had become clear on the 19th that the majority of the committees of the Peter and Paul fortress were unfavourably, or at least dubiously, disposed. Now when the whole garrison is for the Committee and the fortress is caught in a ring, at least politically, it is time to take decisive measures for its conquest. Corporal Blagonravov, the commissar appointed to the fortress, had met resistance. The governmental commandant of the fortress had refused to recognise this Bolshevik guardianship; there were even rumours of his boasting that he would arrest the young guardian. It was necessary to do something and do it quickly. Antonov offered to take a reliable battalion of the Pavlovsky regiment into the fortress and disarm the hostile units. But that was a too drastic operation, one which might be used by the officers to cause bloodshed and break the unity of the garrison. Was it really necessary to adopt such extreme measures? Says Antonov in his memoirs: "Trotsky was called in to consider this question. . . . Trotsky was then playing the decisive rôle. The advice he gave us was a product of his revolutionary intuition; that we capture the fortress from within. 'It cannot be that the troops there are not sympathetic,' he said. And he was right. Trotsky and Lashevich went to a meeting in the fortress." The results of this enterprise, which seemed risky, were awaited in Smolny with the greatest excitement. Trotsky subsequently wrote: "On the 23rd I went to the fortress at about two o'clock in the afternoon. A meeting was in progress in the court. The orators of the right wing were in the highest degree cautious and evasive. . . . The soldiers listened to us and they came with us. On the third floor of Smolny they drew a deep breath when the telephone brought this joyful news: The garrison of Peter and Paul has solemnly promised to take orders henceforth only from the Military Revolutionary Committee.

That change in the mood of the fortress troops was not of course the result of one or two speeches. It had been well prepared in the past. The soldiers turned out to be far to the left of their committees. It was only the cracked shell of the old discipline that held out a little longer behind the fortress walls than in the city barracks. One tap was enough to shatter it.

Blagonravov could now confidently establish himself in the fortress, organise his little headquarters, and set up communications with the Bolshevik soviet of the adjoining district and the committees of the nearest barracks. Meanwhile delegates from the factories and military units were coming up to see what they could do about getting weapons. An indescribable liveliness now prevailed in the fortress. "The telephone rang continually bringing news of our new successes at assemblies and mass meetings." Occasionally an unfamiliar voice would announce the arrival at some railroad station of punitive detachments from the front. Immediate investigation would reveal that this was an invention put in circulation by the enemy.

That day the evening session of the Soviet was distinguished by the exceptional number present and the exalted mood. The occupation of Peter and Paul and the conquest of the Kronverksky arsenal containing 100,000 rifles—this was no small guarantee of success. The spokesman for the Military Revolutionary Committee was Antonov. He drew a picture of the crowding out of the governmental organs step by step by the agents of the Military Revolutionary Committee. These agents, he said, are being received everywhere as natural authorities; they obeyed not through fear but through principle. "From all sides come demands for the appointment of commissars." The backward units are hurrying to catch up to the advanced. The Preobrazhensky, which in July had been the first to fall for the slander about German gold, had now issued through its commissar Chudnovsky a violent protest against the rumour that the Preobrazhentsi are for the government. The very idea is regarded as a malicious insult! . . . To be sure, the customary patrol duties are still being carried out, relates Antonov, but this is done with the consent of the Committee. Orders of headquarters for the delivery of weapons and automobiles are not being carried out. Headquarters thus had ample opportunity to find out who is the master of the capital.

To a question: "Does the committee know about the movement of government troops from the front and the surrounding districts, and what measures have been taken against this?" the spokesman answered: "Cavalry units were sent from the Rumanian front, but they have been held up at Pskov; the 17th Infantry Division, finding out on the road where and why they had been sent, refused to go; in Venden two regiments successfully resisted the attempt to send them against Petrograd; we have as yet no news about the Cossacks and junkers supposed to have been sent from Kiev, or the shock troops summoned from Tsarskoe Selo. They do not dare, and they will not dare, lay hands on the Military Revolutionary Committee." Those words sounded pretty good in the white hall of Smolny. As Antonov read his report, one had the impression that the headquarters of the insurrection was working with wide open doors. As a matter of fact, Smolny had almost nothing to hide. The political set-up of the revolution was so favourable that frankness itself became a kind of camouflage: Surely this isn't the way they make an insurrection? That word "insurrection," however, was not spoken by any one of the leaders. This was not wholly a formal measure of caution, for the term did not fit the actual situation. It was being left to the government of Kerensky, as you might say, to insurrect. In the account in *Izvestia* it does say that Trotsky at the session of the 23rd first acknowledged that the aim of the Military Revolutionary Committee was a seizure of power. It is unquestionably true that the original attitude, when the task of the Committee had been declared to be a testing out of the strategic arguments of Cheremissov, had long been abandoned. The transfer of the regiments was indeed all but forgotten. But on the 23rd the talk was still not about insurrection, but about the "defence" of the coming Congress of Soviets—with armed forces if necessary. It was still in this spirit that the resolution was adopted on the report of Antonov.

How were these events estimated in the governmental upper circles? On the night of the 22nd, in communicating to the chief of the headquarters staff, Dukhonin, the news of the attempt of the Military Revolutionary Committee to get the regiments away from the command, Kerensky added: "I think we can easily handle this." His own departure for headquarters was delayed, he said, not at all through fear of any sort of an insurrection: "That matter could be regulated without me, since everything is organised." To his anxious ministers Kerensky reassuringly declared that he personally, unlike them, was very glad of the coming attack since it would give him the opportunity to "settle once for all with the Bolsheviks." "I would be ready to offer a prayer," says the head of the government to the Kadet Nabokov, a frequent guest at the Winter Palace, "that such an attack may occur." "But are you sure that you will be able to handle them?" "I have more forces than I need. They will be stamped out for good."

In their subsequent ridicule of this optimistic light-mindedness of Kerensky, the Kadets have evidently been a little forgetful. In reality Kerensky was looking at those events through their own eyes. On the 21st, Miliukov's paper wrote that if the Bolsheviks, corroded as they are with a profound inner crisis, dare to come out, they will be put down instantly and without difficulty. Another Kadet paper added: "A storm is coming, but it will perhaps clear the air." Dan testifies that in the couloirs of the Pre-Parliament the Kadets and those grouped around them were talking aloud of their wish that the Bolsheviks might come out as soon as possible: "In an open battle they will be beaten to the last man." Prominent Kadets said to John Reed: After being defeated in an insurrection, the Bolsheviks won't dare lift their heads at the Constituent Assembly.

During the 22nd and 23rd Kerensky took counsel, now with the leaders of the Central Executive Committee, now with headquarters: Would it not be advisable to arrest the Military Revolutionary Committee. The Compromisers did not advise it: they themselves would try to regulate the question about commissars. Polkovnikov also thought it would hardly be worth while to hasten with the arrests: the military forces in case of need are "more than adequate." Kerensky listened to Polkovnikov, but still more to his friends, the Compromisers. He was confidently calculating that in case of danger the Central Executive Committee, in spite of all family misunderstandings, would come to his aid in time. It was so in July and in August. Why should it not continue so?

But now it is no longer July and no longer August. It is October. Cold and raw Baltic winds from the direction of Kronstadt are blowing through the squares and along the quays of Petrograd. Junkers in long coats to their heels are patrolling the streets, drowning their anxiety in songs of triumph.

The mounted police are riding up and down, prancing, their revolvers in brand-new holsters. No. The power still looks imposing enough! Or is this perhaps an optical illusion? At a corner of the Nevsky, John Reed, an American with naïve and intelligent eyes in his head, buys a brochure of Lenin's entitled "Will the Bolsheviks Be Able To Hold the State Power?" paying for it with one of those postage stamps which are now circulating in place of money.

Chapter V

Lenin Summons to Insurrection

Besides the factories, barracks, villages, the front and the soviets, the revolution had another laboratory: the brain of Lenin. Driven underground, Lenin was obliged for a hundred and eleven days—from July 6 to October 25—to cut down his meetings even with members of the Central Committee. Without any immediate intercourse with the masses, and deprived of contacts with any organisations, he concentrated his thought the more resolutely upon the fundamental problems of the revolution, reducing them—as was both his rule and the necessity of his nature—to the key problems of Marxism.

The chief arguments of the democrats, even the most leftward, against seizing the power, was that the toilers were incapable of mastering the machinery of state. Opportunist elements even within the Bolshevik Party cherished the same fears. "The machinery of state!" Every petty bourgeois is brought up in adoration of this mystic principle elevated above people and above classes. And the educated philistine carries in his marrow the same awe that his father did, or his uncle, the shopkeeper or well-off peasant, before these all-powerful institutions where questions of war and peace are decided, where commercial patents are given out, whence issue the whips of the taxes, where they punish and once in a while also pardon, where they legitimise marriages and births, where death itself has to stand in line respectfully awaiting recognition. The machinery of state! Removing in imagination not only his hat but his shoes too, the petty bourgeois comes tip-toeing into the temple of the idol on stockinged feet—it matters not what his name is, Kerensky, Laval, MacDonald or Hilferding—that is the way he comes when personal good-luck or the force of circumstances makes him a minister. Such gracious condescension he can answer with a humble submission before the "machinery of state." The Russian radical intelligentsia who had never dared crawl into the seats of power even during the revolution except behind backs of titled landlords and big business men, gazed with fright and indignation upon the Bolsheviks. Those street agitators, those demagogues, think that they can master the machinery of state!

After the Soviet, confronted by the spineless impotence of the official democracy, had saved the revolution in the struggle against Kornilov, Lenin wrote: "Let those of little faith learn from this example. Shame on those who say, 'We have no machine with which to replace that old one which gravitates inexorably to the defence of the bourgeoisie.' For we have a machine. And that is the soviets. Do not fear the initiative and independence of the masses. Trust the revolutionary organisations of the masses, and you will see in all spheres of the state life that same power, majesty and unconquerable will of the workers and peasants, which they have shown in their solidarity and enthusiasm against Kornilovism."

During the first months of his underground life Lenin wrote a book *The State and Revolution*, the principal material for which he had collected abroad during the war. With the same painstaking care which he dedicated to thinking out the practical problems of the day, he here examines the theoretic problems of the state. He cannot do otherwise: for him theory is in actual fact a guide to action. In this work Lenin has not for a minute proposed to introduce any new word into political theory. On the contrary, he gives his work an extraordinarily modest aspect, emphasising his position as a disciple. His task, he says, is to revive the genuine "teaching of Marxism about the state."

With its meticulous selection of quotations, its detailed polemical interpretations, the book might seem pedantic—to actual pedants, incapable of feeling under the analysis of texts the mighty pulsation of the mind and will. By a mere re-establishment of the class theory of the state on a new and higher historical foundation, Lenin gives to the ideas of Marx a new concreteness and therewith a new significance. But this work on the state derives its immeasurable importance above all from the fact that it constituted the scientific introduction to the greatest revolution in history. This "commentator" of Marx was preparing his party for the revolutionary conquest of a sixth part of the habitable surface of the earth.

If the state could simply re-accommodate itself to the demands of a new historic régime, revolutions would never have arisen. As a fact, however, the bourgeoisie itself has never yet come to power except by way of revolution. Now it is the workers' turn. Upon this question, too, Lenin restored to Marxism its significance as the theoretic weapon of the proletarian revolution.

You say the workers cannot master the machinery of state? But it is not a question—Lenin teaches—of getting possession of the old machine and using it for new aims: that is a reactionary Utopia. The selection of personages in the old machine, their education, their mutual relations, are all in conflict with the historic task of the proletariat. After seizing the power our task is not to re-educate the old machine, but to shatter it to fragments. And with what replace it? With the soviets. From being leaders of the revolutionary masses, instruments of education, the soviets will become organs of the new state order.

In the whirlpool of the revolution this work will find few readers; it will be published, indeed, only after the seizure of power. Lenin is working over the problem of the state primarily for the sake of his own inner confidence and for the future. One of his continual concerns was to preserve the succession of ideas. In July he writes to Kamenev: "*Entre nous.* If they bump me off I ask you to publish my little note-book *Marxism on the State* (stranded in Stockholm). Bound in a blue cover. All the quotations are collected from Marx and Engels, likewise from Kautsky against Pannekoek. There is a whole series of notes and comments. Formulate it. I think you could publish it with a week's work. I think it important, for it is not only Plekhanov and Kautsky who got off the track. My conditions: all this to be absolutely *entre nous.*" The revolutionary leader, persecuted as the agent of a hostile state and figuring on the possibility of attempted assassination by his enemies, concerns himself with the publication of a "blue" note-book with quotations from Marx and Engels. That was to be his secret last will and testament. The phrase "bump me off"[1] was to serve as an antidote against that pathos which he hated, for the commission is pathetic in its very essence.

But while awaiting this blow in the back, Lenin himself was getting ready to deliver a frontal blow. While he was putting in order, between reading the papers and writing letters of instruction, his precious note-book, procured at last from Stockholm, life did not stand still. The hour was approaching when the question of the state was to be decided in practical action.

While still in Switzerland immediately after the overthrow of the monarchy, Lenin wrote: "We are not Blanquists, not advocates of the seizure of power by a minority. . . ." This same

1. Ukokoshit.

thought he developed on his arrival in Russia: "We are now in a minority—the masses do not trust us yet. We know how to wait. . . . They will swing to our side, and after explaining the correlation of forces we will then say to them: Our day is come." The question of the conquest of power was presented during those first months as a question of winning a majority in the soviets.

After the July raids Lenin declared: "The power can be seized henceforth only by an armed insurrection; we must obviously rely in this operation not upon the soviets, demoralised by the Compromisers, but on the factory committees; the soviets as organs of power will have to be created anew after the victory." As a matter of fact, only two months after that the Bolsheviks had won over the soviets from the Compromisers. The nature of Lenin's mistake on this question is highly characteristic of his strategic genius: for the boldest designs he based his calculations upon the least favourable premises. Thus in coming to Russia through Germany in April he counted on going straight to prison from the station. Thus on July 5 he was saying: "They will probably shoot us all." And thus now he was figuring: the Compromisers will not let us get a majority in the soviets.

"There is no man more faint-hearted than I am, when I am working out a military plan," wrote Napoleon to General Berthier. "I exaggerate all dangers and all possible misfortunes. . . . When my decision is taken everything is forgotten except what can assure its success." Except for the pose involved in the inappropriate word faint-hearted, the essence of this thought applies perfectly to Lenin. In deciding a problem of strategy he began by clothing the enemy with his own resolution and farsightedness. The tactical mistakes of Lenin were for the most part by-products of his strategic power. In the present instance, indeed, it is hardly appropriate to use the word mistake. When a diagnostician arrives at the definition of a disease by a method of successive eliminations, his hypothetical assumptions, beginning with the worst possible, are not mistakes but methods of analysis. As soon as the Bolsheviks had got control of the soviets of the two capitals, Lenin said: "Our day is come." In April and July he had applied the brakes; in August he was preparing theoretically the new step; from the middle of September he was hurrying and urging on with all his power. The danger now lay not in acting too soon, but in lagging." In this matter it is now impossible to be premature."

In his articles and letters addressed to the Central Committee, Lenin analyses the situation, always emphasising first of all the international conditions. The symptoms and the facts of an awakening European proletariat are for him, on the background of the war, irrefutable proof that the direct threat against the Russian revolution from the side of foreign imperialism will steadily diminish. The arrest of the socialists in Italy, and still more the insurrections in the German fleet, made him announce a supreme change in the whole world situation: "We stand in the vestibule of the world-wide proletarian revolution."

The epigone historians have preferred to hush up this starting point of Lenin's thought—both because Lenin's calculation has been refuted by events, and because according to the most recent theories the Russian Revolution ought to be sufficient unto itself in all circumstances. As a matter of fact Lenin's appraisal of the international situation was anything but illusory. The symptoms which he observed through the screen of the military censorship of all countries did actually portend the approach of a revolutionary storm. Within a year it shook the old building of the Central Empires to its very foundation. But also in the victor countries, England and France—to say nothing of Italy—it long deprived the ruling classes of their freedom of action. Against a strong, conservative, self-confident capitalistic Europe, the proletarian revolution in Russia, isolated and not yet fortified, could not have held out even for a few months. But that Europe no longer existed. The revolution in the west did not, to be sure, put the proletariat into power—the reformists succeeded in saving the bourgeois régime—but nevertheless it proved powerful enough to defend the Soviet Republic in the first and most dangerous period of its life.

Lenin's deep internationalism was not expressed solely in the fact that he always gave first place to his appraisal of the international situation. He regarded the very conquest of power in Russia primarily as the impetus for a European revolution, a thing which, as he often repeated, was to have incomparably more importance for the fate of humanity than the revolution in backward Russia. With what sarcasm he lashed those Bolsheviks who did not understand their international duty. "Let us adopt a resolution of sympathy for the German insurrectionists," he mocks, "and reject the insurrection in Russia. That will be a genuinely reasonable internationalism!"

In the days of the Democratic Conference, Lenin wrote to the

Central Committee: "Having got a majority in the soviets of both capitals . . . the Bolsheviks can and should seize the state power in their hands. . . ." The fact that a majority of the peasant delegates of the stacked Democratic Conference voted against a coalition with the Kadets, had for him decisive significance: The muzhik who does not want a union with the bourgeoisie has nothing left but to support the Bolsheviks. "The people are tired of the wavering of the Mensheviks and Social Revolutionaries. Only our victory in the capitals will bring the peasants over to us." The task of the party is: "To place upon the order of the day armed insurrection in Petersburg and Moscow, conquest of power, overthrow of the government. . . ." Up to that time nobody had so imperiously and nakedly set the task of insurrection.

Lenin very studiously followed all the elections and votings in the country, carefully assembling those figures which would throw light on the actual correlation of forces. The semi-anarchistic indifference to electoral statistics got nothing but contempt from him. At the same time Lenin never identified the indexes of parliamentarism with the actual correlation of forces. He always introduced a correction in favour of direct action. "The strength of a revolutionary proletariat," he explained, "from the point of view of its action upon the masses and drawing them into the struggle, is infinitely greater in an extra-parliamentary than a parliamentary struggle. This is a very important observation when it comes to the question of civil war."

Lenin with his sharp eye was the first to notice that the agrarian movement had gone into a decisive phase, and he immediately drew all the conclusions from this. The muzhik, like the soldier, will wait no longer. "In the face of such a fact as the peasant insurrection," writes Lenin at the end of September, "all other political symptoms, even if they were in conflict with this ripening of an all-national crisis, would have absolutely no significance at all." The agrarian question is the foundation of the revolution. A victory of the government over the peasant revolt would be the "funeral of the revolution. . . ." We cannot hope for more favourable conditions. The hour of action is at hand. "The crisis is ripe. The whole future of the international workers' revolution for socialism is at stake. The crisis is ripe."

Lenin summons to insurrection. In each simple, prosaic, sometimes angular line, you feel the highest tensity of passion. "The revolution is done for," he writes early in October to the

Petrograd party conference, "if the government of Kerensky is not overthrown by proletarians and soldiers in the near future . . . We must mobilise all forces in order to impress upon the workers and soldiers the unconditional necessity of a desperate, last, resolute struggle to overthrow the government of Kerensky."

Lenin had said more than once that the masses are to the left of the party. He knew that the party was to the left of its own upper layer of "old Bolsheviks." He was too well acquainted with the inner groupings and moods in the Central Committee to expect from it any hazardous steps whatever. On the other hand he greatly feared excessive caution, Fabianism, a letting slip of one of those historic situations which are decades in preparation. Lenin did not trust the Central Committee—without Lenin. In that lies the key to his letters from underground. And Lenin was not so wrong in his mistrust.

Being compelled in a majority of cases to express himself after a decision had already been reached in Petrograd, Lenin was continually criticising the policy of the Central Committee from the left. His opposition developed with the question of insurrection as a background. But it was not limited to that. Lenin thought that the Central Committee was giving too much attention to the compromisist Executive Committee, the Democratic Conference, parliamentary doings in the upper soviet circles in general. He sharply opposed the proposal of the Bolsheviks for a coalition præsidium in the Petrograd Soviet. He branded as "shameful" the decision to participate in the Pre-Parliament. He was indignant at the list of Bolshevik candidates for the Constituent Assembly published at the end of September. Too many intellectuals, not enough workers. "To jam up the Constituent Assembly with orators and littérateurs will mean to travel the worn-out road of opportunism and chauvinism. This is unworthy of the Third International." Moreover there are too many new names among the candidates, members of the party not tried out in the struggle! Here Lenin considers it necessary to make an exception: "It goes without saying that . . . nobody would quarrel with such a candidacy, for example, as that of L. D. Trotsky, for in the first place Trotsky took an internationalist position immediately upon his arrival; in the second place, he fought for amalgamation among the Mezhrayontsi; in the third place, in the difficult July Days he stood at the height of the task and proved a devoted champion of the party of the revolutionary proletariat.

It is clear that this cannot be said of a majority of the yesterday's party members who have been introduced into this list. . . ."

It might seem as though the April Days had returned—Lenin again in opposition to the Central Committee. The questions stand differently, but the general spirit of his opposition is the same: the Central Committee is too passive, too responsive to social opinion among the intellectual circles, too compromisist in its attitude to the Compromisers. And above all, too indifferent, fatalistic, not attacking *à la* Bolshevik the problem of the armed insurrection.

It is time to pass from words to deeds: "Our party has now at the Democratic Conference practically its own congress, and this congress has got to decide (whether it wants to or not) the fate of the revolution." Only one decision is thinkable: Armed overthrow. In this first letter on insurrection Lenin makes another exception: "It is not a question of 'the day' of the insurrection, nor 'the moment' in a narrow sense. This can be decided only by the general voice of those who are in contact with the workers and soldiers, with the masses." But only two or three days later (letters in those days were commonly not dated—for conspirative reasons, not through forgetfulness) Lenin, obviously impressed by the decomposition of the Democratic Conference, insists upon immediate action and forthwith advances a practical plan.

"We ought at once to solidify the Bolshevik faction at the Conference, not striving after numbers. . . . We ought to draw up a short declaration of the Bolsheviks. . . . We ought to move our whole faction to the factories and barracks. At the same time without losing a minute we ought to organise a staff of insurrectionary detachments, deploy our forces, move the loyal regiments into the most important positions, surround the Alexandrinka (the theatre where the Democratic Conference was sitting) occupy Peter and Paul, arrest the General Staff and the government, send against the junkers and the Savage Division those detachments which are ready to die fighting, but not let the enemy advance to the centre of the city; we ought to mobilise the armed workers, summon them to a desperate, final battle, occupy the telegraph and telephone stations at once, install our insurrectionary staff at the central telephone station, placing in contact with it by telephone all the factories, all the regiments, all the chief points of armed struggle, etc." The question of date is no longer placed in dependence upon the "general voice of those who are in contact with the masses." Lenin proposed an immediate act: To leave the Alexandrinsky theatre with an ultimatum and return there at the head of the armed masses. A crushing blow is to be struck not only against the government, but also, simultaneously, against the highest organ of the Compromisers.

"Lenin, who in private letters was demanding the arrest of the Democratic Conference,"—such is the accusation of Sukhanov —"in the press, as we know, proposed a 'compromise': Let the Mensheviks and Social Revolutionaries take over the whole power and then see what the Soviet Congress says. . . . The same idea was insistently defended by Trotsky at the Democratic Conference and around it." Sukhanov sees a double game where there was not the slightest hint of it. Lenin proposed an agreement to the Compromisers immediately after the victory over Kornilov—during the first days of September. The Compromisers passed it up with a shrug of their shoulders. They were engaged in converting the Democratic Conference into a screen for a new coalition with the Kadets against the Bolsheviks. With that the possibility of an agreement fell away absolutely. The question of power could henceforth be decided only in open struggle. Sukhanov mixes up two stages one of which preceded the other by two weeks and politically conditioned it.

But although the insurrection flowed inexorably from the new coalition, nevertheless the sharpness of Lenin's change of front took even the heads of his own party by surprise. To unite the Bolshevik faction at the Conference on the basis of his letter, even without "striving after numbers" was clearly impossible. The mood of the faction was such that it rejected by seventy votes against fifty the proposal to boycott the Pre-Parliament—the first step, that is, on the road to insurrection. In the Central Committee itself Lenin's plan found no support whatever. Four years later at an evening of reminiscences, Bukharin with characteristic exaggerations and witticisms, gave a true account of that episode. "The letter (of Lenin) was written with extraordinary force and threatened us with all sorts of punishments. We all gasped. Nobody had yet posed the question so abruptly. . . . At first all were bewildered. Afterwards, having talked it over, we made a decision. Perhaps that was the sole case in the history of our party when the Central Committee unanimously decided to burn a letter of Lenin. . . . Although we believed unconditionally that in Petersburg and

Moscow we should succeed in seizing the power, we assumed that in the provinces we could not yet hold out, that having seized the power and dispersed the Democratic Conference we could not fortify ourselves in the rest of Russia."

The burning of several copies of this dangerous letter, owing to conspirative considerations, was as a matter of fact not unanimously resolved upon, but by six votes against four with six abstaining. One copy, luckily for history, was preserved. But it is true, as Bukharin relates, that all the members of the Central Committee, although for different motives, rejected the proposal. Some opposed an insurrection in general; others thought that the moment of the conference was the least advantageous of all; others simply vacillated and adopted a waiting attitude.

Having run into this direct resistance, Lenin entered into a sort of conspiracy with Smilga, who was also in Finland and as President of the Regional Committee of the Soviets held a tolerable amount of real power in his hands. Smilga stood in 1917 on the extreme left wing of the party and already in July had been inclined to carry the struggle through to the end. At turning points in his policy Lenin always found somebody to rely on. On September 27 Lenin wrote Smilga a voluminous letter: ". . . What are we doing? Only passing resolutions? We are losing time, we are setting 'dates' (October 20—Congress of Soviets—Isn't it ridiculous to postpone this way? Isn't it ridiculous to rely on that?) The Bolsheviks are not carrying on a systematic work of preparing their armed forces for the overthrow of Kerensky. . . . We must agitate in the party for a serious attitude toward armed insurrection. . . . And further, as to your rôle . . .; To create a secret committee of the most loyal military men, talk the thing over on all sides with them, collect (and yourself verify) the most accurate information about the make-up and position of the troops in and around Petrograd, about the transportation of Finland troops to Petrograd, about the movements of the fleet, etc." Lenin demanded "a systematic propaganda among the Cossacks located here in Finland. . . . We must study all information about the attitude of the Cossacks and organise a sending of agitatorial detachments from our best forces of sailors and soldiers of Finland." And finally: "For a correct preparation of minds we must immediately put into circulation a slogan of this kind: The power must immediately pass to the Petrograd Soviet which will hand it over to the Congress of Soviets. For why endure three more weeks of war and of Kornilovist preparations by Kerensky?"

In this letter we have a new plan of insurrection: A secret committee of the more important military men in Helsingfors as a fighting staff, the Russian troops quartered in Finland as fighting forces. "It seems that the only ones we can fully control and who will play a serious military rôle are the Finland troops and the Baltic Fleet." Thus we see that Lenin counted on dealing the chief blow against the government from outside Petrograd. At the same time a "correct preparation of minds" is necessary, so that an overthrow of the government by military forces from Finland shall not fall unexpectedly upon the Petrograd Soviet, which until the Congress of Soviets was to be the inheritor of power.

This new draft of a plan, like the preceding one, was not realised. But it did not go by without effect. The agitation among the Cossack Divisions soon gave results: we have heard about this from Dybenko. The participation of Baltic sailors in the chief blow against the government also entered into the plan later adopted. But that was not the chief thing: With his extremely sharp posing of the question Lenin permitted nobody to evade or manœuvre. What seemed untimely as a direct tactical proposal became expedient as a test of attitudes in the Central Committee, a support to the resolute against the wavering, a supplementary push to the left.

With all the means at his disposal in his underground isolation Lenin was trying to make the cadres of the party feel the acuteness of the situation and the strength of the mass pressure. He summoned individual Bolsheviks to his hiding-place, put them through partisan cross-questionings, tested out the words and deeds of the leaders, used indirect ways to get his slogans into the party—deep down in it—in order to compel the Central Committee to act in the face of necessity and carry the thing through.

A day after his letter to Smilga, Lenin wrote the above quoted document *The Crisis is Ripe*, concluding it with something in the nature of a declaration of war against the Central Committee. "We must . . . acknowledge the truth that there is in the Central Committee and the upper circles of the party a tendency or an opinion in favour of waiting for the Congress of Soviets, against the immediate seizure of power, against immediate insurrection." This tendency we must overcome at any cost. "Conquer Kerensky first and then summon the Congress."

To lose time waiting for the Congress of Soviets is "complete idiocy or else complete treachery. . . ." There remain more than twelve days until the Congress designated for the 20th: "Weeks and even days are now deciding everything." To postpone the show-down means a cowardly renunciation of insurrection, since during the Congress a seizure of power will become impossible: "They will get together the Cossacks for the day of that stupidly 'appointed' insurrection."

The mere tone of the letter shows how ruinous the Fabianism of the Petrograd leadership seemed to Lenin. But this time he is not satisfied with furious criticism; by way of protest he resigns from the Central Committee. He gives his reasons: the Central Committee has made no response since the beginning of the Conference to his insistence in regard to the seizure of power; the editorial board of the party organ (Stalin) is printing his articles with intentional delays, omitting from them his indication of such "flagrant mistakes of the Bolsheviks as their shameful decision to participate in the Pre-Parliament," etc. This procedure Lenin does not consider it possible to conceal from the party: "I am compelled to request permission to withdraw from the Central Committee, which I hereby do, and leave myself freedom of agitation in the lower ranks of the party and at the party congress."

The documents do not show what further formal action was taken in this matter. Lenin in any case did not withdraw from the Central Committee. By announcing his resignation, an act which could not possibly be with him the fruit of momentary irritation, Lenin obviously wanted to make it possible to free himself in case of need from the internal discipline of the Central Committee. He could be quite sure that as in April a direct appeal to the lower ranks would assure him the victory. But the road of open mutiny against the Central Committee required the preparation of a special session; it required time; and time was just what was lacking. Keeping this announcement of his resignation in reserve, but not withdrawing completely beyond the limits of party legality, Lenin now continued with greater freedom to develop his offensive along internal lines. His letter to the Central Committee he not only sent to the Petrograd and Moscow committees, but he also saw to it that copies fell into the hands of the more reliable party workers of the district locals. Early in October—and now over the heads of the Central Committee—Lenin wrote directly to the Petrograd and the Moscow committees: "The Bolsheviks have no right to await the Congress of Soviets. They ought to seize the power *right now*. . . . Delay is a crime. Waiting for the Congress of Soviets is a childish toying with formalities, a shameful toying with formalities, betrayal of the revolution." From the standpoint of hierarchical attitudes towards action, Lenin was by no means beyond reproach, but the question here was of something bigger than considerations of formal discipline.

One of the members of the Vyborg District Committee, Sveshnikov, remembers: "Ilych from underground was writing and writing untiringly, and Nadyezhda Constantinovna (Krupskaia) often read these manuscripts to us in the district committee. . . . The burning words of the leader would redouble our strength. . . . I remember as though it were yesterday the bending figure of Nadyezhda Constantinovna in one of the rooms of the district administration, where the typists were working, carefully comparing the copy with the original, and right alongside stood Uncle and Gene demanding a copy each." "Uncle" and "Gene" were old conspirative pseudonyms for two leaders of the district. "Not long ago," relates the district worker, Naumov, "we got a letter from Ilych for delivery to the Central Committee. . . . We read the letter and gasped. It seems that Lenin had long ago put before the Central Committee the question of insurrection. We raised a row. We began to bring pressure on them." It was just this that was needed.

In the first days of October, Lenin appealed to a Petrograd party conference to speak a firm word in favour of insurrection. Upon his initiative the conference "insistently requests the Central Committee to take all measures for the leadership of the inevitable insurrection of the workers, soldiers and peasants." In this phrase alone there are two kinds of camouflage, juridical and diplomatic: It speaks of the leadership of an "inevitable insurrection" instead of the direct preparation of insurrection, in order not to place trump cards in the hands of the district attorney; and it "requests the Central Committee"—it does not demand, and it does not protest—this in obvious deference to the prestige of the highest institution of the party. But in another resolution, also written by Lenin, the speech is more frank: "In the upper circles of the party a wavering is to be observed, a sort of dread of the struggle for power, an inclination to replace this struggle with resolutions, protests, and conferences." This is already almost a direct pitting of the party against the Central Committee. Lenin did not decide lightly upon such steps. But it was a question of the fate of the revolution, and all other considerations fell away.

On October 8, Lenin addressed the Bolshevik delegates of the forthcoming Northern Regional Congress: "We must not await the All-Russian Congress of Soviets which the Central Executive Committee is able to postpone even to November. We must not delay and let Kerensky bring in more Kornilov troops." That Regional Conference, at which Finland, the fleet and Reval were represented, should take the initiative in "an immediate move on Petrograd." The direct summons to immediate insurrection was this time addressed to the representatives of scores of soviets. The summons came from Lenin personally. There was no party decision; the higher institutions of the party had not yet expressed themselves.

It required a mighty confidence in the proletariat, in the party, but also a very serious mistrust of the Central Committee, in order over its head, upon his own personal responsibility, from underground, and by means of a few small sheets of note-paper minutely inscribed, to raise an agitation for an armed revolution, for an armed overthrow of the government. How could it happen that Lenin, whom we have seen at the beginning of April isolated among the leaders of his own party, found himself again solitary in the same group in September and early October? This cannot be understood if you believe the unintelligent legend which portrays the history of Bolshevism as an emanation of the pure revolutionary idea. In reality Bolshevism developed in a definite social milieu undergoing its heterogeneous influences and among them the influence of a petty bourgeois environment and of cultural backwardness. To each new situation the party adapted itself only by way of an inner crisis.

In order that the sharp pre-October struggle in the Bolshevik upper circles may come before us in a true light, it is necessary again to look back at those processes in the party of which we spoke in the first volume. This is the more necessary since exactly at this present time the faction of Stalin is making unheard-of efforts, and that, too, on an international scale, to wipe out of historic memory every recollection of how the October revolution was in reality prepared and achieved.

In the years before the war the Bolsheviks had described themselves in the legal press as "consistent democrats." This pseudonym was not accidentally chosen. The slogans of revolutionary democracy, Bolshevism and Bolshevism alone carried through to its logical conclusion. But in its prognosis of the revolution it did not go beyond this. The war, however, inseparably binding up the bourgeois democrats with imperialism, proved conclusively that the programme of "consistent democracy" could be no otherwise enacted than through a proletarian revolution. Every Bolshevik to whom the war did not make this clear was inevitably destined to be caught unaware by the revolution, and converted into a left fellow-traveller of the bourgeois democracy.

However, a careful study of the materials characterising the party life during the war and the beginning of the revolution, notwithstanding the extreme and unprecedented scantiness of these materials—and then beginning with 1923 their increasing disingenuousness—reveals more clearly every day the immense intellectual backsliding of the upper stratum of the Bolsheviks during the war when the proper life of the party practically came to an end. The cause of this backsliding is twofold: isolation from the masses and isolation from those abroad—that is primarily from Lenin. The result was a drowning in isolation and provincialism.

Not one of the old Bolsheviks in Russia, left each to himself, formulated throughout the whole war one document which might be looked upon as even the tiniest beacon-light on the road from the Second International to the Third. "The problems of peace, the character of the coming revolution, the rôle of the party in a future Provisional Government, etc."—thus wrote one of the old members of the party, Antonov-Saratovsky, some years ago—"were conceived by us vaguely enough or did not enter into our field of reflection at all." Up to this time there has not been published one article, not one page of a diary, not one letter in which Stalin, Molotov, or any other of the leaders formulated even indirectly, even very hastily, his views upon the perspectives of the war and the revolution. This does not mean, of course, that the "old Bolsheviks" wrote nothing on these questions during the years of the war, of the collapse of the social democracy and the preparation of the Russian revolution. These historic events too insistently demanded an answer; jail and exile, moreover, gave plenty of leisure for meditation and correspondence. But among all that was written on these themes, not one thing has turned up which might even with stretching be interpreted as an approach to the ideas of the October revolution. It is sufficient to remember that the Institute of Party History has been forbidden to print one line from the pen of Stalin during the years 1914–

1917, and has been compelled to hide carefully the most important documents of March 1917. In the official political biographies of a majority of the ruling stratum, the years of the war present a vacant space. That is the unadorned truth.

One of the most recent young historians, Bayevsky, specially delegated to demonstrate how the upper circles of the party developed during the war in the direction of proletarian revolution, was unable, in spite of his manifest flexibility of scientific conscience, to squeeze out of the materials anything more than the following meagre statement: "It is impossible to follow the course of this process, but certain documents and memoirs indubitably prove that there were subterranean searchings of the party mind in the direction of the April theses of Lenin. . . ." As though it were a question of subterranean searchings, and not of scientific appraisals and political prognoses!

It was possible to arrive *a priori* at the ideas of the October revolution, not in Siberia, not in Moscow, not even in Petrograd, but only at the crossing of the roads of world history. The tasks of a belated bourgeois revolution had to be seen intercrossing with the perspectives of a world proletarian movement, before it could seem possible to advance a programme of proletarian dictatorship for Russia. A higher point of observation was necessary—not a national but an international horizon—to say nothing of a more serious armament than was possessed by the so-called Russian "practicals" of the party.

In their eyes the overthrow of the monarchy was to open the era of a "free" republican Russia, in which they intended, following the example of the western countries, to begin a struggle for socialism. Three old Bolsheviks, Rykov, Skvortzov, and Vegman, "at the direction of the social democrats of the Narym district liberated by the revolution," sent a telegram in March from Tomsk: "We send a greeting to the resurrected *Pravda* which has so successfully prepared the revolutionary cadres for the conquest of political liberty. We express our profound confidence that it will succeed in uniting all around its banner for the further struggle in the name of the national revolution." A whole world-philosophy emerges from this collective telegram. It is separated by an abyss from the April theses of Lenin. The February revolution immediately converted the leading layer of the party, with Kamenev, Rykov and Stalin at their head, into democratic defensists—in motion, moreover, toward the right, in the direction of a rapprochement with the Mensheviks. The future historian of the party, Yaroslavsky, the future head of the Central Control Commission, Ordzhonikidze, and the future president of the Ukrainian Central Executive Committee, Petrovsky, published during March in Yakutsk, in close union with the Mensheviks, a paper called the *Social Democrat*, which stood on the borderland of patriotic reform and liberalism. In recent years the issues of this publication have been carefully collected and destroyed.

The Petersburg *Pravda* tried at the beginning of the revolution to occupy an internationalist position—to be sure, a very contradictory one for it did not transcend the framework of bourgeois democracy. The authoritative Bolsheviks arriving from exile immediately imparted to the central organ a democratical-patriotic policy. Kalinin, in defending himself on the 30th of May against a charge of opportunism, recalled this fact: "Take *Pravda* for example. At the beginning *Pravda* had one policy. Came Stalin, Muranov, Kamenev, and turned the helm of *Pravda* to the other side."

"We must frankly acknowledge," wrote Angarsky, a member of this stratum, when it was still permissible to write such things, "that an enormous number of the old Bolsheviks held fast up to the April party conference to the old Bolshevik views of 1905 as to the character of the revolution of 1917, and that the renunciation of these views, the outgrowing of them, was not so easily accomplished." It would be well to add that those ideas of 1905, having outlived themselves, had ceased in 1917 to be "old Bolshevik views" and had become the ideas of patriotic reform.

"The April theses of Lenin," says an official historic publication, "just simply had no luck in the Petrograd committee. Only two against thirteen voted for these theses, which created an epoch, and one abstained from the vote." "Lenin's argument seemed too bold even for his most rapturous followers," writes Podvoisky. Lenin's speeches—in the opinion of the Petrograd committee and the Military Organisation—"isolated the party of the Bolsheviks, and thus, it goes without saying, damaged the position of the proletariat and the party in the extreme."

"We must say frankly," wrote Molotov some years ago, "the party lacked that clarity and resolution which the revolutionary movement demanded. . . . The agitation and the whole revolutionary party work in general had no firm foundation, since our thoughts had not yet arrived at bold conclusions in regard to the necessity of an immediate struggle for socialism and the socialist revolution." The break began only in the second month of the revolution. "From the time of Lenin's arrival in Russia in April 1917"—so testifies Molotov—"our party felt firm ground under its feet. . . . Up to that moment the party was only weakly and diffidently groping its way."

Stalin at the end of March had spoken in favour of military defence, of conditional support to the Provisional government and the pacifist manifesto of Sukhanov, and of merging with the party of Tseretelli. "This mistaken position," Stalin himself retrospectively acknowledged in 1924, "I then shared with other party comrades, and I renounced it fully only in the middle of April when I adhered to the theses of Lenin. A new orientation was necessary. Lenin gave the party that new orientation in his celebrated April theses."

Kalinin even at the end of April was still standing for a voting bloc with the Mensheviks. At the Petrograd city conference of the party Lenin said: "I am sharply opposed to Kalinin, because a bloc with . . . chauvinists is unthinkable. . . . That is treason to socialism." Kalinin's attitude was not exceptional even in Petrograd. It was said at the conference: "Under the influence of Lenin the amalgamation fumes are dissipating."

In the provinces the resistance to Lenin's theses lasted considerably longer—in a number of provinces almost to October. According to a Kiev worker, Sivtzov, "The ideas set forth in the theses (of Lenin) were not immediately accepted by the whole Kiev Bolshevik organisation. A number of comrades, including G. Piatakov, disagreed with the theses . . ." A railroad worker of Kharkov, Morgunov, says: "The old Bolsheviks enjoyed a great influence among all the roalroad workers. . . . Many of the old Bolsheviks remained outside of our faction. After the February revolution a number of them registered as Mensheviks by mistake, a thing at which they themselves afterwards laughed, wondering how it could have happened." There is no lack of this and similar testimony.

In spite of all this, the mere mention of a re-arming of the party carried out by Lenin in April, is regarded by the present official historians as blasphemy. These most recent historians have substituted for the historic criterion the criterion of honour to the party uniform. On this theme they are deprived of the right to quote even Stalin himself, who was obliged to acknowledge the great depth of the April change. "The famous April theses of Lenin were necessary," he wrote, "in order that the party should come out with one bold step on a new road."

"A new orientation," "a new road"—that means the re-arming of the party. Six years later, however, Yaroslovsky, who ventured in his capacity of historian to recall the fact that Stalin had occupied at the beginning of the revolution "a mistaken position upon fundamental questions" was furiously denounced from all sides. The idol of prestige is the most gluttonous of all monsters!

The revolutionary tradition of the party, the pressure of the workers from below, and Lenin's criticism from above, compelled the upper stratum during the months of April and May —employing the words of Stalin—"to come out on a new road." But one would have to be completely ignorant of political psychology to imagine that a mere voting for the theses of Lenin meant an actual and complete renunciation of the "mistaken position on fundamental questions." In reality those crass democratic views organically fortified during the war, merely accommodated themselves to the new programme, remaining in silent opposition to it.

On the 6th of August Kamenev, contrary to the decision of the April conference of the Bolsheviks, spoke in the Executive Committee in favour of participating in the Stockholm conference of the Social Patriots then in preparation. Kamenev's speech met no opposition in the central organ of the party. Lenin wrote a formidable article, which appeared, however, only ten days after Kamenev's speech. The resolute insistence of Lenin himself and other members of the Central Committee was required to induce the editorial staff, headed by Stalin, to publish the protesting article.

A convulsion of doubt went through the party after the July Days. The isolation of the proletarian vanguard frightened many leaders, especially in the provinces. During the Kornilov days these frightened ones tried to get in contact with the Compromisers, which again evoked a warning cry from Lenin.

On August 20, Stalin, as editor of *Pravda,* printed without dissenting comment an article of Zinoviev, entitled "What Not to Do," an article directed against the preparation of an insurrection. "We must look the truth in the face: In Petrograd there are now many conditions favourable to the outbreak of an insurrection of the type of the Paris Commune of 1871. . . ." On September 3, Lenin—in another connection and without naming Zinoviev but striking him an indirect blow—wrote: "The reference to the Commune is very superficial and even stupid. For in the first place the Bolsheviks after all have learned something since 1871. They would not fail to seize the banks, they would not renounce the offensive against Versailles, and in these conditions even the Commune might have succeeded. Moreover the Commune could not immediately offer the people what the Bolsheviks can if they come to power, namely, land to the peasants and an immediate proposal of peace. . . ." This was a nameless but unequivocal warning not only to Zinoviev, but also to the editor of *Pravda*, Stalin.

The question of the Pre-Parliament split the Central Committee in half. The decision of the Bolshevik faction of the Conference in favour of participating in the Pre-Parliament was ratified by many local committees, if not a majority of them. It was so for instance in Kiev. "On the question of . . . entering the Pre-Parliament," says E. Bosh in her memoirs, "the majority of the committee voted for participation and elected Piatakov as its delegate." In many cases—as for example Kamenev, Rykov, Piatakov and others—it is possible to trace a succession of waverings: against the theses of Lenin in April, against the boycott of the Pre-Parliament in September, against the insurrection in October. On the other hand, the next lower stratum of the Bolsheviks, standing nearer to the masses and being more fresh politically, easily accepted the slogan of boycott and compelled the committees, including the Central Committee itself, to make an about-face. Under the influence of letters from Lenin, the city conference of Kiev voted with an overwhelming majority against their committee. Similarly at almost all sharp political turning-points Lenin relied upon the lower strata of the party machine against the higher, or on the party mass against the machine as a whole.

In these circumstances the pre-October waverings could least of all catch Lenin unawares. He was armed in advance with a sharp-eyed suspicion, was watching for alarming symptoms, was making the worst possible assumptions; and he considered it more expedient to bring excess pressure than to be indulgent.

It was at the suggestion of Lenin beyond a doubt that the Moscow Regional Bureau adopted at the end of September a bitter resolution against the Central Committee, accusing it of irresolution, wavering and introducing confusion into the ranks of the party, and demanding that it "take a clear and definite course toward insurrection." In the name of the Moscow Bureau, Lomov on the 3rd of October reported this decision to the Central Committee. The minutes remark: "It was decided not to debate the question." The Central Committee was still continuing to dodge the question what to do. But Lenin's pressure, brought to bear through Moscow, had its result: After two days the Central Committee decided to withdraw from the Pre-Parliament.

That this step meant entering the road of insurrection was clear to the enemies and opponents. "Trotsky in leading his army out of the Pre-Parliament," writes Sukhanov, "was definitely steering a course towards violent revolution." The report of the Petrograd Soviet on withdrawal from the Pre-Parliament ended with the cry: "Long live the direct and open struggle for revolutionary power in the country!" That was October 9th.

On the following day, upon the demand of Lenin, occurred the famous session of the Central Committee where the question of insurrection was flatly posed. From the beginning of that session Lenin placed his further policy in dependence upon its outcome: either through the Central Committee or against it. "O new jest of the merry muse of history!" writes Sukhanov. "That high-up and decisive session was held in my apartment, still on the same Karpovka (32, Apartment 31). But all this was without my knowledge." The wife of the Menshevik, Sukhanov, was a Bolshevik. "That time special measures were taken to assure my sleeping outside the house: at least my wife made carefully sure of my intention, and gave me friendly and impartial advice—not to tire myself out after my work with the long journey home. In any case the lofty assemblage was completely safe from any invasion from me." What was more important, it proved safe from invasions from Kerensky's police.

Twelve of the twenty-one members of the Central Committee were present. Lenin came in wig and spectacles without a beard. The session lasted about ten hours—deep into the night. In the intervals there were tea with bread and sausage for reinforcement. And reinforcement was needed: it was a question of seizing the power in the former empire of the czars. The session began, as always, with an organisational report from Sverdlov. This time his communication was devoted to the front—and evidently by previous agreement with Lenin, in order to give him support for the necessary inferences. This was quite in accord with Lenin's methods. Representatives of the army of the northern front gave warning through Sverdlov of preparations by the counter-revolutionary command for some sort of "shady plot involving a withdrawal of troops inland"; from Minsk, the headquarters of the western front, it was reported that a new Kornilov insurrection was in preparation; in view of the revolutionary character of the local garrison, headquarters had surrounded the city with Cossack troops. "Some sort of negotiations of a suspicious character are in progress between headquarters and the general staff"; it is quite possible to seize the headquarters in Minsk: the local garrison is ready to disarm the Cossack ring; they are also in a position to send a revolutionary corps from Minsk to Petrograd; the mood on the front is for the Bolsheviks; they will go against Kerensky.—Such was Sverdlov's report. It was not in every part sufficiently definite, but it was entirely encouraging in character.

Lenin immediately took the offensive: "From the beginning of September there has been a kind of indifference to the question of insurrection." References are made to the cooling off and disappointment of the masses. No wonder. "The masses are tired of words and resolutions." We must take the situation as a whole. Events in the city are now taking place against the background of a gigantic peasant movement. The government would require colossal forces in order to quell the agrarian insurrection. "The political situation is thus ready. We must talk of the technical side. That is the whole thing. Meanwhile in the manner of the defensists we are inclined to regard the systematic preparation of insurrection as something in the nature of a political sin." The speaker was obviously restraining himself: He had too much feeling piled up in him. "We must make use of the northern regional congress and the proposal from Minsk in order to start a decisive action."

The northern congress opened exactly on the day of this session of the Central Committee, and was to close in two or three days. The beginning of "decisive action" Lenin presented as the task of the next days. We must not wait. We must not postpone. On the front—as we have heard from Sverdlov—they are preparing an overturn. Will the Congress of Soviets ever be held? We do not know. We must seize the power immediately and not wait for any congresses. "Never to be communicated or reproduced," wrote Trotsky several years later, "was the general spirit of those tense and passionate impromptu speeches, saturated with a desire to instil into the objecting, the wavering, the doubtful, his thought, his will, his confidence, his courage. . . ."

Lenin expected strong resistance, but his fears were soon dispelled. The unanimity with which the Central Committee had rejected the proposal of immediate insurrection in September had been episodic: The left wing had been against the "surrounding of the Alexandrinka" for temporary reasons; the right for reasons of general strategy, although these were not as yet thoroughly thought out. During the three weeks following there had been a considerable shift to the left in the Central Committee. Ten against two voted for the insurrection. That was a big victory!

Soon after the revolution, at a new stage in the inner party struggle, Lenin recalled during a debate in the Petrograd committee how up to that session of the Central Committee, he "had fears of opportunism from the side of the internationalist fusionists, but these were dissipated. In our party, however, certain members (of the Central Committee) did not agree. This grieved me deeply." Aside from Trotsky, whom Lenin could hardly have had in mind, the only "internationalists" in the Central Committee were Joffé, the future ambassador in Berlin, Uritzky the future head of the Cheka in Petrograd, and Sokolnikov, the future inventor of the Chervonetz. All three took the side of Lenin. His opponents were two old Bolsheviks, closest of all to Lenin in their past work: Zinoviev and Kamenev. It is to them he referred when he said "this grieved me very much." That session of the 10th reduced itself almost entirely to a passionate polemic against Zinoviev and Kamenev. Lenin led the attack, and the rest joined in one after the other.

The resolution, written hastily by Lenin with the gnawed end of a pencil on a sheet of paper from a child's notebook ruled in squares, was very unsymmetrical in architecture, but nevertheless gave firm support to the course towards insurrection. "The Central Committee recognizes that both the international situation of the Russian revolution (the insurrection in the German fleet, as the extreme manifestation of the growth throughout Europe of a world-wide socialist revolution, and also the threat of a peace between the imperialists with the aim of strangling the revolution in Russia)—and the military situation (the indubitable decision of the Russian bourgeoisie and Kerensky and Co. to surrender Petersburg to the Germans)—all this in connection with the peasant insurrection and the swing of popular confidence to our party (the elections in Moscow), and finally the obvious preparation of a second Kornilov attack (the withdrawal of troops from Petersburg, the importation of Cossacks into Petersburg, the surrounding of Minsk with Cossacks, etc.)—all this places armed insurrection on the order of the day. Thus recognising that the armed insurrection is inevitable and fully ripe, the Central Committee recommends to all organisations of the party that they be guided by this, and from this point of view consider and decide all practical questions (the Congress of Soviets of the Northern Region, the withdrawal of troops from Petersburg, the coming-out of Moscow and Minsk)."

A remarkable thing here as characterising both the moment and the author is the very order in which the conditions of the insurrection are enumerated. First comes the ripening of the world revolution; the insurrection in Russia is regarded only as the link in a general chain. That was Lenin's invariable starting-point, his major premise: he could not reason otherwise. The task of insurrection he presented directly as the task of the party. The difficult question of bringing its preparation into accord with the soviets is as yet not touched upon. The All-Russian Congress of Soviets does not get a word. To the northern regional congress and the "coming out of Moscow and Minsk" as points of support for the insurrection was added, upon the insistence of Trotsky, "the withdrawal of troops from Petersburg." This was the sole hint of that plan of insurrection which was subsequently dictated by the course of events in the capital. Nobody proposed any tactical amendments to the resolution, which defined only the strategical starting-point of the insurrection, as against Zinoviev and Kamenev who rejected the very necessity of insurrection.

The very recent attempt of official historians to present this matter as though the whole guiding stratum of the party except Zinoviev and Kamenev stood for the insurrection, goes to pieces when confronted by facts and documents. Aside from the fact that those voting for insurrection were much of the time inclined to push it off into an indefinite future, the open enemies of the insurrection, Zinoviev and Kamenev, were not alone even in the Central Committee. Rykov and Nogin who were absent at the session of the 10th stood wholly upon their point of view, and Miliutin was close to them. "In the upper circles of the party a wavering is to be observed, a sort of dread of the struggle for power"—such is the testimony of Lenin himself. According to Antonov-Saratovsky, Miliutin, arriving in Saratov after the 10th, "told about the letter of Ilych demanding that we 'begin,' about the waverings in the Central Committee, the preliminary 'failure' of Lenin's proposal, about his indignation, and finally about how the course was taken towards insurrection." The Bolshevik, Sadovsky, wrote later about "a certain vagueness and lack of confidence which prevailed at that time. Even among our Central Committee of those days, as is well known, there were debates and conflicts about how to begin and whether to begin at all."

Sadovsky himself was during that period one of the leaders of the military section of the Soviet and Military Organisation of the Bolsheviks. But it was exactly these members of the Military Organisation—as appears from numerous memoirs—who were most exceptionally prejudiced in October against the idea of insurrection. The specific character of the organisation inclined its leaders to under-estimate the political conditions and over-estimate the technical. On the 16th of October, Krylenko reported: "The larger part of the bureau (the Military Organisation) think that we should not force the issue practically, but the minority think that we can take the initiative." On the 18th another prominent member of the Military Organisation, Lashevich, said: "Ought we not to seize the power immediately? I think that we ought not to speed up the course of events. . . . There is no guarantee that we will succeed in holding the power. . . . The strategic plan proposed by Lenin limps on all four legs." Antonov-Ovseënko tells about a meeting of the chief military workers with Lenin: "Podvoisky expressed doubt; Nevsky at first seconded him, but then fell into the confident tone of Ilych; I described the situation in Finland. . . . Lenin's confidence and firmness had a fortifying effect upon me and cheered up Nevsky, but Podvoisky remained stubbornly dubious." We must not forget that in all recollections of this kind, the doubts are painted in with water colours and the confidence in heavy oil.

Chudnovsky spoke decisively against the insurrection. The sceptical Manuilsky warningly asserted that "the front is not with us." Tomsky was against the insurrection. Volodarsky supported Zinoviev and Kamenev. Moreover by no means all the opponents of the insurrection spoke openly. At a session of the Petrograd Committee on the 15th, Kalinin said: "The resolution of the Central Committee was one of the best resolutions ever adopted by the Central Committee. . . . We are practically approaching the armed insurrection. But when it will be possible—perhaps a year from now—is unknown." This kind of "agreement" with the Central Committee, although perfectly characteristic of Kalinin, was not peculiar to him. Many adhered to the resolution in order in that way to insure their struggle against the insurrection.

In Moscow least of all was there unanimity among the leaders. The regional bureau supported Lenin. In the Moscow committee there were very considerable hesitations; the prevailing mood was in favour of delay. The provincial committee occupied an indefinite position, but in the regional bureau, according to Yakovleva, they thought that at the decisive moment the provincial committee would swing over to the opponents of insurrection.

Lebedev from Saratov tells how in visiting Moscow not long before the revolution, he took a walk with Rykov, and how the latter, pointing to the stone houses, the rich stores, the business-like excitement about them, complained of the difficulty of the coming task. "Here in the very centre of bourgeois Moscow we really seem to be pygmies thinking of moving a mountain."

In every organisation of the party, in every one of its provincial committees, there were people of the same mood as Zinoviev and Kamenev. In many committees they were the majority. Even in proletarian Ivanovo-Voznesensk, where the Bolsheviks ruled alone, the disagreement among the ruling circles took an extraordinarily sharp form. In 1925, when memoirs had already accommodated themselves to the demands of the new course, Kisselev, an old worker Bolshevik, wrote: "The workers' part of the party, with the exception of certain individuals, went with Lenin. Against Lenin, however, was a small group of party intellectuals and solitary workers." In public discussion the opponents of insurrection repeated the same arguments as those of Zinoviev and Kamenev. "But in private arguments," writes Kisselev, "the polemic took a more acute and candid form, and here they went so far as to say that 'Lenin is a crazy man; he is pushing the working-class to certain ruin. From this armed insurrection we will get nothing; they will shatter us, exterminate the party and the working-class, and that will postpone the revolution for years and years, etc.'" Such was the attitude of Frunze in particular, a man of great personal courage but not distinguished by a wide outlook.

Even the victory of the insurrection in Petrograd was far from breaking everywhere the inertia of the waiting policy and the direct resistance of the right wing. The wavering of the leaders subsequently almost shipwrecked the insurrection in Moscow. In Kiev, the committee headed by Piatakov, which had been conducting a purely defensive policy, turned over the initiative in the long run—and afterward the power also—to the Rada. "The organisation of our party in Voronezh," says Vrachev, "wavered very considerably. The actual overturn in

Voronezh . . . was carried out not by a committee of the party, but by its active minority with Moiseiev at the head." In a whole series of provincial cities the Bolsheviks formed in October a bloc with the Compromisers "against the counter-revolution." As though the Compromisers were not at that moment one of its chief supports! Almost everywhere a push was required both from above and below to shatter the last indecisiveness of the local committee, compel it to break with the Compromisers and lead the movement. "The end of October and the beginning of November were verily days of 'the great turmoil' in our party circles. Many quickly surrendered to moods." Thus reports Shliapnikov, who himself made no small contribution to these waverings.

All those elements which, like the Kharkov Bolsheviks, had found themselves in the Menshevik camp in the beginning of the revolution and afterwards themselves wondered "just how that could have happened," found no place for themselves at all as a general rule in the October Days but merely wavered and waited. These people have now all the more confidently advanced their claims as "old Bolsheviks" in the period of intellectual reaction. In spite of the vast work that has been done in recent years towards concealing these facts, and even without the secret archives which are now inaccessible to the investigator, plenty of testimony has been preserved in the newspapers, memoirs and historic journals of that time, to prove that on the eve of the overturn the official machine even of this most revolutionary party put up a big resistance. Conservatism inevitably finds its seat in a bureaucracy. The machine can fulfil a revolutionary function only so long as it remains an instrument in the service of the party, so long as it remains subordinate to an idea and is controlled by the mass.

The resolution of October 10th became immensely important. It promptly put the genuine advocates of insurrection on the firm ground of party right. In all the party organisations, in all its nuclei, the most resolute elements began to be advanced to the responsible posts. The party organisations, beginning with Petrograd, pulled themselves together, made an inventory of their forces and material resources, strengthened their communications, and gave a more concentrated character to the campaign for an overturn.

But the resolution did not put an end to disagreements in the Central Committee. On the contrary, it only formulated them and brought them to the surface. Zinoviev and Kamenev, who but yesterday had felt surrounded in a certain section of the leading circles by an atmosphere of sympathy, observed with fright how swiftly things were shifting to the left. They decided to lose no more time, and on the very next day distributed a voluminous address to the members of the party. "Before history, before the international proletariat, before the Russian revolution and the Russian working-class," they wrote, "we have no right to stake the whole future at the present moment upon the card of armed insurrection."

Their plan was to enter as a strong opposition party into the Constituent Assembly, which "in its revolutionary work can rely only upon the soviets." Hence their formula: "Constituent Assembly and soviets—that is, the combined type of state institution toward which we are travelling." The Constituent Assembly where the Bolsheviks, it was assured, would be a minority, and the soviets where the Bolsheviks were a majority—that is, the organ of the bourgeoisie and the organ of the proletariat—were to be "combined" in a peaceful system of dual power. That had not succeeded even under the leadership of the Compromisers. How could it succeed when the soviets were Bolshevik?

"It is a profound historic error," concluded Zinoviev and Kamenev, "to pose the question of the transfer of power to the proletarian party—either now or at any time. No, the party of the proletariat will grow, its programme will become clear to broader and broader masses."

This hope for a further unbroken growth of Bolshevism regardless of the actual course of class conflicts, crashed head on against Lenin's leit-motif in those days: "The success of the Russian and world revolution depends upon a two or three days' struggle."

It is hardly necessary to explain that the truth in this dramatic dialogue was wholly on Lenin's side. A revolutionary situation cannot be preserved at will. If the Bolsheviks had not seized the power in October and November, in all probability they would not have seized it at all. Instead of firm leadership the masses would have found among the Bolsheviks that same disparity between word and deed which they were already sick of, and they would have ebbed away in the course of two or three months from this party which had deceived their hopes, just as they had recently ebbed away from the Social Revolutionaries and Mensheviks. A part of the workers would have fallen into indifferentism, another part would have burned up their force in convulsive movements in anarchistic flare-ups, in guerrilla skirmishes, in a Terror dictated by revenge and despair. The breathing-spell thus offered would have been used by the bourgeoisie to conclude a separate peace with the Hohenzollern, and stamp out the revolutionary organisations. Russia would again have been included in the circle of capitalist states as a semi-imperialist, semi-colonial country. The proletarian revolution would have been deferred to an indefinite future. It was his keen understanding of this prospect that inspired Lenin to that cry of alarm: "The success of the Russian and world revolution depends upon a two or three days' struggle."

But now, since the 10th of the month, the situation in the party had radically changed. Lenin was no longer an isolated "oppositionist" whose proposals were set aside by the Central Committee. It was the right wing that was isolated. Lenin no longer had to gain the right of free agitation at the price of resigning from the Central Committee. The party legality was on his side. Zinoviev and Kamenev, on the other hand, circulating their document attacking a decision adopted by the majority of the Central Committee, were now the violators of discipline. And Lenin in a struggle never left unpunished the oversights of his enemy—even far slighter ones than that!

At the session of the 10th, upon the proposal of Dzerzhinsky, a political bureau of seven men was elected: Lenin, Trotsky, Zinoviev, Kamenev, Stalin, Solkolnikov, Bubnov. This new institution, however, turned out completely impracticable. Lenin and Zinoviev were still in hiding; Zinoviev, moreover, continued to wage a struggle against the insurrection, and so did Kamenev. The political bureau in its October membership never once assembled, and it was soon simply forgotten—as were other organisations created *ad hoc* in the whirlpool of events.

No practical plan of insurrection, even tentative, was sketched out in the session of the 10th. But without introducing the fact into the resolution, it was agreed that the insurrection should precede the Congress of Soviets and begin, if possible, not later than October 15th. Not all eagerly agreed to that date. It was obviously too short for the take-off planned in Petrograd. But to insist on a delay would have been to support the right wing and mix the cards. Besides, it is never too late to postpone!

The fact of this preliminary setting of the date at the 15th was first made public in Trotsky's recollections of Lenin in 1924, seven years after the event. The statement was soon disputed by Stalin, and the question has become an acute one in Russian historic literature. As is known, the insurrection actually occurred only on the 25th, and consequently the date originally set was not held to. The epigone historians consider it impossible that there should be a mistake in the policy of the Central Committee, or even a delay in the matter of a date. "It would follow," writes Stalin upon this theme, "that the Central Committee set the date of the insurrection for October 15th and afterwards itself violated (!) this resolution, delaying the date of the insurrection to October 25th. Is this true? No, it is not true." Stalin comes to the conclusion that "Trotsky's memory has betrayed him." In proof of this he cites the resolution of October 10th which did not set any date.

This debated question of the chronology of the insurrection is very important to an understanding of the rhythm of events and demands clarification. That the resolution of the 10th contained no date is quite true. But this general resolution had to do with an insurrection throughout the whole country, and was destined for hundreds and thousands of leading party workers. To include in it the conspirative date of an insurrection to be carried out in the next few days in Petrograd, would have been unreasonable in the extreme. We must remember that out of caution Lenin did not in those days even put a date on his letters. In the given case it was a question of so important, and withal so simple, a decision that none of the participants could have any difficulty in remembering it—especially seeing that it was a question only of a few days. Stalin's reference to the text of the resolution shows thus a complete failure to understand.

We are prepared to concede, however, that the reference of one of the participants to his own memory, especially when his statement is disputed by another participant, is not sufficient for the historic investigator. Luckily the question is decided beyond possible doubt upon another level—that of an analysis of conditions and documents.

The Congress of Soviets was to open on the 20th of October. Between the session of the Central Committee and the date of the Congress, there remained an interval of ten days. The Congress was not to agitate in favour of power to the soviets but seize it. A few hundred delegates all by themselves, however, were powerless to conquer the power; it was necessary to seize it for the Congress and before the Congress. "First conquer Kerensky and then summon the Congress"—that thought had stood in the centre of Lenin's whole agitation since the middle of September. All those agreed with it in principle who stood for the seizure of power in general. Consequently the Central Committee could not help setting itself the task of attempting to carry an insurrection between the 10th and 20th of October. And since it was impossible to foresee how many days the struggle would last, the beginning of the insurrection was set for the 15th. "About the actual date," wrote Trotsky in his recollections of Lenin, "there was, as I remember, almost no dispute. All understood that the date was approximate, and set, as you might say merely for purposes of orientation, and that it might be advanced or retarded at the dictation of events. But this could be a question of days only, and not more. The necessity of a date, and that, too, a near one, was completely obvious."

This testimony of political logic essentially exhausts the question. But there is no lack of supplementary proof. Lenin insistently and frequently proposed that the party avail itself of the Northern Regional Congress of the Soviets for the beginning of military activities. The resolution of the Central Committee adopted this idea. But the Regional Congress, which had opened on the 10th, was to close just before the 15th.

At the conference on the 16th, Zinoviev, while insisting upon the revocation of the resolution adopted six days before, made this demand: "We must say to ourselves frankly that in the next five days we will not make an insurrection." He was referring to the five days still remaining before the Congress of Soviets. Kamenev, arguing at the same conference that "the appointing of an insurrection is adventurism," reminded the conference that "it was said before that the action ought to come before the 20th." Nobody objected to this statement and nobody could object. It was the very delay of the insurrection which Kamenev was interpreting as a failure of Lenin's resolution. According to his words, "nothing has been done during this week" towards an insurrection. That is obviously an exaggeration. The setting of the date had compelled all to make their plans more strict and hasten the tempo of their work. But it is indubitable that the five-day interval indicated at the session of the 10th had turned out too short. The postponement was already a fact. It was only on the 17th that the Central Executive Committee transferred the opening of the Soviet Congress to the 25th. That postponement was as opportune as anything could be.

Lenin, to whom in his isolation all these inner hindrances and frictions, inevitably presented themselves in an exaggerated form, was alarmed by the delay, and insisted upon the calling of a new meeting of the Central Committee with representatives from the more important branches of the party work in the capital. It was at this conference, held on the 16th in the outskirts of the city, in Lesnoi, that Zinoviev and Kamenev advanced the arguments quoted above for revoking the old date and against naming a new.

The dispute was reopened with redoubled vigour. Miliutin's opinion was: "We are not ready to strike the first blow .... Another prospect arises: Armed conflict.... It is growing, its possibility is drawing near. And we ought to be ready for this conflict. But this prospect is a different thing from insurrection." Miliutin occupied that defensive position which was more concisely defended by Zinoviev and Kamenev. Shotman, an old Petrograd worker who lived through the whole history of the party, has asserted that at this city conference, both in the party committee and in the Military Revolutionary Committee, the mood was far less militant than in the Central Committee. "We cannot come out but we ought to get ready." Lenin attacked Miliutin and Shotman for their pessimistic appraisal of the correlation of forces: "It is not a question of a struggle with the army, but a struggle of one part of the army with another.... The facts prove that we have the advantage over the enemy. Why cannot the Central Committee begin?"

Trotsky was not present at this meeting. During those same hours he was carrying through the Soviet the resolution on the Military Revolutionary Committee. But the point of view which had firmly crystallized in Smolny during the past days was defended by Krylenko, who had just been conducting hand in hand with Trotsky and Antonov-Ovseënko the Northern Regional Congress of Soviets. Krylenko had no doubt that "the water is boiling hard enough." To take back the resolution in favour of insurrection "would be the greatest possible mistake." He disagreed with Lenin, however, "on the question who shall begin it and how it shall begin?" To set the date of the insurrection definitely now is still inexpedient. "But the question of the removal of the troops is just that fighting issue upon which the struggle is taking place.... The attack upon us is thus already a fact, and this we can make use of.... It is not necessary to worry about who shall begin, for the thing is already begun." Krylenko was expounding and defending the policy laid down by the Military Revolutionary Committee and the Garrison Conference. It was along this road that the insurrection continued to develop.

Lenin did not respond to the words of Krylenko. The living picture of the last six days in Petrograd had not passed before his eyes. Lenin feared delay. His attention was fixed upon the outright opponents of insurrection. All by-remarks, conditional formulæ, inadequately categorical answers, he was inclined to interpret as an indirect support to Zinoviev and Kamenev, who were opposing him with the determination of people who have burned their bridges behind them. "The week's results," argued Kamenev, "testify that the data for an insurrection are now lacking. We have no machine of insurrection. The enemy's machine is far stronger and has probably grown still greater during this week. . . . Two tactics are in conflict here: the tactic of conspiracy and the tactic of faith in the motive forces of the Russian revolution." Opportunists always believe in those motive forces whenever it becomes necessary to fight.

Lenin replied: "If you consider that an insurrection is right, it is not necessary to argue about conspiracy. If an insurrection is politically inevitable, then we must relate ourselves to insurrection as to an art." It was along this line that the fundamental and really principled dispute in the party took place—the dispute upon whose decision, upon whose resolution one way or the other, depended the fate of the revolution. However, within the general frame of Lenin's formula, which united the majority of the Central Committee, there arose subordinate, but very important, questions: How on the basis of the ripened political situation are we to approach the insurrection? How find a bridge from the politics to the technique of revolution? And how lead the masses along that bridge?

Joffé, who belonged to the left wing, had supported the resolution of the 10th. But he opposed Lenin in one point: "It is not true that the question is now purely technical. Now, too, the moment of insurrection must be considered from the political point of view." This very last week has shown that for the party, for the Soviet, for the masses, the insurrection has not yet become a mere question of technique. For that very reason we failed to keep to the date set on the 10th.

Lenin's new resolution summoning "all organisations and all workers and soldiers to an all-sided and most vigorous preparation of armed insurrection," was adopted by 20 voices against 2, Zinoviev and Kamenev, with 3 abstaining. The official historians cite these figures as proof of the complete insignificance of the opposition. But they simplify the matter. The shift to the left in the depths of the party was already so strong that the opponents of insurrection, not daring to come out openly, felt it to their interest to remove any barrier of principle between the two camps. If the overthrow, in spite of the date set before, has not been realised by the 16th, can we not bring it about that in the future, too, the thing will be limited to a platonic "course toward insurrection"? That Kalinin was not so utterly alone was very clearly revealed in that same session. The resolution of Zinoviev to the effect that "any action before a conference with the Bolshevik section of the Congress of Soviets is inadmissible," was rejected by 15 votes against 6, with 3 abstaining. This is where you find the real test of opinions. Some of the "defenders" of the resolution of the Central Committee really wanted to delay the decision until the Congress of Soviets, and until a new conference with the Bolsheviks of the provinces who were in their majority more moderate. Of these "defenders," counting also those abstaining, there were 9 men out of 24—more, that is, than a third. That, of course, is still a minority, but as a headquarters rather an important one. The hopeless weakness of this headquarters lay in the fact that it had no support in the lower ranks of the party or the working class.

On the next day Kamenev, in agreement with Zinoviev, gave to Korky's paper a declaration attacking the decision adopted the night before. "Not only Zinoviev and I, but also a number of practical comrades,"—thus wrote Kamenev—"think that to take the initiative in an armed insurrection at the present moment, with the given correlation of social forces, independently of and several days before the Congress of Soviets, is an inadmissible step ruinous to the proletariat and the revolution. . . . To stake everything . . . on the card of insurrection in the coming days would be an act of despair. And our party is too strong, it has too great a future before it, to take such a step. . . ." Opportunists always feel "too strong" to go into a fight.

Kamenev's letter was a direct declaration of war against the Central Committee, and that, too, upon a question upon which nobody was joking. The situation immediately became extraordinarily acute. It was complicated by several other personal episodes having a common political source. At a session of the Petrograd Soviet on the 18th, Trotsky, in answer to a question raised by the enemy, declared that the Soviet had not set the date for an insurrection in the coming days, but that if it became necessary to set one, the workers and soldiers would come out as one man. Kamenev, sitting next to Trotsky in the præsidium, immediately arose for a short statement: He wanted to sign his name to Trotsky's every word. That was a cunning ruse. Whereas Trotsky was juridically screening a policy of attack with a speciously defensive formula, Kamenev tried to make use of Trotsky's formula—with which he was in radical disagreement—in order to screen a directly opposite policy.

In order to annul the effect of Kamenev's manœuvre, Trotsky said on the same day in a speech to the All-Russian Conference of Factory and Shop Committees: "A civil war is inevitable. We have only to organise it as painlessly as possible. We can achieve this not by wavering and vacillation, but only by a stubborn and courageous struggle for power." All understood that those words about waverings were directed against Zinoviev, Kamenev and their colleagues.

Besides that, Trotsky referred the question of Kamenev's speech in the Soviet to investigation by the next session of the Central Committee. In the interval Kamenev, desiring to free his hands for agitation against the insurrection, resigned from the Central Committee. The question was taken up in his absence. Trotsky insisted that "the situation created is absolutely intolerable," and moved that Kamenev's resignation be accepted.[1]

Sverdlov, supporting Trotsky's motion, read a letter of

1. In the minutes of the Central Committee for 1917, published in 1929, it says that Trotsky explained his declaration to the Soviet on the ground that "it was forced by Kamenev." Here there is obviously an erroneous record, or the record was subsequently incorrectly edited. The declaration of Trotsky needed no special explanation; it flowed from the circumstances. By a curious accident the Moscow Regional Committee, which wholly supported Lenin, found itself obliged to publish in the Moscow party paper on the same day, the 18th, a declaration almost verbally identical with the formula of Trotsky: "We are not a conspirative party and we do not set the date for our actions secretly. . . . When we decide to come out, we will say so in our printed organ. . . ." It was impossible to reply otherwise to the direct queries of the enemy. But although the declaration of Trotsky was not, and could not have been, forced by Kamenev, it was consciously compromised by Kamenev's false solidarity and that moreover under circumstances which deprived Trotsky of the possibility of putting the missing dots on the i's.

Lenin branding Zinoviev and Kamenev as strikebreakers for their declaration in Gorky's paper, and demanding their expulsion from the party. "Kamenev's trick at the session of the Petrograd Soviet," writes Lenin, "was something positively vile. He is in complete accord, says he, with Trotsky! But is it hard to understand that Trotsky *could* not, had no right, to say before the enemy any more than he did say? Is it hard to understand that ... a decision as to the necessity of an armed insurrection, as to the fact that it is fully ripe, as to its all-sided preparation, etc.... makes it *necessary* in public speeches to shoulder off not only the blame, but also the initiative, upon the enemy.... Kamenev's trick was plain petty cheating...."

When sending his indignant protest through Sverdlov, Lenin could not yet know that Zinoviev, in a letter to the editors of the central organ, had announced that his views "are very far from those which Lenin combats," and that he "subscribes to yesterday's declaration of Trotsky in the Petrograd Soviet." Lunacharsky, a third opponent of insurrection, came out in the press to the same effect. To complete the malicious confusion, a letter of Zinoviev's printed in the central organ on the very day of the session of the Central Committee, the 20th, was accompanied by a sympathetic remark from the editors: "We in our turn express the hope that with the declaration made by Zinoviev (and also the declaration of Kamenev in the Soviet) the question may be considered settled. The sharpness of tone of Lenin's article does not alter the fact that in fundamentals we remain of one opinion." That was a new blow in the back, and moreover from a direction from which no one was expecting it. At the time when Zinoviev and Kamenev were coming out in a hostile press with open agitation against the decision of the Central Committee in favour of insurrection, the central organ of the party condemns the "sharpness" of Lenin's tone and registers its solidarity with Zinoviev and Kamenev "in fundamentals." As though at that moment there could be a more fundamental question than the question of insurrection! According to the brief minutes, Trotsky declared at the session of the Central Committee: "The letters of Zinoviev and Lunacharsky to the central organ, and also the remark of the editors are intolerable." Sverdlov supported the protest.

The editors at that time were Stalin and Solkolnikov. The minutes read: "Solkolnikov states that he had no part in the declaration of the editors on the subject of Zinoviev's letter, and considers this declaration an error." It thus became known that Stalin personally and alone—against the other member of the editorial board and a majority of the Central Committee—supported Kamenev and Zinoviev at the most critical moment, four days before the beginning of the insurrection, with a sympathetic declaration. The indignation at this was great.

Stalin spoke against the acceptance of Kamenev's resignation, arguing that "our whole situation is self-contradictory." That is, he took upon himself the defence of that confusion which the members of the Central Committee coming out against the insurrection had introduced into people's minds. Kamenev's resignation was accepted by 5 votes against 3. By 6 votes, again with Stalin opposing, a decision was adopted forbidding Kamenev and Zinoviev to carry on a struggle against the policy of the Central Committee. The minutes read: "Stalin announces that he withdraws from the editorial board." In order not to complicate an already difficult situation, the Central Committee refused to accept Stalin's resignation.

This conduct on the part of Stalin might seem inexplicable in the light of the legend which has been created around him. In reality it fully corresponds to his spiritual mould and his political methods. When faced by great problems, Stalin always retreats—not through lack of character as in the case of Kamenev, but through narrowness of horizon and lack of creative imagination. His suspicious caution almost organically compels him at moments of great decision and deep difference of opinion to retire into the shadow, to wait, and if possible to insure himself against both outcomes. Stalin voted with Lenin for the insurrection; Zinoviev and Kamenev were openly fighting against the insurrection. But nevertheless—aside from the "sharpness of tone" of Lenin's criticism—"in fundamentals we remain of one opinion." Stalin made this editorial comment by no means through light-mindedness. On the contrary he was carefully weighing the circumstances and the words. But on the 20th of October he did not think it advisable to burn irrevocably his bridge to the camp of the enemies of the uprising.

The testimony of these minutes, which we are compelled to quote, not from the original, but from the official text as worked up by Stalin's secretariat, not only demonstrates the actual position of the figures in the Bolshevik Central Committee, but also, in spite of its brevity and dryness, unfolds before us an authentic panorama of the party leadership as it existed in reality, with all its inner contradictions and inevitable personal waverings. Not only history as a whole, but even its very boldest turns, are accomplished by people to whom nothing human is alien. But does this after all lessen the importance of what is accomplished?

If we were to unfold on a screen the most brilliant of Napoleon's victories, the film would show us, side by side with genius, scope, ingenuity, heroism, also the irresolution of individual marshals, the confusion of generals unable to read the map, the stupidity of officers, and the panic of whole detachments, even down to the bowels relaxed with fright. This realistic document would only testify that the army of Napoleon consisted not of the automatons of legend, but of living Frenchmen born and brought up during the break between two epochs. And the picture of human weaknesses would only the more plainly emphasise the grandeur of the whole.

It is easier to theorise about a revolution afterward than absorb it into your flesh and blood before it takes place. The approach of an insurrection has inevitably produced, and always will produce, crisis in the insurrectionary parties. This is demonstrated by the experience of the most tempered and revolutionary party that history has up to this time known. It is enough that, a few days before the battle, Lenin found himself obliged to demand the expulsion from the party of his two closest and most prominent disciples. The recent attempts to reduce this conflict to "accidents" of a personal character have been dictated by a purely churchly idealisation of the party's past. Just as Lenin more fully and resolutely than others expressed in the autumn months of 1917 the objective necessity of an insurrection, and the will of the masses of revolution, so Zinoviev and Kamenev more frankly than others incarnated the blocking tendencies of the party, the moods of irresolution, the influence of petty bourgeois connections, and the pressure of the ruling classes.

If all the conferences, debates, personal quarrels, which took place in the upper layer of the Bolshevik party during October alone had been taken down by a stenographer, posterity might convince itself with what intense inner struggle the determination necessary for the overthrow was crystallized among the heads of the party. The stenographic report would show at the same time how much a revolutionary party has need of internal democracy. The will to struggle is not stored up in advance, and is not dictated from above—it has on every occasion to be independently renewed and tempered.

Citing the assertion of the author of this book that "the party is the fundamental instrument of proletarian revolution," Stalin asked in 1924: "How could our revolution conquer if its 'fundamental instrument' was no good?" His irony did not conceal the primitive falsity of this objection. Between the saints as the church paints them and the devils as the candidates for sainthood portray them, there are to be found living people. And it is they who make history. The high temper of the Bolshevik party expressed itself not in an absence of disagreements, waverings, and even quakings, but in the fact that in the most difficult circumstances it gathered itself in good season by means of inner crises, and made good its opportunity to interfere decisively in the course of events. That means that the party as a whole was a quite adequate instrument of revolution.

In practice a reformist party considers unshakable the foundations of that which it intends to reform. It thus inevitably submits to the ideas and morals of the ruling class. Having risen on the backs of the proletariat, the social democrats became merely a bourgeois party of the second order. Bolshevism created the type of the authentic revolutionist, who subordinates to historic goals irreconcilable with contemporary society the conditions of his personal existence, his ideas, and his moral judgments. The necessary distance from bourgeois ideology was kept up in the party by a vigilant irreconcilability, whose inspirer was Lenin. Lenin never tired of working with his lancet, cutting off those bonds which a petty bourgeois environment creates between the party and official social opinion. At the same time Lenin taught the party to create its own social opinion, resting upon the thoughts and feelings of the rising class. Thus by a process of selection and education, and in continual struggle, the Bolshevik party created not only a political but a moral medium of its own, independent of bourgeois social opinion and implacably opposed to it. Only this permitted the Bolsheviks to overcome the waverings in their own ranks and reveal in action that courageous determination without which the October victory would have been impossible.

Chapter VI

The Art of Insurrection

People do not make revolution eagerly any more than they do war. There is this difference, however, that in war compulsion plays the decisive rôle, in revolution there is no compulsion except that of circumstances. A revolution takes place only when there is no other way out. And the insurrection, which rises above a revolution like a peak in the mountain chain of its events, can no more be evoked at will than the revolution as a whole. The masses advance and retreat several times before they make up their minds to the final assault.

Conspiracy is ordinarily contrasted to insurrection as the deliberate undertaking of a minority to a spontaneous movement of the majority. And it is true that a victorious insurrection, which can only be the act of a class called to stand at the head of the nation, is widely separated both in method and historic significance from a governmental overturn accomplished by conspirators acting in concealment from the masses.

In every class society there are enough contradictions so that a conspiracy can take root in its cracks. Historic experience proves, however, that a certain degree of social disease is necessary—as in Spain, for instance, or Portugal, or South America—to supply continual nourishment for a régime of conspiracies. A pure conspiracy even when victorious can only replace one clique of the same ruling class by another—or still less, merely alter the governmental personages. Only mass insurrection has ever brought the victory of one social régime over another. Periodical conspiracies are commonly an expression of social stagnation and decay, but popular insurrections on the contrary come usually as a result of some swift growth which has broken down the old equilibrium of the nation. The chronic "revolutions" of the South American republics have nothing in common with the Permanent Revolution; they are in a sense the very opposite thing.

This does not mean, however, that popular insurrection and conspiracy are in all circumstances mutually exclusive. An element of conspiracy almost always enters to some degree into any insurrection. Being historically conditioned by a certain stage in the growth of a revolution, a mass insurrection is never purely spontaneous. Even when it flashes out unexpectedly to a majority of its own participants, it has been fertilised by those ideas in which the insurrectionaries see a way out of the difficulties of existence. But a mass insurrection can be foreseen and prepared. It can be organised in advance. In this case the conspiracy is subordinate to the insurrection, serves it, smoothes its path, hastens its victory. The higher the political level of a revolutionary movement and the more serious its leadership, the greater will be the place occupied by conspiracy in a popular insurrection.

It is very necessary to understand the relations between insurrection and conspiracy, both as they oppose and as they supplement each other. It is especially so, because the very use of the word conspiracy, even in Marxian literature, contains a superficial contradiction due to the fact that it sometimes implies an independent undertaking initiated by the minority, at others a preparation by the minority of a majority insurrection.

History testifies, to be sure, that in certain conditions a popular insurrection can be victorious even without a conspiracy. Arising "spontaneously" out of the universal indignation, the scattered protests, demonstrations, strikes, street fights, an insurrection can draw in a part of the army, paralyse the forces of the enemy, and overthrow the old power. To a certain degree this is what happened in February 1917 in Russia. Approximately the same picture is presented by the development of the German and Austro-Hungarian revolutions of the autumn of 1918. Since in these events there was no party at the head of the insurrectionaries imbued through and through with the interests and aims of the insurrection, its victory had inevitably to transfer the power to those parties which up to the last moment had been opposing it.

To overthrow the old power is one thing; to take the power in one's own hands is another. The bourgeoisie may win the power in a revolution not because it is revolutionary, but because it is bourgeois. It has in its possession property, education, the press, a network of strategic positions, a hierarchy of institutions. Quite otherwise with the proletariat. Deprived in the nature of things of all social advantages, an insurrectionary proletariat can count only on its numbers, its solidarity, its cadres, its official staff.

Just as a blacksmith cannot seize the red hot iron in his naked hand, so the proletariat cannot directly seize the power; it has to have an organisation accommodated to this task. The co-ordination of the mass insurrection with the conspiracy, the subordination of the conspiracy to the insurrection, the organisation of the insurrection through the conspiracy, constitutes that complex and responsible department of revolutionary politics which Marx and Engels called "the art of insurrection." It presupposes a correct general leadership of the masses, a flexible orientation in changing conditions, a thought-out plan of attack, cautiousness in technical preparation, and a daring blow.

Historians and politicians usually give the name of *spontaneous insurrection* to a movement of the masses united by a common hostility against the old régime, but not having a clear aim, deliberated methods of struggle, or a leadership consciously showing the way to victory. This spontaneous insurrection is condescendingly recognised by official historians—at least those of democratic temper—as a necessary evil the responsibility for which falls upon the old régime. The real reason for their attitude of indulgence is that "spontaneous" insurrection cannot transcend the framework of the bourgeois régime.

The social democrats take a similar position. They do not reject revolution at large as a social catastrophe, any more than they reject earthquakes, volcanic eruptions, eclipses and epidemics of the plague. What they do reject—calling it "Blanquism," or still worse, Bolshevism—is the conscious preparation of an overturn, the plan, the conspiracy. In other words, the social democrats are ready to sanction—and that only *ex post facto*—those overturns which hand the power to the bourgeoisie, but they implacably condemn those methods which might alone bring the power to the proletariat. Under this pretended objectivism they conceal a policy of defence of the capitalist society.

From his observations and reflections upon the failure of the many insurrections he witnessed or took part in, Auguste Blanqui derived a number of tactical rules which if violated will make the victory of any insurrection extremely difficult, if not impossible. Blanqui demanded these things: a timely creation of correct revolutionary detachments, their centralised command and adequate equipment, a well calculated placement of barricades, their definite construction, and a systematic, not a mere episodic, defence of them. All these rules, deriving from the military problems of the insurrection, must of course change with social conditions and military technique, but in themselves they are not by any means "Blanquism" in the sense that this word approaches the German "putschism," or revolutionary adventurism.

Insurrection is an art, and like all arts it has its laws. The rules of Blanqui were the demands of a military revolutionary realism. Blanqui's mistake lay not in his direct but his inverse theorem. From the fact that tactful weakness condemns an insurrection to defeat, Blanqui inferred that an observance of the rules of insurrectionary tactics would itself guarantee the victory. Only from this point on is it legitimate to contrast Blanquism with Marxism. Conspiracy does not take the place of insurrection. An active minority of the proletariat, no matter how well organised, cannot seize the power regardless of the general conditions of the country. In this point history has condemned Blanquism. But only in this. His affirmative theorem retains all its force. In order to conquer the power, the proletariat needs more than a spontaneous insurrection. It needs a suitable organisation, it needs a plan; it needs a conspiracy. Such is the Leninist view of this question.

Engels' criticism of the fetishism of the barricade was based upon the evolution of military technique and of technique in general. The insurrectionary tactic of Blanquism corresponded to the character of the old Paris, the semi-handicraft proletariat, the narrow streets and the military system of Louis Philippe. Blanqui's mistake in principle was to identify revolution with insurrection. His technical mistake was to identify insurrection with the barricade. The Marxian criticism has been directed against both mistakes. Although at one with Blanquism in regarding insurrection as an art, Engels discovered not only the subordinate place occupied by insurrection in a revolution, but also the declining rôle of the barricade in an insurrection. Engels' criticism had nothing in common with a renunciation of the revolutionary methods in favour of pure parliamentarism, as the philistines of the German Social Democracy, in co-operation with the Hohenzollern censorship, attempted in their day to pretend. For Engels the question about barricades remained a question about one of the technical elements of an uprising. The reformists have attempted to infer from his rejection of the decisive importance of the barricade a rejection of revolutionary violence in general. That is about the same as to infer the destruction of militarism from considerations of the probable decline in importance of trenches in future warfare.

The organisation by means of which the proletariat can both overthrow the old power and replace it, is the soviets. This afterwards became a matter of historic experience, but was up to the October revolution a theoretical prognosis—resting, to be sure, upon the preliminary experience of 1905. The soviets are organs of preparation of the masses for insurrection, organs of insurrection, and after the victory organs of government.

However, the soviets by themselves do not settle the question. They may serve different goals according to the programme and leadership. The soviets receive their programme from the party. Whereas the soviets in revolutionary conditions—and apart from revolution they are impossible—comprise the whole class with the exception of its altogether backward, inert or demoralised strata, the revolutionary party represents the brain of the class. The problem of conquering the power can be solved only by a definite combination of party with soviets—or with other mass organisations more or less equivalent to soviets.

When headed by a revolutionary party the soviet consciously and in good season strives towards a conquest of power. Accommodating itself to changes in the political situation and the mood of the masses, it gets ready the military bases of the insurrection, unites the shock troops upon a single scheme of action, works out a plan for the offensive and for the final assault. And this means bringing organised conspiracy into mass insurrection.

The Bolsheviks were compelled more than once, and long before the October revolution, to refute accusations of conspiracy and Blanquism directed against them by their enemies. Moreover, nobody waged a more implacable struggle against the system of pure conspiracy than Lenin. The opportunists of the international social democracy more than once defended the old Social Revolutionary tactic of individual terror directed against the agents of czarism, when this tactic was ruthlessly criticised by the Bolsheviks with their insistence upon mass insurrection as opposed to the individual adventurism of the intelligentsia. But in refuting all varieties of Blanquism and anarchism, Lenin did not for one moment bow down to any "sacred" spontaneousness of the masses. He thought out before anybody else, and more deeply, the correlation between the objective and subjective factors in a revolution, between the spontaneous movement and the policy of the party, between the popular masses and the progressive class, between the proletariat and its vanguard, between the soviets and the party, between insurrection and conspiracy.

But if it is true that an insurrection cannot be evoked at will, and that nevertheless in order to win it must be organised in advance, then the revolutionary leaders are presented with a task of correct diagnosis. They must feel out the growing insurrection in good season and supplement it with a conspiracy. The interference of the midwife in labour pains—however this image may have been abused—remains the clearest illustration of this conscious intrusion into an elemental process. Herzen once accused his friend Bakunin of invariably in all his revolutionary enterprises taking the second month of pregnancy for the ninth. Herzen himself was rather inclined to deny even in the ninth that pregnancy existed. In February the question of determining the date of birth hardly arose at all, since the insurrection flared up unexpectedly without centralised leadership. But exactly for this reason the power did not go to those who had accomplished the insurrection, but to those who had applied the brakes. It was quite otherwise with the second insurrection. This was consciously prepared by the Bolshevik Party. The problem of correctly seizing the moment to give the signal for the attack was thus laid upon the Bolshevik staff.

Moment here is not to be taken too literally as meaning a definite day and hour. Physical births also present a considerable period of uncertainty—their limits interesting not only to the art of the midwife, but also to the casuistics of the Surrogate's Court. Between the moment when an attempt to summon an insurrection must inevitably prove premature and lead to a revolutionary miscarriage, and the moment when a favourable situation must be considered hopelessly missed, there exists a certain period—it may be measured in weeks, and sometimes in a few months—in the course of which an insurrection may be carried out with more or less chance of success. To discriminate this comparatively short period and then choose the definite moment—now in the more accurate sense of the very day and hour—for the last blow, constitutes the most responsible task of the revolutionary leaders. It can with full justice be called the key problem, for it unites the policy of revolution with the technique of insurrection—and it is needless to add that insurrection, like war, is a continuation of politics with other instruments.

Intuition and experience are necessary for revolutionary leadership, just as for all other kinds of creative activity. But much more than that is needed. The art of the magician can also successfully rely upon intuition and experience. Political magic is adequate, however, only for epochs and periods in which routine predominates. An epoch of mighty historic upheavals has no use for witch-doctors. Here experience, even illumined by intuition, is not enough. Here you must have a synthetic doctrine comprehending the interactions of the chief historic forces. Here you must have a materialistic method permitting you to discover, behind the moving shadows of programme and slogan, the actual movement of social bodies.

The fundamental premise of a revolution is that the existing social structure has become incapable of solving the urgent problems of development of the nation. A revolution becomes possible, however, only in case the society contains a new class capable of taking the lead in solving the problems presented by history. The process of preparing a revolution consists of making the objective problems involved in the contradictions of industry and of classes find their way into the consciousness of living human masses, change this consciousness and create new correlation of human forces.

The ruling classes, as a result of their practically manifested incapacity to get the country out of its blind alley, lose faith in themselves; the old parties fall to pieces; a bitter struggle of groups and cliques prevails; hopes are placed in miracles or miracle workers. All this constitutes one of the political premises of a revolution, a very important although a passive one.

A bitter hostility to the existing order and a readiness to venture upon the most heroic efforts and sacrifices in order to bring the country out upon an upward road—this is the new political consciousness of the revolutionary class, and constitutes the most important active premise of a revolution.

These two fundamental camps, however—the big property holders and the proletariat—do not exhaust the population of a country. Between them lie broad layers of the petty bourgeoisie, showing all the colours of the economic and political rainbow. The discontent of these intermediate layers, their disappointment with the policy of the ruling class, their revolutionary initiative on the part of the proletariat, constitute the third political premise of a revolution. It is partly passive—in that it neutralizes the upper strata of the petty bourgeoisie—but partly also active, for it impels the lower strata directly into the struggle side by side with the workers.

That these premises condition each other is obvious. The more decisively and confidently the proletariat acts, the better will it succeed in bringing after it the intermediate layer, the more isolated will be the ruling class, and the more acute its demoralisation. And, on the other hand, a demoralisation of the rulers will pour water into the mill of the revolutionary class.

The proletariat can become imbued with the confidence necessary for a governmental overthrow only if a clear prospect opens before it, only if it has had an opportunity to test out in action a correlation of forces which is changing to its advantage, only if it feels above it a far-sighted, firm and confident leadership. This brings us to the last premise—by no means the last in importance—of the conquest of power: the revolutionary party as a tightly welded and tempered vanguard of the class.

Thanks to a favourable combination of historic conditions both domestic and international, the Russian proletariat was headed by a party of extraordinary political clarity and unexampled revolutionary temper. Only this permitted that small and young class to carry out a historic task of unprecedented proportions. It is indeed the general testimony of history—the Paris Commune, the German and Austrian revolutions of 1918, the Soviet revolutions in Hungary and Bavaria, the Italian revolution of 1919, the German crisis of 1923, the Chinese revolution of 1925–1927, the Spanish revolution of 1931—that up to now the weakest link in the chain of necessary conditions has been the party. The hardest thing of all is for the working class to create a revolutionary organisation capable of rising to the height of its historic task. In the older and more civilised countries powerful forces work toward the weakening and demoralisation of the revolutionary vanguard. An important constituent part of this work is the struggle of the social democrats against "Blanquism," by which name they designate the revolutionary essence of Marxism.

Notwithstanding the number of great social and political crises, a coincidence of all the conditions necessary to a victorious and stable proletarian revolution has so far occurred but once in history: in Russia in October 1917. A revolutionary situation is not long-lived. The least stable of the premises of a revolution is the mood of the petty bourgeoisie. At a time of national crises the petty bourgeoisie follows that class which inspires confidence not only in words but deeds. Although capable of impulsive enthusiasm and even of revolutionary fury, the petty bourgeoisie lacks endurance, easily loses heart under reverses, and passes from elated hope to discouragement. And these sharp and swift changes in the mood of the petty bourgeoisie lend their instability to every revolutionary situation. If the proletarian party is not decisive enough to convert the hopes and expectations of the popular masses into revolutionary action in good season, the flood tide is quickly followed by an ebb: the intermediate strata turn away their eyes from the revolution and seek a saviour in the opposing camp. And just as at flood tide the proletariat draws after it the petty bourgeoisie, so during the ebb the petty bourgeoisie draws after it considerable layers of the proletariat. Such is the dialectic of the communist and fascist waves observable in the political evolution of Europe since the war.

Attempting to ground themselves upon the assertion of Marx that no régime withdraws from the stage of history until it has exhausted all its possibilities, the Mensheviks denied the legitimacy of a struggle for proletarian dictatorship in backward Russia where capitalism had far from exhausted itself. This argument contained two mistakes, both fatal. Capitalism is not a national but a world-wide system. The imperialist war and its consequences demonstrated that the capitalist system had exhausted itself on a world scale. The revolution in Russia was a breaking of the weakest link in the system of world-wide capitalism.

But the falsity of this Menshevik conception appears also from a national point of view. From the standpoint of economic abstraction, it is indeed possible to affirm that capitalism in Russia has not exhausted its possibilities. But economic processes do not take place in the ether, but in a concrete historical medium. Capitalism is not an abstraction, but a living system of class relations requiring above all things a state power. That the monarchy, under whose protection Russian capitalism developed, had exhausted its possibilities is not denied even by the Mensheviks. The February revolution tried to build up an intermediate state régime. We have followed its history: in the course of eight months it exhausted itself completely. What sort of state order could in these conditions guarantee the further development of Russian capitalism.

"The bourgeois republic, defended only by socialists of moderate tendencies, finding no longer any support in the masses . . . could not maintain itself. Its whole essence had evaporated. There remained only an external shell." This accurate definition belongs to Miliukov. The fate of this evaporated system was necessarily, according to his words, the same as that of the czarist monarchy: "Both prepared the ground for a revolution, and on the day of revolution neither could find a single defender."

As early as July and August Miliukov characterised the situation by presenting a choice between two names: Kornilov or Lenin? But Kornilov had now made his experiment and it had ended in a miserable failure. For the régime of Kerensky there was certainly no place left. With all the varieties of mood, says Sukhanov, "the one thing upon which all united was hate for the Kerensky régime." Just as the czarist monarchy had toward the end become impossible in the eyes of the upper circle of the nobility and even the grand dukes, so the government of Kerensky became odious even to the direct inspiritors of his régime, the "grand dukes" of the compromisist upper crust. In this universal dissatisfaction, this sharp political nerve-tension of all classes, we have one of the symptoms of a ripe revolutionary situation. In the same way every muscle, nerve and fibre of an organism is intolerably tensed just before an abscess bursts.

The resolution of the July congress of the Bolsheviks, while warning the workers against premature encounters had at the same time pointed out that the battle must be joined "whenever the general national crisis and the deep mass enthusiam have created conditions favourable to the going over of the poor people of the city and country to the side of the workers." That moment arrived in September and October.

The insurrection was thenceforth able to believe in its success, for it could rely upon a genuine majority of the people. This, of course, is not to be understood in a formal sense. If a referendum could have been taken on the question of insurrection, it would have given extremely contradictory and uncertain results. An inner readiness to support a revolution is far from identical with an ability clearly to formulate the necessity of it. Moreover, the answer would have depended to a vast degree upon the manner in which the question was presented, the institution which conducted the referendum—or, to put it more simply, the class which held the power.

There is a limit to the application of democratic methods. You can inquire of all the passengers as to what type of car they like to ride in, but it is impossible to question them as to whether to apply the brakes when the train is at full speed and accident threatens. If the saving operation is carried out skilfully, however, and in time, the approval of the passengers is guaranteed in advance.

Parliamentary consultations of the people are carried out at a single moment, whereas during a revolution the different layers of the population arrive at the same conclusion one after another and with inevitable, although sometimes very slight, intervals. At the moment when the advanced detachment is burning with revolutionary impatience the backward layers have only begun to move. In Petrograd and Moscow all the mass organisations were under the leadership of the Bolsheviks. In Tambov province, which has over three million population—that is, a little less than both capitals put together—a Bolshevik faction first appeared in the Soviet only a short time before the October revolution.

The syllogisms of the objective development are far from coinciding—day by day—with the syllogisms of the thought process of the masses. And when a great practical decision becomes unpostponable, in the course of events, that is the very moment when a referendum is impossible. The difference in level and mood of the different layers of the people is overcome in action. The advance layers bring after them the wavering and isolate the opposing. The majority is not counted up, but won over. Insurrection comes into being at exactly that moment when direct action alone offers a way out of the contradictions.

Although lacking the power to draw by themselves the necessary political inferences from their war against the landlords, the peasants had by the very fact of the agrarian insurrection already adhered to the insurrection of the cities, had evoked it and were demanding it. They expressed their will not with the white ballot, but with the red cock—a more serious referendum. Within those limits in which the support of the peasantry was necessary for the establishment of a soviet dictatorship, the support was already at hand. "The dictatorship"—as Lenin answered the doubters—"would give land to the peasants and all power to the peasant committees in the localities. How can you in your right mind doubt that the peasant would support that dictatorship?" In order that the soldiers, peasants and oppressed nationalities, floundering in the snow-storm of an elective ballot, should recognise the Bolsheviks in action, it was necessary that the Bolsheviks seize the power.

But what correlation of forces was necessary in order that the proletariat should seize the power? "To have at the decisive moment, at the decisive point, an overwhelming superiority of force," wrote Lenin later, interpreting the October revolution, "—this law of military success is also the law of political success, especially in that seething and bitter war of classes which is called revolution. The capitals, or generally speaking, the biggest centres of trade and industry . . . decide to a considerable degree the political fate of the people—that is, of course, on condition that the centres are supported by sufficient local rural forces, although this support need not be immediate." It was in this dynamic sense that Lenin spoke of the majority of the people, and that was the sole real meaning of the concept of majority.

The enemy democrats comforted themselves with the thought that the people following the Bolsheviks were mere raw material, mere historic clay. The potters were still to be these same democrats acting in co-operation with the educated bourgeoisie. "Can't those people see," asked a Menshevik paper, "that the Petrograd proletariat and garrison were never before so isolated from all other social strata?" The misfortune of the proletariat and the garrison was that they were "isolated" from those classes from whom they intended to take the power!

But was it really possible to rely upon the sympathy and support of the dark masses in the provinces and at the front? "Their Bolshevism," wrote Sukhanov scornfully, "was nothing but hatred for the coalition and longing for land and peace." As though that were little! Hatred for the coalition meant a desire to take the power from the bourgeoisie. Longing for land and peace was the colossal programme which the peasant and soldier intended to carry out under the leadership of the workers. The insignificance of the democrats, even the most leftward, resulted from this very distrust—the distrust of "educated" sceptics—in those dark masses who grasp a phenomenon wholesale, not bothering about details and nuances. This intellectual, pseudo-aristocratic, squeamish attitude toward the people was foreign to Bolshevism, hostile to its very nature. The Bolsheviks were not lily-handed, literary friends of the masses, not pedants. They were not afraid of those backward strata now for the first time lifting themselves out of the dregs. The Bolsheviks took the people as preceding history had created them, and as they were called to achieve the revolution. The Bolsheviks saw it as their mission to stand at the head of that people. Those against the insurrection were "everybody"—except the Bolsheviks. But the Bolsheviks were the people.

The fundamental political force of the October revolution was the proletariat, and the first place in its ranks was occupied by the workers of Petrograd. In the vanguard of these workers stood the Vyborg district. The plan of the insurrection chose this fundamental proletarian district as the point of departure for its offensive.

Compromisers of all shades, beginning with Martov, attempted after the revolution to portray Bolshevism as a soldier movement. The European social democrats grabbed up this theory with delight. But fundamental historic facts were here ignored: the fact that the proletariat was the first to come over to the Bolsheviks; that the Petrograd workers were showing the road to the workers of all countries; that the garrison and front much longer than the workers remained bulwarks of compromise; that the Social Revolutionaries and Mensheviks created all kinds of privileges for the soldier at the expense of the worker in the soviet system, struggled against the arming of the workers and incited the soldiers against them; that the break in the troops was brought about only by the influence of workers; that at the decisive moment the leadership of the soldiers was in the hands of the workers; and finally that a year later the social democrats of Germany, following the example of their Russian colleagues, relied on the soldiers in their struggle against the workers.

By autumn the Right Compromisers had ceased even to be able to make speeches in the factories and barracks. But the Lefts were still trying to convince the masses of the madness of insurrection. Martov, who in the struggle against the counter-revolutionary offensive in July had found a path to the minds of the masses, was now again serving a hopeless cause. "We cannot expect"—he himself acknowledged on the 14th of October, at a meeting of the Central Executive Committee—"We cannot expect the Bolsheviks to listen to us." Nevertheless he considered it his duty to "warn the masses." The masses, however, wanted action and not moral admonition. Even where they did patiently listen to their well-known adviser, they "thought their own thoughts as before," as Mstislavsky acknowledges. Sukhanov tells how he made an effort in a drizzling rain to convince the Putilov men that they could fix things up without an insurrection. Impatient voices interrupted him. They would listen for two or three minutes and interrupt again. "After a few attempts I gave it up," he says, "It was no use . . . and the rain was drizzling down on us heavier and heavier." Under that impatient October sky the poor Left Democrats, even as described in their own writings, look like wet hens.

The favourite political argument of the "Left" opponents of the revolution—and this even among the Bolsheviks—was a reference to the absence of fighting enthusiasm among the lower ranks. "The mood of the labouring and soldier masses," write Zinoviev and Kamenev on October 11, "is far from comparable even to the mood which existed before the 3rd of July." This assertion was not unfounded: there was a certain depression in the Petrograd proletariat as a result of waiting too long. They were beginning to feel disappointed even in the Bolsheviks: Can it be that they are going to cheat us too? On October 16 Rakhia, one of the fighting Petrograd Bolsheviks, a Finn by birth, said at a conference of the Central Committee: "Our slogan is evidently already getting a little out of date, for there exists a doubt as to whether we will do the thing for which we are calling." But this weariness of waiting, which looked like listlessness, lasted only up to the first fighting signal.

The first task of every insurrection is to bring the troops over to its side. The chief means of accomplishing this are the general strike, mass processions, street encounters, battles at the barricades. The unique thing about the October revolution, a thing never before observed in so complete a form, was that, thanks to a happy combination of circumstances, the proletarian vanguard had won over the garrison of the capital before the moment of open insurrection. It had not only won them over, but had fortified this conquest through the organisation of the Garrison Conference. It is impossible to understand the mechanics of the October revolution without fully realising that the most important task of the insurrection, and the one most difficult to calculate in advance, was fully accomplished in Petrograd before the beginning of the armed struggle.

This does not mean, however, that insurrection had become superfluous. The overwhelming majority of the garrison was, it is true, on the side of the workers. But a minority was against the workers, against the revolution, against the Bolsheviks. This small minority consisted of the best trained elements in the army: the officers, the junkers, the shock battalions, and perhaps the Cossacks. It was impossible to win these elements politically; they had to be vanquished. The last part of the task of the revolution, that which has gone into history under the name of the October insurrection, was therefore purely military in character. At this final stage rifles, bayonets, machine-guns, and perhaps cannon, were to decide. The party of the Bolsheviks led the way on this road.

What were the military forces of the approaching conflict? Boris Sokolov, who directed the military work of the Social Revolutionary Party, says that in the period preceding the overturn, "in the regiments all the party organisations except those of the Bolsheviks had disintegrated, and conditions were not at all favourable to the organisation of new ones. The mood of the soldiers was tending definitely toward the Bolsheviks. But their Bolshevism was passive and they lacked any tendency whatever toward active armed movements." Sokolov does not fail to add: "One or two regiments wholly loyal and capable of fighting would have been enough to hold the whole garrison in obedience." Literally all of them, from the monarchist generals to the "socialistic" intelligentsia, wanted only those "one or two regiments" and they would have put down the proletarian revolution! But it is quite true that the garrison, although deeply hostile to the government in its overwhelming mass, was not capable of fighting even on the side of the Bolsheviks. The cause of this lay in the hostile break between the old military structure of the troops, and their new political structure. The backbone of a fighting unit is its commanding staff. The commanding staffs were against the Bolsheviks. The political backbone of the troops was composed of Bolsheviks. The latter, however, not only did not know how to command, but in the majority of cases hardly knew how to handle a gun. The soldier crowd was not homogeneous. The active fighting elements were, as always, a minority. The majority of the soldiers sympathised with the Bolsheviks, voted for them, elected them, but also expected them to decide things. The elements hostile to the Bolsheviks in the troops were too insignificant to venture upon any initiative whatever. The political condition of the garrison was thus exceptionally favourable for an insurrection. But its fighting weight was not large—that was clear from the beginning.

However, it was not necessary to dismiss the garrison entirely from the military count. A thousand soldiers ready to fight on the side of the revolution were scattered here and there among the more passive mass, and for that very reason more or less drew it after them. Certain individual units, more happily constituted, had preserved their discipline and fighting capacity. Strong revolutionary nuclei were to be found even in the disintegrating regiments. In the Sixth Reserve Battalion, consisting of about 10,000 men, out of five companies, the first invariably distinguished itself, being known as Bolshevik almost from the beginning of the revolution and rising to the heights in the October Days. The typical regiments of the garrison did not really exist as regiments; their administrative mechanism had broken down; they were incapable of prolonged military effort; but they were nevertheless a horde of armed men a majority of whom had been under fire. All the units were united by a single sentiment: Overthrow Kerensky as soon as possible, disperse, and go home and institute a new land system. Thus that completely demoralised garrison was to rally once more in the October Days, and rattle its weapons suggestively, before completely going to pieces.

What force did the Petrograd workers offer from a military point of view? This raises the question of the Red Guard. It is time to speak of this in greater detail, for the Red Guard is soon to come out on the great arena of history.

Deriving its tradition from 1905, the Workers' Guard was reborn with the February revolution and subsequently shared the vicissitudes of its fate. Kornilov, while Commander of the Petrograd military district, asserted that during the days of the overthrow of the monarchy, 30,000 revolvers and 40,000 rifles disappeared from the military stores. Over and above that, a considerable quantity of weapons came into the possession of the people during the disarming of the police and by the hands of friendly regiments. Nobody responded to the demand to restore the weapons. A revolution teaches you to value a rifle. The organised workers, however, had received only a small part of this blessing.

During the first four months the workers were not in any way confronted with the question of insurrection. The democratic régime of the dual power gave the Bolsheviks an opportunity to win a majority in the soviets. Armed companies of workers formed a constituent part of the militia. This was, however, more form than substance. A rifle in the hands of a worker involves a totally different historic principle than the same rifle in the hands of a student.

The possession of rifles by the workers alarmed the possessing classes from the very beginning, since it shifted the correlation of forces sharply to the advantage of the factory. In Petrograd, where the state apparatus supported by the Central Executive Committee was at first an indubitable power, the Workers' Militia was not much of a menace. In the provincial industrial regions, however, a reinforcement of the Workers' Guard would involve a complete change of all relations, not only within the given plant but all around it. Armed workers would remove managers and engineers, and even arrest them. Upon resolutions adopted by a factory meeting the Red Guard would not infrequently receive pay out of the factory exchequer. In the Urals, with their rich tradition of guerilla fighting in 1905, companies of the Red Guard led by the old veterans established law and order. Armed workers almost unnoticeably dissolved the old government and replaced it with soviet institutions. Sabotage on the part of the property owners and administrators shifted to the workers the task of protecting the plants—the machines, stores, reserves of coal and raw materials. Rôles were here interchanged: the worker would tightly grip his rifle in defence of the factory in which he saw the source of his power. In this way elements of a workers' dictatorship were inaugurated in the factories and districts some time before the proletariat as a whole seized the state power.

Reflecting as always the fright of the property owners, the Compromisers tried with all their might to oppose the arming of the Petrograd workers or reduce it to a minimum. According to Minichev, all the arms in the possession of the Narva district consisted of "fifteen or twenty rifles and a few revolvers." At that time robberies and deeds of violence were increasing in the capital. Alarming rumours were spreading everywhere heralding new disturbances. On the eve of the July demonstration it was generally expected that the district would be set fire to. The workers were hunting for weapons, knocking at all doors and sometimes breaking them in.

The Putilov men brought back a trophy from the demonstration of July 3rd: a machine-gun with five cases of cartridge-belt. "We were happy as children," said Minichev. Certain individual factories were somewhat better armed. According to Lichkov, the workers of his factory had 80 rifles and 20 big revolvers. Riches indeed! Through the Red Guard headquarters they got two machine-guns. They put one in the dining-room, one in the attic. "Our commander," says Lichkov, "was Kocherovsky, and his first assistants were Tomchak, who was killed by White Guards in the October Days near Tsarskoe Selo, and Efimov, who was shot by White bands near Hamburg." These scant words enable us to glance into the factory laboratory where the cadres of the October revolution and the future Red Army were forming, where the Tomchaks and Efimovs were being chosen out, tempered, and were learning to command, and with them those hundreds and thousands of nameless workers who won the power, loyally defended it from its enemy, and fell subsequently on all the fields of battle.

The July Days introduced a sudden change in the situation of the Red Guard. The disarming of the workers was now carried out quite openly—not by admonition but by force. However, what the workers gave up as weapons was mostly old rubbish. All the very valuable guns were carefully concealed. Rifles were distributed among the most reliable members of the party. Machine-guns smeared with tallow were buried in the ground. Detachments of the Guard closed up shop and went underground, closely adhering to the Bolsheviks.

The business of arming the workers was originally placed in the hands of the factory and district committees of the party. It was only after the recovery from the July Days that the Military Organisation of the Bolsheviks, which had formerly worked only in the garrison and at the front, took up the organisation of the Red Guard, providing the workers with military instructors and in some cases with weapons. The prospect of armed insurrection put forward by the party gradually prepared the advanced workers for a new conception of the function of the Red Army. It was no longer a militia of the factories and workers' districts, but the cadres of a future army of insurrection.

During August, fires in the shops and factories multiplied. Every new crisis is preceded by a convulsion of the collective mind, sending forth waves of alarm. The factory and shop committees developed an intense labour of defending the plants from attacks of this kind. Concealed rifles came out into the open. The Kornilov insurrection conclusively legalised the Red Guard. About 25,000 workers were enrolled in companies and armed—by no means fully, to be sure—with rifles, and in part with machine-guns. Workers from the Schlüsselberg powder factory delivered on the Neva a bargeful of hand grenades and explosives—against Kornilov! The compromisist Central Executive Committee refused this gift of the Greeks! The Red Guards of the Vyborg side distributed the gift by night throughout the district.

"Drill in the art of handling a rifle," says the worker Skorinko, "formerly carried on in flats and tenements, was now brought out into the light and air, into the parks, the boulevards." "The shops were turned into camps," says another worker, Rakitov. . . . "The worker would stand at his bench with knapsack on his back and rifle beside him." Very soon all those working in the bomb factory except the old Social Revolutionaries and Mensheviks were enrolled in the Guard. After the whistle all would draw up in the court for drill. "Side by side with a bearded worker you would see a boy apprentice, and both of them attentively listening to the instructor. . . ." Thus while the old czarist army was disintegrating, the foundation of a future Red Army was being laid in the factories.

As soon as the Kornilov danger passed, the Compromisers tried to slow up on the fulfilment of their promises. To the 30,000 Putilov men, for instance, only 500 rifles were given out. Soon the giving out of weapons stopped altogether. The danger now was not from the right, but the left; protection must be sought not among the proletarians but the junkers.

An absence of immediate practical aims combined with the lack of weapons caused an ebbing of workers from the Red Guard, but this only for a short interval. The foundation cadres had been laid down solidly in every plant; firm bonds had been established between the different companies. These cadres now knew from experience that they had serious reserves which could be brought to their feet in case of danger.

The going over of the Soviet to the Bolsheviks again radically changed the position of the Red Guard. From being persecuted or tolerated, it now became an official instrument of the Soviet already reaching for the power. The workers now often found by themselves a way to weapons, asking only the sanction of the Soviet. From the end of September on, and more especially from the 10th of October, the preparation of an insurrection was openly placed on the order of the day. For a month before the revolution in scores of shops and factories of Petrograd an intense military activity was in progress—chiefly rifle practice. By the middle of October the interest in weapons had risen to a new height. In certain factories almost every last man was enrolled in a company.

The workers were more and more impatiently demanding weapons from the Soviet, but the weapons were infinitely fewer than the hands stretched out for them. "I came to Smolny every day," relates the engineer, Kozmin, "and observed how both before and after the sitting of the Soviet, workers and sailors would come up to Trotsky, offering and demanding weapons for the arming of the workers, making reports as to how and where these weapons were distributed, and putting the question: 'But when does business begin?' The impatience was very great. . . ."

Formally the Red Guard remained non-party. But the nearer the final day came, the more prominent were the Bolsheviks. They constituted the nucleus of every company; they controlled the commanding staff and the communications with other plants and districts. The non-party workers and Left Social Revolutionaries followed the lead of the Bolsheviks.

However, even now, on the eve of the insurrection, the ranks of the Guard were not numerous. On the 16th, Uritzky, a member of the Bolshevik Central Committee, estimated the workers' army of Petrograd at 40,000 bayonets. The figure is probably exaggerated. The resources of weapons remained still very limited. In spite of the impotence of the government it was impossible to seize the arsenals without taking the road of open insurrection.

On the 22nd, there was held an all-city conference of the Red Guard, its hundred delegates representing about twenty thousand fighters. The figure is not to be taken too literally—not all those registered had shown any sign of activity. But at a moment of alarm volunteers would pour into the companies in large numbers. Regulations adopted the next day by the conference defined the Red Guard as "an organisation of the armed forces of the proletariat for the struggle against counter-revolution and the defence of the conquests of the revolution." Observe this: that twenty-four hours before the insurrection the task was still defined in terms of defence and not attack.

The basic military unit was the ten; four tens was a squad, three squads, a company; three companies, a battalion. With its commanding staff and special units, a battalion numbered over 500 men. The battalions of a district constituted a division.[1] Big factories like the Putilov had their own divisions. Special technical commands—sappers, bicycles, telegraphers, machine-gunners and artillery men—were recruited in the corresponding factories, and attached to the riflemen—or else acted independently according to the nature of the given task. The entire

1. Otryad.

commanding staff was elective. There was no risk in this: all were volunteers here and knew each other well.

The working women created Red Cross divisions. At the shops manufacturing surgical supplies for the army, lectures were announced on the care of the wounded. "Already in almost all the factories," writes Tatiana Graff, "the working women were regularly on duty as nurses with the necessary first-aid supplies." The organisation was extremely poor in money and technical equipment. By degrees, however, the factory committees sent material for hospital bases and ambulances. During the hours of the revolution these weak nuclei swiftly developed. An imposing technical equipment was suddenly found at their disposal. On the 24th the Vyborg district soviet issued the following order: "Immediately requisition all automobiles. . . . Take an inventory of all first-aid supplies, and have nurses on duty in all clinics."

A growing number of non-party workers were now going out for shooting drill and manœuvres. The number of posts requiring patrol duty was increasing. In the factories sentries were on duty night and day. The headquarters of the Red Guard were transferred to more spacious rooms. On the 23rd at a pipe foundry they held an examination of the Red Guard. An attempt of a Menshevik to speak against the insurrection was drowned in a storm of indignation: Enough, enough! The time for argument is passed! The movement was irresistible. It was seizing even the Mensheviks. "They were enrolling in the Red Guard," says Tatiana Graff, "participating in all duties and even developing some initiative." Skorinko tells how on the 23rd, Social Revolutionaries and Mensheviks, old and young, were fraternising with the Bolsheviks, and how Skorinko himself joyfully embraced his own father, who was a worker in the same factory. The worker Peskovoi says that in his armed detachment, "there were young workers of sixteen and old men of fifty." The variety of ages gave "good cheer and fighting courage."

The Vyborg side was especially fervent in preparing for battle. Having stolen the keys of the drawbridges, studied out the vulnerable points of the district, and elected their military-revolutionary committee, the factory committees established continuous patrols. Kayurov writes with legitimate pride of the Vyborg men: "They were the first to go to battle with the autocracy, they were the first to institute in their district the eight-hour day, the first to come out with a protest against the ten minister-capitalists, the first to raise a protest on July 7th against the persecution of our party, and they were not the last on the decisive day of October 25th." What is true is true!

The history of the Red Guard is to a considerable extent the history of the dual power. With its inner contradictions and conflicts, the dual power helped the workers to create a considerable armed force even before the insurrection. To cast up the general total of the workers' detachments throughout the country at the moment of insurrection is hardly possible, at least at the present moment. In any case, tens and tens of thousands of armed workers constituted the cadres of the insurrection. The reserves were almost inexhaustible.

The organisation of the Red Guard remained, of course, extremely far from complete. Everything was done in haste, in the rough, and not always skilfully. The Red Guard men were in the majority little trained; the communications were badly organised; the supply system was lame; the sanitary corps lagged behind. But the Red Guard, recruited from the most self-sacrificing workers, was burning to carry the job through this time to the end. And that was the decisive thing. The difference between the workers' divisions and the peasant regiments was determined not only by the social ingredients of the two—many of those clumsy soldiers after returning to their villages and dividing the landlords' land will fight desperately against the White Guards, first in guerrilla bands and afterwards in the Red Army. Beside the social difference there existed another more immediate one: Whereas the garrison represented a compulsory assemblage of old soldiers defending themselves against war, the divisions of the Red Guard were newly constructed by individual selection on a new basis and with new aims.

The Military Revolutionary Committee had at its disposal a third kind of armed force: the sailors of the Baltic Fleet. In their social ingredients they are far closer to the workers than the infantry are. There are a good many Petrograd workers among them. The political level of the sailors is incomparably higher than that of the soldiers. In distinction from the none too belligerent reserves who have forgotten all about rifles, these sailors have never stopped actual service.

For active operations it was possible to count firmly upon the armed Bolsheviks, upon the divisions of the Red Guard, upon the advanced group of the sailors, and upon the better preserved regiments. The different elements of this collective army supplemented each other. The numerous garrisons lacked the will to fight. The sailor detachments lacked numbers. The Red Guard lacked skill. The workers together with the sailors contributed energy, daring and enthusiasm. The regiments of the garrison constituted a rather inert reserve, imposing in its numbers and overwhelming in its mass.

In contact as they were from day to day with workers, soldiers and sailors, the Bolsheviks were aware of the deep qualitative difference between the constituent parts of this army they were to lead into battle. The very plan of the insurrection was based to a considerable degree upon a calculation of these differences.

The possessing classes constituted the social force of the other camp. This means that they were its military weakness. These solid people of capital, the press, the pulpit—where and when have they ever fought? They are accustomed to find out by telegraph or telephone the results of the battles which settle their fate. The younger generation, the sons, the students? They were almost all hostile to the October revolution. But a majority of them too stood aside. They stood with their fathers awaiting the outcome of the battle. A number of them afterward joined the officers and junkers—already largely recruited from among the students. The property holders had no popular masses with them. The workers, soldiers, peasants had turned against them. The collapse of the Compromise Parties meant that the possessing classes were left without an army.

In proportion to the significance of railroads in the life of modern states, a large place was occupied in the political calculations of both camps by the question of the railroad workers. Here the hierarchical constitution of the personnel leaves room for an extraordinary political variegation, creating favourable conditions for the diplomats of the Compromisers. The lately formed Vikzhel had kept a considerably more solid root among the clerks and even among the workers than, for instance, the army committees at the front. In the railroads only a minority followed the Bolsheviks, chiefly workers in the stations and yards. According to the report of Schmidt, one of the Bolshevik leaders of the trade union movement, the railroad workers of the Petrograd and Moscow junctions stood closest of all to the party.

But even among the compromisist mass of clerks and workers there was a sharp shift to the left from the date of the railroad strike at the end of September. Dissatisfaction with the Vikzhel, which had compromised itself by talking and wavering, was more and more evident in the lower ranks. Lenin remarked: "The army of railroad and postal clerks continues in a state of sharp conflict with the government." From the standpoint of the immediate tasks of the insurrection that was almost enough.

Things were less favourable in the post and telegraph service. According to the Bolshevik, Boky, "the men in the Post and Telegraph Offices are mostly Kadets." But here too the lower personnel had taken a hostile attitude toward the upper ranks. There was a group of mail carriers ready at a critical moment to seize the Post Office.

It would have been hopeless in any case to try to change the minds of the railroad and postal clerks with words. If the Bolsheviks should prove indecisive, the advantage would remain with the Kadets and the compromisist upper circles. With a decisive revolutionary leadership the lower ranks must inevitably carry with them the intermediate layers, and isolate the upper circles of the Vikzhel. In revolutionary calculations statistics alone are not enough; the co-efficient of living action is also essential.

The enemies of the insurrection in the ranks of the Bolshevik party itself found, however, sufficient ground for pessimistic conclusions. Zinoviev and Kamenev gave warning against an under-estimation of the enemy's forces. "Petrograd will decide, and in Petrograd the enemy has . . . considerable forces: 5,000 junkers, magnificently armed and knowing how to fight, and then the army headquarters, and then the shock troops, and then the Cossacks, and then a considerable part of the garrison, and then a very considerable quantity of artillery spread out fanwise around Petrograd. Moreover the enemy with the help of the Central Executive Committee will almost certainly attempt to bring troops from the front. . . ." The list sounds imposing, but it is only a list. If an army as a whole is a copy of society, then when society openly splits, both armies are copies of the two warring camps. The army of the possessors contained the wormholes of isolation and decay.

The officers crowding the hotels, restaurants and brothels had been hostile to the government ever since the break between Kerensky and Kornilov. Their hatred of the Bolsheviks, however, was infinitely more bitter. As a general rule, the monarchist officers were most active on the side of the government. "Dear Kornilov and Krymov, in what you failed to do perhaps with God's help we shall succeed. . . ." Such was the prayer of officer Sinegub, one of the most valiant defenders of the Winter Palace on the day of the uprising. But in spite of the vast number of officers, only single individuals were really ready to fight. The Kornilov plot had already proven that these completely demoralised officers were not a fighting force.

The junkers were not homogeneous in social make-up, and there was no unanimity among them. Along with hereditary fighters, sons and grandsons of officers, there were many accidental elements gathered up under pressure of war-needs even during the monarchy. The head of an engineering school said to an officer: "I must die with you. . . . We are nobles, you know, and cannot think otherwise." These lucky gentlemen, who did after all succeed in evading a noble death, would speak of the democratic junkers as low-breeds, as muzhiks "with coarse stupid faces." This division into the blue blood and the black penetrated deeply into the junker schools, and it is noticeable that here too those who came out most zealously in defence of the republican government were the very ones who most mourned the loss of the monarchy. The democratic junkers declared that they were not for Kerensky but for the Central Executive Committee. The revolution had first opened the doors of the junker schools to the Jews. And in trying to hold their own with the privileged upper circles, the sons of the Jewish bourgeoisie became extraordinarily warlike against the Bolsheviks. But, alas, this was not enough to save the régime—not even to defend the Winter Palace. The heterogeneousness of these military schools and their complete isolation from the army brought it about that during the critical hours the junkers began to hold meetings. They began to ask questions: How are the Cossacks behaving? Is anybody coming out besides us? Is it worth while anyway to defend the Provisional Government? According to a report of Podvoisky, there were about 120 socialist junkers in the Petrograd military schools at the beginning of October, and of these 42 or 43 were Bolsheviks. "The junkers say that the whole commanding staff of the schools is counter-revolutionary. They are being definitely prepared in case anything happens to put down the insurrection. . . ." The number of socialists, and especially Bolsheviks, was wholly insignificant, but they made it possible for Smolny to know everything of importance that went on among the junkers. In addition to that, the location of the military schools was very disadvantageous. The junkers were sandwiched in among the barracks, and although they spoke scornfully of the soldiers, they looked upon them with a great deal of dread.

The junkers had plenty of ground for caution. Thousands of hostile eyes were watching them from the neighbouring barracks and the workers' districts. This observation was the more effective in that every school had its soldier group, neutral in words but in reality inclining toward the insurrection. The school storerooms were in the hands of non-combatant soldiers. "Those scoundrels," writes an officer of the Engineering School, "not satisfied with losing the key to the storeroom so that I had to give order to break in the door, also removed the breech-blocks from the machine-guns and hid them somewhere." In these circumstances you could hardly expect miracles of heroism from the junkers.

But would not a Petrograd insurrection be threatened from without, from the neighbouring garrisons? In the last days of its life the monarchy had never ceased to put its hope in that small military ring surrounding the capital. The monarchy had missed its guess, but how would it go this time? To guarantee conditions excluding every possible danger would have been to make the very insurrection unnecessary. After all, its aim was to break down the obstacles which could not be dissolved politically. Everything could not be calculated in advance, but all that could be, was.

Early in October a conference of the soviets of Petrograd province was held in Kronstadt. Delegates from the garrisons of the environs of the capital—Gatchina, Tsarskoe, Krasnoe, Oranienbaum, Kronstadt itself—took the very highest note set by the tuning-fork of the Baltic sailors. Their resolution was adhered to by the deputies of Petrograd province. The muzhiks were veering sharply through the Left Social Revolutionaries toward the Bolsheviks.

At a conference of the Central Committee on the 16th, a party worker in the province, Stepanov, drew a somewhat variegated picture of the state of the forces, but nevertheless with a clear predominance of Bolshevik colours. In Sestroretsk and Kolpino the workers are under arms; their mood is militant. In Novy Peterhoff the work in the regiment has fallen off; the regiment is disorganised. In Krasnoe Selo the 176th regiment is Bolshevik (the same regiment which patrolled the Tauride Palace on July 4th), the 172nd is on the side of the Bolsheviks, "and, besides, there is cavalry there." In Luga the garrison of 30,000, after swinging over to the Bolsheviks, is wavering in part; the soviet is still defensist. In Gdov the regiment is Bolshevik. In Kronstadt the mood has declined; the garrison boiled over during the preceding months; the better part of the sailors are in the active fleet. In Schlüsselburg, within 60 versts of Petrograd, the soviet long ago became the sole power; the workers of the powder factory are ready at any moment to support the capital.

In combination with the results of that Kronstadt conference of soviets, this information about the first line reserves may be considered entirely encouraging. The radiation of the February insurrection had been sufficient to dissolve discipline over a wide area. And it was now possible to look with confidence upon the near-by garrisons, their conditions being adequately known in advance.

The troops of Finland and the Northern front were among the second line reserves. Here conditions were still more favourable. The work of Smilga, Antonov, Dybenko had produced invaluable results. Along with the garrison of Helsingfors the fleet had become a sovereign in Finnish territory. The government had no more power there. The two Cossack divisions quartered in Helsingfors—Kornilov had intended them for a blow at Petrograd—had come in close contact with the sailors and were supporting the Bolsheviks, or the Left Social Revolutionaries, who in the Baltic Fleet were becoming less and less distinguishable from Bolsheviks.

Helsingfors was extending its hand to the sailors of the Reval naval base, whose attitude up to that time had been indefinite. The Congress of Soviets of the Northern Region, in which also apparently the Baltic Fleet had taken the initiative, had united the soviets of the garrisons surrounding Petrograd in such a wide circle that it took in Moscow on one side and Archangel on the other. "In this manner," writes Antonov, "the idea was realised of armouring the capital of the revolution against possible attacks from Kerensky's troops." Smilga returned from the Congress to Helsingfors to organise a special detachment of sailors, infantry and artillery to be sent to Petrograd at the first signal. The Finland flank of the Petrograd insurrection was thus protected to the last degree. On this side no blow was to be expected, only strong help. On other portions of the front, too, things were wholly favourable—at least far more favourable than the most optimistic of the Bolsheviks in those days imagined. During October committee elections were held throughout the army, and everywhere they showed a sharp swing to the

Bolsheviks. In the corps quartered near Dvinsk the "old reasonable soldiers" were completely snowed under in the elections to the regimental and company committees; their places were taken by "gloomy, grey creatures . . . with angry piercing eyes and wolfish snouts." The same thing happened in other sectors. "Committee elections are in progress everywhere, and everywhere only Bolsheviks and defeatists are elected." The governmental commissars began to avoid making trips to their units.

"Their situation is now no better than ours." We are quoting Baron Budberg. Two cavalry regiments of his corps, the Hussar and Ural Cossacks, who remained longest of all in the control of the commanders, and had not refused to put down mutinous units, suddenly changed colour and demanded "that they be relieved of the function of punitive troops and gendarmes." The threatening sense of this warning was clear to the Baron and to everybody else. "You can't command a flock of hyenas, jackals and sheep by playing on a violin," he wrote. "The only salvation lies in a mass application of the hot iron. . . ." And here follows the tragic confession: ". . . a thing which we haven't got and is nowhere to be gotten."

If we do not cite similar testimony about other corps and divisions, it is only because their chiefs were not as observant as Budberg, or they did not keep diaries, or these diaries have not yet come to light. But the corps standing near Dvinsk was distinguished in nothing but the trenchant style of its commander from the other corps of the 5th Army, which in its turn was but little in advance of the other armies.

The compromisist committee of the 5th Army, which had long been hanging in the air, continued to send telegraphic threats to Petrograd to the effect that it would restore order in the rear with the bayonet. "All that was mere braggadocio and hot air," writes Budberg. The committee was actually living its last days. On the 23rd it failed of re-election. The president of the new Bolshevik committee was Doctor Skliansky, a magnificent young organiser who soon developed his talent widely in the work of creating the Red Army, and who died subsequently an accidental death while canoeing on one of the American lakes.

The assistant of the government Commissar of the Northern front reports to the War Minister on the 22nd of October that the ideas of Bolshevism are making great headway in the army, that the mass wants peace, and that even the artillery which has held out to the very last moment has become "hospitable to defeatist propaganda." This too is no unimportant symptom. "The Provisional Government has no authority"—reports its own direct agent three days before the revolution.

To be sure, the Military Revolutionary Committee did not then know of all these documents. But what it did know was amply sufficient. On the 23rd, representatives of various units at the front filed past the Petrograd Soviet and demanded peace. Otherwise, they answered, they would march to the rear and "destroy all the parasites who want to keep on fighting for another ten years." Seize the power, the front men said to the Soviet, "the trenches will support you."

In the more remote and backward fronts, the South-western and Rumanian, Bolsheviks were still rare specimens, curiosities. But the mood of the soldiers here was the same as elsewhere. Efgenia Bosh tells how in the 2nd Corps of the Guards, quartered in the vicinity of Zhmerinka, among 60,000 soldiers, there was one young communist and two sympathisers. This did not prevent the corps from coming out in support of the insurrection in the October days.

To the very last hour the government circles rested their hope in the Cossacks. But the less blind among the politicians of the right camp understood that here too things were in a very bad way. The Cossack officers were Kornilovists almost to a man. The rank-and-file were tending more and more to the left. In the government they did not understand this, imagining that the coolness of the Cossack regiments to the Winter Palace was caused by injured feelings about Kaledin. In the long run, however, it became clear even to the Minister of Justice, Maliantovich, that "only the Cossack officers" were supporters of Kaledin. The rank-and-file Cossacks, like all the soldiers, were simply going Bolshevik.

Of that front which in the early days of March had kissed the hands and feet of liberal priests, had carried Kadet ministers on its shoulders, got drunk on the speeches of Kerensky, and believed that the Bolsheviks were German agents—of that there was nothing left. Those rosy illusions had been drowned in the mud of the trenches, which the soldiers refused to go on kneading with their leaky boots. "The denouement is approaching," wrote Budberg on the very day of the Petrograd insurrection, "and there can be no doubt of its outcome. On our front there is not one single unit . . . which would not be in the control of the Bolsheviks."

Chapter VII

The Conquest of the Capital

All is changed and yet all remains as before. The revolution has shaken the country, deepened the split, frightened some, embittered others, but not yet wiped out a thing or replaced it. Imperial St. Petersburg seems drowned in a sleepy lethargy rather than dead. The revolution has stuck little red flags in the hands of the cast-iron monuments of the monarchy. Great red streamers are hanging down the fronts of the government buildings. But the palaces, the ministries, the headquarters, seem to be living a life entirely apart from those red banners, tolerably faded, moreover, by the autumn rains. The two-headed eagles with the sceptre of empire have been torn down where possible, but oftener draped or hastily painted over. They seem to be lurking there. All the old Russia is lurking, its jaws set in rage.

The slight figures of the militia-men at the street corners remind one of the revolution that has wiped out the old "Pharaohs," who used to stand there like live monuments. Moreover Russia has now for almost two months been called a republic. And the Czar's family is in Tobolsk. Yes, the February whirlwind has left its traces. But the czarist generals remain generals, the senators senatorialise, the privy councillors defend their dignity, the Table of Precedence is still in effect. Coloured hatbands and cockades recall the bureaucratic hierarchy; yellow buttons with an eagle still distinguish the student. And yet more important—the landlords are still landlords, no end of the war is in sight, the Allied diplomats are impudently jerking official Russia along on a string.

All remains as before and yet nobody knows himself. The aristocratic quarters feel that they have been moved out into the backyard; the quarters of the liberal bourgeoisie have moved nearer the aristocracy. From being a patriotic myth, the Russian people have become an awful reality. Everything is billowing and shaking under foot. Mysticism flares up with sharpened force in those circles which not long ago were making fun of the superstitions of the monarchy.

Brokers, lawyers, ballerinas are cursing the oncoming eclipse of public morals. Faith in the Constituent Assembly is evaporating day by day. Gorky in his newspaper is prophesying the approaching downfall of culture. The flight from raving and hungry Petrograd to a more peaceful and well-fed province, on the increase ever since the July Days, now becomes a stampede. Respectable families who have not succeeded in getting away from the capital, try in vain to insulate themselves from reality behind stone wall and under iron roof. But the echoes of the storm penetrate on every side: through the market, where everything is getting dear and nothing to be had; through the respectable press, which is turning into one yelp of hatred and fear; through the seething streets where from time to time shootings are to be heard under the windows; and finally through the back entrance, through the servants, who are no longer humbly submissive. It is here that the revolution strikes home to the most sensitive spot. That obstreperousness of the household slaves destroys utterly the stability of the family régime.

Nevertheless the everyday routine defends itself with all its might. School-boys are still studying the old text-books, functionaries drawing up the same useless papers, poets scribbling the verses that nobody reads, nurses telling the fairy-tales about Ivan Czarevich. The nobility's and merchants' daughters, coming in from the provinces, are studying music or hunting husbands. The same old cannon on the wall of the Peter and Paul fortress continues to announce the noon hour. A new ballet is going on in the Mariinsky Theatre, and the Minister of Foreign Affairs, Tereshchenko, stronger on choreography than diplomacy, finds time, we may assume, to admire the steel toes of the ballerina and thus demonstrate the stability of the régime.

The remnants of the old banquet are still very plentiful and everything can be had for big money. The Guard officers still click their spurs accurately and go after adventures. Wild parties are in progress in the private dining-rooms of expensive restaurants. The shutting-off of the electric lights at midnight does not prevent the flourishing of gambling-clubs where champagne sparkles by candlelight, where illustrious peculators swindle no less illustrious German spies, where monarchist conspirators call the bets of Semitic smugglers, and where the astronomical figures of the stakes played for indicate both the scale of debauchery and the scale of inflation.

Can it be that a mere tram-car, run-down, dirty, dilatory, draped with clusters of people, leads from this St. Petersburg in its death-agony into the workers' quarters so passionately and tensely alive with a new hope? The blue-and-gold cupola of Smolny Convent announces from afar the headquarters of the insurrection. It is on the edge of the city where the tram-line ends and the Neva describes a sharp turn south, separating the centre of the capital from the suburbs. That long grey three-story building, an educative barrack for the daughters of the nobility, is now the stronghold of the soviets. Its long echoing corridors seem to have been made for teaching the laws of perspective. Over the doors of many of the rooms along the corridors little enamelled tablets are still preserved: "Teacher's Room," "Third Grade," "Fourth Grade," "Grade Supervisor." But alongside the old tablets, or covering them, sheets of paper have been tacked up as best they might, bearing the mysterious hieroglyphics of the revolution: Tz-K P-S-R, S-D Mensheviki, S-D-Bolsheviki, Left S-R, Anarchist-Communists, Despatching Room of the Tz-I-K, etc., etc. The observant John Reed notices a placard on the walls: "Comrades, for the sake of your own health, observe cleanliness." Alas, nobody observes cleanliness, not even nature. October Petrograd is living under a canopy of rain. The streets, long unswept, are dirty. Enormous puddles are standing in the court of Smolny. The mud is carried into the corridors and halls by the soldiers' boots. But nobody is looking down now underfoot. All are looking forward.

Smolny is more and more firmly and imperiously giving commands, for the passionate sympathy of the masses is lifting her up. However, the central leadership grasps directly only the topmost links of that revolutionary system which as a connected whole is destined to achieve the change. The most important processes are taking place below, and somehow of their own accord. The factories and barracks are the chief forges of history in these days and nights. As in February, the Vyborg district focuses the basic forces of the revolution. But it has to-day a thing it lacked in February—its own powerful organisation open and universally recognised. From the dwellings, the factory lunch-rooms, the clubs, the barracks, all threads lead to the house numbered 33 Samsonevsky Prospect, where are located the district committee of the Bolsheviks, the Vyborg Soviet, and the military headquarters. The district militia is fusing with the Red Guard. The district is wholly in the control of the workers. If the government should raid Smolny, the Vyborg district alone could re-establish a centre and guarantee the further offensive.

The denouement was approaching close, but the ruling circles thought, or pretended to think, that they had no special cause for anxiety. The British Embassy, which had its own reasons for following events in Petrograd with some attention, received, according to the Russian ambassador in London, reliable information about the coming insurrection. To the anxious inquiries of Buchanan at the inevitable diplomatic luncheon, Tereshchenko replied with warm assurance: "Nothing of the kind" is possible; the government has the reins firmly in hand. The Russian Embassy in London found out about the revolution in Petrograd from the despatches of a British telegraph agency.

The mine owner, Auerbach, paying a visit during those days to the deputy-minister, Palchinsky, inquired in passing—after a conversation about more serious matters—as to the "dark clouds on the political horizon." He received a most reassuring answer: The next storm in a series, and nothing more; it will pass over and all will be clear—"sleep well." Palchinsky himself was going to pass one or two sleepless nights before he got arrested.

The more unceremoniously Kerensky treated the Compromise leaders, the less did he doubt that in the hour of danger they would come punctually to his aid. The weaker the Compromisers grew, the more carefully did they surround themselves with an atmosphere of illusion. Exchanging words of neutral encouragement between their Petrograd turrets and their upper-crust organisations in the provinces and the front, the Mensheviks and Social-Revolutionaries created a simulacrum of public opinion, and thus disguising their own impotence, fooled not so much their enemy as themselves.

The cumbersome and good-for-nothing state apparatus, representing a combination of March socialist with czarist bureaucrat, was perfectly accommodated to the task of self-deception. The half-baked March socialist dreaded to appear to the bureaucrat a not wholly mature statesman. The bureaucrat dreaded lest he show a lack of respect to the new ideas. Thus was created a web of official lies, in which generals, district attorneys, newspaper-men, commissars, aides-de-camp, lied the more, the nearer they stood to the seats of power. The commander of the Petrograd military district made comforting reports, for the reason that Kerensky, faced by an uncomforting reality, had great need of them.

The traditions of the dual power worked in the same direction. Were not the current orders of the military headquarters, when countersigned by the Military Revolutionary Committee, implicitly obeyed? The patrolling squads throughout the city were filled out by the troops of the garrison in the usual order—and we must add, it had been long since the troops had done their patrol duty with such zeal as now. Discontent among the masses? But "slaves in revolt" are always discontented. Only the scum of the garrison and the workers' districts will take part in mutinous attempts. The soldiers' sections are against headquarters? But the military department of the Central Executive Committee is for Kerensky. The whole organised democracy, with the exception of the Bolsheviks, supports the government. Thus the rosy March nimbus had turned into a grey vapour, hiding the actual traits of things.

It was only after the break between Smolny and headquarters that the government tried to adopt a more serious attitude toward the situation. There is, of course, no immediate danger, they said, but this time we must avail ourselves of the opportunity to put an end to the Bolsheviks. Besides, the bourgeois Allies were bringing every pressure to bear on the Winter Palace. On the night of the 24th the government summoned up its courage and passed a resolution: to institute legal proceedings against the Military Revolutionary Committee; to shut down the Bolshevik papers advocating insurrection; to summon reliable military detachment from the environs and from the front. The proposal to arrest the Military Revolutionary Committee as a body, although adopted in principle, was postponed in execution. For so large an undertaking, they decided, it was necessary to secure in advance the support of the Pre-Parliament.

The rumour of the government's decision spread immediately through the town. In the building of the main headquarters alongside the Winter Palace, the soldiers of the Pavlovsky regiment, one of the most reliable units of the Military Revolutionary Committee, were on sentry duty during the night of the 24th. Conversations went on in their presence about summoning the junkers, about lifting the bridges, about arrests. All that the Pavlovtsi managed to hear and remember they immediately passed on to Smolny. Those in the revolutionary centre did not always know how to make use of the communications of this self-constituted Intelligence Service. But it fulfilled an invaluable function. The workers and soldiers of the whole city were made aware of the intentions of the enemy, and reinforced in their readiness to resist.

Early in the morning the authorities began their preparations for aggressive action. The military schools of the capital were ordered to make ready for battle. The cruiser *Aurora* moored in the Neva, its crew favourable to the Bolsheviks, was ordered to put out and join the rest of the fleet. Military detachments were called in from neighbouring points: a battalion of shock troops from Tsarskoe Selo, the junkers from Oranienbaum, the artillery from Pavlovsk. The headquarters of the Northern front was asked to send reliable troops to the capital immediately. In the way of direct measures of military precaution, the following orders were given: to increase the guard of the Winter Palace; to raise the bridges over the Neva; to have all automobiles inspected by the junkers; to cut Smolny out of the telephone system. The Minister of Justice, Maliantovich, gave an order for the immediate arrest of those Bolsheviks released under bail who had again brought themselves to attention by anti-governmental activity. This blow was aimed primarily at Trotsky. The fickleness of the times is well illustrated by the fact that Maliantovich—as also his predecessor, Zarudny—had been Trotsky's defence counsel in the trial of the St. Petersburg Soviet of 1905. Then, too, it had been a question of the leadership of the Soviet. The indictments were identical in the two cases, except that the former defenders when they became accusers, added the little point about German gold.

Headquarters developed a particularly feverish activity in the sphere of typography. Document followed document. No coming-out will be permitted; the guilty will be held strictly responsible; detachments of the garrison not to leave their barracks without orders from headquarters; "all commissars of the Petrograd Soviet to be removed"; their illegal activities to be investigated "with a view to court martial." In these formidable orders it was not indicated who was to carry them out or how. Under threat of personal liability the commander demanded that owners of automobiles place them at the disposal of headquarters "with a view of preventing unlawful seizures," but nobody moved a finger in response.

The Central Executive Committee was also prolific of warnings and forbiddings. And the peasant executive committee, the city duma, the central committees of the Mensheviks and Social-Revolutionaries followed in its steps. All these institutions were sufficiently rich in literary resources. In the proclamations which plastered the walls and fences, the talk was invariably about a handful of lunatics, about the danger of bloody encounters, about the inevitability of counter-revolution.

At five-thirty in the morning a government commissar with a detachment of junkers showed up at the Bolshevik printing-plant, and after manning the exits, presented an order of headquarters for the immediate suppression of the central organ and the soldiers' paper.—What? Headquarters? Does that still exist? No orders are recognised here without the sanction of the Military Revolution Committee. But that did not help. The stereotypes were smashed, the building sealed. The government had scored its first success.

A worker and a working-girl from the Bolshevik printing-plant ran panting to Smolny and there found Podvoisky and Trotsky. If the Committee would give them a guard against the junkers, the workers would bring out the paper. A form was soon found for the first answer to the government offensive. An order was issued to the Litovsky regiment to send a company immediately to the defence of the workers' press. The messengers from the printing-plant insisted that the 6th battalion of sappers be also ordered out: these were near neighbours and loyal friends. Telephonograms were immediately sent to the two addresses. The Litovtsi and the sappers came out without delay. The seals were torn from the building, the moulds again poured, and the work went on. With a few hours' delay the newspaper suppressed by the government came out under protection of the troops of a committee which was itself liable to arrest. That was insurrection. That is how it developed.

During this same time the cruiser *Aurora* had addressed a question to Smolny: Shall we go to sea or remain in the Neva? The very same sailors who had guarded the Winter Palace against Kornilov in August were now burning to settle accounts with Kerensky. The government order was promptly countermanded by the Committee and the crew received Order No. 1218: "In case of an attack on the Petrograd garrison by the counter-revolutionary forces, the cruiser *Aurora* is to protect herself with tugs, steam-boats, and cutters." The cruiser enthusiastically carried out this order, for which it had only been waiting.

These two acts of resistance, suggested by workers and sailors, and carried out, thanks to the sympathy of the garrison, with complete impunity, became political events of capital importance. The last remnants of the fetishism of authority crumbled to dust. "It became instantly clear," says one of the participants, "that the job was done!" If not yet done, it was at least proving much simpler than anyone had imagined yesterday.

An attempt to suppress the papers, a resolution to prosecute the Military Revolutionary Committee, an order removing commissars, the cutting-out of Smolny's telephones—these pinpricks were just sufficient to convict the government of preparing a counter-revolutionary *coup d'état*. Although an insurrection can win on the offensive, it develops better, the more it looks like self-defence. A piece of official sealing-wax on the door of the Bolshevik editorial-rooms—as a military measure that is not much. But what a superb signal for battle! Telephonograms to all districts and units of the garrison announced the event: "The enemy of the people took the offensive during the night. The Military Revolutionary Committee is leading the resistance to the assault of the conspirators." The conspirators—these were the institutions of the official government. From the pen of revolutionary conspirators this term came as a surprise, but it wholly corresponded to the situation and to the feelings of the masses. Crowded out of all its positions, compelled to undertake a belated defence, incapable of mobilising the necessary forces, or even finding out whether it had such forces, the government had developed a scattered, unthought-out, unco-ordinated action, which in the eyes of the masses inevitably looked like a malevolent attempt. The Committee's telephonograms gave the command: "Make the regiment ready for battle and await further orders." That was the voice of a sovereign power. The commissars of the Committee, themselves liable to removal by the government, continued with redoubled confidence to remove those whom they thought it necessary to remove.

The *Aurora* in the Neva meant not only an excellent fighting unit in the service of the insurrection, but a radio-station ready for use. Invaluable advantage! The sailor Kurkov has remembered: "We got word from Trotsky to broadcast . . . that the counter-revolution had taken the offensive." Here too the defensive formulation concealed a summons to insurrection addressed to the whole country. The garrisons guarding the approaches to Petrograd were ordered by radio from the *Aurora* to hold up the counter-revolutionary echelons, and, in case admonitions were inadequate, to employ force. All revolutionary organisations were placed under obligation "to sit continually, accumulating all possible information as to the plans and activities of the conspirators." There was no lack of proclamations, however, the word was not divorced from the deed, but was a comment on it.

Somewhat belatedly the Military Revolutionary Committee undertook a more serious fortification of Smolny. In leaving the building at three o'clock on the night of the 24th, John Reed noticed machine-guns at the entrances and strong patrols guarding the gates and the adjacent street corners. The patrols had been reinforced the day before by a company of the Litovsky regiment and a company of machine-gunners with twenty-four machine-guns. During the day the guard increased continually. "In the Smolny region," writes Shliapnikov, "I saw a familiar picture, reminding me of the first days of the February revolution around the Tauride Palace." The same multitude of soldiers, workers and weapons of all kinds. Innumerable cords of firewood had been piled up in the court—a perfect cover against rifle-fire. Motor-trucks were bringing up foodstuffs and munitions. "All Smolny," says Raskolnikov, "was converted into an armed camp. Cannon were in position out in front of the columns. Machine-guns alongside them. . . . Almost on every step those same 'maxims,' looking like toy-cannon. And through all the corridors . . . the swift, loud, happy tramp of workers, soldiers, sailors and agitators." Sukhanov, accusing the organisers of the insurrection—not without foundation—of insufficient military precaution, writes: "Only now, in the afternoon and evening of the 24th, did they begin to bring up armed detachments of Red Guards and soldiers to Smolny to defend the headquarters of the insurrection. . . . By the evening of the 24th the defence of Smolny began to look like something."

This matter is not without importance. In Smolny, whence the compromisist Executive Committee had managed to steal away to the headquarters of the government staff, there were now concentrated the heads of all the revolutionary organisations led by the Bolsheviks. Here assembled on that day the all-important meeting of the Central Committee of the Bolsheviks to take the final decision before striking the blow. Eleven members were present. Lenin had not yet turned up from his refuge in the Vyborg district. Zinoviev also was absent from the session. According to the temperamental expression of Dzerzhinsky, he was "hiding and taking no part in the party work."

Kamenev, on the other hand, although sharing the views of Zinoviev, was very active in the headquarters of the insurrection. Stalin was not present at the session. Generally speaking he did not appear at Smolny, spending his time in the editorial office of the central organ. The session, as always, was held under the chairmanship of Sverdlov. The official minutes of the session are scant, but they indicate everything essential. For characterising the leading participants in the revolution, and the distribution of functions among them, they are irreplaceable.

It was a queston of taking full possession of Petrograd in the next twenty-four hours. That meant to seize those political and technical institutions which were still in the hands of the government. The Congress of Soviets must hold its session under the Soviet power. The practical measures of the nocturnal assault had been worked out, or were being worked out, by the Military Revolutionary Committee and the Military Organisations of the Bolsheviks. The Central Committee was to underline the final points.

First of all a proposal of Kamenev was adopted: "To-day no member of the Central Committee can leave Smolny without a special resolution." It was decided over and above that, to keep on duty here members of the Petrograd Committee of the party. The minutes read further: "Trotsky proposes that they place at the disposal of the Military Revolutionary Committee two members of the Central Committee for the purpose of establishing communications with the postal and telegraph workers and the railroad workers; a third member to keep the Provisional Government under observation." It was resolved to delegate Dzerzhinsky to the postal and telegraph workers, Bubnov to the railroad workers. At first, and obviously at Sverdlov's suggestion, it was proposed to allot the watch over the Provisional Government to Podvoisky. The minutes read: "Objections to Podvoisky; Sverdlov is appointed." Miliutin, who passed as an economist, was appointed to organise the supply of food for the period of the insurrection. Negotiations with the Left Social-Revolutionaries were entrusted to Kamenev, who had the reputation of a skilful although too yielding parliamentary. "Yielding," of course, only from a Bolshevik criterion. "Trotsky proposes"—we read further—"that a reserve headquarters be established in the Peter and Paul fortress, and that one member of the Central Committee be sent there for that purpose." It was resolved: "To appoint Lashevich and Blagonravov for general observation; to commission Sverdlov to keep in continual touch with the fortress." Further: "To supply all members of the Central Committee with passes to the fortress."

Along party lines all threads were held in the hands of Sverdlov, who knew the cadres of the party as no one else did. He kept Smolny in touch with the party apparatus, supplied the Military Revolutionary Committee with the necessary workers, and was summoned into the Committee for counsel at all critical moments. Since the Committee had a too broad, and to some extent fluid, membership, the more conspirative undertakings were carried out through the heads of the Military Organisation of the Bolsheviks, or through Sverdlov, who was the unofficial but all the more real "general secretary" of the October insurrection.

The Bolshevik delegates arriving in those days for the Soviet Congress would come first into the hands of Sverdlov, and would not be left for one unnecessary hour without something to do. On the 24th there were already two or three hundred provincial delegates in Petrograd, and the majority of them were included one way or another in the mechanics of the insurrection. At two o'clock in the afternoon, they assembled at a caucus in Smolny to hear a report from the Central Committee of the party. There were waverers among them who, like Zinoviev and Kamenev, preferred a waiting policy; there were also newcomers who were merely not sufficiently reliable. There could be no talk of expounding before this caucus the whole plan of the insurrection. Whatever is said at a large meeting inevitably gets abroad. It was still impossible even to throw off the defensive envelope of the attack without creating confusion in the minds of certain units of the garrison. But it was necessary to make the delegates understand that a decisive struggle had already begun, and that it would remain only for the Congress to crown it.

Referring to recent articles of Lenin, Trotsky demonstrated that "a conspiracy does not contradict the principles of Marxism," if objective relations make an insurrection possible and inevitable. "The physical barrier on the road to power must be overcome by a blow. . . ." However, up till now the policy of the Military Revolutionary Committee has not gone beyond the policy of self-defence. Of course this self-defence must be understood in a sufficiently broad sense. To assure the publication of the Bolshevik press with the help of armed forces, or to retain the *Aurora* in the waters of the Neva—"Comrades, is that not self-defence?—It is defence!" If the government intends to arrest us, we have machine-guns on the roof of Smolny in preparation for such an event. "That also, comrades, is a measure of defence." But how about the Provisional Government? says one of the written questions. What if Kerensky tries not to submit to the Congress of Soviets? The spokesman replied: If Kerensky should attempt not to submit to the Congress of Soviets, then the resistance of the government would have created "not a political but a police question." That was in essence almost exactly what happened.

At that moment Trotsky was called out to consult with a deputation just arrived from the city duma. In the capital, to be sure, it was still quiet, but alarming rumours were on foot. The mayor put these questions: Does the Soviet intend to make an insurrection, and how about keeping order in the city? And what will become of the duma itself if it does not recognise the revolution? These respected gentlemen wanted to know too much. The answer was: The question of power is to be decided by the Congress of Soviets. Whether this will lead to an armed struggle "depends not so much upon the soviets as upon those who, in conflct with the unanimous will of the people, are retaining the state of power in their hands." If the Congress declines the power, the Petrograd Soviet will submit. But the government itself is obviously seeking a conflict. Orders have been issued for the arrest of the Military Revolutionary Committee. The workers and soldiers can only reply with ruthless resistance. What about looting and violence from criminal gangs? An order of the Committee issued to-day reads: "At the first attempt of criminal elements to bring about disturbances, looting, knifing or shooting on the streets of Petrograd, the criminals will be wiped off the face of the earth." As to the city duma, it will be possible in case of a conflict to employ constitutional methods—dissolution and a new election. The delegation went away dissatisfied. But what had they as a matter of fact expected?

That official visit of the City Fathers to the camp of the rebels was only too candid a demonstration of the impotence of the ruling groups. "Remember, comrades," said Trotsky upon returning to the Bolshevik caucus, "that a few weeks ago when we won the majority, we were only a trade-name—without a printing press, without a treasury, without departments—and now the city duma sends a deputation to the arrested Military Revolutionary Committee" for information as to the destiny of the city and the state.

The Peter and Paul fortress, won over politically only yesterday, is to-day completely taken possession of by the Military Revolutionary Committee. The machine-gun crew, the most revolutionary unit, is being brought into fighting trim. A mighty work of cleaning the Colt machine-guns is in progress—there are eighty of them. Machine-guns are set up on the fortress wall to command the quay and the Troitsky bridge. The sentry guard at the gates is reinforced. Patrols are sent out into the surrounding districts. But in the heat of these morning hours it suddenly becomes known that within the fortress itself the situation is not assured. The uncertainty lies in a bicycle battalion. Recruited, like the cavalry, from well-to-do and rich peasants, the bicycle men, coming from the intermediate city layers, constituted a most conservative part of the army. A theme for idealistic psychologists: Let a man find himself, in distinction from others, on top of two wheels with a chain—at least in a poor country like Russia—and his vanity begins to swell out like his tyres. In America it takes an automobile to produce this effect.

Brought in from the front to put down the July movement, the bicycle battalion had zealously stormed the Palace of Kshesinskaia, and afterward been installed in Peter and Paul as one of the most reliable detachments. It was learned that at yesterday's meeting which settled the fate of the fortress, the bicycle men had not been present. The old discipline still held in the battalion to such an extent that the officers had succeeded in keeping the soldiers from going into the fortress court. Counting on these bicycle men, the commandant of the fortress held his chin high, frequently got into telephone connection with Kerensky's headquarters, and even professed to be about to arrest the Bolshevik commissar. The situation must not be left indefinite for an extra minute. Upon an order from Smolny, Blagonravov confronts the enemy: the colonel is subjected to house arrest, the telephones are removed from all officers' apartments. The government staff calls up excitedly to know why the commandant is silent, and in general what is going on in the fortress. Blagonravov respectfully reports over the telephone that the fortress henceforward fulfils only the orders of the Military Revolutionary Committee, with which it behoves the government in the future to get in connection.

All the troops of the fortress garrison accepted the arrest of the commandant with complete satisfaction, but the bicycle men bore themselves evasively. What lay concealed behind their sulky silence: a hidden hostility or the last waverings? "We decided to hold a special meeting for the bicycle men," writes Blagonravov, "and invite our best agitational forces, and above all Trotsky, who had enormous authority and influence over the soldier masses." At four o'clock in the afternoon the whole battalion met in the neighbouring building of the Cirque Moderne. As governmental opponent, Quartermaster-General Poradelov, considered to be a Social-Revolutionary, took the floor. His objections were so cautious as to seem equivocal; and so much the more destructive was the attack of the Committee's representatives. This supplementary oratorical battle for the Peter and Paul fortress ended as might have been foreseen: by all voices except thirty the battalion supported the resolution of Trotsky. One more of the potential bloody conflicts was settled before the fighting and without bloodshed. That was the October insurrection. Such was its style.

It was now possible to rely upon the fortress with tranquil confidence. Weapons were given out from the arsenal without hindrance. At Smolny, in the Factory and Shop Committee room, delegates from the plants stood in line to get orders for rifles. The capital had seen many queues during the war years —now it saw rifle-queues for the first time. Trucks from all the districts of the city were driving up to the arsenal. "You would hardly have recognised the Peter and Paul fortress," writes the worker Skorinko. "It's renowned silence was broken by the chugging automobiles, shouts, and the creak of wagons. There was a special bustle in the storehouses. . . . Here too they led by us the first prisoners, officers and junkers."

The meeting in the Cirque Moderne had another result. The bicycle men who had been guarding the Winter Palace since July withdrew, announcing that they would no longer consent to protect the government. That was a heavy blow. The bicycle men had to be replaced by junkers. The military support of the government was more and more reducing itself to the officers' schools—a thing which not only narrowed it extremely, but also conclusively revealed its social constitution.

The workers of the Putilov wharf—and not they alone— were insistently urging Smolny to disarm the junkers. If this measure had been taken after careful preparation, in co-operation with the non-combatant units of the schools, on the night of the 25th, the capture of the Winter Palace would have offered no difficulties whatever. If the junkers had been disarmed even on the night of the 26th, after the capture of the Winter Palace, there would have been no attempted counter-insurrection on the 29th of October. But the leaders were still in many directions revealing a "magnanimous spirit"—in reality an excess of optimistic confidence—and did not always listen attentively enough to the sober voice of the lower ranks. In this Lenin's absence, too, was felt. The masses had to correct these omissions and mistakes, with unnecessary losses on both sides. In a serious struggle there is no worse cruelty than to be magnanimous at an inopportune time.

At an afternoon session of the Pre-Parliament, Kerensky sings his swan-song. During recent days, he says, the population of Russia, and especially of the capital, has been in a constant state of alarm. "Calls for insurrection appear daily in the Bolshevik papers." The orator quotes the articles of the wanted state criminal, Vladimir Ulianov Lenin. The quotations are brilliant and irrefutably prove that the above-named individual is inciting to insurrection. And when? At a moment when the government is just taking up the question of transferring the land to the peasant committees, and of measures to bring the war to an end. The authorities have so far made no haste to put down the conspirators, wishing to give them the opportunity to correct their own mistakes. "That is just what is wrong!" comes from the section where Miliukov is leader. But Kerensky is unabashed. "I prefer in general," he says, "that a government should act more slowly, and thus more correctly, and at the necessary moment more decisively." From those lips the words have a strange sound! At any rate: "All days of grace are now past"; the Bolsheviks have not only not repented, but they have called out two companies, and are independently distributing weapons and cartridges. This time the government intends to put an end to the lawlessness of the rabble. "I choose my words deliberately: rabble." This insult to the people is greeted on the right with loud applause. He, Kerensky, has already given orders, he says, for the necessary arrests. "Special attention must be given to the speeches of the President of the Soviet, Bronstein-Trotsky." And be it known that the government has more than adequate forces; telegrams are coming in continually from the front demanding decisive measures against the Bolsheviks. At this point Konovalov hands the speaker the telephonogram from the Military Revolutionary Committee to the troops of the garrison, instructing them to "make the regiment ready for battle and await further orders." After reading the document Kerensky solemnly concludes: "In the language of the law and of judicial authority that is called a state of insurrection." Miliukov bears witness: "Kerensky pronounced these words in the complacent tone of a lawyer who has at last succeeded in getting evidence against his opponent." "Those groups and parties who have dared to lift their hands against the state," he concludes, "are liable to immediate, decisive and permanent liquidation." The entire hall, except the extreme left, demonstratively applauded. The speech ended with a demand: that this very day, in this session, an answer be given to the question, "Can the government fulfil its duty with confidence in the support of this lofty assemblage?" Without awaiting the vote, Kerensky returned to headquarters—confident, according to his own account, that an hour would not pass before he would receive the needed decision. For what purpose it was needed remains unknown.

However, it turned out otherwise. From two to six o'clock the Mariinsky Palace was busy with factional and interfactional conferences, striving to work out a formula. The conferees did not understand that they were working out a formula for their own funeral. Not one of the compromisist groups had the courage to identify itself with the government. Dan said: "We Mensheviks are ready to defend the Provisional Government with the last drop of our blood; but let the government make it possible for the democracy to unite around it." Towards evening the left faction of the Pre-Parliament, worn out with the search for a solution, united on a formula borrowed by Dan from Martov, a formula which laid the responsibility for insurrection not only on the Bolsheviks, but also on the government, and demanded immediate transfer of the land to the Land Committees, intercession with the Allies in favour of peace negotiations, etc. Thus the apostles of moderation tried at the last moment to counterfeit those slogans which only yesterday they had been denouncing as demagogy and adventurism. Unqualified support to the government was promised by the Kadets and Cossacks—that is, by those two groups who intended to throw Kerensky over at the very first opportunity—but they were a minority. The support of the Pre-Parliament could have added little to the government, but Miliukov is right: this refusal of support robbed the government of the last remnants of its authority. Had not the government itself only a few weeks before determined the composition of the Pre-Parliament?

While they were seeking a salvation formula in the Mariinsky

Palace, the Petrograd Soviet was assembling in Smolny for purposes of information. The spokesman considered it necessary to remind the Soviet that the Military Revolutionary Committee had arisen "not as an instrument of insurrection, but on the basis of revolutionary self-defence." The Committee had not permitted Kerensky to remove the revolutionary troops from Petrograd, and it had taken under its protection the workers' press. "Was this insurrection?" The *Aurora* stands to-day where she stood last night. "Is this insurrection?" We have to-day a semi-government, in which the people do not believe, and which does not believe in itself, because it is inwardly dead. This semi-government is awaiting that swish of the historic broom that will clear the space for an authentic government of the revolutionary people. To-morrow the Congress of Soviets will open. It is the duty of the garrison and the workers to put all their forces at the disposal of the Congress. "If, however, the government attempts to employ the twenty-four hours remaining to it in plunging a knife into the back of the revolution then we declare once more: The vanguard of the revolution will answer blow with blow and iron with steel." This open threat was at the same time a political screen for the forthcoming night attack. In conclusion Trotsky informed the meeting that the Left Social-Revolutionary faction of the Pre-Parliament, after to-day's speech from Kerensky and a mouse-riot among the Compromise factions, had sent a delegation to Smolny to express its readiness to enter officially into the staff of the Military Revolutionary Committee. In this shift of the Left Social Revolutionaries the Soviet joyfully welcomed a reflection of deeper processes: the widening scope of the peasant war and the successful progress of the Petrograd insurrection.

Commenting on this speech of the President of the Petrograd Soviet, Miliukov writes: "Probably this was Trotsky's original plan—having prepared for battle, to confront the government with the 'unanimous will of the people' as expressed in the Congress of Soviets, and thus give the new power the appearance of a legal origin. But the government proved weaker than he expected, and the power fell into his hands of its own accord before the Congress had time to assemble and express itself." What is true here, is that the weakness of the government exceeded all expectations. But from the beginning the plan had been to seize the power before the Congress opened. Miliukov recognises this, by the way, in a different connection. "The actual intentions of the leaders of the revolution," he says, "went much further than these official announcements of Trotsky. The Congress of Soviets was to be placed before a *fait accompli*."

The purely military plan consisted originally of guaranteeing a united action of the Baltic sailors and the armed Vyborg workers. The sailors were to come by railroad and detrain at the Finland station, which is in the Vyborg district, and then from this base by way of a further assimilation of the Red Guard and units of the garrison, the insurrection was to spread to other districts of the city, and having seized the bridges, to advance into the centre for the final blow. This scheme—naturally deriving from the circumstances, and formulated, it seems, by Antonov—was drawn up on the assumption that the enemy would be able to put up a considerable resistance. It was just this premise that soon fell away. It was unnecessary to start from a limited base, because the government proved open to attack wherever the insurrectionists found it necessary to strike a blow.

The strategic plan underwent changes in the matter of dates also, and that in two directions: the insurrection began earlier and ended later than had been indicated. The morning attacks of the government called out by way of self-defence an immediate resistance from the Military Revolutionary Committee. The impotence of the authorities, thus revealed, impelled Smolny during the same day to offensive actions—preserving, to be sure, a half-way, semi-disguised and preparatory character. The main blow as before was prepared during the night: in that sense the plan held good. It was transgressed, however, in the process of fulfilment—but now in an opposite direction. It had been proposed to occupy during the night all the commanding summits, and first of all the Winter Palace where the central power had taken refuge. But time-calculations are even more difficult in insurrection than in regular war. The leaders were many hours late with the concentration of forces, and the operations against the palace, not even begun during the night, formed a special chapter of the revolution ending only on the night of the 26th—that is, a whole twenty-four hours late. The most brilliant victories are not achieved without duds.

After Kerensky's speech at the Pre-Parliament the authorities tried to broaden their offensive. The railroad stations were occupied by detachments of junkers. Pickets were posted at the big street-crossings and ordered to requisition the private automobiles not turned over to headquarters. By three o'clock in the afternoon the bridges were raised, except for the Dvortsovy which remained open under heavy guard for the movement of the junkers. This measure, adopted by the monarchy at all critical moments and for the last time in the February Days, was dictated by fear of the workers' districts. The raising of the bridges was received by the population as an official announcement of the beginning of the insurrection. The headquarters of the districts concerned immediately answered this military act of the government in their own way by sending armed detachments to the bridges. Smolny had only to develop their initiative. This struggle for the bridges assumed the character of a test for both sides. Parties of armed workers and soldiers brought pressure to bear on the junkers and Cossacks, now persuading and now threatening. The guard finally yielded without hazarding a straight-out fight. Some of the bridges were raised and lowered several times.

The *Aurora* received a direct order from the Military Revolutionary Committee: "With all means at your command restore movement on the Nikolaevsky Bridge." The commander of the cruiser at first refused to carry out the order, but, after a symbolic arrest of himself and all his officers, obediently brought the ship to the bridge. Cordons of sailors spread out along both quays. By the time the *Aurora* had dropped anchor before the bridge, relates Korkov, the tracks of the junkers were already cold. The sailors themselves lowered the bridge and posted guards. Only Dvortsovy Bridge remained several hours in the hands of the government patrols.

Notwithstanding the manifest failure of its first experiments, individual branches of the government tried to deal further blows. A detachment of militia appeared in the evening at a big private printing-plant to suppress the newspaper of the Petrograd Soviet, *Worker and Soldier*. Twelve hours before, the workers of the Bolshevik press had run for help in a like case to Smolny. Now there was no need of it. The printers, together with two sailors who happened by, immediately captured the automobile loaded with papers; a number of the militia joined them on the spot; the inspector of militia fled. The captured paper was successfully delivered at Smolny. The Military Revolutionary Committee sent two squads of the Preobrazhentsi to protect the publication. The frightened administration thereupon turned over the management of the printing-plant to the soviet of worker-overseers.

The legal authorities did not even think of penetrating

Smolny to make arrests: it was too obvious that this would be the signal for a civil war in which the defeat of the government was assured in advance. There was made, however, as a kind of administrative convulsion, an attempt to arrest Lenin in the Vyborg district, where, generally speaking, the authorities were afraid even to look in. Late in the evening a certain colonel with a dozen junkers accidentally entered a workers' club instead of the Bolshevik editorial rooms located in the same house. The brave boys had for some reason imagined that Lenin would be waiting for them in the editorial rooms. The club immediately informed the district headquarters of the Red Guard. While the colonel was wandering around from one storey to another, arriving once even among the Mensheviks, a detachment of Red Guards, rushing up, arrested him along with his junkers, and brought them to the headquarters of the Vyborg district, and thence to the Peter and Paul fortress. Thus the loudly proclaimed campaign against the Bolsheviks, meeting insuperable difficulties at every step, turned into disconnected jumps and small anecdotes, evaporated, and came to nothing.

During this time the Military Revolutionary Committee was working day and night. Its commissars were on continual duty in the military units. The population was notified in special proclamations where to turn in case of counter-revolutionary attempts or pogroms: "Help will be given on the instant." A suggestive visit to the telephone exchange from the commissar of the Keksgolmsky regiment proved sufficient to get Smolny switched back into the system. Telephone communications, the swiftest of all, gave confidence and regularity to the developing operations.

Continuing to plant its own commissars in those institutions which had not yet come under its control, the Military Revolutionary Committee kept broadening and reinforcing its bases for the coming offensive. Dzerzhinsky that afternoon handed the old revolutionist Pestkovsky a sheet of paper in the form of credentials appointing him to the office of commissar of the central telegraph station. But how shall I get possession of the telegraph station?—asked the new commissar in some surprise. The Keksgolmsky regiment is supplying sentries there and it is on our side! Pestkovsky needed no further illumination. Two Keksgolmsti, standing by the commutator with rifles, proved sufficient to attain a compromise with the hostile telegraph officials, among whom were no Bolsheviks.

At nine o'clock in the evening another commissar of the Military Revolutionary Committee, Stark, with a small detachment of sailors under the command of the former emigré Savin, also a seaman, occupied the government news agency and therewith decided not only the fate of that institution, but also to a certain degree his own fate: Stark became the first Soviet director of the agency, before being appointed Soviet ambassador to Afghanistan.

Were these two modest operations acts of insurrection, or were they only episodes in the two-power system—transferred, to be sure, from the compromisist to the Bolshevik rails? The question may perhaps reasonably be regarded as casuistic, but for the purpose of camouflaging an insurrection it had a certain importance. The fact is that even the intrusion of armed sailors into the building of the news agency had still a sort of half-way character: it was not yet a question of seizing the institution, but only of establishing a censorship over despatches. Thus right up to the evening of the 24th, the umbilical cord of "legality" was not conclusively severed. The movement was still disguising itself with the remnants of the two-power tradition.

In working out the plans of the insurrection, Smolny rested great hopes on the Baltic sailors as a fighting detachment combining proletarian resolution with strict military training. The arrival of the sailors in Petrograd had been dated in advance to coincide with the Congress of Soviets. To call the Baltic sailors in earlier would have meant to take openly the road of insurrection. Out of this arose a difficulty which subsequently turned into a delay.

During the afternoon of the 24th, two delegates from the Kronstadt Soviet, the Bolshevik Flerovsky and the anarchist Yarchuk, who was keeping step with the Bolsheviks, arrived in Smolny for the Congress. In one of the rooms of Smolny they ran into Chudnovsky, who had just returned from the front, and who, alluding to the mood of the soldiers, spoke against insurrection in the near future. "At the height of the argument," relates Flerovsky, "Trotsky came into the room. . . . Calling me aside, he advised me to return immediately to Kronstadt: 'Events are maturing so fast that everyone must be at his post. . . .' In this curt order I felt keenly the discipline of the advancing insurrection." The argument was cut short. The impressionable and hot-headed Chudnovsky laid aside his doubts in order to take part in drawing up the plans of the fight. On the heels of Flerovsky and Yarchuk went a telephonogram: "The armed forces of Kronstadt are to come out at dawn for the defence of the Congress of Soviets."

Through Sverdlov the Military Revolutionary Committee sent a telegram that night to Helsingfors, to Smilga, the president of the regional Committee of the Soviets: "Send regulations." That meant: Send immediately 1,500 chosen Baltic sailors armed to the teeth. Although the sailors could reach Petrograd only during the next day, there was no reason to postpone military action; the internal forces were adequate. Yes, and a postponement was impossible. Operations had already begun. If reinforcements should come from the front to help the government, then the sailors would arrive in time to deal them a blow in the flank or rear.

The tactical plans for the conquest of the capital were worked out chiefly by the staff of the Military Organisation of the Bolsheviks. Officers of the general staff would have found many faults in them, but military academicians do not customarily take part in the preparation of a revolutionary insurrection. The essentials at any rate were taken care of. The city was divided into military divisions, each subordinate to the nearest headquarters. At the most important points companies of the Red Guard were concentrated in co-ordination with the neighbouring military units, where companies on duty were awake and ready. The goal of each separate operation, and the forces for it, were indicated in advance. All those taking part in the insurrection from top to bottom—in this lay its power, in this also at times its Achilles' heel—were imbued with absolute confidence that the victory was going to be won without casualties.

The main operation began at two o'clock in the morning. Small military parties, usually with a nucleus of armed workers or sailors under the leadership of commissars, occupied simultaneously, or in regular order, the railroad stations, the lighting plant, the munition and food stores, the waterworks, Dvortsovy Bridge, the Telephone Exchange, the State Bank, the big printing-plants. The Telegraph Station and the Post Office were completely taken over. Reliable guards were placed everywhere.

Meagre and colourless is the record of the episodes of that October night. It is like a police report. All the participants were shaking with a nervous fever. There was no time to observe and record and no one to do it. The information flowing in at headquarters was not always jotted down, and if so it was done carelessly. Notes got lost. Subsequent recollections were dry and not always accurate, since they came for the most part from accidental people. Those workers, sailors, and soldiers who really inspired and lead the operation took their places soon after at the head of the first detachments of the Red Army, and the majority laid down their lives in the various theatres of the civil war. In the attempt to determine the sequence of separate episodes, the investigator runs into a vast confusion, which is still more complicated by the accounts in the newspapers. At times it seems as though it was easier to capture Petrograd in the autumn of 1917 than to recount the process fourteen years later.

To the first company of the sapper battalion, the strongest and most revolutionary, was given the task of seizing the nearby Nikolaevsky railroad station. In less than a quarter of an hour the station was occupied by strong guards without a blow. The government squad simply evaporated in the darkness. The keenly cold night was full of mysterious movements and suspicious sounds. Suppressing a sharp alarm in their hearts, the soldiers would conscientiously stop all passers-by, on foot or in vehicles, meticulously inspecting their documents. They did not always know what to do. They hesitated—most often let them go. But confidence increased with every hour. About six in the morning the sappers held up two truckloads of junkers—about sixty men—disarmed them, and sent them to Smolny.

That same sapper battalion was directed to send fifty men to guard the food warehouses, twenty-one to guard the Power Station, etc. Order followed order, now from Smolny, now from the district. Nobody offered a murmur of objection. According to the report of the commissar, the orders were carried out "immediately and exactly." The movement of the soldiers acquired a precision long unseen. However rickety and crumbly that garrison was—good only for scrap-iron in a military sense—on that night the old soldierly drill re-awoke, and for one last moment tensed every nerve and muscle in the service of the new goal.

Commissar Uralov received two authorisations: one, to occupy the printing-plant of the reactionary paper *Russkaia Volia*, founded by Protopopov a little while before he became the last Minister of the Interior of Nicholas II; the other, to get a troop of soldiers from the Semenov Guard regiment which the government for old times' sake was still considering its own. The Semenovtsi were needed for the occupation of a printing-plant. The printing-plant was needed to issue the Bolshevik paper in large format and with a big circulation. The soldiers had already lain down to sleep. The commissar briefly told them the object of his visit. "I hadn't stopped talking when a shout of 'Hurrah!' went up on all sides. The soldiers were jumping out of their bunks and crowding around me in a close circle." A truck loaded with Semenovtsi approached the printing-plant. The workers of the night-shift quickly assembled in the rotary-press room. The commissar explained why he had come. "And here, as in the barracks, the workers answered with shouts of 'Hurrah! Long live the Soviets!' " The job was done. In much the same manner the other institutions were seized. It was not necessary to employ force, for there was no resistance. The insurrectionary masses lifted their elbows and pushed out the lords of yesterday.

The commander of the district reported that night to general headquarters and the headquarters of the Northern front over the military wire: "The situation in Petrograd is frightful. There are no street demonstrations or disorders, but a regulated seizure of institutions, railroad stations, also arrests, is in progress. . . . The junkers' patrols are surrendering without resistance. . . . We have no guarantee that there will not be an attempt to seize the Provisional Government." Polkovnikov was right: they had no guarantee of that.

In military circles the rumour was going round that agents of the Military Revolutionary Committee had stolen from the desk of the Petrograd commandant the password for the sentries of the garrison. That was not at all improbable. The insurrection had many friends among the lower personnel of all institutions. Nevertheless this tale about stealing the password is apparently a legend which arose in the hostile camp to explain the too humiliating ease with which the Bolshevik patrols got possession of the city.

An order was sent out through the garrison from Smolny during the night: Officers not recognising the authority of the Military Revolutionary Committee to be arrested. The commanders of many regiments fled of their own accord, and passed some nervous days in hiding. In other units the officers were removed or arrested. Everywhere special revolutionary committees or staffs were formed and functioned hand in hand with the commissars. That this improvised command did not stand very high in a military sense, goes without saying. Nevertheless it was reliable, and the question here was decided primarily in the political court.

It is necessary to add, however, that with all their lack of experience the staffs of certain units developed a considerable military initiative. The committee of the Pavlovsky regiment sent scouts into the Petrograd district headquarters to find out what was going on there. The chemical reserve battalion kept careful watch of its restless neighbours, the junkers of the Pavlovsky and Vladimirsky schools, and the students of the cadet corps. The chemical men from time to time disarmed junkers in the street and thus kept them cowed. Getting into connection with the soldier personnel of the Pavlovsky school, the staff of the chemical battalion saw to it that the keys of the weapons were in the hands of the soldiers.

It is difficult to determine the number of forces directly engaged in this nocturnal seizure of the capital—and this not only because nobody counted them or noted them down, but also because of the character of the operations. Reserves of the second and third order almost merged with the garrison as a whole. But it was only occasionally necessary to have recourse to the reserves. A few thousand Red Guards, two or three thousand sailors—to-morrow with the arrivals from Kronstadt and Helsingfors there will be about treble the number—a score of infantry companies: such were the forces of the first and second order with whose aid the insurrectionists occupied the governmental high points of the capital.

At 3.20 in the morning the chief of the political administration of the War Ministry, the Menshevik Sher, sent the following information by direct wire to the Caucasus: "A meeting of the Central Executive Committee together with the delegates to the Congress of Soviets is in progress with an overwhelming majority of Bolsheviks. Trotsky has received an ovation. He has announced that he hopes for a bloodless victory of the insurrection, since the power is in their hands. The Bolsheviks have begun active operations. They have seized the Nikolaevsky Bridge and posted armoured cars there. The Pavlovsky regiment has posted pickets on Milliony Street near the Winter Palace, is stopping everybody, arresting them, and sending them to Smolny Institute. They have arrested Minister Kartashev and the general administrator of the Provisional Government, Halperin. The Baltic railroad station is also in the hands of the Bolsheviks. If the front does not intervene, the government will be unable to resist with the forces on hand."

The joint session of the Executive Committees about which Lieutenant Sher's communication speaks, opened in Smolny after midnight in unusual circumstances. Delegates to the Congress of Soviets brimmed the hall in the capacity of invited guests. Reinforced guards occupied the entrances and corridors. Trench-coats, rifles, machine-guns filled the windows. The members of the Executive Committees were drowned in this many-headed and hostile mass of provincials. The high organ of the "democracy" looked already like a captive of the insurrection. The familiar figure of the president, Cheidze, was absent. The invariable spokesman, Tseretelli, was absent. Both of them, frightened by the turn of events, had surrendered their responsible posts, and abandoning Petrograd, left for their Georgian homeland. Dan remained as leader of the Compromise bloc. He lacked the sly good humour of Cheidze, and likewise the moving eloquence of Tseretelli. But he excelled them both in obstinate short-sightedness. Alone in the president's chair the Social Revolutionary, Gotz, opened the session. Dan took the floor amid an utter silence which seemed to Sukhanov languid—to John Reed "almost threatening." The spokesman's hobby was a new resolution of the Pre-Parliament, which had tried to oppose the insurrection with the dying echo of its own slogans. "It will be too late if you do not take account of this decision," cried Dan, trying to frighten the Bolsheviks with the inevitable hunger and the degeneration of the masses. "Never before has the counter-revolution been so strong as at the given moment," he said—that is, on the night before October 25, 1917. The frightened petty-bourgeois confronted by great events sees nothing but dangers and obstacles. His sole recourse is the pathos of alarm. "In the factories and barracks the Black Hundred press is enjoying a far more considerable success than the socialist press." Lunatics are leading the revolution to ruin just as in 1905 "when this same Trotsky stood at the head of the Petrograd Soviet." But no, he cried, the Central Executive Committee will not permit an insurrection. "Only over its dead body will the hostile camps cross their bayonets." Shouts from the benches: "Yes, it's been dead a long time!" The entire hall felt the appropriateness of that exclamation. Over the corpse of Compromise the bayonets of the bourgeoisie and the proletariat had already crossed. The voice of the orator is drowned in a hostile uproar, his pounding on the table is futile, his appeals do not move, his threats do not frighten. Too late! Too late!

Yes, it is an insurrection! Replying in the name of the Military Revolutionary Committee, the Bolshevik party, the Petrograd workers and soldiers, Trotsky now throws off tthe last qualification. Yes, the masses are with us, and we are leading them to the assault! "If you do not weaken there will be no civil war, for the enemy is already capitulating, and you can assume the place of master of the Russian land which of right belongs to you." The astounded members of the Central Executive Committee found no strength even to protest. Up to now the defensive phraseology of Smolny had kept up in them, in spite of all the facts, a glimmering spark of hope. Now that too was extinguished. In those hours of deep night the insurrection lifted its head high.

That session so rich in episodes closed at four o'clock in the morning. The Bolshevik speakers would appear in the tribune only to return immediately to the Military Revolutionary Committee, where from all corners of the city news uniformly favourable was pouring in. The patrols in the streets were doing their work, the government institutions were being occupied one after the other; the enemy was offering no resistance anywhere.

It had been assumed that the central Telephone Exchange would be specially well fortified, but at seven in the morning it was taken without a fight by a company from the Keksgolmsky regiment. The insurrectionists could now not only rest easy about their own communications, but control the telephone connections of the enemy. The apparatus of the Winter Palace and of central headquarters was promptly cut out.

Almost simultaneously with the seizure of the Telephone Exchange a detachment of sailors from the Marine Guard, about forty strong, seized the building of the State Bank on the Ekaterininsky Canal. The bank clerk Ralzevich recalls that the sailors "worked with expedition," immediately placing sentries at each telephone to cut off possible help from outside. The occupation of the building was accomplished "without any resistance, in spite of the presence of a squad from the Semenovsky regiment." The seizure of the bank had to some extent a symbolic importance. The cadres of the party had been brought up on the Marxian criticism of the Paris Commune of 1871, whose leaders, as is well known, did not venture to lay hands on the State Bank. "No we will not make that mistake," many Bolsheviks had been saying to themselves long before October 25. News of the seizure of the most sacred institution of the bourgeois state swiftly spread through the districts, raising a warm wave of joy.

In the early morning hours the Warsaw railroad station was occupied, also the printing-plant of the *Stock Exchange News,* and Dvortsovy Bridge under Kerensky's very windows. A commissar of the Committee presented the soldier patrol from the Volinsky regiment in Kresty Prison with a resolution demanding the liberation of a number of prisoners according to the lists of the Soviet. The prison administration tried in vain to get instructions from the Minister of Justice: he was too busy. The liberated Bolsheviks, among them the young Kronstadt leader, Roshal, immediately received military appointments.

In the morning, a party of junkers who had left the Winter Palace in a truck in search of provisions, and been held up by the sappers at Nikolaevsky station, were brought to Smolny. Podvoisky relates the following: "Trotsky told them that they were free on condition that they give a promise not to take further action against the Soviet power, and that they might go back to their school and get to work. The youngsters, who had expected a bloody end, were unspeakably surprised at this." To what extent their immediate liberation was wise, remains in doubt. The victory was not yet finally achieved. The junkers were the chief force of the enemy. On the other hand, with the wavering moods in the military schools, it was important to prove by example that a surrender to the mercy of the victor would not threaten the junkers with punishment. The arguments in both directions seemed about equal.

From the War Ministry, not yet occupied by the insurrectionists, General Levitsky sent word by direct wire to General Dukhonin at headquarters: "The troops of the Petrograd garrison . . . have gone over to the Bolsheviks. The sailors and a light-armed cruiser have come from Kronstadt. They have lowered the raised bridges. The whole town is covered with sentry guards from the garrison. But there has been no coming-out. (!) The Telephone Exchange is in the hands of the garrison. The troops in the Winter Palace are defending it only in a formal sense, since they have decided not to come out actively. The general impression is that the Provisional Government finds itself in the capital of a hostile state which has finished mobilisation but not yet begun active operations." Invaluable military and political testimony! To be sure, the general anticipates events when he says the sailors have arrived from Kronstadt: they will arrive a few hours later. The bridge was really let down by the crew of the *Aurora.* The hope expressed in conclusion that the Bolsheviks, "having long been actually in a position to get rid of us . . . will not dare come into conflict with the opinion of the army at the front," is rather naïve. However, these illusions about the front were about all that the rear generals had left, or the rear democrats either. At any rate that image of the Provisional Government finding itself in the capital of a hostile state will go into the history of the revolution for ever as the best possible explanation of the October event.

Meetings were continuous in Smolny. Agitators, organisers, leaders of factories, regiments, districts, would appear for an hour or two, sometimes for a few minutes, to get news, to check up on their own activities and return to their posts. Before room 18, the quarters of the Bolshevik faction of the Soviet, there was an indescribable jam. Tired to death, those arriving would often fall asleep right in the assembly hall, leaning their unbearably heavy heads against a white column, or against the walls in the corridors, with both arms around their rifles—or sometimes they would simply stretch out in piles on the dirty wet floor. Lashevich was receiving the military commissars and giving them their last instructions. In the quarters of the Military Revolutionary Committee on the third floor, reports coming in from all sides would be converted into orders. Here beat the heart of the insurrection.

The district centres reproduced the picture of Smolny on a smaller scale. In the Vyborg district opposite the headquarters of the Red Guard on Samsonevsky Prospect a whole camp was created: the street was jammed full of wagons, passenger-cars and trucks. The institutions of the district were swarming with armed workers. The soviet, the duma, the trade unions, the factory and shop committees—everything in this district—were serving the cause of the insurrection. In the factories and barracks and various institutions the same thing was happening in a smaller way as throughout the whole capital: they were crowding out some and electing others, breaking the last threads of the old ties, strengthening the new. The backward ones were adopting resolutions of submission to the Military Revolutionary Committee. The Mensheviks and Social-Revolutionaries timidly shrank aside along with the factory administrations and the commanding staff of the troops. At continuous meetings fresh information was given out, fighting confidence kept up and ties reinforced. The human masses were crystallizing along new axes; a revolution was achieving itself.

Step by step we have tried to follow in this book the development of the October insurrection: the sharpening discontent of the worker masses, the coming over of the soviets to the Bolshevik banners, the indignation of the army, the campaign of the peasants against the landlords, the flood-tide of the national movement, the growing fear and distraction of the possessing and ruling classes, and finally the struggle for the insurrection within the Bolshevik party. The final act of the revolution seems, after all this, too brief, too dry, too business-like—somehow out of correspondence with the historic scope of the events. The reader experiences a kind of disappointment. He is like a mountain climber, who, thinking the main difficulties are still ahead, suddenly discovers that he is already on the summit or almost there. Where is the insurrection? There is no picture of the insurrection. The events do not form themselves into a picture. A series of small operations, calculated and prepared in advance, remain separated one from another both in space and time. A unity of thought and aim unites them, but they do not fuse in the struggle itself. There is no action of great masses. There are no dramatic encounters with the troops. There is nothing of all that which imaginations brought up upon the facts of history associate with the idea of insurrection.

The general character of the revolution in the capital subsequently moved Masaryk, among many others, to write: "The October revolution . . . was anything but a popular mass movement. That revolution was the act of leaders working from above and behind the scenes." As a matter of fact it was the most popular mass-insurrection in all history. The workers had no need to come out into the public square in order to fuse together: they were already politically and morally one single whole without that. The soldiers were even forbidden to leave their barracks without permission: upon that point the order of the Military Revolutionary Committee fell in with the order of Polkovnikov. But those invisible masses were marching more than ever before in step with the events. The factories and barracks never lost connection for a minute with the district headquarters, nor the districts with Smolny. The Red Guard detachments felt at their back the support of the factories. The soldier squad returning to the barracks found the new shifts ready. Only with heavy reserves behind them could revolutionary detachments go about their work with such confidence.

The scattered government patrols, in contrast, being convinced in advance of their own isolation, renounced the very idea of resistance. The bourgeois classes had expected barricades, flaming conflagrations, looting, rivers of blood. In reality a silence reigned more terrible than all the thunders of the world. The social ground shifted noiselessly like a revolving stage, bringing forward the popular masses, carrying away to limbo the rulers of yesterday.

As early as ten o'clock on the morning of the 25th, Smolny considered it possible to broadcast through the capital and throughout the whole country a triumphant announcement: "The Provisional Government is overthrown. The state power has passed into the hands of the Military Revolutionary Committee." In a certain sense this declaration was very premature. The government still existed, at least within the territory of the Winter Palace. Headquarters existed; the provinces had not expressed themselves; the Congress of Soviets had not yet opened. But the leaders of an insurrection are not historians; in order to prepare events for the historians they have to anticipate them. In the capital the Military Revolutionary Committee was already complete master of the situation. There could be no doubt of the sanction of the Congress. The provinces were awaiting Petrograd's initiative. In order to get complete possession of the power it was necessary to act as a power. In a proclamation to the military organisations of the front and rear, the Committee urged the soldiers to watch vigilantly over the conduct of the commanding staff, to arrest officers not adhering to the revolution, and not to stop at the use of force in case of attempts to throw hostile divisions against Petrograd.

The chief commissar of headquarters, Stankevich, having arrived the night before from the front and not wishing to remain wholly inactive, placed himself at the head of a half-company of military engineering students in the morning, and undertook to clean the Bolsheviks out of the Telephone Exchange. It was in this way that the junkers first found out who had possession of the telephone connections. "There is a model of energy for you," exclaimed officer Sinegub, grinding his teeth. "But where did they get such leadership?" The sailors occupying the telephone building could easily have shot down the junkers through the windows. But the insurrectionists were striving with all their might to avoid bloodshed, and Stankevich had given strict orders not to open fire lest the junkers be accused of shooting at the people. The commanding officer thought to himself: "Once order is restored, who will dare to peep?" and concluded his meditations with an exclamation: "Damned clowns!" This is a good formula for the attitude of the officers to the government. On his own initiative Sinegub sent to the Winter Palace for hand grenades and sticks of pyroxyle. In the interval a monarchist lieutenant got into an argument at the gates of the Exchange with a Bolshevik ensign. Like the heroes of Homer they exchanged mighty epithets before the battle. Finding themselves between two fires—for the time only wordy ones—the telephone girls gave free reign to their nerves. The sailors let them go home. "What's this? Women? . . ." They fled with hysterical screams through the gates. "The deserted Morskaia," relates Sinegub, "was suddenly enlivened with running and jumping skirts and hats." The sailors managed somehow to handle the work of the switchboard. An armoured car from the Reds soon entered the court of the Exchange, doing no damage to the frightened junkers. They on their side seized two trucks and barricaded the gates of the Exchange from the outside. A second armoured car appeared from the direction of the Nevsky, and then a third. It all came down to manœuvres and attempts to frighten each other. The struggle for the Exchange was decided without pyroxyle: Stankevich raised the seige after negotiating a free passage for his junkers.

Weapons in general are still serving merely as an external sign of power: they are not being brought into action. On the road to the Winter Palace a half-company of junkers runs into a crew of sailors with rifles cocked. The enemies only measure each other with their eyes. Neither side wants to fight: the one through consciousness of strength, the other of weakness. But where chance offers, the insurrectionists—especially the workers—promptly disarm the enemy. A second half-company of those same engineering junkers was surrounded by Red Guards and soldiers, disarmed by them with the help of armoured cars, and taken prisoner. Even here, however, there was no conflict; the junkers did not put up a fight. "Thus ended," says the initiator of it, "the sole attempt, so far as I know, at active resistance to the Bolsheviks." Stankevich has in mind, of course, operations outside the Winter Palace region.

By noon the streets around the Mariinsky Palace were occupied by troops of the Military Revolutionary Committee. Members of the Pre-Parliament were just assembling for a meeting. The præsidium made an attempt to get the latest news; their hearts sank when they learned that the telephones of the palace had been cut out. The Council of Elders went into session to decide what to do. The deputies murmured meanwhile in the corners. Avksentiev offered consolation: Kerensky has gone to the front, and will be back soon and fix everything. An armoured car drew up at the entrance. Soldiers of the Litovsky and Keksgolmsky regiments and sailors of the Marine Guard entered the building, formed in line on the staircase, and occupied the first hall. The commander of the detachment suggested to the deputies that they leave the palace at once. "The impression created was appalling," testifies Nabokov. The members of the Pre-Parliament decided to disperse, "temporarily suspending their activities," Forty-eight right wing members voted against submitting to violence, quite evidently knowing they would be in a minority. The deputies peacefully descended the magnificent stairway between two rows of rifles. An eye-witness testifies: "In all this there was no attempt at dramatics." "Ordinary, meaningless, obtuse, malicious physiognomies," writes the liberal patriot, Nabokov, of these Russian soldiers and sailors. Down below at the entrance the soldiers inspected their papers and let them all through. "A sorting of members and some arrests have been expected," writes Miliukov himself let out with the others. "But the revolutionary headquarters had other things to worry about." It was not only that. The revolutionary staff had little experience. The instructions read: Arrest members of the government if found. But none were found. The members of the Pre-Parliament were freely released, among them some who soon became organisers of the civil war.

This parliamentary hybrid, which ended its existence twelve hours in advance of the Provisional Government, had lived in the world for eighteen days. That was the interval between the withdrawal of the Bolsheviks from the Mariinsky Palace to the streets and the entry of the armed street forces into the Mariinsky Palace. . . . Of all the parodies of popular representation in which history is so rich, this Council of the Russian Republic was perhaps the most absurd.

After leaving the unlucky building, the Octobrist Shidlovsky went strolling through the town to see the fights—for these gentlemen believed that the people were going to rise in their defence. But no fighting was to be seen. Instead, according to Shidlovsky, the public in the streets—the select crowd, that is, along the Nevsky Prospect—were to the last man laughing.

"Have you heard about it? The Bolsheviks have seized the power. Well, that won't last more than three days. Ha, ha, ha!" Shidlovsky decided to remain in the capital "during the period which social rumour designated for the rule of the Bolsheviks."

The Nevsky public had begun to laugh, it may be remarked, only towards evening. In the morning such a mood of alarm had prevailed that hardly anybody in the bourgeois districts dared go into the streets at all. At about nine o'clock a journalist, Knizhnik, ran out on Kamenoöstrovsky Prospect in search of newspapers, but could find no stands. In a little group of citizens he learned that the Bolsheviks had occupied the telephone, the telegraph, and the Bank during the night. A soldier patrol listened to them and asked them not to make so much noise. "But even without that everybody was unusually subdued." Armed detachments of workers were going by. The tramcars moved as usual—that is, slowly. "The scarcity of passers-by oppressed me," writes Knizhnik about the Nevsky. Food could be had in the restaurants, but for the most part in back rooms. At noon the cannon from the walls of Peter and Paul, now safely occupied by the Bolsheviks, thundered out neither louder nor more gently than usual. The walls and fences were pasted over with proclamations warning against insurrection, but other proclamations were already making their way, announcing the victory of the insurrection. There was no time yet to paste them up; they were tossed out from automobiles. Just off the press, these handbills smelled of fresh inks as though of the events themselves.

Companies of the Red Guard had emerged from their districts. The worker with a rifle, the bayonet above hat or cap, the rifle-belt over a civilian coat—that is the essential image of the 25th of October. Cautiously and still diffidently, the armed worker was bringing order into the capital conquered by him.

The tranquillity of the street instilled tranquillity in the heart. The philistines began to dribble down from their houses. Towards evening they felt even less anxious than during the preceding days. Business, to be sure, had come to an end in the governmental and social institutions, but many stores remained open. Others were closed rather through excessive caution than necessity. Can this be insurrection? Is an insurrection like this? The February sentries have merely been replaced by those of October.

By evening the Nevsky was even fuller than usual of that public which was giving the Bolsheviks three days of life. The soldiers of the Pavlovsky regiment, although their patrols were reinforced by armoured cars and even anti-aircraft guns, had already ceased to inspire fear. To be sure, something serious was going on around the Winter Palace and they would not let you through there, but still an insurrection could not very well all be concentrated on Winter Palace square. An American journalist saw old men in rich fur coats shake their gloved fists at the Pavlovtsi, and handsomely dressed women scream abuse in their faces. "The soldiers argued feebly with embarrassed grins." They were obviously at a loss on that elegant Nevsky, not yet converted into the "Prospect of the Twenty-Fifth of October."

Claude Anet, the official French journalist in Petrograd, was sincerely surprised that these absurd Russians should make a revolution not at all as he had read about it in the old books. "The city is quiet." He calls up his friends on the telephone, receives visitors, and at noon leaves the house. The soldiers who block his road on Moika Street march in perfect order "as under the old régime." There are innumerable patrols on Milliony Street. There is no shooting anywhere. The immense square of the Winter Palace at this noon hour is still almost empty. There are patrols on Morskaia and Nevsky. The soldiers carry themselves in military style, and are dressed irreproachably. At first glance it seems certain that these are government troops. On Mariinsky Square, whence Anet intends to make his way into the Pre-Parliament, he is stopped by soldiers and sailors. "Mighty polite, I assure you." Two streets leading up to the palace are barricaded with automobiles and wagons—here, too, an armoured car. These are all under Smolny. The Military Revolutionary Committee has sent out patrols through the town, posted sentries, dissolved the Pre-Parliament, taken command of the capital, and established therein a state of order "unseen since the revolution began." In the evening the janitress informs her French lodger that telephone numbers have been sent over from Soviet headquarters, by which at any moment he can summon military help in case of attack, suspicious search-parties, etc. "As a fact they never guarded us better."

At 2.35 in the afternoon—the foreign journalists looked at their watches, the Russians were too busy—an emergency session of the Petrograd Soviet was opened with a report by Trotsky, who in the name of the Military Revolutionary Committee announced that the Provisional Government no longer existed. "They told us that an insurrection would drown the revolution in torrents of blood. . . . We do not know of a single casualty." There is no example in history of a revolutionary movement involving such gigantic masses being so bloodless. "The Winter Palace is not yet taken, but its fate will be settled in the course of the next few minutes." The following twelve hours were to show that this prediction was too optimistic.

Trotsky said: "Troops have been moved against Petrograd from the front; it is necessary at once to send commissars of the soviets to the front, and throughout the country, to make known that the revolution has occurred." Voices from the small right sector: "You are anticipating the will of the Congress of Soviets." The speaker answered: "The will of the Congress has been anticipated by the colossal fact of an insurrection of the Petrograd workers and soldiers. It now remains only to develop our victory."

Lenin, who appeared here publicly for the first time after emerging from underground, briefly outlined the programme of the revolution: To break up the old governmental apparatus; to create a new system of administration through the soviets; to take measures for the immediate cessation of war, relying upon revolutionary movements in other countries; to abolish the landlords' property rights and thus win the confidence of the peasants; to establish workers' control over production. "The third Russian revolution," he said, "must in the end lead to the victory of socialism."

Chapter VIII

The Capture of the Winter Palace

Kerensky was in a great state of excitement when he met Stankevich arriving with his report from the front. He had just returned from a mutiny of the Council of the Republic where the insurrection of the Bolsheviks had been conclusively exposed.—Insurrection! Don't you know that we have an armed insurrection?—Stankevich laughed: Why the streets are perfectly quiet; surely that isn't the way a real insurrection ought to look? But anyway we must put an end to these everlasting disturbances.—To this Kerensky heartily agreed, he was only waiting for the resolution of the Pre-Parliament.

At nine in the evening the government assembled in the Malachite Chamber of the Winter Palace to work out methods for a "resolute and final liquidation" of the Bolsheviks. Stankevich, returning from the Mariinsky Palace where he had been sent to hurry things up, reported with indignation the passing of the resolution of semi-non-confidence. Even the struggle against insurrection the resolution of the Pre-Parliament proposed to entrust not to the government, but to a special committee of public safety. Kerensky hotly announced that under those circumstances "he would not remain a minute longer at the head of the government." The Compromise leaders were immediately summoned to the palace by telephone. The possibility of Kerensky's resignation surprised them no less than their resolution had surprised Kerensky. Avksentiev presented their excuses: they had, you know, regarded the resolution "as purely theoretical and accidental, and had not believed it would lead to practical steps." Moreover they now themselves saw that the resolution was "perhaps not quite happily worded." Those people never missed an opportunity to show what they were worth.

This nocturnal conversation of the democratic leaders with the head of the State seems absolutely unbelievable on the background of the developing insurrection. Dan, one of the chief grave-diggers of the February régime, demanded that the government immediately, by night, plaster the town with posters announcing that it had proposed immediate peace negotiations to the Allies. Kerensky reported that the government had no need of such counsels. It is quite possible to believe that the government would have preferred a sharp division; but Dan could not offer that. Kerensky, of course, was attempting to throw the responsibility for the insurrection upon his interlocutors. Dan answered that the government was exaggerating events under the influence of its "reactionary staff." At any rate there was no need of resigning: the disagreeable resolution had been necessary in order to break the mood of the masses. The Bolsheviks will be compelled "not later than to-morrow" to dissolve their headquarters, if the government follows Dan's suggestion. "At that very moment," adds Kerensky in describing this conversation with legitimate irony, "the Red Guard was occupying the government buildings one after another."

This so weighty conference with his Left friends had hardly ended when Kerensky's friends from the Right appeared in the form of a delegation from the Council of the Cossack Troops. The officers pretended that the conduct of the three Cossack regiments in Petrograd depended upon their wills, and presented Kerensky with conditions diametrically opposite to those of Dan: No concessions to the Soviet; this time the settlement with the Bolsheviks must be carried through to the end, and not handled as in July when the Cossacks suffered in vain. Kerensky, himself desiring nothing better, promised everything they asked and apologised to his interlocutors for the fact that up to now owing to considerations of prudence he had not arrested Trotsky, the president of the Soviet of Deputies. The delegates departed, assuring him that the Cossacks would do their duty. An order was issued from headquarters to the Cossack regiment: "In the name of freedom, honour and the glory of the homeland come to the help of the Central Executive Committee, the Provisional Government, and save Russia from ruin." That bigoted government which had so jealously defended its independence of the Central Executive Committee was compelled to hide humbly behind its back at a moment of danger. Beseeching commands were also sent to the military schools in Petrograd and the environs. The railroads were instructed: "to despatch echelons of troops coming toward Petrograd from the front ahead of all other trains, cutting off passenger traffic if necessary."

When the government dispersed at two o'clock in the morning, having done all it could, there remained with Kerensky in the palace only his vice-minister, the liberal Moscow merchant,

Konovalov. The commander of the district, Polkovnikov, came to them with a proposal to organise with the help of the loyal soldiers an immediate expedition for the seizure of Smolny. Kerensky accepted this admirable plan without hesitation, but from the words of the commander it was absolutely impossible to make out upon just what forces he was counting. Only now did Kerensky realise, according to his own confession, that the reports of Polkovnikov during the last ten or twelve days about his complete preparedness for the struggle with the Bolsheviks were "based on absolutely nothing." As though Kerensky had no other sources for an appraisal of the political and military situation but the secretarial reports of a mediocre colonel whom he had placed—nobody knows why—at the head of the district. During the aggrieved meditations of the head of the government the commissar of the city government, Rogovsky, brought a series of communications: A number of ships from the Baltic Fleet have entered the Neva in fighting array; some of them have come as far as the Nikolaevsky Bridge and occupied it; detachments of the insurrectionaries are advancing on Dvortsovy Bridge. Rogovsky called Kerensky's special attention to the circumstances that "the Bolsheviks are carrying out their whole plan in complete order, meeting nowhere the slightest resistance on the part of the government troops." Just what troops were meant by the word "government" was not quite clear in any case from the man's report.

Kerensky and Konovalov rushed from the palace to headquarters: "We must not lose another minute," they cried. The impressive red building was brimful of officers. They had come here not on the business of their troops, but to hide from them. Civilians unknown to anybody were also poking their noses in among this military crowd. A new report from Polkovnikov finally convinced Kerensky that it was impossible to rely upon the commander or his officers. The head of the government decided to gather around his own person "all those loyal to their duty." Remembering that he was the member of a party—as others remember only on their death beds about the church—Kerensky called up the Social Revolutionaries on the telephone and demanded that they send fighting companies immediately. Before this unexpected appeal to the armed forces of the party could give any results, however—supposing it could do so at all—it would inevitably, as Miliukov says, "repel from Kerensky all the Right Wing elements, who even without that were unfriendly enough." Kerensky's isolation, plainly enough exposed already in the Kornilov insurrection, assumed here a more fatal aspect. "The long hours of that night dragged torturingly," says Kerensky, repeating his autobiographic phrase.

Reinforcements arrived from nowhere. The Cossacks held sittings. Representatives of this regiment said that, generally speaking, they might come out—why not?—but for this it was necessary to have machine-guns, armoured cars, and, above all, infantry. Kerensky, without a thought, promised them armoured cars which were getting ready to abandon him, and infantry of which he had none. In answer he was told that the regiments would soon decide all questions and "begin to saddle their horses." The fighting forces of the Social Revolutionaries gave no signs of life. Did they indeed still exist? Where in fact was the boundary between the real and the spectral? The officers assembled in headquarters adopted a "more and more challenging" attitude toward the commander-in-chief and head of the government. Kerensky even asserts that there was talk among the officers of arresting him. The headquarters building was, as before, unguarded. Official negotiations were carried on before outsiders in the intervals between excited private conversations. The mood of hopelessness and disintegration soaked through from headquarters into the Winter Palace. The junkers began to get nervous. The armoured car crews became excited. There is no support below, there is no head above. In such circumstances can anything but destruction follow?

At five o'clock in the morning Kerensky summoned to headquarters the general director of the War Ministry, Manikovsky. At the Troitsky Bridge General Manikovsky was stopped by patrols and taken to the barracks of the Pavlovsky regiment, but there after brief explanation he was set free. The general convinced them, we may assume, that his arrest might upset the whole administrative mechanism and entail damage to the soldiers at the front. At about the same time the automobile of Stankevich was stopped near the Winter Palace, but the regimental committee released him also. "These were insurrectionaries," relates Stankevich, "but they behaved very irresolutely. I telegraphed about it from my house to the Winter Palace, but received tranquillising assurances that this had been a mistake." The real mistake was the release of Stankevich: In a few hours he will try, as we know, to get the telephone station away from the Bolsheviks.

Kerensky demanded from headquarters in Moghiliev and from the staff of the Northern front at Pskov the immediate despatch of loyal regiments. Dukhonin assured him over the direct wire that all measures had been taken for the despatch of troops to Petrograd, and that certain units ought already to be arriving. But the units were not arriving. The Cossacks were still "saddling their horses." The situation in the city was getting worse from hour to hour. When Kerensky and Konovalov returned to the palace to rest a little, a courier handed them an urgent communication! All the palace telephones were cut off; Dvortsovy bridge under Kerensky's very windows, was occupied by pickets of sailors. The square in front of the Winter Palace remained deserted as before. "Of the Cossacks neither hide nor hair was to be seen." Kerensky again rushed over to headquarters, but here, too, he got uncomforting news. The junkers had received from the Bolsheviks a demand that they abandon the palace, and were greatly excited. The armoured cars had broken order inopportunely exposing the "loss" of certain important units. There was still no news of the echelons from the front. The close approaches to the palace and headquarters were absolutely unguarded. If the Bolsheviks had not yet penetrated this far it was only through lack of information. The building, brimmed with officers since evening, had been rapidly vacated. Everyone was saving himself in his own way. A delegation from the junkers appeared: They were ready to do their duty in the future "only if there is hope of the arrival of some sort of reinforcement." But reinforcements were just exactly what were lacking.

Kerensky hastily summoned his ministers to headquarters. The majority of them had no automobiles. These important instruments of locomotion, which impart a new tempo to modern insurrection, had either been seized by the Bolsheviks or cut off from the ministers by cordons of insurrectionaries. Only Kishkin arrived, and some time later Maliantovich. What should the head of the government do? Go out at once to meet the echelons and bring them forward no matter what the obstacles might be. Nobody could think of anything else.

Kerensky ordered out his "magnificent open touring-car." But here a new factor entered into the chain of events, demonstrating the indestructible solidarity uniting the governments of the Entente in weal and woe. "In what manner I do not know, but the news of my departure had reached the Allied embassies." The representatives of Great Britain and the United States had immediately expressed the desire that with the head of the government in making his get-away from the capital, "there should go an automobile carrying the American flag." Kerensky himself thought the proposal excessive, and was even embarrassed, but accepted it as an expression of the solidarity of the Allies.

The American ambassador, David Francis, gives a different account—not so much like a Christmas story. According to him an automobile containing a Russian officer followed the American automobile to the embassy, and the officer demanded that they turn over the embassy automobile to Kerensky for a journey to the front. Taking counsel together, the officials of the embassy arrived at the conclusion that since the automobile had already been practically "seized"—which was not at all true—there was nothing left but to bow to the force of circumstance. The Russian officer—in spite, they say, of protests from the diplomatic gentlemen—refused to remove the American flag. And no wonder: it was only that colourful bit which made the automobile inviolable. Francis approved the action of the embassy officials, but told them "to say nothing about it to anybody."

By juxtaposing these two testimonies, which intersect with the line of truth at different angles, a sufficiently clear picture can be made to emerge. It was not the Allies, of course, who imposed the automobile upon Kerensky, but he himself who requested it: but since diplomats are obliged to pay a certain homage to the hypocrisy of non-interference in domestic affairs it was agreed that the automobile had been "seized," and that the embassy had "protested" against the misuse of the flag. After this delicate matter had been arranged, Kerensky took a seat in his own automobile; the American car followed as a reserve. "It is needless to say," says Kerensky further, "that the whole street—both the passers-by and the soldiers—immediately recognised me. I saluted as always, a little carelessly and with an easy smile." Incomparable picture! Carelessly and smiling—thus the February régime passed into the Kingdom of Shades. At the gates of the city everywhere stood pickets and patrols of armed workers. At sight of the madly flying automobile the Red Guards rushed into the highway, but did not venture to shoot. In general, shootings were still being avoided. Maybe, too, the little American flag held them back. The automobile succeessfully rushed on.

And does this mean that there are no troops in Petrograd prepared to defend the Provisional Government? asked the astonished Maliantovich, who had up to that moment dwelt in the kingdom of the eternal truths of law. I know nothing, Konovalov answered, shrugging his shoulders. It's pretty bad, he added. And what are these troops that are on their way? insisted Maliantovich. A bicycle battalion, it seems. The minister sighed. There were 200,000 soldiers in Petrograd and in the environs. Things were going badly with the régime, if the head of the government had to fly off with an American flag at his back to meet a bicycle battalion.

The ministers would have sighed deeper if they had known that this third bicycle battalion sent from the front had stopped at Peredolskaia and telegraphed the Petrograd Soviet to know for just what purpose it was being sent. The Military Revolutionary Committee telegraphed the battalion a brotherly greeting and asked them to send their representatives immediately. The authorities sought and did not find the bicycle men, whose delegates arrived that same day in Smolny.

It had been proposed in the preliminary calculations to occupy the Winter Palace on the night of the 25th, at the same time with the other commanding high points of the capital. A special trio had been formed already as early as the 23rd to take the lead in seizing the palace, Podvoisky and Antonov being the central figures. The engineer Sadovsky, a man in military service, was included as a third, but soon fell away, being preoccupied with the affairs of the garrison. He was replaced by Chudnovsky, who had come with Trotsky in May from the concentration camp in Canada, and had spent three months at the front as a soldier. Lashevich also took an important part in the operations—an old Bolshevik who had done enough service in the army to become a non-commissioned officer. Three years later Sadovsky remembered how Podvoisky and Chudnovsky quarrelled furiously in his little room in Smolny over the map of Petrograd and the best form of action against the palace. It was finally decided to surround the region of the palace with an uninterrupted oval, the longer axis of which should be the quay of the Neva. On the riverside the circle should be closed up by the Peter and Paul fortress, the *Aurora*, and other ships summoned from Kronstadt and the navy. In order to prevent or paralyse the attempts to strike at the rear with Cossacks and junker detachments, it was decided to establish imposing flank defences composed of revolutionary detachments.

The plan as a whole was too heavy and complicated for the problem it aimed to solve. The time allotted for preparation proved inadequate. Small inco-ordinations and omissions came to light at every step, as might be expected. In one place the direction was incorrectly indicated, in another the leader came late, having misread the instructions; in a third they had to wait for a rescuing armoured car. To call out the military units, unite them with the Red Guards, occupy the fighting positions, make sure of communications among them all and with headquarters—all this demanded a good many hours more than had been imagined by the leaders quarelling over their map of Petrograd.

When the Military Revolutionary Committee announced at about ten o'clock in the morning that the government was overthrown, the extent of this delay was not yet clear even to those in direct command of the operation. Podvoisky had promised the fall of the palace "not later than twelve o'clock." Up to that time everything had run so smoothly on the military side that nobody had any reason to question the hour. But at noon it turned out that the besieging force was still not filled out, the Kronstadters had not arrived, and that meanwhile the defence of the palace had been reinforced. This loss of time, as almost always happens, made new delays necessary. Under urgent pressure from the Committee the seizure of the palace was now set for three o'clock—and this time "conclusively." Counting on this new decision, the spokesman of the Military Revolutionary Committee expressed to the afternoon session of the Soviet the hope that the fall of the Winter Palace would be a matter of the next few minutes. But another hour passed and brought no decision. Podvoisky, himself in a state of white heat, asserted over the telephone that by six o'clock the palace would be taken no matter what it cost. His former confidence, however, was lacking. And indeed the hour of six did strike and the denouement had not begun. Beside themselves with the urgings of Smolny, Podvoisky and Antonov now refused to set any hour at all. That caused serious anxiety. Politically it was considered necessary that at the moment of the opening of the Congress the whole capital should be in the hands of the Military Revolutionary Committee: That was to simplify the task of dealing with the opposition at the Congress, placing them before an accomplished fact. Meanwhile the hour appointed for opening the Congress had arrived, had been postponed, and arrived again, and the Winter Palace was still holding out. Thus the siege of the palace, thanks to its delay, became for no less than twelve hours the central problem of the insurrection.

The main staff of the operation remained in Smolny, where Lashevich held the threads in his hands. The field headquarters was in the Peter and Paul fortress, where Blagonravov was the responsible man. There were three subordinate headquarters, one on the *Aurora*, another in the barracks of the Pavlovsky regiment, another in the barracks of the sailors. In the field of action the leaders were Podvoisky and Antonov—apparently without any clear order of priority.

In the quarters of the general staff a trio was also bending over the map: the commander of the district Colonel Polkovnikov, the chief of his staff General Bagratuni, and General Alexeiev, especially invited in as a high authority. Notwithstanding this so well qualified commanding staff the plans of the defence were incomparably less definite than those of the attack. It is true that the inexperienced marshals of the insurrection did not know how to concentrate their forces rapidly and deal a punctual blow. But the forces were there. The marshals of the defence had cloudy hopes in place of forces: maybe the Cossacks will make up their minds; maybe loyal units will be found in the neighbouring garrison; maybe Kerensky will bring troops from the front. The feelings of Polkovnikov are known from his night telegrams to headquarters: he thought that the game was up. Alexeiev, still less inclined to optimism, soon abandoned the rotten ship.

Delegates from the military schools were brought into headquarters for the purpose of keeping in touch, and an attempt was made to raise their spirits with assurances that troops would soon arrive from Gatchina, Tsarskoe and the front. However they did not much believe in these misty promises, and a depressing rumour began to creep through the schools: "There is a panic in headquarters, nobody is doing anything." And it was so. Cossack officers coming to headquarters to propose that they seize the armoured cars in the Mikailovsky Riding Academy found Polkovnikov sitting on the window-seat in a condition of complete prostration. Seize the riding academy? "Seize it. I have nobody. I can't do anything alone."

While this languid mobilisation of the schools for the defence of the Winter Palace was going on, the ministers assembled at a meeting. The square before the palace and its adjacent streets were still free from insurrectionists. On the corner of Morskaia and Nevsky armed soldiers were holding up passing automobiles and ejecting their passengers. The crowd was making queries: "Are these soldiers of the government or the Military

Revolutionary Committee?" The ministers had for this once the full benefit of their own unpopularity: Nobody was interested in them and hardly anybody recognised them on their way. They all assembled except Prokopovich who was accidentally arrested in a cab—and was, by the way, released again during the day.

The old servants still remained in the palace, having seen much and ceased to be surprised, although not yet cured of fright. Strictly trained, dressed in blue with red collars and gold braids, these relics of the old kept up an atmosphere of order and stability in the luxurious building. They alone perhaps on this alarming morning still gave the ministers an illusion of power.

Not before eleven o'clock in the morning, did the government finally decide to place one of its members at the head of the defence. General Iznikovsky had already refused this honour, offered to him by Kerensky at dawn. Another military man in the staff of the government, Admiral Verderevsky, was still less materially inclined. It thus fell to a civilian to captain the defence—the Minister of Public Charities, Kishkin. An order of the senate confirming his appointment was immediately drawn up and signed by all. Those people had plenty of time to occupy themselves with bureaucratic fandangles. Moreover it never occurred to any of them that Kishkin as a member of the Kadet Party was doubly hated by the soldiers both front and rear. Kishkin in turn selected as his assistants Palchinsky and Ruthenberg. An appointee of the capitalists and protector of lock-outs, Palchinsky enjoyed the hatred of the workers. The engineer Ruthenberg was an aide-de-camp of Savinkov, and Savinkov even the all-embracing party of the Social Revolutionaries had expelled as a Kornilovist. Polkovnikov, under suspicion of treason, was discharged. In his place they appointed General Bagratuni who differed from him in nothing.

Although the city telephones of the Winter Palace and headquarters had been cut off, the palace remained in connection with the more important institutions by its own wire—particularly with the War Ministry which had a direct wire to headquarters. Evidently some of the city apparatus also had not been cut out in the hurry of the moment. In a military sense, however, the telephone connections gave nothing to the government, and in a moral sense they damaged rather than improved its situation for it robbed them of their illusions.

From morning on, the leaders of the defence kept demanding local reinforcements while awaiting reinforcements from the front. Certain people in the city tried to help them. A Doctor Feit who took an active part in this, a member of the Central Committee of the Social Revolutionary Party, told some years later at a legal proceeding about the "astonishing lightning-like change in the mood of the military units." You would learn, he said, from the most reliable sources of the readiness of this or that regiment to come to the defence of the government, but as soon as you called the barracks directly on the telephone, one unit after another would flatly refuse. "The result is known to you," said the old Narodnik. "Nobody came out and the Winter Palace was captured." The fact of the matter is that no lightning-like changes in the garrison took place, but the remaining illusions of the governmental parties did crumble to the ground with lightning speed.

The armoured cars upon which they were especially counting in the Winter Palace and headquarters, were divided into two groups: Bolsheviks and pacifists. None of them was in favour of the government. On the way to the Winter Palace a half-company of engineering junkers ran into two armoured cars which they awaited with a feeling of hope and fear: Are they friends or enemies? It turned out that they were neutral, and had come into the street with the purpose of preventing conflicts between the two sides. Out of the six armoured cars in the Winter Palace only one remained to guard the palace property; the other five departed. In proportion as the insurrection succeeded the number of Bolshevik armoured cars increased, and the neutral army melted away. Such is the fate of pacifism in any serious struggle.

Noon is approaching. The vast square before the Winter Palace is vacant as before. The government has nobody to fill it with. The troops of the Committee do not occupy it, because they are absorbed in carrying out their too complicated plan. Military units, workers' detachments, armoured cars, are still assembling for this wide encirclement. The palace district begins to look like a plague spot which is being encircled far away to avoid direct contact with the infection.

The court of the palace opening on the square is piled up with logs of wood like the court of Smolny. Black three-inch field guns are set up to left and right. Rifles are stacked up in several different places. The small guard of the palace clings close to the building. In the court and the first story, two schools of ensigns from Oranienbaum and Peterhoff are quartered—

not the whole school by any means—and a squad from the Constantinovsky Artillery School wtih six cannon.

During the afternoon a battalion of junkers from the engineering school arrived, having lost half a company on the road. The picture presented when they arrived could in no wise have increased the fighting spirit of the junkers which, according to Stankevich, was inadequate even before. Inside the palace they found a lack of provisions. Even of this nobody had thought in time. A truckload of bread had been seized, it turned out, by patrols of the Committee. Some of the junkers did sentry duty; the rest lay around inactive, uncertain and hungry. No leadership whatever made itself felt. In the square before the palace, and on the quay on the other side, little groups of apparently peaceful passers-by began to appear, and they would snatch the rifles from the junker sentries, threatening them with revolvers.

"Agitators" also began to appear among the junkers. Had they gotten in from the outside? No, these were still evidently internal trouble-makers. They succeeded in starting a ferment among the Oranienbaum and Peterhoff students. The committees of the school called a conference in the White Hall, and demanded that representatives of the government come in and make an explanation. All the ministers came in, with Konovalov at their head. The argument lasted a whole hour. Konovalov was heckled and stopped talking. The Minister of Agriculture, Maslov, made a speech as an old revolutionist. Kishkin explained to the junkers that the government had decided to stand firm as long as possible. According to Stankevich one of the junkers was about to express his readiness to die for the government, but "the obvious coolness of the rest of his comrades held him back." The speech of the other ministers produced actual irritation among the junkers, who interrupted, shouted and even, it seems, whistled. The blue-bloods explained the conduct of the majority of the junkers by their low social origin: "They were all from the plough, half-illiterate, ignorant beasts, cattle. . . ."

The meeting in the besieged palace ended nevertheless in conciliation. The junkers, after they had been promised active leadership and correct information about what was happening, agreed to stay. The chief at the engineering school, appointed commander of the defence, ran his pencil over the plan of the palace, writing in the names of the units. The forces on hand were distributed in fighting positions. The majority of the junkers were stationed on the first floor where they could train their guns on Winter Palace Square through the windows. But they were forbidden to fire first. A battalion of the engineering school was brought out into the courtyard to cover the artillery. Squads were appointed for barricade work. A communication squad was formed with four men from each unit. The artillery squad was directed to defend the gate in case of a breach. Fortifications of fire-wood were laid up in the court and before the gates. Something like order was established. The sentries felt more confident.

A civil war in its first steps before real armies have been formed and before they are tempered, is a war of naked nerves. As soon as a little activity developed on the side of the junkers, —their clearing of the square with gun fire from behind the barricades—the forces and equipment of the defence were enormously over-estimated in the attacking camp. In spite of the dissatisfaction of the Red Guard and the soldiers, the leaders now decided to postpone the assault until they had concentrated their reserves; they were chiefly awaiting the arrival of the sailors from Kronstadt.

The delay of a few hours thus created brought some small reinforcements to the besieged. After Kerensky's promise of infantry to the Cossack delegation the Council of the Cossack Troops had gone into session, the regimental committees had gone into session, and the general assembly of the regiments had gone into session. Decision: Two squadrons and the machine-gun crew of the Uralsky regiment, brought in from the front in July to crush the Bolsheviks, should immediately enter the Winter Palace, the rest not until the promise was actually fulfilled, that is, not until after the arrival of infantry reinforcements. But even with the two squadrons this was not accomplished without argument. The Cossack youth objected. The "old men" even had to lock the young ones up in the stable, where they could not hinder them from equipping themselves for the march. Only at twilight, when they were no longer expected, did these bearded Uraltsi appear in the palace. They were met like saviours. They themselves, however, looked sulky. They were not accustomed to fight about palaces. Yes, and it was not quite clear which side was right.

Some time later there arrived unexpectedly forty of the Knights of St. George under command of a staff captain on a cork leg. Patriotic cripples acting as the last reserves of democracy. . . . But even so they felt better. Soon came also a shock company of the Women's Battalion. What encouraged them most of all was that these reinforcements had made their way through without fighting. The cordon of the besieging forces could not, or did not dare, deny them access to the palace. Quite obviously, therefore, the enemy was weak. "Glory be to God the thing is beginning to pull itself together," said the officers, comforting themselves and the junkers. The new arrivals received their military allotments, replacing those who were tired. However, the Uraltsi glanced with no great approval upon those "wenches" with rifles. Where is the real infantry?

The besiegers were obviously losing time. The Kronstadters were late—not, to be sure, through their own fault. They had been summoned too late. After a tense night of preparation they had begun to embark at dawn. The destroyer *Amur* and the cruiser *Yastreb* had made straight for Petrograd. The old armoured cruiser *Tzaria Svobodi,* after landing marines at Oranienbaum, where it was proposed to disarm the junkers, was to anchor at the entrance to the Morskoy Canal, in order, in case of need, to bombard the Baltic railroad. Five thousand sailors and soldiers disembarked early in the morning from the Island of Kotlin in order to embark on the social revolution. In the officers' cabin a solemn silence reigns: These officers are being taken along to fight for a cause which they hate. The commissar of the detachment, the Bolshevik, Flerovsky, announced to them: "We do not count upon your sympathy, but we demand that you be at your posts. . . . We will spare you any unnecessary unpleasantness." He received the brief naval answer: "Aye, aye, sir!" All took their places. The commander ascended the bridge.

Upon arriving in the Neva a triumphal hurrah: the sailors are greeting their own. A band strikes up on the *Aurora,* anchored in midstream. Antonov addresses the new arrivals with a brief greeting: "There is the Winter Palace. . . . We must take it." In the Kronstadt detachment the most resolute and bold choose themselves out automatically. These sailors in black blouses with rifles and cartridge belts will go all the way. The disembarkation on Konnogvardeisky Boulevard takes but a few moments. Only a military watch remains on the ship.

The forces are now more than adequate on the Nevsky. There are strong outposts on the bridge of the Ekaterininsky Canal and on the bridge of the Moika armoured automobiles and Zenith guns aimed at the Winter Palace. On this side of the Moika the workers have set up machine-guns behind screens.

An armoured car is on duty on Morskaia. The Neva and its crossings are in the hands of the attackers. Chudnovsky and Ensign Dashkevich are ordered to send troops from the Guard regiments to hold Mars Field. Blagonravov from the fortress, after crossing the bridge, is to get into contact with the troops on Mars Field. The sailors just arrived are to keep in contact with the fortress and the crew of the *Aurora*. After artillery fire the storm is to begin.

At the same time five ships of war arrive from the Baltic battle fleet: a cruiser, two destroyers, and two smaller vessels. "However sure we may have been of winning with the forces on hand," writes Flerovsky, "this gift from the navy raised everybody's spirits." Admiral Verderovsky, looking from the windows of the Malachite Hall, could probably see an imposing mutinous flotilla, dominating not only the palace and the surrounding district but also the principal approaches to Petrograd.

About four o'clock in the afternoon Konovalov summoned to the palace by telephone the political leaders standing close to the government. The besieged ministers had need at least of moral support. Of all those invited only Nabokov appeared. The rest preferred to express their sympathy by telephone. Minister Tretiakov complained against Kerensky and against fate: The head of the ministry has fled leaving his colleagues without defence. But perhaps reinforcements will come? Perhaps. However, why aren't they here? Nabokov expressed his sympathy, glancing stealthily at his watch, and hastened to take his farewell. He got out just in time. Shortly after six the Winter Palace was at last solidly surrounded by the troops of the Military Revolutionary Committee. There was no longer any passage either for reinforcements or for individuals.

From the direction of Konnogvardeisky Boulevard, the Admiralty Quay, Morskaia Street, Nevsky Prospect, Mars Field, Milliony Street and Dvortsovy Quay, the oval of the besiegers thickened and contracted. Imposing cordons extended from the iron fences of the Winter Palace garden, still in the hands of the besieged, from the arch between Palace Square and Morskaia Street, from the canal by the Hermitage, from the corners of the Admiralty, and the Nevsky near by the palace. Peter and Paul fortress frowned threateningly from the other side of the river. The *Aurora* looked in from the Neva with her six-inch guns. Destroyers steamed back and forth patrolling the river.

The insurrection looked at that moment like a military manœuvre in the grand style.

On Palace Square, cleared by the junkers three hours before, armoured automobiles now appeared and occupied the entrances and exits. The old patriotic names were still visible on the armour under the new designations painted hastily in red. Under the protection of these steel monsters the attackers felt more and more confident on the square. One of the armoured cars approached the main entrance of the palace, disarmed the junkers guarding it, and withdrew unhindered.

In spite of the complete blockade now at last established, the besieged still kept in touch with the outside world by telephone. To be sure, as early as five o'clock a company of the Keksgolmsky regiment had already occupied the War Ministry, through which the Winter Palace had kept in touch with headquarters. But even after that an officer still remained apparently for some hours at the apparatus of the South-western front, located in an attic chamber of the ministry where the captors never thought of looking. However, as before, this contact was of no help. The answers from the Northern front had become more and more evasive. The reinforcements had not turned up. The mysterious bicycle battalion never arrived. Kerensky himself seemed to have disappeared like a diver. The city friends confined themselves to briefer and briefer expressions of sympathy. The ministers were sick at heart. There was nothing to talk about, nothing to hope for. The ministers disagreed with each other and with themselves. Some sat still in a kind of stupor, others automatically paced up and down the floor. Those inclined to generalisation looked back into the past, seeking a culprit. He was not hard to find: the democracy! It was the democracy which had sent them into the government, laid a mighty burden on them, and at the moment of danger left them without support. For this once the Kadets were fully at one with the socialists. Yes, the democracy was to blame! To be sure, in forming the Coalition both groups had turned their back to an institution as near to them as the Democratic Conference. Independence of the democracy had indeed been the chief idea of the Coalition. But never mind: what does a democracy exist for, if not to rescue a bourgeois government when it gets into trouble? The Minister of Agriculture Maslov, a Right Social Revolutionary, made a note which he himself described as a dying utterance. He solemnly promised to die with a curse to the democracy upon his lips. His colleagues hastened to communicate this fateful intention to the Duma by telephone. His death, to be sure, remained only a project, but there was no lack of curses right on hand.

Up above near the chambers of the commandant there was a dining-room where the court servants served the officer gentlemen a "divine dinner and wine." One could forget unpleasantnesses for a time. The officers figured out seniorities, made envious comparisons, and cursed the new power for its slow promotions. They gave it to Kerensky especially: yesterday at the Pre-Parliament he was vowing to die at his post, and today he beats it out of town dressed up as a sister of mercy. Certain of the officers demonstrated to the members of the government the folly of any further resistance. The energetic Palchinsky declared such officers Bolsheviks, and tried even to arrest them.

The junkers wanted to know what was going to happen next, and demanded from the government explanations which it was not in a position to give. During this new conference between the junkers and the ministers, Kishkin arrived from staff headquarters, bringing an ultimatum signed by Antonov and delivered from the Peter and Paul fortress to the Quartermaster-General, Poradelov, by a bicycle man: Surrender and disarm the garrison of the Winter Palace; otherwise fire will be opened from the guns of the fortress and the ships of war; twenty minutes for reflection. This period had seemed small. Poradelov had managed to extract another ten minutes. The military members of the government, Manikovsky and Verderevsky, approached the matter simply: Since it is impossible to fight, they said, we must think of surrendering—that is, accept the ultimatum. But the civilian ministers remained obstinate. In the end they decided to make no answer to the ultimatum, and to appeal to the city duma as the only legal body existing in the capital. This appeal to the duma was the last attempt to wake up the drowsy conscience of the democracy.

Poradelov, considering it necessary to end the resistance, asked for his discharge: he lacked "confidence in the correctness of the course chosen by the Provisional Government." The hesitations of the officer were put an end to before his resignation could be accepted. In about half an hour a detachment of Red Guards, sailors and soldiers, commanded by an ensign of the Pavlovsky regiment, occupied the staff headquarters without resistance, and arrested the faint-hearted Quartermaster-General. This seizure of the headquarters might have been carried out some time before since the building was completely undefended from within. But until the arrival of armoured cars on the Square the besiegers feared a sortie of junkers from the palace which might cut them off.

After the loss of headquarters the Winter Palace felt still more orphaned. From the Malachite Room, whose windows opened on the Neva, and seemed, as it were, to invite a few shells from the *Aurora,* the ministers removed themselves to one of the innumerable apartments of the palace with windows on the court. The lights were put out. Only a lonely lamp burned on the table, its light shut off from the windows by newspapers.

What will happen to the palace if the *Aurora* opens fire? asked the ministers of their naval colleague. It will be a pile of ruins, exclaimed the admiral readily, and not without a feeling of pride in his naval artillery. Verderevsky preferred a surrender, and was not unwilling to frighten these civilians out of their untimely bravery. But the *Aurora* did not shoot. The fortress also remained silent. Maybe the Bolsheviks after all will not dare carry out their threat?

General Bagratuni, appointed in place of the insufficiently steadfast Polkovnikov, considered this the appropriate moment to announce that he refused any longer to occupy the post of commander of the district. At Kishkin's order the general was demoted "as unworthy," and was requested immediately to leave the palace. On emerging from the gates the former commander fell into the hands of the sailors, who took him to the barracks of the Baltic crew. It might have gone badly with the general, but that Podvoisky, making the rounds of his front before the final attack, took the unhappy warrior under his wing.

From the adjacent streets and quays many noticed how the palace which had just been glimmering with hundreds of electric lights was suddenly drowned in darkness. Among these observers were friends of the government. One of the colleagues of Kerensky, Redemeister, has written: "The darkness in which the palace was drowned presented an alarming enigma." The friends did not take any measures toward solving this enigma. We must confess, however, that the possibilities were not great.

Hiding behind their piles of firewood the junkers followed tensely the cordon forming on Palace Square, meeting every movement of the enemy with rifle and machine-gun fire. They were answered in kind. Towards night the firing became hotter. The first casualties occurred. The victims, however, were only a few individuals. On the square, on the quays, on Milliony, the besiegers accommodated themselves to the situation, hid behind projections, concealed themselves in hollows, clung along the walls. Among the reserves the soldiers and Red Guards warmed themselves around camp fires which they had kindled at nightfall, abusing the leaders for going so slow.

In the palace the junkers were taking up positions in the corridors, on the stairway, at the entrances, and in the court. The outside sentries clung along the fence and walls. The building would hold thousands, but it held hundreds. The vast quarters behind the sphere of defence seemed dead. Most of the servants had scattered, or were hiding. Many of the officers took refuge in the buffet, where they compelled those servants who had not yet made their get-away to set out continual batteries of wines. This drunken debauch of the officers in the agonising palace could not remain a secret to the junkers, Cossacks, cripples and women soldiers. The denouement was preparing not only from without but from within.

An officer of the artillery squad suddenly reported to the commandent of the defence: The junkers have left their weapons in the entrance and are going home, in obedience to orders received from the commandant of the Constantinovsky school. That was a treacherous blow! The commandant tried to object: nobody but he could give orders here. The junkers understood this, but nevertheless preferred to obey the commandant of the school, who in his turn was acting under pressure from the commissar of the Military Revolutionary Committee. A majority of the artillery men, with four of the six guns, abandoned the palace. Held up on the Nevsky by a soldier patrol, they attempted to resist, but a patrol of the Pavlovsky regiment, arriving just in time with an armoured car, disarmed them and sent them to its barracks with two of the guns. The other two were set up on the Nevsky and the bridge over the Moika and aimed at the Winter Palace.

The two squadrons of the Uraltsi were waiting in vain for the arrival of their comrades. Savinkov, who was closely associated with the Council of the Cossack Troops, and had even been sent by it as a delegate to the Pre-Parliament, attempted with the co-operation of General Alexeiev to get the Cossacks in motion. But the chiefs of the Cossack Council, as Miliukov justly observes "could as little control the Cossack regiment as the staff could the troops of the garrison." Having considered the question from all sides, the Cossack regiment finally announced that they would not come out without infantry, and offered their services to the Military Revolutionary Committee for the purpose of guarding the government property. At the same time the Uralsky regiment decided to send delegates to the Winter Palace to call its two squadrons back to the barracks. This suggestion fell in admirably with the new quite well-defined mood of the Uralsky's "old men." There was nobody but strangers around: junkers—among them a number of Jews—invalid officers—yes, and then these female shock troops. With angry and frowning faces the Cossacks gathered up their saddle-bags. No further arguments could move them. Who remained to defend Kerensky? "Yids and wenches. . . . But the Russian people has stayed over there with Lenin." It turned out that the Cossacks were in touch with the besiegers, and they got free passes through an exit till then unknown to the defenders. It was about nine o'clock in the evening when the Uraltsi left the palace. Only their machine-guns they agreed to leave for the defence of a hopeless cause.

By this same entrance too, coming from the direction of Milliony Street, Bolsheviks had before this got into the palace for the purpose of demoralising the enemy. Oftener and oftener mysterious figures began to appear in the corridors beside the junkers. It is useless to resist. The insurrectionists have captured the city and the railroad stations; there are no reinforcements; in the palace they "only keep on lying through inertia. . . ." What are we to do next? asked the junkers. The government refused to issue any direct commands. The ministers themselves would stand by their old decision; the rest could do as they pleased. That meant free egress from the palace for those who wanted it. The government had neither will nor idea left; the ministers passively awaited their fate. Miliantovich subsequently related: "We wandered through the gigantic mousetrap, meeting occasionally, either all together or in small groups, for brief conversations—condemned people, lonely, abandoned by all. . . . Around us vacancy, within us vacancy, and in this grew up the soulless courage of placid indifference."

Antonov-Ovseënko had agreed with Blagonravov that after the encirclement of the palace was completed, a red lantern should be raised on the flagpole of the fortress. At this signal the *Aurora* would fire a blank volley in order to frighten the palace. In case the besieged were stubborn the fortress should begin to bombard the palace with real shells from the light guns. If the palace did not surrender even then, the *Aurora* would open a real fire from its six-inch guns. The object of this gradation was to reduce to a minimum the victims and the damage, supposing they could not be altogether avoided. But the too complicated solution of a simple problem threatened to lead to an opposite result. The difficulty of carying this plan out is too obvious. They are to begin with a red lantern: It turns out that they have none on hand. They lose time hunting for it, and finally find it. However, it is not so simple to tie a lantern to a flagpole in such a way that it will be visible in all directions. Efforts are renewed and twice renewed with a dubious result, and meanwhile the precious time is slipping away.

The chief difficulty developed, however, in connection with the artillery. According to a report made by Blagonravov the bombardment of the capital had been possible on a moment's notice ever since noon. In reality it was quite otherwise. Since there was no permanent artillery in the fortress, except for that rusty-muzzled cannon which announces the noon hour, it was necessary to lift field guns up to the fortress walls. That part of the programme had actually been carried out by noon. But a difficulty arose about finding gunners. It had been known in advance that the artillery company—one of those which had not come out on the side of the Bolsheviks in July—was hardly to be relied on. Only the day before it had meekly guarded a bridge under orders from headquarters. A blow in the back was not to be expected from it, but the company had no intention of going through fire for the soviets. When the time came for action the ensign reported: The guns are rusty; there is no oil in the compressors; it is impossible to shoot. Very likely the guns really were not in shape, but that was not the essence of it. The artillerists were simply dodging the responsibility, and leading the inexperienced commissars by the nose. Antonov dashes up on a cutter in a state of fury. Who is sabotaging the plan? Blagonravov tells him about the lantern, about the oil, about the ensign. They both start to go up to the cannon. Night, darkness, puddles in the court from the recent rains. From the other side of the river comes hot rifle fire and the rattle of machine-guns. In the darkness Blagonravov loses the road. Splashing through the puddles, burning with impatience, stumbling and falling in the mud, Antonov blunders after the commissar through the dark court. "Beside one of the weakly glimmering lanterns," relates Blagonravov . . . "Antonov suddenly stopped and peered inquiringly at me over his spectacles, almost touching my face. I read in his eyes a hidden alarm." Antonov had for a second suspected treachery where there was only carelessness.

The position of the guns was finally found. The artillery men were stubborn: Rust. . . . Compressors. . . . Oil. Antonov gave orders to bring gunners from the naval polygon and also to fire a signal from the antique cannon which announced the noon hour. But the artillery men were suspiciously long monkeying with the signal cannon. They obviously felt that the commanders too, when not far-off at the telephone but right beside them, had no firm will to resort to heavy artillery. Even under the very clumsiness of this plan for artillery fire the same thought is to be felt lurking: Maybe we can get along without it.

Somebody is rushing through the darkness of the court. As he comes near he stumbles and falls in the mud, swears a little but not angrily, and then joyfully and in a choking voice cries out: "The palace has surrendered and our men are there." Rapturous embraces. How lucky there was a delay! "Just what we thought!" The compressors are immediately forgotten. But why haven't they stopped shooting on the other side of the river? Maybe some individual groups of junkers are stubborn about surrendering. Maybe there is a misunderstanding? The misunderstanding turned out to be good news: not the Winter Palace was captured, but only the general staff. The siege of the palace continued.

By secret agreement with a group of junkers of the Oranienbaum school the irrepressible Chudnovsky gets into the palace for negotiations: this opponent of the insurrection never misses a chance to dash into the firing line. Palchinsky arrests the daredevil, but under pressure from the Oranienbaum students is compelled to release both Chudnovsky and a number of the junkers. They take away with them a few of the Cavaliers of St. George. The unexpected appearance of these junkers on the square throws the cordons into confusion. But there is no end of joyful shouting, when the besiegers know that these are surrendering troops. However only a small minority surrenders. The remainder continue to fire from behind their cover. The shooting of the attackers has increased. The bright electric light in the court makes a good mark of the junkers. With difficulty they succeed in putting out the light. Some unseen hand again switches on the light. The junkers shoot at the light, and then find the electrician and make him switch off the current.

The Women's Battalion suddenly announce their intention to make a sortie. According to their information the clerks in General Headquarters have gone over to Lenin, and after disarming some of the officers have arrested General Alexeiev—the sole man who can save Russia. He must be rescued at any cost. The commandant is powerless to restrain them from this hysterical undertaking. At the moment of their sortie the lights again suddenly flare up in the high electric lanterns on each side of the gate. Seeking an electrician the officer jumps furiously upon the palace servants: in these former lackeys of the czar he sees agents of revolution. He puts still less trust in the court electrician: "I would have sent you to the next world long ago if I hadn't needed you." In spite of revolver threats, the electrician is powerless to help. His switch-board is disconnected. Sailors have occupied the electric station and are controlling the light. The women soldiers do not stand up under fire and the greater part of them surrender. The commandant of the defence sends a corporal to report to the government that the sortie of the women's battalion has "led to their destruction," and that the palace is swarming with agitators. The failure of the sortie causes a lull lasting approximately from ten to eleven. The besiegers are busied with the preparation of artillery fire.

The unexpected lull awakens some hopes in the besieged. The ministers again try to encourage their partisans in the city and throughout the country: "The government in full attendance, with the exception of Prokopovich, is at its post. The situation is considered favourable. . . . The Palace is under fire, but only rifle fire and without results. It is clear that the enemy is weak." In reality the enemy is all-powerful but cannot make up his mind to use his power. The government sends out through the country communications about the ultimatum, about the *Aurora*, about how it, the government, can only transfer the power to the Constituent Assembly, and how the first assault on the Winter Palace has been repulsed. "Let the army and the people answer!" But just how they are to answer the ministers do not suggest.

Lashevich meantime has sent two sailor gunners to the fortress. To be sure, they are none too experienced, but they are at least Bolsheviks, and quite ready to shoot from rusty guns without oil in the compressors. That is all that is demanded of them. A noise of artillery is more important at the moment than a well-aimed blow. Antonov gives the order to begin. The gradations indicated in advance are completely followed out. "After a signal shot from the fortress," relates Flerovsky, "the *Aurora* thundered out. The boom and flash of blank fire are much bigger than from a loaded gun. The curious onlookers jumped back from the granite parapet of the quay, fell down and crawled away. . . ." Chudnovsky promptly raises the question: How about proposing to the besieged to surrender. Antonov as promptly agrees with him. Again an interruption. Some group of women and junkers are surrendering. Chudnovsky wants to leave them their arms, but Antonov revolts in time against this too beautiful magnanimity. Laying the rifles on the sidewalk the prisoners go out under convoy along Milliony Street.

The palace still holds out. It is time to have an end. The order is given. Firing begins—not frequent and still less effectual. Out of thirty-five shots fired in the course of an hour and a half or two hours, only two hit the mark, and they only injure the plaster. The other shells go high, fortunately not doing any damage in the city. Is lack of skill the real cause? They were shooting across the Neva with a direct aim at a target as impressive as the Winter Palace: that does not demand a great deal of artistry. Would it not be truer to assume that even Lashevich's artillerymen intentionally aimed high in the hope that things would be settled without destruction and death? It is very difficult now to hunt out any trace of the motive which guided the two nameless sailors. They themselves have spoken no word. Have they dissolved in the immeasurable Russian land, or, like so many of the October fighters, did they lay down their heads in the civil wars of the coming months and years?

Shortly after the first shots, Palchinsky brought the ministers a fragment of shell. Admiral Verderevsky recognised the shell as his own—from a naval gun, from the *Aurora*. But they were shooting blank from the cruiser. It had been thus agreed, was thus testified by Flerovsky, and thus reported to the Congress of Soviets later by a sailor. Was the admiral mistaken? Was the sailor mistaken? Who can ascertain the truth about a cannon shot fired in the thick of night from a mutinous ship at a czar's palace where the last government of the possessing classes is going out like an oilless lamp.

The garrison of the palace was greatly reduced in number. If at the moment of the arrival of the Uraltsi, the cripples and the women's battalion, it rose to a thousand and a half, or perhaps even two thousand, it was now reduced to a thousand, and perhaps considerably less. Nothing can save the day now but a miracle. And suddenly into the despairing atmosphere of the Winter Palace there bursts—not, to be sure, a miracle, but the news of its approach. Palchinsky announces: They have just telephoned from the City Duma that the citizens are getting ready to march from there for the rescue of the government. "Tell everybody," he gives orders to Sinegub, "that the people are coming." The officer runs up and down stairs and through the corridors with the joyful news. On the way he stumbles upon some drunken officers fighting each other with rapiers—shedding no blood, however. The junkers lift up their heads. Passing from mouth to mouth the news becomes more colourful and impressive. The public men, the merchantry, the people, with the clergy at their head, are marching this way to free the beleaguered palace. The people with the clergy! "That will be strikingly beautiful!" A last remnant of energy flares up: "Hurrah! Long live Russia!" The Oranienbaum junkers, who by that time had quite decided to leave, changed their minds and stayed.

But the people with the clergy come very slowly. The number of agitators in the palace is growing. In a minute the *Aurora* will open fire. There is a whispering in the corridors. And this whisper passes from lip to lip. Suddenly two explosions. Sailors have got into the palace and either thrown or dropped from the gallery two hand grenades, lightly wounding two junkers. The sailors are arrested and the wounded bound up by Kishkin, a physician by profession.

The inner resolution of the workers and sailors is great, but it has not yet become bitter. Lest they call it down on their heads, the besieged, being the incomparably weaker side, dare not deal severely with these agents of the enemy who have penetrated the palace. There are no executions. Uninvited guests now begin to appear no longer one by one, but in groups. The palace is getting more and more like a sieve. When the junkers fall upon these intruders, the latter permit themselves to be disarmed. "What cowardly scoundrels!" says Palchinsky scornfully. No, these men were not cowardly. It required a high courage to make one's way into that palace crowded with officers and junkers. In the labyrinth of an unknown building, in dark corridors, among innumerable doors leading nobody knew where, and threatening nobody knew what, the daredevils had nothing to do but surrender. The number of captives grows. New groups break in. It is no longer quite clear who is surrendering to whom, who is disarming whom. The artillery continues to boom.

With the exception of the district immediately adjoining the Winter Palace, the life of the streets did not cease until late at night. The theatres and moving-picture houses were open. To the respectable and educated strata of the capital it was of no consequence apparently that their government was under fire. Redemeister on the Troitsky Bridge saw quietly approaching pedestrians whom the sailors stopped. "There was nothing unusual to be seen." From acquaintances coming from the direction of the People's House Redemeister learned, to the tune of a cannonade, that Chaliapin had been incomparable in *Don Carlos*. The ministers continued to tramp the floors of their mousetrap.

"It is clear that the attackers are weak"; maybe if we hold out an extra hour reinforcements will still arrive. Late at night Kishkin summoned Assistant-Minister of Finance Khrushchev, also a Kadet, to the telephone, and asked him to tell the leaders of the party that the government needed at least a little bit of help in order to hold out until the morning hours, when Kerensky ought finally to arrive with the troops. "What kind of a party is this," shouts Kishkin indignantly, "that can't send us three hundred armed men!" And he is right. What kind of a party is it? These Kadets who had assembled tens of thousands of votes at the elections in Petrograd, could not put out three hundred fighters at the moment of mortal danger to the bourgeois régime. If the ministers had only thought to hunt up in the palace library the books of the materialist Hobbes, they could have read in his dialogues about civil war that there is no use expecting or demanding courage from store-keepers who have gotten rich, "since they see nothing but their own momentary advantage . . . and completely lose their heads at the mere thought of the possibility of being robbed." But after all Hobbes was hardly to be found in the czar's library. The ministers, too, were hardly up to the philosophy of history. Kishkin's telephone call was the last ring from the Winter Palace.

Smolny was categorically demanding an end. We must not drag out the siege till morning, keep the city in a tension, rasp the nerves of the Congress, put a question-mark against the whole victory. Lenin sends angry notes. Call follows call from the Military revolutionary Committee. Podvoisky talks back. It is possible to throw the masses against the palace. Plenty are eager to go. But how many victims will there be, and what will be left of the ministers and the junkers? However, the necessity of carrying the thing though is too imperious. Nothing remains but to make the naval artillery speak. A sailor from Peter and Paul takes a slip of paper to the *Aurora*. Open fire on the palace immediately. Now, it seems, all will be clear. The gunners on the *Aurora* are ready for business, but the leaders still lack resolution. There is a new attempt at evasion. "We decided to wait just another quarter of an hour," writes Flerovsky, "sensing by instinct the possibility of a change of circumstances." By "instinct" here it is necessary to understand a stubborn hope that the thing would be settled by mere demonstrative methods. And this time "instinct" did not deceive. Towards the end of that quarter of an hour a new courier arrived straight from the Winter Palace. The palace is taken!

The palace did not surrender but was taken by storm—this, however, at a moment when the power of resistance of the besieged had already completely evaporated. Hundreds of enemies broke into the corridor—not by the secret entrance this time but through the defended door—and they were taken by the demoralised defenders for the Duma deputation. Even so they were successfully disarmed. A considerable group of junkers got away in the confusion. The rest—at least a number of them—still continued to stand guard. But the barrier of bayonets and rifle-fire between the attackers and defenders is finally broken down.

That part of the palace adjoining the Hermitage is already filled with the enemy. The junkers make an attempt to come at them from the rear. In the corridors phantasmagoric meetings and clashes take place. All are armed to the teeth. Lifted hands hold revolvers. Hand-grenades hang from belts. But nobody shoots and nobody throws a grenade. For they and their enemy are so mixed together that they cannot drag themselves apart. Never mind: the fate of the palace is already decided.

Workers, sailors, soldiers are pushing up from outside in chains and groups, flinging the junkers from the barricades, bursting through the court, stumbling into the junkers on the staircase, crowding them back, toppling them over, driving them upstairs. Another wave comes on behind. The square pours into the court. The court pours into the palace, and floods up and down stairways and through corridors. On the befouled parquets, among mattresses and chunks of bread, people, rifles, hand-grenades are wallowing. The conquerors find out that Kerensky is not there, and a momentary pang of disappointment interrupts their furious joy. Antonov and Chudnovsky are now in the palace. Where is the government? That is the door—there where the junkers stand frozen in the last pose of resistance. The head sentry rushes to the ministers with a question: Are we commanded to resist to the end? No, no, the ministers do not command that. After all, the palace is taken. There is no need of bloodshed. We must yield to force. The ministers desire to surrender with dignity, and sit at the table in imitation of a session of the government. The commandant has already surrendered the palace, negotiating for the lives of the junkers, against which in any case nobody had made the slightest attempt. As to the fate of the government, Antonov refuses to enter into any negotiations whatever.

The junkers at the last guarded doors were disarmed. The victors burst into the room of the ministers. "In front of the crowd and trying to hold back the onpressing ranks strode a rather small, unimpressive man. His clothes were in disorder, a wide-brimmed hat askew on his head, eyeglasses balanced uncertainly on his nose, but his little eyes gleamed with the joy of victory and spite against the conquered." In these annihilating strokes the conquered have described Antonov. It is not hard to believe that his clothes and his hat were in disorder: It is sufficient to remember the nocturnal journey through the puddles of the Peter and Paul fortress. The joy of victory might also doubtless have been read in his eyes; but hardly any spite against the conquered in those eyes—I announce to you, members of the Provisional Government, that you are under arrest—exclaimed Antonov in the name of the Military Revolutionary Committee. The clock then pointed to 2.10 in the morning of October 26.—The members of the Provisional Government submit to force and surrender in order to avoid bloodshed—answered Konovalov. The most important part of the ritual was thus observed.

Antonov summoned twenty-five armed men, choosing them from the first detachments to break into the palace, and turned over to them the defence of the ministry. After drawing up a minute of the proceeding, the arrestees were led out into the square. In the crowd, which had made its sacrifice of dead and wounded, there was in truth a flare up of spite against the conquered. "Death to them! Shoot them!" Individual soldiers tried to strike the ministers. The Red Guards quieted the intemperate ones: Do not stain the proletarian victory! Armed workers surrounded the prisoners and their convoy in a solid ring. "Forward!" They had not far to go—through Milliony and across the Troitsky Bridge. But the excitement of the crowd made that short journey long and full of danger. Minister Nikitin wrote later very truly that but for the energetic intercession of Antonov the consequences might have been "very serious." To conclude their misadventure, the procession while on the bridge was fired on by accident and the arrestees and their convoy had to lie down on the pavement. But here too, nobody was injured. Somebody was evidently shooting in the air as a warning.

In the narrow quarters of the garrison club of the fortress, lighted with a smoky kerosene lamp because the electricity had refused to function that day, forty or fifty men are crowded. Antonov, in the presence of the commissar of the fortress, calls the roll of the ministers. There are eighteen of them, including the highest assistants. The last formalities are concluded; the prisoners are distributed in the rooms of the historic Trubetskoy Bastion. None of the defenders had been arrested: the officers and junkers were paroled on their word of honour that they would not take any action against the soviet power. Only a few of them kept their word.

Immediately after the capture of the Winter Palace rumours went round in bourgeois circles about the execution of junkers, the raping of the women's battalion, the looting of the riches of the palace. All these fables had long ago been refuted when Miliukov wrote this in his *History*: "Those of the Women's Battalion who had not died under fire were seized by the Bolsheviks, subjected during that evening and night to the frightful attentions of the soldiers, to violence and execution." As a matter of fact there were no shootings and, the mood of both sides being what it was at that period, there could not have been any shootings. Still less thinkable were acts of violence, especially within the palace where alongside of various accidental elements from the streets, hundreds of revolutionary workers came in with rifles in their hands.

Attempts at looting were actually made, but it was just these attempts which revealed the discipline of the victors. John Reed, who did not miss one of the dramatic episodes of the revolution, and who entered the palace on the heels of the first cordons, tells how in the basement stores a group of soldiers were prying drawers open with the butts of their guns and dragging out carpets, linen, china, glassware. It is possible that regular robbers were working in the disguise of soldiers, as they did invariably during the last years of the war, concealing their identity in trenchcoats and *papakhi*. The looting had just begun when somebody shouted: "Comrades, keep your hands off, that is the property of the people." A soldier sat down at a table by the entrance with pen and paper: two Red Guards with revolvers stood behind him. Everyone going out was searched, and every object stolen was taken back and listed. In this way they recovered little statues, bottles of ink, daggers, cakes of soap, ostrich feathers. The junkers were also subjected to a careful search, and their pockets turned out to be full of stolen bric-a-brac. The junkers were abused and threatened by the soldiers, but that was as far as it went. Meanwhile a palace guard was formed with the sailor Prikhodko at the head. Sentries were posted everywhere. The palace was cleared of outsiders. In a few hours Chudnovsky was appointed commandant of the Winter Palace.

But what had become of the people, advancing with the clergy at their head to liberate the palace? It is necessary to tell about this heroic attempt, the news of which had for a moment so touched the hearts of the junkers. The city duma was the centre of the anti-Bolshevik forces; its building on the Nevsky was boiling like a cauldron. Parties, factions, sub-factions, groups, remnants and mere influential individuals were there discussing this criminal adventure of the Bolsheviks. From time to time they would call up the ministry languishing in the palace, and tell them that under the weight of universal condemnation the insurrection must inevitably expire. Hours were devoted to dissertations on the moral isolation of the Bolsheviks. Meanwhile the artillery began to speak. The minister Prokopovich, arrested in the morning but soon released, complained to the duma with a weeping voice that he had been deprived of the possibility of sharing the fate of his comrades. He aroused warm sympathy, but the expression of this sympathy used up time.

From the general confusion of ideas and speeches a practical plan is at last produced, and wins stormy applause from the whole meeting. The duma must march in a body to the Winter Palace in order to die there, if necessary, with the government.

The Social Revolutionaries, Mensheviks and Co-operators are all alike seized with a willingness either to save the ministers or fall by their sides. The Kadets, not generally inclined to risky undertakings, this time decide to lay down their heads with the rest. Some provincials accidentally turning up in the hall, the duma journalists, and one man from the general public, request permission in more or less eloquent language to share the fate of the duma. The permission is granted.

The Bolshevik faction tries to offer a prosaic piece of advice: Why wander through the streets in the dark seeking death? Better call up the ministers and persuade them to surrender before blood is shed. But the democrats are indignant: These agents of insurrection want to tear from our hands not only the power, but our right to a heroic death. Meanwhile the members decided, in the interest of history, to take a vote by roll call. After all, one cannot die too late—even though the death be glorious. Sixty-two members of the duma ratify the decision: yes, they are actually going to die under the ruins of the Winter Palace. To this the fourteen Bolsheviks answer that it is better to conquer with Smolny than to die in the Winter Palace, and immediately set off for the meeting of the Soviet Congress. Only three Menshevik-Internationalists decide to remain within the walls of the duma: They have nowhere to go and nothing to die for.

The members of the duma are just on the point of setting out on their last journey when the telephone rings and news comes that the whole of the Executive Committee of the Peasants' Deputies is coming to join them. Unending applause. Now the picture is complete and clear: The representatives of one hundred million peasants, together with the representatives of all classes of the city population are going to die at the hands of an insignificant gang of thugs. There is no lack of speeches and applause.

After the arrival of the Peasants' Deputies the column finally set out along the Nevsky. At the head of the column march the burgomaster, Schreider, and the minister Prokopovich. Among the marchers John Reed noticed the Social Revolutionary, Avksentiev, president of the Peasant Executive Committee, and the Menshevik leaders, Khinchuk and Abramovich, the first of whom was considered Right, the second Left. Prokopovich and Schreider each carried a lantern: it had been so agreed by telephone with the ministers, in order that the junkers should not take friends for enemies. Prokopovich carried besides this an umbrella, as did many others. The clergy were not present. The clergy had been created out of misty fragments of the history of the fatherland by the none too opulent imagination of the junkers. But the people also were absent. Their absence determined the character of the whole scheme. Three or four hundred "representatives" and not one man of those whom they represented! "It was a dark night," remembers the Social Revolutionary, Zenzinov, "and the lights on the Nevsky were not burning. We marched in a regular procession and only our singing of the 'Marseillaise' was to be heard. Cannon shots resounded in the distance: that was the Bolsheviks continuing to bombard the Winter Palace."

At the Ekaterininsky Canal a patrol of armed sailors was stretched out across the Nevsky, blocking the way for this column of the democracy. "We are going forward," declared the condemned, "What can you do to us?" The sailors answered frankly that they would use force: "Go home and leave us alone." Someone of the marchers suggested that they die right there on the spot. But in the decision adopted by a roll call vote in the duma this variant had not been foreseen. The minister Prokopovich clambered up on some sort of elevation and "waving his umbrella"—rains are frequent in the autumn in Petrograd—urged the demonstrators not to lead into temptation those dark and deceived people who might actually resort to arms. "Let us return to the duma and talk over methods of saving the country and the revolution."

This was truly a wise proposal. To be sure, the original plan would then remain unfulfilled. But what can you do with armed ruffians who will not permit the leaders of the democracy to die a heroic death? "They stood around for a while, got chilly and decided to go back," writes Stankevich mournfully. He too was a marcher in this procession. Without the "Marseillaise" now —on the contrary in a glum silence—the procession moved back along the Nevsky to the duma building. There at last it would surely find "methods of saving the country and the revolution."

With the capture of the Winter Palace the Military Revolutionary Committee came into full possession of the capital. But just as the nails and hair continue to grow on a corpse, so the overthrown government continued to show signs of life through its official press. *The Herald of the Provisional Government*, which on the 24th had announced the retirement of the Privy Councillors with their uniform and pince-nez, had suddenly disappeared on the 25th—an event which, to be sure, nobody noticed. But on the 26th it appeared again as if nothing had happened. On the first page it carried a rubric: "In consequence of the shutting off of the electric current the issue of October 25 did not appear." In all other respects except only the electric current, the governmental life was going on in due order, and the *Herald* of a government now located in the Trubetskoy Bastion announced the appointment of a dozen new senators. In its column of "administrative information" a circular of the Minister of the Interior, Nikitin, advised the commissars of the provinces "not to be influenced by false rumours of events in Petrograd where all is tranquil." The minister was not after all so far wrong. The days of the revolution went by peacefully enough, but for the cannonading, whose effect was only acoustic. But just the same the historian will make no mistake if he says that on October 25th not only was the electric current shut off in the government printing plant, but an important page was turned in the history of mankind.

CHAPTER IX

The October Insurrection

Physical analogies with revolution come so naturally that some of them have become worn-out metaphors: "Volcanic eruption," "birth of a new society," "boiling point." . . . Under the simple literary image there is concealed here an intuitive grasp of the laws of dialectic—that is, the logic of evolution.

Armed insurrection stands in the same relation to revolution that revolution as a whole does to evolution. It is the critical point when accumulating quantity turns with an explosion into quality. But insurrection itself again is not a homogeneous and indivisible act: it too has its critical points, its inner crises and accelerations.

An extraordinary importance both political and theoretical attaches to that short period immediately preceding the "boiling point"—the eve, that is, of the insurrection. Physics teaches that the steady increase of temperature suddenly comes to a stop; the liquid remains for a time at the same temperature, and boils only after absorbing an additional quantity of heat. Everyday language also comes to our aid here, designating this condition of pseudo-tranquil concentration preceding an explosion as "the lull before the storm."

When an unqualified majority of the workers and soldiers of Petrograd had come over to the Bolsheviks, the boiling temperature, it seemed, was reached. It was then that Lenin proclaimed the necessity of immediate insurrection. But it is striking to observe that something was still lacking to the insurrection. The workers, and especially the soldiers, had to absorb some additional revolutionary energy.

The contradiction between word and deed is unknown to the masses, but the passing over from word to deed—even to a simple strike, and so much the more to insurrection—inevitably calls out inner frictions and molecular regroupings: some move forward, others have to crowd back. Civil war in general is distinguished in its first steps by an extraordinary indecisiveness. Both camps are as though stuck fast in the same national soil; they cannot break away from their own environment with its intermediate groupings and moods of compromise.

The lull before the storm in the lower ranks produced a sudden hesitation among the guiding groups. Those organs and institutions which had been formed in the comparatively tranquil period of preparation—for revolution has like war its peaceful period, its days of calm—proved even in the most tempered party inadequate, or at least not wholly adequate, to the tasks of insurrection. A certain reconstruction and shifting about is unavoidable at the critical moment. Far from all the delegates of the Petrograd Soviet who voted for a soviet government were really imbued with the idea that an armed insurrection had become the task of the day. In order to convert the Soviet into a machine of insurrection, it was necessary with as little disturbance as possible to bring them over to this new course. In the circumstances of a matured crisis this did not require months, or even many weeks. But just in those last days it was most dangerous to fall out of step, to give orders for a jump some days before the Soviet was ready to make it, to bring confusion into one's own ranks, to cut off the party from the Soviet even for 24 hours.

Lenin more than once repeated that the masses are far to the left of the party, just as the party is to the left of the Central Committee. Applied to the revolution as a whole this was perfectly true. But these correlations too, have their deep inward oscillations. In April, in June, and especially at the beginning of July, the workers and soldiers were impatiently pushing the party along the path toward decisive action. After the July raids the masses became more cautious. They wanted a revolution as before, and more than before, but having badly burnt themselves once, they feared another failure. Throughout July, August and September, the party was daily holding back the workers and soldiers, whom the Kornilovists on their part were challenging into the streets with all their might. The political experience of those last months had greatly developed the inhibitory centres not only of the leaders, but of the led. The unbroken success of the agitation had nourished in its turn the inertia of the time-biding-attitude. A new political orientation was not enough for the masses: they had need of a psychological readjustment. An insurrection takes in broader masses, the more the commands of the revolutionary party fuse with the command of circumstances.

The difficult problem of passing from the political preparation to the actual technique of insurrection arose throughout the whole country in different forms, but in essence it was everywhere the same. Muralov tells how in the Moscow military organisation of the Bolsheviks opinion as to the necessity of a seizure of power was unanimous; however "the attempt to decide concretely how this seizure should be carried out remained unresolved." The last connecting link was lacking.

During those days when Petrograd was full of the transfer of the garrison, Moscow was living in an atmosphere of continual strike conflicts. On the initiative of a factory committee the Bolshevik faction of the soviet put forward a plan to settle economic conflicts by means of decrees. The preparatory steps took a good deal of time. Only on the 23rd of October was "Revolutionary Decree No. 1" adopted by the soviet bodies. It provided that: Workers and clerks in factories and shops shall henceforth be employed and discharged only with the consent of the shop committees. This meant that the soviet had begun to function as a state power. The inevitable resistance of the government would, according to the design of the initiators, unite the masses more closely round the soviet and lead to an open conflict. This idea never came to the test because the revolution in Petrograd gave Moscow, together with all the rest of the country, a far more imperative motive for insurrection—the necessity of coming promptly to the support of the newly formed society government.

The attacking side is almost always interested in seeming on the defensive. A revolutionary party is interested in legal coverings. The coming Congress of Soviets, although in essence a Soviet of revolution, was nevertheless for the whole popular mass indubitably endowed, if not with the whole sovereignty, at least with a good half of it. It was a question of one of the elements of a dual power making an insurrection against the other. Appealing to the Congress as the source of authority, the Military Revolutionary Committee accused the government in advance of preparing an attempt against the soviets. This accusation flowed logically from the whole situation. In so far as the government did not intend to capitulate without a fight, it could not help getting ready to defend itself. But by this very fact it became liable to the accusation of conspiracy against the highest organ of the workers, soldiers and peasants. In its struggle against the Congress of Soviets which was to overthrow Kerensky, the government lifted its hand against that source of power from which Kerensky had issued.

It would be a serious mistake to regard all this as juridical hair-splitting of no interest to the people. On the contrary, it was in just this form that the fundamental facts of the revolution reflected themselves in the minds of the masses. It was necessary to make full use of this extraordinary advantageous tie-up. In thus giving a great political goal to the natural disinclination of the soldier to pass from the barracks to the trenches, and in mobilising the garrison for the defence of the Soviet Congress, the revolutionary leaders did not bind their hands in the slightest degree regarding the date of the insurrection. The choice of the day and hour depended upon the further course of the conflict. The freedom to manœuvre belonged to the strongest.

"First conquer Kerensky and then call the Congress," Lenin kept repeating, fearing that insurrection would be replaced with constitutional by-play. Lenin had obviously not yet appreciated the new factor which had intruded into the preparation of the insurrection and changed its whole character, the sharp conflict between the Petrograd garrison and the government. If the Congress of Soviets was to decide the question of power; if the government wanted to dismember the garrison in order to prevent the Congress from becoming the power; if the garrison without awaiting the Congress of Soviets had refused to obey the government, why this meant that in essence the insurrection had begun, and begun without waiting for the Congress, although under cover of its authority. It would have been wrong politically, therefore, to separate the preparation of the insurrection from the preparation for the Congress of Soviets.

The peculiarities of the October revolution can best be understood by contrasting it with the February revolution. In making this comparison it is not necessary, as in other cases, to assume conditionally the identity of a whole series of circumstances. They are in reality identical. The scene is Petrograd in both cases: the same arena, the same social groupings, the same proletariat, and the same garrison. The victory in both cases was attained by the going over of a majority of the reserve regiments to the side of the workers. But within the framework of these fundamental traits what an enormous difference! The two Petrograd revolutions, historically completing each other in the course of eight months, seem in their contrasting traits almost predestined to promote an understanding of the nature of insurrection in general.

The February insurrection is called spontaneous. We have introduced in their due place all the necessary limitations to this description. But it is true in any case that in February nobody laid out the road in advance, nobody voted in the factories and barracks on the question of revolution, nobody summoned the masses from above to insurrection. The indignation accumulated for years broke to the surface unexpectedly, to a considerable degree, even to the masses themselves.

It was quite otherwise in October. For eight months the masses had been living an intense political life. They had not only been creating events, but learning to understand their connections. After each action they had critically weighed its results. Soviet parliamentarism had become the daily mechanics of the political life of the people. When they were deciding by a vote questions of strikes, of street manifestations, of the transfer of regiments to the front, could the masses forgo an independent decision on the question of insurrection?

From this invaluable and sole substantial conquest of the February revolution there arose, however, new difficulties. It was impossible to summon the masses to battle in the name of the Soviet without raising the question formally in the Soviet—that is, without making the problem of insurrection a subject of public debate, and that too, with the participation of representatives of the hostile camp. The necessity of creating a special, and to the extent possible a disguised, soviet organ for the leadership of the insurrection was obvious. But this too demanded democratic procedures, with all their advantages and all their delays. The resolution on the Military Revolutionary Committee adopted on the 9th of October was carried out only on the 20th. But that was not the chief difficulty. To take advantage of the majority in the Soviet and compose the Committee of Bolsheviks alone, would have provoked discontent among the non-party men, to say nothing of the Left Social Revolutionaries and certain groups of anarchists. The Bolsheviks in the Military Revolutionary Committee would submit to the decisions of their party—although not always without resistance—but it was impossible to demand discipline of the non-party men and the Left Social Revolutionaries. To get an *a priori* resolution of insurrection at a definite date from them was not to be thought of. And moreover it was extremely imprudent even to put the question to them. By means of the Military Revolutionary Committee, therefore, it was possible only to draw the masses into insurrection, sharpening the situation from day to day and making the conflict irrevocable.

Would it not have been simpler in that case to summon the insurrection directly in the name of the party? This form of action undoubtedly has weighty advantages. But its disadvantages are hardly less obvious. In those millions upon whom the party legitimately counted it is necessary to distinguish three layers: one which was already with the Bolsheviks on all conditions; another, more numerous, which supported the Bolsheviks in so far as they acted through the soviets; a third which followed the soviets in spite of the fact that they were dominated by Bolsheviks.

These three layers were different not only in political level, but to a considerable degree also in social ingredients. Those standing for the Bolsheviks as a party were above all industrial workers, with the hereditary proletarians of Petrograd in the front rank. Those standing for the Bolsheviks in so far as they had a legal soviet cover, were a majority of the soldiers. Those standing for the soviets, independently and regardless of the fact that an overplus of Bolsheviks dominated them, were the more conservative groups of workers—former Mensheviks and Social Revolutionaries, who dreaded to break away from the rest of the masses—the more conservative parts of the army even including the Cossacks, and the peasants who had freed themselves from the leadership of the Social Revolutionary party and were adhering to its left flank.

It would be an obvious mistake to identify the strength of the Bolshevik party with the strength of the soviets led by it. The latter was much greater than the former. However, without the former it would have been mere impotence. There is nothing mysterious in this. The relations between the party and the Soviet grew out of the disaccord inevitable in a revolutionary epoch between the colossal political influence of Bolshevism and its narrow organisational grasp. A lever correctly applied makes the human arm capable of lifting a weight many times exceeding its living force, but without the living arm the lever is nothing but a dead stick.

At a Moscow regional conference of the Bolsheviks at the end of September, one of the delegates reported: "In Yegorevsk the influence of the Bolsheviks is undivided. . . . But the party organisation as such is weak. It is in complete neglect; their is neither regular registration nor membership dues." This disproportion between influence and organisation, although not everywhere so marked, was a general phenomenon. Broad masses knew of the Bolshevik slogans and the soviet organisation. The two fused completely in their minds in the course of September and October. What the people were waiting for was that the soviets should show them when and how to carry out the programme of the Bolsheviks.

The party itself systematically educated the masses in this spirit. In Kiev, when the rumour went round that an insurrection was preparing, the Bolshevik Executive Committee immediately came out with a denial: "No action without the summons of the Soviet must take place. . . . Not a step without the Soviet!" In denying on the 18th of October the rumours of an insurrection alleged to have been appointed for the 22nd, Trotsky said: "The Soviet is an elective institution and . . . cannot make a decision which is unknown to the workers and soldiers. . . ." Repeated daily and reinforced by practical action, such formulæ entered into the flesh and blood of the masses.

According to the report of Ensign Berezin, at an October military conference of the Bolsheviks in Moscow the delegates were saying: "It is hard to know whether the troops will come out at the summons of the Moscow committee of the Bolsheviks. At the summons of the Soviet they might all come out." Nevertheless even in September the Moscow garrison had voted 90 per cent. Bolshevik. At a conference of October 16th in Petrograd, Boky made this report in the name of the party committee: In the Moscow district "they will come out at the summons of the Soviet, but not of the party"; in the Nevsky district "all will follow the Soviet." Volodarsky thereupon summarised the state of mind in Petrograd in the following words: "The general impression is that nobody is eager to go into the streets, but all will appear at the call of the Soviet." Olga Ravich corrected him: "Some say also at the call of the party." At a Petrograd Garrison Conference on the 18th, delegates reported that their regiments were awaiting the summons of the Soviet to come out. Nobody mentioned the party, notwithstanding that the Bolsheviks stood at the head of many units. Thus unity in the barracks could be preserved only by uniting the sympathetic, the wavering, and the semi-hostile under the discipline of the Soviet. The grenadier regiment even declared that it would come out only at the command of the Congress of Soviets. The very fact that agitators and organisers in estimating the state of mind of the masses always alluded to the distinction between the Soviet and the party, shows what great significance this question had from the standpoint of the summons to insurrection.

The chauffeur Mitrevich tells how in a squad of motor-trucks, where they did not succeed in carrying a resolution in favour of insurrection, the Bolsheviks put through a compromise proposal: "We will not come out either for the Bolsheviks or the Mensheviks, but . . . we will carry out without delay all the demands of the Second Congress of Soviets." These Bolsheviks were applying on a small scale to the motor-truck squad the same enveloping tactics which were being applied at large by the Military Revolutionary Committee. Mitrevich is not arguing but telling a story—the more convincing his testimony!

Attempts to lead the insurrection directly through the party nowhere produced results. A highly interesting piece of testimony is preserved regarding the preparation of the uprising in Kineshma, a considerable centre of the textile industry. After insurrection in the Moscow region had been placed on the order of the day, the party committee in Kineshma elected a special trio to take an inventory of the military forces and supplies, and prepare for armed insurrection—calling them for some reason "the Directory." "We must say, however," writes one of the members of this directory, "that little appears to have been done by the elected trio. Events took a somewhat different course. . . . The regional strike wholly took possession of us, and when the decisive events came, the organisational centre was transferred to the strike committee and the soviet." On the modest provincial scale the same thing was repeated here which occurred in Petrograd.

The party set the soviets in motion, the soviets set in motion the workers, soldiers, and to some extent the peasantry. What was gained in mass was lost in speed. If you represent this conducting apparatus as a system of cog-wheels—a comparison to which Lenin had recourse at another period on another theme—you may say that the impatient attempt to connect the party wheel directly with the gigantic wheel of the masses—omitting the medium-sized wheel of the soviets—would have given rise to the danger of breaking the teeth of the party wheel, and nevertheless not setting sufficiently large masses in motion.

The opposite danger was, however, no less real—the danger of letting slip a favourable situation as a result of inner frictions in the soviet system. Speaking theoretically, the most favourable opportunity for an insurrection reduces itself to such and such a point in time. There can be no thought of practically lighting upon this ideal point. The insurrection may develop with success on the rising curve approaching this ideal culmination—but also on the descending curve, before the correlation of forces has yet radically changed. Instead of a "moment" we have then a section of time measured in weeks, and sometimes months. The Bolsheviks could have seized the power in Petrograd at the beginning of July. But if they had done so they could not have held it. Beginning with the middle of September they could hope not only to seize the power but also to keep hold of it. If the Bolsheviks had delayed the insurrection beyond the end of October they would probably—although far from surely—have still been able for a certain time to make up for the omission. We may assume conditionally that for a period of three or four months—September to December approximately—the political premises for a revolution were at hand. The thing had ripened but not yet fallen apart. Within these bounds, which are easier to establish after the fact than in the course of action, the party had a certain freedom of choice which gave rise to inevitable and sometimes sharp disagreements of a practical character.

Lenin proposed to raise the insurrection in the days of the Democratic Conference. At the end of September he considered any delay not only dangerous but fatal. "Waiting for the Congress of Soviets," he wrote at the beginning of October, "is a childish toying with formalities—a shameful toying with formalities, betrayal of the revolution." It is not likely, however, that anybody among the Bolshevik leaders was guided in this question by formal considerations. When Zinoviev, for example, demanded a preliminary conference with the Bolshevik faction of the Soviet Congress, he was not seeking a formal sanction, but simply counting on the political support of the provincial delegates against the Central Committee. But the fact is that the dependence of the party on the Soviet—which, in its turn, was appealing to the Congress of Soviets—introduced an element of indefiniteness into the insurrection which greatly and quite justly alarmed Lenin.

The question when to summon the insurrection, was closely bound up with the question who should summon it. The advantages of summoning it in the name of the Soviet were only too clear to Lenin, but he understood sooner than others what difficulties would arise along that road. He could not but fear, especially from a distance, that the hindering elements would prove still stronger in the soviet summits than in the Central Committee, whose policy even without that he considered irresolute. Lenin approached the question who should begin, the Soviet or the party, as a choice between two possible alternatives, but in the first weeks he was decidedly in favour of the independent initiative of the party. In this there was not the shadow of a thought of contrasting the two plans in principle. It was a question of two approaches to an insurrection resting upon one and the same basis, in one and the same situation, for one and the same goal. But nevertheless these were two different approaches.

Lenin's proposal to surround the Alexandrinka and arrest the Democratic Conference flowed from the assumption that the insurrection would be headed not by the soviets, but by the party appealing directly to the factories and barracks. It could not have been otherwise. To carry such a plan through by way of the Soviet was absolutely unthinkable. Lenin was clearly aware that even among the heads of the party his plan would meet resistance; he recommended in advance that they should "not strive after numbers," in the Bolshevik faction of the Conference. With determination up above, the numbers would be guaranteed by the lower ranks. Lenin's bold plan had the indubitable advantages of swiftness and unexpectedness, but it laid the party too bare, incurring the risk that within certain limits it would set itself over against the masses. Even the Petrograd Soviet, taken unawares, might at the first failure lose its still unstable Bolshevik majority.

The resolution of October 10th proposed to the local organisations of the party to decide all questions practically from the point of view of an approaching insurrection. There is not a word in the resolution of the Central Committee about the soviets as organs of the insurrection. At the conference of the 16th, Lenin said: "Facts show that we have the advantage over the enemy. Why cannot the Central Committee begin?" This question on Lenin's lips was by no means rhetorical. It meant: Why lose time accommodating ourselves to the complicated soviet transmission if the Central Committee can give the signal immediately. However, this time the resolution proposed by Lenin concluded with an expression of "confidence that the Central Committee and the Soviet will indicate in good season the favourable moment and expedient methods of action." The mention of the Soviet together with the party, and the more flexible formulation of the question of date, were the result of Lenin's having felt out through the party leaders the resistance of the masses.

The next day in his polemic with Zinoviev and Kamenev, Lenin summed up as follows the debates of the day before: "All agreed that at the summons of the soviets and for the defence of the soviets the workers will come out as one man." This meant: Even if not all are in agreement with him, Lenin, that you can issue the summons in the name of the party, all are agreed that you can do it in the name of the soviets.

"Who is to seize the power?" writes Lenin on the evening of the 24th. "That is now of no importance. Let the Military Revolutionary Committee take it, or 'some other institution,' which will declare that it will surrender the power only to the genuine representatives of the interests of the people." "Some other institution" enclosed in mysterious quotation-marks—that is a conspirative designation for the Central Committee of the Bolsheviks. Lenin here renews his September proposal that action be taken directly in the name of the Central Committee—this time in case soviet legality should hinder the Military Revolutionary Committee from placing the Congress before the accomplished fact of an overthrow.

Although this whole struggle about dates and methods of insurrection continued for a week, not all those who took part in it were clearly aware of its sense and significance. "Lenin proposed the seizure of power through the soviets whether in Leningrad or Moscow, and not behind the back of the soviets," wrote Stalin in 1924. "For what purposes did Trotsky require this more than strange legend about Lenin?" And again: "The party knows Lenin as the greatest Marxist of our times . . . strange to any tinge of Blanquism." Whereas Trotsky "gives us not the great Lenin, but some sort of a dwarf Blanquist. . . ." Not only a Blanquist but a dwarf! In reality the question in whose name to raise an insurrection, and in the hands of what institution to seize the power, is not in the least predetermined by any doctrine. When the general conditions for a revolution are at hand, insurrection becomes a practical problem of art, a problem which can be solved by various methods. This part of the disagreements in the Central Committee was analogous to the quarrel of the officers of a general staff educated in the same military doctrine and appraising alike the strategic situation, but proposing different ways of solving their most immediate—extraordinarily important, to be sure, but nevertheless particular—problem. To mix in here the question of Marxism and Blanquism is only to reveal a lack of understanding of both.

Professor Pokrovsky denies the very importance of the alternative: Soviet or party. Soldiers are no formalists, he laughs: they did not need a Congress of Soviets in order to overthrow Kerensky. With all its wit such a formulation leaves unexplained the problem: Why create soviets at all if the party is enough? "It is interesting," continues the professor, "that nothing at all came of this aspiration to do everything almost legally, with soviet legality, and the power at the last moment was taken not by the Soviet, but by an obviously 'illegal' organisation created *ad hoc*." Pokrovsky here cites the fact that Trotsky was compelled "in the name of the Military Revolutionary Committee," and not the Soviet, to declare the government of Kerensky non-existent. A most unexpected conclusion! The Military Revolutionary Committee was an elected organ of the Soviet. The leading rôle of the Committee in the overturn did not in any sense violate that soviet legality which the professor makes fun of but of which the masses were extremely jealous. The Council of People's Commissars was also created *ad hoc*. But that did not prevent it from becoming and remaining an organ of the soviet power, including Pokrovsky himself in its staff as deputy People's Commissar of Education.

The insurrection was able to remain on the ground of soviet legality, and to a certain degree even within the limits of the tradition of the dual power, thanks mainly to the fact that the Petrograd garrison had almost wholly submitted to the Soviet before the revolution. In numberless memoirs, anniversary articles and early historic essays, this fact, confirmed by manifold documents, was taken as indubitable. "The conflict in Petrograd developed about the question of the fate of the garrison," says the first book about October—a book written upon the basis of fresh recollections by the author of the present work in the intervals between sessions of the Brest-Litovsk conference, a book which for several years served the party as a text-book of history. "The fundamental question about which the whole movement in October was built up and organised" —this is the still more definite expression of Sadovsky, one of the direct organisers of the uprising—"was the question of the transfer of the Petrograd garrison to the Northern front." Not one of the closest leaders of the insurrection then taking part in a collective conversation with the immediate purpose of reviving and establishing the course of events, took it into his head to object to this statement of Sadovsky or correct it. Only after 1924 did it suddenly become known that Trotsky had overestimated the significance of the peasant garrison to the detriment of the Petrograd workers—a scientific discovery which most happily supplements the accusation that he underestimated the peasantry. Scores of young historians with Professor Pokrovsky at their head have explained to us in recent years the importance of the proletariat in a proletarian revolution, have waxed indignant that we do not speak of the workers when we are talking about the soldiers, have arraigned us for analysing the real course of events instead of repeating copybook phrases. Pokrovsky condenses the results of this criticism in the following conclusion: "In spite of the fact that Trotsky very well knows that the armed insurrection was decided upon by the party . . . and it was perfectly clear that the pretext to be found for the action was a secondary matter, nevertheless for him the Petrograd garrison stands at the centre of the whole picture . . . as though, if it hadn't been for that, there would have been no thought of an insurrection." For our historian the "decision of the party" regarding the insurrection is alone significant, and how the insurrection took place in reality is "a secondary matter." A pretext he says, can always be found. Pokrovsky gives the name of pretext to the method by which the troops were won over—to the solution, that is, of the very problem which summarises the fate of every insurrection. The proletarian revolution would undoubtedly have taken place even without the conflict about the transfer of the garrison—in that the professor is right. But that would have been a different insurrection and would have demanded a different exposition. We have in view the events which actually happened.

One of the organisers and afterward a historian of the Red Guard, Malakhovsky, insists that it was the armed workers in distinction to the semi-passive garrison which showed initiative, determination and endurance in the insurrection. "The Red Guard detachments during the October revolution," he writes, "occupied the governmental institutions, the Post Office, the telegraph, and they were in the front rank during the battles, etc. . . ." All that is indubitable. It is not difficult to understand, however, that if the Red Guard was able to simply "occupy" these institutions, that is only because the garrison was at one with them; it supported or at least did not hinder them. This decided the fate of the insurrection.

The very broaching of such a question as who was more important to the insurrection, the soldiers or the workers, shows that we are on so miserably low a theoretic level that there is hardly room for argument. The October revolution was a struggle of the proletariat against the bourgeoisie for power, but the outcome of the struggle was decided in the last analysis by the muzhik. That general schema, which prevailed throughout the country, found its most perfect expression in Petrograd. What here gave the revolution the character of a brief blow with a minimum number of victims, was the combination of a revolutionary conspiracy, a proletarian insurrection, and the struggle of a peasant garrison for self-preservation. The party led the uprising; the principal motive force was the proletariat; the armed detachments of workers were the first of the insurrection; but the heavy-weight peasant garrison decided the outcome of the struggle.

It is upon just this question that a contrasting of the February with the October revolution is most indispensable. On the eve of the overthrow of the monarchy the garrison represented for both sides a great unknown; the soldiers themselves did not yet know how they would react to an insurrection of the workers. Only a general strike could create the necessary arena for mass encounters of the workers with the soldiers, for the trying-out of the soldiers in action, for the coming over of the soldiers to the side of the workers. In this consisted the dramatic content of the five February days.

On the eve of the overthrow of the Provisional Government the overwhelming majority of the garrison were standing openly on the side of the workers. Nowhere in the whole country was the government so isolated as in its own residence. No wonder it struggled to get away. But in vain: the hostile capital would not let go. With its unsuccessful attempt to push out the revolutionary regiments the government conclusively destroyed itself.

To explain the passive policy of Kerensky before the uprising solely by his personal qualities, is merely to slide over the surface of things. Kerensky was not alone. There were people in the government like Palchinsky not lacking in energy. The leaders of the Executive Committee well knew that the victory of the Bolsheviks meant political death for them. All of them, however, jointly and singly, turned out to be paralysed, fell like Kerensky into a kind of heavy half-sleep—that sleep in which, in spite of the danger hanging over him, a man is powerless to lift a hand to save himself.

The fraternisation of the workers and soldiers in October did not grow out of open street encounters as in February, but preceded the insurrection. If the Bolsheviks did not now call a general strike, it was not because they were unable, but because they did not feel the need. The Military Revolutionary Committee before the uprising already felt itself master of the situation; it knew every part of the garrison, its mood, its inner groupings; it was receiving reports every day—not for show, but expressing the actual facts; it could at any time send a plenipotentiary commissar, a bicycle man with an order, to any regiment; it could summon to its office by telephone the committee of the unit, or give orders to the company on duty. The Military Revolutionary Committee occupied in relation to the troops the position of a governmental headquarters, not the headquarters of conspirators.

To be sure, the commanding summits of the state remained in the hands of the government. But the material foundation was removed from under them. The ministries and the headquarters were hanging over an empty space. The telephones and telegraph continued to serve the government—so did the State Bank. But the government no longer had the military forces to retain possession of these institutions. It was as though the Winter Palace and Smolny had changed places. The Military Revolutionary Committee had placed the phantom government in such a position that it could do nothing at all without breaking up the garrison. But every attempt of Kerensky to strike at the troops only hastened his end.

However, the task of the revolution still remained unachieved. The spring and the whole mechanism of the watch were in the hands of the Military Revolutionary Committee, but it lacked the hands and face. And without these details a clock cannot fulfil its function. Without the telegraph and telephone, without the bank and headquarters, the Military Revolutionary Committee could not govern. It had almost all the real premises and elements of power, but not the power itself.

In February the workers had thought, not of seizing the banks and the Winter Palace, but of breaking the resistance of the army. They were fighting not for individual commanding summits, but for the soul of the soldier. Once the victory was won in this field, all remaining problems solved themselves. Having surrendered its guard battalions, the monarchy no longer made an attempt to defend either its court or its headquarters.

In October the government of Kerensky, having irrevocably lost the soul of the soldier, still clung to the commanding summits. In its hands the headquarters, the banks, the telephone, were only the façade of power. When they should come into the hands of the soviets, they would guarantee the conquest of complete power. Such was the situation on the eve of the insurrection, and it decided the forms of activity during the last twenty-four hours.

Demonstrations, street fights, barricades—everything comprised in the usual idea of insurrection—were almost entirely absent. The revolution had no need of solving a problem already solved. The seizure of the governmental machine could be carried through according to plan with the help of comparatively small armed detachments guided from a single centre. The barracks, the fortress, the storehouses, all those enterprises in which workers and soldiers functioned, could be taken possession of by their own internal forces. But the Winter Palace, the Pre-Parliament, the district headquarters, the ministries, the military schools, could not be captured from within. This was true also of the telephone, the telegraph, the Post Office and the State Bank. The workers in these institutions, although of little weight in the general combination of forces, nevertheless ruled within their four walls, and these were, moreover, strongly guarded with sentries. It was necessary to penetrate these bureaucratic high points from without. Political conquest was here replaced by forcible seizure. But since the preceding crowding-out of the government from its military bases had made resistance almost impossible, this military seizure of the final commanding heights passed off as a general rule without conflicts.

To be sure, the thing was not after all settled without fighting. The Winter Palace had to be taken by storm. But the very fact that the resistance of the government came down to a defence of the Winter Palace, clearly defines the place occupied by October 25th in the whole course of the struggle. The Winter Palace was the last redoubt of a régime politically shattered during its eight months' existence, and conclusively disarmed during the preceding two weeks.

Conspiratorial elements—understanding by this term, plan and centralised leadership—occupied an insignificant place in the February revolution. This resulted from the mere weakness and scatteredness of the revolutionary groups under the press of czarism and the war. So much the greater was the task laid upon the masses. The insurrectionaries were not human locusts. They had their political experience, their traditions, their slogans, their nameless leaders. But while the scattered elements of leadership in the insurrection proved adequate to overthrow the monarchy, they were far from adequate to give the victors the fruits of their victory.

The tranquillity of the October streets, the absence of crowds and battles, gave the enemy a pretext to talk of the conspiracy of an insignificant minority, of the adventure of a handful of Bolsheviks. This formula was repeated unnumbered times in the days, months, and even years, following the insurrection. It is obviously with a view to mending the reputation of the proletarian revolution that Yaroslavsky writes of the 25th of October: "Thick masses of the Petrograd proletariat summoned by the Military Revolutionary Committee stood under its banners and overflowed the streets of Petrograd." This official historian only forgets to explain for what purpose the Military Revolutionary Committee had summoned these masses to the streets, and just what they did when they got there.

From the combination of its strong and weak points has grown up an official idealisation of the February revolution as an all-national revolution, in contrast to the October one which is held to be a conspiracy. But in reality the Bolsheviks could reduce the struggle for power at the last moment to a "conspiracy," not because they were a small minority, but for the opposite reason—because they had behind them in the workers' districts and the barracks an overwhelming majority, consolidated, organised, disciplined.

The October revolution can be correctly understood only if you do not limit your field of vision to its final link. During the last days of February the chess game of insurrection was played out from the first move to the last—that is to the surrender of the enemy. At the end of October the main part of the game was already in the past. And on the day of insurrection it remained to solve only a rather narrow problem: mate in two moves. The period of revolution, therefore, must be considered to extend from the 9th of October, when the conflict about the garrison began, or from the 12th, when the resolution was passed to create a Military Revolutionary Committee. The enveloping manœuvre extended over more than two weeks. The more decisive part of it lasted five to six days – from the birth of the Military Revolutionary Committee to the capture of the Winter Palace. During this whole period hundreds of thousands of workers and soldiers took direct action, defensive in form, but aggressive in essence. The final stage, when the insurrectionaries at last threw off the qualifications of the dual power with its dubious legality and defensive phraseology, occupied exactly twenty-four hours: from 2 o'clock on the night of the 25th to 2 o'clock on the night of the 26th. During this period the Military Revolutionary Committee openly employed arms for the conquest of the city and the capture of the government. In these operations, generally speaking, as many forces took part as were needed to solve the limited problem—hardly more than 25 or 30 thousand at the most.

An Italian author who writes books not only about *The Eunuchs' Nights*, but also about the highest problems of state, visited soviet Moscow in 1929, misunderstood what little he learned at second or tenth hand, and upon this basis has created a book: *Coup d'État: The Technique of Revolution.* The name of this writer, Malaparte, makes it easy to distinguish him from a certain other specialist in state insurrections called Bonaparte.

In contrast to "the strategy of Lenin" which was bound up with the social and political conditions of Russia in 1917, "Trotsky's tactics," according to Malaparte, "were not bound up with the general conditions of the country." To Lenin's opinions about the political premises of a revolution the author makes Trotsky reply: "Your strategy demands too many favourable circumstances: an insurrection needs nothing, it is self-sufficient." It would be hard to imagine a more self-sufficient absurdity. Malaparte many times repeats that it was not the strategy of Lenin that won in October, but the tactics of Trotsky. And these tactics still threaten the tranquillity of the European states. "The strategy of Lenin does not constitute an immediate danger to the governments of Europe. The real and, moreover, permanent danger to them is the tactics of Trotsky." And still more concretely: "Put Poincaré in Kerensky's place, and the Bolsheviks' state revolution of October 1917 would succeed just as well." It would be futile to try to find out what is the use of Lenin's strategy, which depends upon historic conditions, if Trotsky's tactics will solve the same problem in any circumstances. It remains to add that this remarkable book has already appeared in several languages. The statesmen are evidently learning from it how to repulse a state revolution. We wish them all success.

A criticism of the purely military operations of October 25th has not yet been made. What exists in soviet literature upon this theme is not critical, but purely apologetic in character. Compared with the writings of the Epigones, even Sukhanov's criticism, in spite of all its contradictions is favourably distinguished by an attentive attitude to facts.

In judging the organisation of the October uprising, Sukhanov has presented in the course of two years two views diametrically opposed to each other. In his work on the February revolution he says: "I will write some day, from personal reminiscences, a description of the October revolution, which was carried through like a piece of music played from notes." Yaroslavsky repeats this comment of Sukhanov word for word. "The insurrection in Petrograd," he says, "was well prepared and played through by the party as though from notes." Claude Anet, a hostile and not profound, but nevertheless attentive, observer, speaks even more emphatically: "The state revolution of November 7 permits only ecstatic praise. Not one mis-step, not one rift; the government was overthrown before it could say 'ouch!' " On the other hand, in his volume devoted to the October revolution Sukhanov tells how Smolny "stealthily feeling its way, cautiously, and without system" undertook the liquidation of the Provisional Government.

There is exaggeration in both these comments. But from a broader point of view it may be conceded that both appraisals, however they contradict each other, find some support in the facts. The planned character of the October revolution grew chiefly out of objective relations, out of the maturity of the revolution as a whole, the place occupied by Petrograd in the country, the place occupied by the government in Petrograd, out of the whole preceding work of the party, and finally out of the correct political leadership of the revolution. But there remained the problems of military technique. Here there were no few particular failings, and if you join them all together it is possible to create the impression of a job done blindly.

Sukhanov has several times called attention to the military defencelessness of Smolny itself during the last days before the insurrection. It is true that as late as the 23rd the headquarters of the revolution was little better defended than the Winter Palace. The Military Revolutionary Committee assured its inviolability primarily by strengthening its bonds with the garrison, and by thus being able to follow all the military movements of the enemy. More serious measures of a technical military character were undertaken by the Committee approximately twenty-four hours before the government undertook them. Sukhanov feels sure that during the 23rd and the night of the 24th the government, had it shown some initiative, could have captured the Committee. "A good detachment of 500 men," he says, "would have been enough to liquidate Smolny and everybody in it." Possibly. But in the first place, for this the government would have required determination and daring, qualities inconsistent with its nature. In the second place, it would have had to have that "good detachment of 500 men." Where were they to get it? Make it up out of officers? We have observed them towards the end of August in the character of conspirators: they had to be hunted up in the night clubs. The fighting companies of the Compromisers had disintegrated. In the military schools every acute question produced conflicting groups. Things were still worse with the Cossacks. To create a detachment by the method of individual selection from various units would have involved giving oneself away ten times before the thing could be finished.

However, even the existence of such a detachment would still not have settled things. The first shot in the region of Smolny would have resounded in the workers' districts and barracks with a shocking reverberation. Tens of thousands of armed and half-armed men would have run to the help of the threatened centre of the revolution at any hour of the day or night. And finally, even the capture of the Military Revolutionary Committee would not have saved the government. Beyond the walls of Smolny there remained Lenin, and in communication with him the Central Committee and the Petrograd committee. There was a second headquarters in the Peter and Paul fortress, a third on the *Aurora*, and each district had its headquarters. The masses would not have been without leadership. And the workers and soldiers in spite of their slowness to move were determined to conquer at any cost.

It is indubitable, however, that supplementary measures of military precaution might and should have been taken some few days earlier. In this respect Sukhanov's criticism is just. The military apparatus of a revolution functions clumsily, with delays and omissions, and the general leadership is too much inclined to put politics in the place of technique. Lenin's eyes were much lacking in Smolny. Others had not yet learned.

Sukhanov is also right in asserting that it would have been infinitely easier to capture the Winter Palace on the night of the 25th, or the morning of that day, than during the second half of it. The palace, and also the neighbouring headquarters building, were defended by the usual detachment of junkers: a sudden attack would almost certainly have been successful. Kerensky had got away unhindered that morning in an automobile. This alone proved that there was no serious reconnoitring in progress in regard to the Winter Palace. Here obviously was a bad slip.

The task of keeping watch over the Provisional Government

had been laid upon Sverdlov—too late to be sure, on the 24th! —with Lashevich and Blagonravov as assistants. It is doubtful if Sverdlov, exploding in pieces even without that, ever occupied himself with this additional business at all. It is even possible that the very decision, although inscribed in the minutes, was forgotten in the heat of those hours.

In the Military Revolutionary Committee, in spite of everything, the military resources of the government, and particularly the defences of the Winter Palace, were over-estimated. And even had the direct leaders of the siege known the inner forces of the palace, they might still have feared the arrival of reinforcements at the first alarm: junkers, Cossacks, shock-battalions. The plan for capturing the palace was worked out in the style of a large operation. When civil and semi-civil people undertake the solution of a purely military problem, they are always inclined to excessive strategic ingenuities. And along with their superfluous pedantry, they cannot but prove extraordinarily helpless in carrying them out.

The mis-steps in the capture of the Palace are explained to a certain degree by the personal qualities of the principal leaders. Podvoisky, Antonov-Ovseënko and Chudnovsky, are men of heroic mould. But after all they are far from being men of system and disciplined thought. Podvoisky, having been too impetuous in the July Days, had become far more cautious and even sceptical about immediate prospects. But in fundamentals he remained true to himself. Confronted with any practical task whatever, he inclined organically to break over its bounds, to broaden out the plan, drag in everybody and everything, give a maximum where a minimum was enough. In the element of hyperbole contained in the plan it is easy to see the impress of his spirit. Antonov-Ovseënko was naturally an impulsive optimist, far more apt at improvisation than calculation. As a former petty officer he possessed a certain amount of military information. An emigré during the Great War, he had conducted in the Paris paper *Nashe Slovo* a review of the military situation, and frequently revealed a gift for guessing out strategy. His impressionable amateurism in this field could not, however, counterbalance the excessive flights of Podvoisky. The third of these military chiefs, Chudnovsky, had spent some months as an agitator on an inactive front—that was the whole of his military training. Although gravitating toward the right wing, Chudnovsky was the first to get into the fight and always sought the place where it was hottest. Personal daring and political audacity are not always, as is well known, in perfect equilibrium. Some days after the revolution Chudnovsky was wounded near Petrograd in a skirmish with Kerensky's Cossacks, and some months later he was killed in the Ukraine. It is clear that the talkative and impulsive Chudnovsky could not make up for what was lacking in the other two leaders. No one of them had an eye to detail, if only for the reason that no one of them had ever learned the secrets of the trade. Feeling their own weakness in matters of reconnoitring, communications, manœuvring, these Red martials felt obliged to roll up against the Winter Palace such a superiority of forces as removed the very possibility of practical leadership. An incongruous grandeur of plan is almost equivalent to no plan at all. What has been said does not in the least mean, however, that it would have been possible to find in the staff of the Military Revolutionary Committee, or around it, any more able military leaders. It would certainly have been impossible to find more devoted and selfless ones.

The struggle for the Winter Palace began with the enveloping of the whole district on a wide circle. Owing to the inexperience of the commanders, the interruption of communications, the unskilfulness of the Red Guard detachments, and the listlessness of the regular units, this complicated operation developed at an extraordinarily slow pace. During those same hours when the detachments were gradually filling up their circle and accumulating reserves behind them, companies of junkers, the Cossack squadrons, the Knights of St. George, and the Women's Battalion made their way into the palace. A resisting fist was being formed simultaneously with the attacking ring. You may say that the very problem arose from the too roundabout way in which it was being solved. A bold attack by night or a daring approach by day would hardly have cost more victims than this prolonged operation. The moral effect of the *Aurora's* artillery might at any rate have been tried out twelve or even twenty-four hours sooner than it was. The cruiser stood ready in the Neva, and the sailors were not complaining of any lack of gun-oil. But the leaders of the operation were hoping that the problem could be solved without a battle, were sending parliamentaries, presenting ultimatums and then not living up to their dates. It did not occur to them to examine the artillery in the Peter and Paul fortress in good season for the simple reason that they were counting on getting along without it.

The unpreparedness of the military leadership was still more clearly revealed in Moscow, where the correlation of forces had been considered so favourable that Lenin even insistently advised beginning there: "The victory is sure and there is nobody to fight." In reality it was in Moscow that the insurrection took the form of extended battles lasting with intervals for eight days. "In this hot work," writes Muralov, one of the chief leaders of the Moscow insurrection, "we were not always and in everything firm and determined. Having an overwhelming numerical advantage, ten to one, we dragged the fight out for a whole week . . . owing to a lack of ability to direct fighting masses, to the undiscipline of the latter, and to a complete ignorance of the tactics of the street fight both on the part of the commanders and on the part of the soldiers." Muralov has a habit of naming things with their real names: no wonder he is now in Siberian exile. But in the present instance in refusing to load off the responsibility upon others, Muralov lays upon the military command a lion's share of the blame which belongs to the political leadership—very shaky in Moscow and receptive to the influence of the compromisist circles. We must not lose sight, either, of the fact that the workers of old Moscow, textile and leather workers, were extremely far behind the Petrograd proletariat. In February no insurrection in Moscow had been necessary: the overthrow of the monarchy had rested entirely with Petrograd. In July again Moscow had remained peaceful. This found its expression in October: the workers and soldiers lacked fighting experience.

The technique of insurrection carries through what politics has not accomplished. The gigantic growth of Bolshevism had undoubtedly weakened the attention paid to the military side of things. The passionate reproaches of Lenin were well founded enough. The military leadership proved incomparably weaker than the political. Could it indeed have been otherwise? For a number of months still, the new revolutionary government will show extreme awkwardness in all those cases where it is necessary to resort to arms.

Even so, the military authorities of the governmental camp in Petrograd gave a very flattering judgment of the military leadership of the revolution. "The insurrectionaries are preserving order and discipline," stated the War Ministry over the direct wire to headquarters immediately after the fall of the Winter Palace. "There have been no cases at all of destruction or pogroms. On the contrary, patrols of insurrectionists have detained strolling soldiers. . . . The plan of the insurrection was undoubtedly worked out in advance and carried through inflexibly and harmoniously." Not altogether "from the notes" as Sukhanov and Yaroslavsky have written, nor yet altogether "without system," as the former has subsequently affirmed. Moreover, even in the court of the most austere critic success is the best praise.

Chapter X

The Congress of the Soviet Dictatorship

In Smolny on the 25th of October the most democratic of all parliaments in the world's history was to meet. Who knows—perhaps also the most important.

Having got free of the influence of compromisist intellectuals, the local soviets had sent up for the most part workers and soldiers. The majority of them were people without big names, but who had proved themselves in action and won lasting confidence in their own localities. From the active army it was almost exclusively rank-and-file soldiers who had run the blockade of army committees and headquarters and come here as delegates. A majority of them had begun to live a political life with the revolution. They had been formed by an experience of eight months. They knew little, but knew it well. The outward appearance of the Congress proclaimed its make-up. The officers' chevrons, the eye-glasses and neckties of intellectuals to be seen at the first Congress had almost completely disappeared. A grey colour prevailed uninterruptedly, in costumes and in faces. All had worn out their clothes during the war. Many of the city workers had provided themselves with soldiers' coats. The trench delegates were by no means a pretty picture: long unshaven, in old torn trench-coats, with heavy *papakhi*[1] on their dishevelled hair, often with cotton sticking out through a hole, with coarse weatherbeaten faces, heavy cracked hands, fingers yellowed with tobacco, buttons torn off, belts hanging loose, and long unoiled boots wrinkled and rusty. The plebeian nation had for the first time sent up an honest representation made in its own image and not retouched.

The statistics of this Congress which assembled during the hours of insurrection are very incomplete. At the moment of opening there were 650 delegates with votes: 390 fell to the lot of the Bolsheviks—by no means all members of the party, but they were of the flesh and blood of the masses, and the masses had no roads left but the Bolshevik road. Many of the delegates who had brought doubts with them were maturing fast in the red-hot atmosphere of Petrograd.

1. Tall fur hats.

How completely had the Mensheviks and Social Revolutionaries squandered the political capital of the February revolution! At the June Congress of Soviets the Compromisers had a majority of 600 votes out of the whole number of 832 delegates. Now the compromisist opposition of all shades made up less than a quarter of the Congress. The Mensheviks, with the national group adhering to them, amounted to only 80 members—about half of them "Lefts." Out of 159 Social Revolutionaries—according to other reports 190—about three-fifths were Lefts, and moreover the Right continued to melt fast during the very sitting of the Congress. Toward the end the total number of delegates, according to several lists, reached 900. But this figure, while including a number of advisory members, does not on the other hand include all those with votes. The registration was carried on intermittently; documents have been lost; the information about party affiliations was incomplete. In any case the dominant position of the Bolsheviks in the Congress remains indubitable.

A straw-vote taken among the delegates revealed that 505 soviets stood for the transfer of all power to the soviets; 86 for a government of the "democracy"; 55 for a coalition; 21 for a coalition, but without the Kadets. Although eloquent even in this form, these figures give an exaggerated idea of the remains of the Compromisers' influence. Those for democracy and coalition were soviets from the more backward districts and least important points.

From early in the morning of the 25th caucuses of the factions were held in Smolny. Only those attended the Bolshevik caucus who were free from fighting duties. The opening of the Congress was delayed: the Bolshevik leaders wanted to finish with the Winter Palace first. But the opposing factions, too, were in no hurry. They themselves had to decide what to do, and that was not easy. Hours passed. Sub-factions were disputing within the factions. The split among the Social Revolutionaries took place after a resolution to withdraw from the Congress had been rejected by 92 votes against 60. It was only late in the evening that the Right and Left Social Revolutionaries began to sit in different rooms. At 8 o'clock the Mensheviks demanded a new delay: they had too many opinions. Night came on. The operations at the Winter Palace were dragging out. But it became impossible to wait longer. It was necessary to say some clear word to the aroused and watchful nation.

The revolution had taught the art of filling space. Delegates, guests, guards, jammed into the commencement hall of the noble maidens, making room for more and more. Warnings of the danger of the floor's collapsing had no effect, nor did appeals to smoke a little less. All crowded closer and smoked twice as much. John Reed with difficulty fought his way through the noisy crowd around the doors. The hall was not heated, but the air was heavy and hot.

Jamming the entries and the side exits, sitting on all the window sills, the delegates now patiently await the president's gong. Tseretelli, Cheidze, Chernov—none of them is on the platform. Only leaders of the second rank have come to their funeral. A short man in the uniform of a military doctor opens the session at 10.40 in the evening in the name of the Executive Committee. The Congress, he says, assembles in such "exceptional circumstances" that he, Dan, obeying the directions of the Central Executive Committee, will refrain from making a political speech. His party friends are now indeed under fire in the Winter Palace "while loyally fulfilling their duty as ministers." The last thing these delegates are expecting is a blessing from the Central Executive Committee. They look up at the platform with hostility. If those people still exist politically, what have they got to do with us and our business?

In the name of the Bolsheviks a Moscow delegate, Avanessov, moves that the præsidium be elected upon a proportional basis: 14 Bolsheviks, 7 Social Revolutionaries, 3 Mensheviks and 1 Internationalist. The Right immediately declines to enter the præsidium. Martov's group sits tight for the time being; it has not decided. Seven votes go over to the Left Social Revolutionaries. The Congress watches these introductory conflicts with a scowl.

Avanessov announces the Bolshevik candidates for the præsidium: Lenin, Trotsky, Zinoviev, Kamenev, Rykov, Nogin, Skliansky, Krylenko Antonov-Ovseënko, Riazanov, Muranov, Lunacharsky, Kollontai, Stuchka. "The præsidium," writes Sukhanov, "consisted of the principal Bolshevik leaders and six (in reality seven) Left Social Revolutionaries." Zinoviev and Kamenev were included in the præsidium as authoritative party names in spite of their active opposition to the insurrection; Rykov and Nogin as representatives of the Moscow Soviet; Lunacharsky and Kollontai as popular agitators of that period; Riazanov as a representative of the trade unions; Muranov as an old worker-Bolshevik who had carried himself courageously during the trial of the deputies of the State Duma; Stuchka as head of the Lettish organisation; Krylenko and Skliansky as representatives of the army; Antonov-Ovseënko as a leader of the Petrograd battles. The absence of Sverdlov's name is obviously explained by the fact that he himself drew up the list, and in the confusion nobody corrected it. It is characteristic of the party morals of the time that the whole headquarters of the opponents of the insurrection turned up in the præsidium: Zinoviev, Kamenev, Nogin, Rykov, Lunacharsky, Riazanov. Of the Left Social Revolutionaries only the little fragile and courageous Spiridonova, who had served long years at hard labour for assassinating the subduer of the Tombovsk peasants, enjoyed an all-Russian renown. The Left Social Revolutionaries had no other "name." The Rights, on the other hand, had now little or nothing but names left.

The Congress greeted its præsidium with enthusiasm. While the factions had been assembling and conferring, Lenin with his make-up still on, in wig and big spectacles, was sitting in the passage-way in the company of two or three Bolsheviks. On the way to a meeting of their faction Dan and Skobelev stopped still, opposite the table where the conspirators were sitting, stared at Lenin, and obviously recognised him. Time, then, to take the make-up off. But Lenin was in no hurry to appear publicly. He preferred to look round a little and gather the threads into his hands while remaining behind the scenes. In his recollections of Lenin published in 1924, Trotsky writes: "The first session of the Second Congress of Soviets was sitting in Smolny. Lenin did not appear here. He remained in one of the rooms of Smolny in which, as I remember, there was for some reason no furniture, or almost none. Later somebody spread blankets on the floor and put two cushions on them, Vladimir Ilych and I took a rest there lying side by side. But in just a few minutes I called: 'Dan is talking and you must answer him.'[1] Returned after my reply, I again lay down beside Vladimir Ilych, who of course had no thought of going to sleep. Was that indeed possible? Every five or ten minutes somebody would run in from the assembly hall to tell us what was going on."

The president's chair is occupied by Kamenev, one of those phlegmatic types designed by nature herself for the office of chairman. There are three questions, he announces, on the order of the day: organisation of a government; war and

1. Evidently the name here should be Martov, to whom Trotsky did make a reply.

peace: convocation of the Constituent Assembly. An unusual, dull, alarming rumble breaks into the noise of the meeting from outside. This is Peter and Paul fortress ratifying the order of the day with artillery fire. A high tension current runs through the Congress, which now suddenly feels and realises what it really is: the convention of a civil war.

Lozovsky, an opponent of the insurrection, demanded a report from the Petrograd Soviet. But the Military Revolutionary Committee was a little behind hand. Replying artillery testified that the report was not ready. The insurrection was in full swing. The Bolshevik leaders were continually withdrawing to the rooms of the Military Revolutionary Committee to receive communications or give orders. Echoes of the fighting would burst up through the assembly like tongues of flame. When votes were taken hands would be raised among bristling bayonets, A blue-grey acrid tobacco smoke hid the beautiful white columns and chandeliers.

The verbal battles of the two camps were extraordinarily impressive against a background of cannon-shots. Martov demanded the floor. The moment when the balance is still oscillating is his moment—this inventive statesman of eternal waverings. With his hoarse tubercular voice Martov makes instant rejoinder to the metallic voice of the guns: "We must put a stop to military action on both sides. . . . The question of power is beginning to be decided by conspiratorial methods. All the revolutionary parties have been placed before a *fait accompli*. . . . A civil war threatens us with an explosion of counter-revolution. A peaceful solution of the crisis can be obtained by creating a government which will be recognised by the whole democracy." A considerable portion of the Congress applauds. Sukhanov remarks ironically: "Evidently many and many a Bolshevik, not having absorbed the spirit of the teachings of Lenin and Trotsky, would have been glad to take that course." The Left Social Revolutionaries and a group of United Internationalists support the proposal of peace negotiations. The Right Wing, and perhaps also the close associates of Martov, are confident that the Bolsheviks will reject this proposal. They are wrong. The Bolsheviks send Lunacharsky to the tribune, the most peace-loving, the most velvety of their orators. "The Bolshevik faction," he says, "has absolutely nothing against Martov's proposal." The enemy are astonished. "Lenin and Trotsky in thus giving way a little to their own masses," comments Sukhanov, "are at the same time cutting the ground from under the Right Wing." Martov's proposal is adopted unanimously. "If the Mensheviks and Social Revolutionaries withdraw now," runs the comment in Martov's group, "they will bury themselves." It is possible to hope, therefore, that the Congress "will take the correct road of creating a united democratic front." Vain hope! A revolution never moves on diagonals.

The Right Wing immediately violates the just-approved initiation of peace negotiations. The Menshevik Kharash, a delegate from the 12th Army with a captain's star on his shoulders, makes a statement: "These political hypocrites propose that we decide the question of power. Meanwhile it is being decided behind our backs. . . . Those blows at the Winter Palace are driving nails in the coffin of the party which has undertaken such an adventure. . . ." The captain's challenge is answered by the Congress with a grumble of indignation.

Lieutenant Kuchin, who had spoken at the State Conference in Moscow in the name of the front, tries here also to wield the authority of the army organisations: "This Congress is untimely and even unauthorised." "In whose name do you speak?" shout the tattered trench-coats, their credentials written all over them in the mud of the trenches. Kuchin carefully enumerates eleven armies. But here this deceives nobody. At the front as at the rear the generals of compromise are without soldiers. The group from the front, continues the Menshevik lieutenant, "declines to assume any responsibility for the consequences of this adventure." That means a complete break with the revolution. "Henceforth the arena of struggle is transferred to the localities." That means fusion with the counter-revolution against the soviets. And so the conclusion: "The front group . . . withdraws from this Congress."

One after another the representatives of the Right mount the tribune. They have lost the parishes and churches, but they still hold the belfries, and they hasten for the last time to pound the cracking bells. These socialist and democrats, having made a compromise by hook and crook with the imperialist bourgeoisie, to-day flatly refuse to compromise with the people in revolt. Their political calculations are laid bare. The Bolsheviks will collapse in a few days, they are thinking: We must separate ourselves from them as quickly as possible, even help to overthrow them, and thus to the best of our ability insure ourselves and our future.

In the name of the Right Menshevik faction, Khinchuk, a

former president of the Moscow Soviet and a future Soviet ambassador in Berlin, reads a declaration: "The military conspiracy of the Bolsheviks . , . will plunge the country into civil dissension, demolish the Constituent Assembly, threaten us with a military catastrophe, and lead to the triumph of the counter-revolution." The sole way out: "Open negotiations with the Provisional Government for the formation of a power resting on all layers of the democracy." Having learned nothing, these people propose to the Congress to cross off the insurrection and return to Kerensky. Through the uproar, bellowing, and even hissing, the words of the representative of the Right Social Revolutionaries are hardly distinguishable. The declaration of his party announces "the impossibility of work in collaboration" with the Bolsheviks, and declares the very Congress of Soviets, although convoked and opened by the compromisist Central Executive Committee, to be without authority.

This demonstration of the Right Wing does not cow anybody, but causes alarm and irritation. The majority of the delegates are too sick and tired of these bragging and narrow-minded leaders who fed them first with phrases and then with measures of repression. Can it be that the Dans, Khinchuks and Kuchins still expect to instruct and command us? A Lettish soldier, Peterson, with a tubercular flush on his cheeks and burning hatred in his eyes, denounces Kharash and Kuchin as imposters. "The revolution has had enough gab! We want action! The power should be in our hands. Let the imposters leave the congress—the army is through with them!" This voice tense with passion relieves the mind of the Congress, which has received nothing so far but insults. Other front-line soldiers rush to the support of Peterson. "These Kuchins represent the opinions of little gangs who have been sitting in the army committees since April. The army long ago demanded new elections." Those who live in the trenches are impatiently awaiting the transfer of power to the soviets."

But the Rights still hold the belfries. A representative of the Bund declares that "all that has happened in Petrograd is a misfortune." and invites the delegates to join the members of the duma who have decided to march unarmed to the Winter Palace in order to die with the government. "Gibes were to be heard in the general uproar, writes Sukhanov. "some coarse and some poisonous." The unctuous orator has obviously mistaken his audience. "Enough from you!" "Deserters!" shout the delegates, guests, Red Guards and sentries at the door to the withdrawing delegates. "Join Kornilov!" "Enemies of the people!"

The withdrawal of the Rights did not leave any vacant space. Evidently the rank-and-file delegates had refused to join the officers and junkers for a struggle against the workers and soldiers. Only about 70 delegates—that is, a little more than half of the Right Wing faction—went out. The waverers took their place with the intermediate groups who had decided not to leave the Congress. Whereas before the opening of the Congress the Social Revolutionaries of all tendencies had numbered not over 190 men, during the next few hours the number of Left Social Revolutionaries alone rose to 180. They were joined by all those who had not yet decided to join the Bolsheviks although ready to support them.

The Mensheviks and Social Revolutionaries were quite ready to remain in a Provisional Government or some sort of a Pre-Parliament under any circumstances. Can one after all break with cultured society? But the soviets—that is only the people. The soviets are all right while you can use them to get a compromise with the bourgeoisie, but can one possibly think of tolerating soviets which have suddenly imagined themselves masters of the country? "The Bolsheviks were left alone," wrote the Social Revolutionary, Zenzinov, subsequently, "and from that moment they began to rely only upon crude physical force." Moral principle undoubtedly slammed the door along with Dan and Gotz. Moral principle will march in a procession of 300 men with two lanterns to the Winter Palace, only to run into the crude physical force of the Bolsheviks and—back down.

The motion adopted by the Congress in favour of peace negotiations was left hanging in the air. If the Rights had admitted the possibility of compromising with a victorious proletariat, they would have been in no hurry to break with the Congress. Martov could not have failed to understand this. Nevertheless he clung to the idea of a compromise—the thing upon which his whole policy always stands or falls. "We must put a stop to the bloodshed . . ." he begins again. "Those are only rumours!" voices call out. "It is not only rumours that we hear," he answers. "If you come to the windows you will hear cannon-shots." This is undeniable. When the Congress quiets down, shots are audible without going to the windows.

Martov's declaration, hostile through and through to the Bolsheviks, and lifeless in its arguments, condemns the revolution as "accomplished by the Bolshevik party alone by the method of a purely military plot," and demands that the Congress suspend its labours until an agreement has been reached with all the socialists parties. To try to find the resultant of a parallelogram of forces in a revolution is worse than trying to catch your own shadow!

At that moment there appeared in the Congress the Bolshevik faction of the city duma, those who had refused to seek a problematic death under the walls of the Winter Palace. They were led by Joffé, subsequently the first Soviet ambassador at Berlin. The Congress again crowded up, giving its friends a joyful welcome.

But it was necessary to put up a resistance to Martov. This task fell to Trotsky. "Now since the exodus of the Rights," concedes Sukhanov, "his position is as strong as Martov's is weak." The opponents stand side by side in the tribune, hemmed in on all sides by a solid ring of excited delegates. "What has taken place," says Trotsky, is an insurrection, not a conspiracy. An insurrection of the popular masses needs no justification. We have tempered and hardened the revolutionary energy of the Petrograd workers and soldiers. We have openly forged the will of the masses to insurrection, and not conspiracy. . . . Our insurrection has conquered, and now you propose to us: Renounce your victory; make a compromise. With whom? I ask: With whom ought we to make a compromise? With that pitiful handful who just went out? . . .Haven't we seen them through and through. There is no longer anybody in Russia who is for them. Are the millions of workers and peasants represented in this Congress, whom they are ready now as always to turn over for a price to the mercies of the bourgeoisie, are they to enter a compromise with these men? No, a compromise is no good here. To those who have gone out, and to all who made like proposals, we must say, 'You are pitiful isolated individuals; you are bankrupts; your rôle is played out. Go where you belong from now on—into the rubbish-can of history!' "

"Then we will go!" cries Martov without awaiting the vote of the Congress. "Martov in anger and affectation," regrets Sukhanov. "began to make his way from the tribune towards the door. And I began to gather together my faction for a conference in the form of an emergency session. . . ." It was not wholly a matter of affectation. The Hamlet of democratic socialism, Martov, would make a step forward when the revolution fell back as in July; but now when the revolution was ready for a tiger's leap, Martov would fall back. The withdrawal of the Rights had deprived him of the possibility of parliamentary manœuvring, and that put him instantly out of his element. He hastened to abandon the Congress and break with the insurrection. Sukhanov replied as best he could. The faction split in half: Martov won by 14 votes against 12.

Trotsky introduced a resolution—an act of indictment against the Compromisers: They prepared the ruinous offensive of June 18; they supported the government of treason to the people; they screened the deception of the peasants on the land question; they carried out the disarming of the workers; they were responsible for the purposeless dragging out of the war; they permitted the bourgeoisie to deepen the economic ruin of the country; having lost the confidence of the masses, they resisted the calling of a soviet congress; and finally, finding themselves in a minority, they broke with the soviets.

Here again the order of the day is suspended for a declaration. Really the patience of the Bolshevik præsidium has no bounds. The president of the executive committee of the peasant soviet has come to summon the peasants to abandon this "untimely" congress, and go to the Winter Palace "to die with those who were sent there to do our will." This summons to die in the ruins of the Winter Palace is getting pretty tiresome in its monotony. A sailor just arrived from the *Aurora* ironically announces that there *are* no ruins, since they are only firing blanks from the cruiser. "Proceed with your business in peace," he says. The soul of the Congress finds rest in the admirable black-bearded sailor, incarnating the simple and imperious will of the insurrection. Martov with his mosaic of thoughts and feelings belongs to another world. That is why he breaks with the Congress.

Still another special declaration—this time half friendly. "The Right Social Revolutionaries," says Kamkov, "have gone out, but we, the Lefts, have remained." The Congress welcomes those who have remained. However, even they consider it necessary to achieve a united revolutionary front, and come out against Trotsky's sharp resolution shutting the door against a compromise with the moderate democracy.

Here too the Bolsheviks made a concession. Nobody ever saw them before, it seems, in such a yielding mood. No wonder: they are the masters of the situation and they have no need to insist upon the forms of words. Again Lunacharsky takes the tribune. "The weight of the task which has fallen upon us is not subject to any doubt," he says. A union of all the genuinely revolutionary elements of the democracy is necessary. But have we, the Bolsheviks, taken any steps whatever to repel the other groups? Did we not adopt Martov's proposal unanimously? For this we have been answered with accusations and threats. Is it not obvious that those who have left the Congress "are ceasing even their compromisist work and openly going over to the camp of the Kornilovists?"

The Bolsheviks did not insist upon an immediate vote on Trotsky's resolution. They did not want to hinder the attempts to reach an agreement on a soviet basis. The method of teaching by object-lesson can be successfully applied even to the accompaniment of artillery! As before with the adoption of Martov's proposal, so now the concession of Kamkov only revealed the impotence of these conciliatory labour pains. However, in distinction from the Left Mensheviks, the Left Social Revolutionaries did not quit the Congress: they were feeling too directly the pressure of the villages in revolt.

A mutual feeling-out has taken place. The primary positions have been occupied. There comes a pause in the evolution of the Congress. Shall we adopt the basic decrees and create a soviet government? It is impossible: the old government is still sitting there in the semi-darkness of a chamber in the Winter Palace, the only lamp on the table carefully barricaded with newspapers. Shortly after two o'clock in the morning the præsidium declares a half-hour recess.

The red marshals employed the short delay accorded to them with complete success. A new wind was blowing in the atmosphere of the Congress when its sitting was renewed. Kamenev read from the tribune a telephonogram just received from Antonov. The Winter Palace has been captured by the troops of the Revolutionary Military Committee; with the exception of Kerensky the whole Provisional Government with the dictator Kishkin at its head is under arrest. Although everybody had already learned the news as it passed from mouth to mouth, this official communication crashed in heavier than a cannon salute. The leap over the abyss dividing the revolutionary class from power has been made. Driven out of the Palace of Kshesinskaia in July, the Bolsheviks have now entered the Winter Palace as rulers. There is no other power now in Russia but the power of the soviets. A complex tangle of feelings breaks loose in applause and shouting: triumph, hope, but also anxiety. Then come new and more confident bursts of applause. The deed is done. Even the most favourable correlation of forces contains concealed surprises, but the victory becomes indubitable when the enemy's staff is made prisoner.

Kamenev impressively reads the list of those arrested. The better known names bring hostile or ironic exclamations from the Congress. Especially bitter is the greeting of Tereshchenko who has guided the foreign destinies of Russia. And Kerensky? Kerensky? It has become known that at ten o'clock this morning he was orating without great success to the garrison of Gatchina. "Where he went from there is not exactly known; rumour says to the front."

The fellow-travellers of the revolution feel bad. They foresee that now the stride of the Bolsheviks will become more firm. Somebody from the Left Social Revolutionaries objects to the arrest of the socialist ministers. A representative of the United Internationalists offers a warning—"lest the Minister of Agriculture Maslov, turn up in the same cell in which he sat under the monarchy." He is answered by Trotsky, who was imprisoned during the ministry of Maslov in the same "Kresty" as under Nicholas: "Political arrest is not a matter of vengeance; it is dictated . . . by considerations of expediency. The government . . . should be indicted and tried, first of all for its indubitable connection with Kornilov . . . The socialist ministers will be placed only under house arrest." It would have been simpler and more accurate to say that the seizure of the old government was dictated by the demands of the still unfinished struggle. It was a question of the political beheading of the hostile camp, and not of punishment for past sins.

But this parliamentary query as to the arrests was immediately crowded out by another infinitely more important episode. The 3rd Bicycle Battalion sent by Kerensky against Petrograd had come over to the side of the revolutionary people! This too favourable news seemed unbelievable, but that was exactly what had happened. This selected military unit, the first to be chosen out from the whole active army, adhered to the insurrection before ever reaching the capital. If there had been a shade of restraint in its joy at the arrest of the ministers, the Congress was now seized with unalloyed and irrepressible rapture.

The Bolshevik commissar of Tsarskoe Selo together with a delegate from the bicycle battalion ascended the tribune. They had both just arrived to make a report to the Congress: "The garrison of Tsarkoe Selo is defending the approaches to Petrograd." The defensists withdrew from the soviet. "All the work rested upon us alone." Learning of the approach of the bicycle men, the Soviet of Tsarskoe Selo prepared to resist, but the alarm happily turned out to be false. "Among the bicycle men are no enemies of the Congress of Soviets." Another battalion will soon arrive at Tsarskoe, and friendly greeting is already in preparation there. The Congress drinks down this report in great gulps.

The representative of the bicycle men is greeted with a storm, a whirlwind, a cyclone. This 3rd Battalion, he reports, was suddenly sent from the South-western front to the North under telegraphic orders "for the defence of Petrograd." The bicycle men advanced "with eyes blindfolded," only confusedly guessing what was up. At Peredolsk they ran into an echelon of the 5th Bicycle Battalion, also moving on the capital. At a joint meeting held right there at the station, it became clear that "among all the bicyclists there is not one man to be found who would consent to take action against his brothers." It was jointly decided not to submit to the government.

"I tell you concretely," says the bicycle soldier, "we will not give the power to a government at the head of which stand the bourgeoisie and the landlords!" That word concretely," introduced by the revolution into the everyday language of the people, sounded fine at this meeting!

How many hours was it since they were threatening the Congress from that same tribune with punishment from the front? Now the front itself had spoken its "concrete" word. Suppose the army committees do sabotage the Congress. Suppose the rank-and-file soldier mass only succeeds in getting its delegates there rather as an exception. Suppose in many regiments and divisions they have not yet learned to distinguish a Bolshevik from a Social Revolutionary. Never mind! The voice from Peredolsk is the authentic, unmistakable, irrefutable voice of the army. From this verdict there is no appeal. The Bolsheviks, and they only, had understood in time that the soldier-cook of the bicycle battalion infinitely better represented the front than all the Kharashes and Kuchins with their wilted credentials. A portentous change occurred here in the mood of the delegates. "They began to feel," writes Sukhanov, "that things were going to go smoothly and well, that the horrors promised on the Right would not after all be so terrible, and that the leaders might be correct in everything else too."

The unhappy Mensheviks selected this moment to draw attention to themselves. They had not yet, it seems, withdrawn. They had been considering in their faction what to do. Out of a desire to bring after him the wavering groups, Kapelinsky, who had been appointed to inform the congress of the decision adopted, finally spoke aloud the most candid reason for breaking with the Bolsheviks: "Remember that the troops are riding towards Petrograd; we are threatened with catastrophe." "What! Are you still here?"—the question was shouted from all corners of the hall. "Why, you went out once!" The Mensheviks moved in a tiny group towards the entrance, accompanied by scornful farewells. "We went out," grieves Sukhanov, completely untying the hands of the Bolsheviks, turning over to them the whole arena of the revolution." It would have made little difference if they had stayed. In any case they went to the bottom. The waves of events closed ruthlessly over their heads.

It was time for the Congress to address a manifesto to the people, but the session continued to consist only of special declarations. Events simply refused to fit into the order of the day. At 5.17 in the morning Krylenko, staggering tired, made his way to the tribune with a telegram in his hand: The 12th Army sends greetings to the Congress and informs it of the creation of a military revolutionary committee which has undertaken to stand guard in the Northern front. Attempts of the government to get armed help have broken against the resistance of the army. The commander-in-chief of the Northern front, General Cheremissov, has submitted to the Committee. The commissar of the Provisional Government, Voitinsky, has resigned, and awaits a substitute. Delegations from the echelons moved against Petrograd have one after another announced to the Military Revolutionary Committee their solidarity with the Petrograd garrison. "Pandemonium," says Reed, "men weeping, embracing each other."

Lunacharsky at last got a chance to read a proclamation addressed to the workers, soldiers and peasants. But this was not merely a proclamation. By its mere exposition of what had happened and what was proposed, this hastily written document laid down the foundations of a new state structure. "The authority of the compromisist Central Executive Committee is at an end. The Provisional Government is deposed. The Congress assumes the power. . . ." The Soviet Government proposes immediate peace. It will transfer the land to the peasant, democratise the army, establish control over production, promptly summon the Constituent Assembly, guarantee the right of the nations of Russia to self-determination. "The Congress resolves: That all power in the localities goes over to the soviets." Every phrase as it is read turns into a salvo of applause. "Soldiers! Be on your guard! Railway workers! Stop all echelons sent by Kerensky against Petrograd! . . . The fate of the revolution and the fate of the democratic peace is in your hands!"

Hearing the land mentioned, the peasants pricked up their ears. Acording to its constitution the Congress represented only soviets of workers and soldiers; but there were delegates present from individual peasant soviets. They now demanded that they be mentioned in the document. They were immediately given a right to vote. The representative of the Petrograd peasant soviet signed the proclamation "with both hands and both feet." A member of Avksentiev's Executive Committee, Berezin, silent until now, stated that out of 68 peasant soviets replying to a telegraphic questionnaire, one-half had expressed themselves for a Soviet government, the other half for the transfer of power to the Constituent Assembly. If this was the mood of the provincial soviets, half composed of governmental functionaries, could there be any doubt that a future peasant congress would support the Soviet power?

While solidifying the rank-and-file delegates, the proclamation frightened and even repelled some of the fellow-travellers by its irrevocableness. Small factions and remnants again filed through the tribune. For the third time a group of Mensheviks, obviously the most leftward now, broke away from the Congress. They withdrew, it seems, only in order to be in a position to save the Bolsheviks: "Otherwise you will destroy yourselves and us and the revolution." The president of the Polish Socialist party, Lapinsky, although he remained at the Congress in order to "defend his point of view to the end," gave essential adherence to the declaration of Martov: "The Bolsheviks will not be able to wield the power which they are assuming." The United Jewish Workers party abstained from the vote—likewise the United Internationalists. How much, though, did all these "united" amount to altogether? The proclamation was adopted almost unanimously, only two dissenting, with twelve abstaining! The delegates had hardly strength left to applaud.

The session finally came to an end at about six o'clock. A grey and cold autumn morning was dawning over the city. The hot spots of the camp-fires were fading out in the gradually lightening streets. The greying faces of the soldiers and the workers with rifles were concentrated and unusual. If there were astrologers in Petrograd, they must have observed portentous signs in the heavens.

The capital awoke under a new power. The everyday people, the functionaries, the intellectuals, cut off from the arena of events, rushed for the papers early to find out to which shore the wave had tossed during the night. But it was not easy to make out what had happened. To be sure, the papers reported the seizure by conspirators of the Winter Palace and the ministers, but only as a passing episode. Kerensky has gone to headquarters; the fate of the government will be decided by the front. Reports of the Soviet Congress reproduce only the declarations of the Right Wing, enumerate those who withdrew, and expose the impotence of those who remained. The political editorials, written before the seizure of the Winter Palace, exude a cloudless optimism.

The rumours of the street do not wholly coincide with the tone of the newspapers. Whatever you say, the ministers are after all locked up in the fortress. Reinforcements from Kerensky are not yet in sight. Functionaries and officers confer anxiously. Journalists and lawyers ring each other up. Editors try to collect their thoughts. The drawing-room oracles say: "We must surround the usurpers with a blockade of universal contempt. Storekeepers don't know whether to do business or refrain. The new authorities give orders to do business. The restaurants open; the tramcars move; the banks languish with evil forebodings; the seismograph of the Stock Exchange describes a convulsive curve. Of course the Bolsheviks will not hold out long, but they may do damage before they tumble.

The reactionary French journalist, Claude Anet, wrote on this day: "The victors are singing a song of victory. And quite rightly too. Among all these blabbers they alone acted. . . . Today they are reaping the harvest. Bravo! Fine work." The Mensheviks estimated the situation quite otherwise "Twenty-four hours have passed since the 'victory' of the Bolsheviks," wrote Dan's paper, "and the historic fates have already begun to take their cruel revenge. . . . Around them is an emptiness created by themselves. . . . They are isolated from all. . . . The entire clerical and technical machinery refuses to serve them. . . . They . . . are sliding at the very moment of their triumph into the abyss."

The liberal and compromisist circles, encouraged by the sabotage of the functionaries and their own light-mindedness, believed strangely in their own impunity. They spoke and wrote of the Bolsheviks in the language of the July Days. "Hirelings of Wilhelm"—"the pockets of the Red Guard full of German marks"—"German officers in command of the insurrection." . . . The new government had to show these people a firm hand before they began to believe in it. The more unbridled papers were detained already on the night of the 26th. Some others were confiscated on the following day. The socialist press for the time being was spared: it was necessary to give the Left Social Revolutionaries, and also some elements of the Bolshevik party, a chance to convince themselves of the groundlessness of the hope for coalition with the official democracy.

The Bolsheviks developed their victory amid sabotage and chaos. A provisional military headquarters, organised during the night, undertook the defence of Petrograd in case of an attack from Kerensky. Military telephone men were sent to the central exchange where a strike had begun. It was proposed to the armies that they create their own military revolutionary committees. Gangs of agitators and organisers, freed by the victory, were sent to the front and to the provinces. The central organ of the party wrote: "The Petrograd Soviet has acted; it is the turn of the other soviets."

News came during the day which has especially disturbed the soldiers. Kornilov has escaped. As a matter of fact, the lofty captive, who had been living in Bykhov, guarded by Tekintsi, loyal to him, and kept in touch with all events by Kerensky's headquarters, decided on the 26th that things were taking a serious turn, and without the slightest hindrance from anybody abandoned his pretended prison. The connections between Kerensky and Kornilov were thus again obviously confirmed in the eyes of the masses. The Military Revolutionary Committee summoned the soldiers and the revolutionary officers by telegram to capture both former commanders-in-chief and deliver them in Petrograd.

As had the Tauride Palace in February, so now Smolny became the focal point for all functions of the capital and the state. Here all the ruling institutions had their seat. Here orders were issued and hither people came to get them. Hence a demand went out for weapons, and hither came rifles and revolvers confiscated from the enemy. Arrested people were brought in here from all ends of the city. The injured began to flow in seeking justice. The bourgeois public and its frightened cab-drivers made a great yoke-shaped detour to avoid the Smolny region.

The automobile is a far more genuine sign of present-day sovereignty than the orb and sceptre. Under the régime of dual power the automobiles had been divided between the government, the Central Executive Committee and private owners. Now all confiscated motors were dragged into the camp of the insurrection. The Smolny district looked like a giant military garage. The best of automobiles smoked in those days from the low-grade petrol. Motor-cycles chugged impatiently and threateningly in the semi-darkness. Armoured-cars shrieked their sirens. Smolny seemed like a factory, a railroad and power station of the revolution.

A steady flood of people poured along the sidewalks of the adjoining streets. Bonfires were burning at the outer and inner gates. By their wavering light armed workers and soldiers were belligerently inspecting passes. A number of armoured-cars stood shaking with the action of their own motors in the court. Nothing wanted to stop moving, machines or people. At each entrance stood machine-guns abundantly supplied with cartridge-belts. The endless, weakly lighted, gloomy corridors echoed with the tramping of feet, with exclamations and shouts. The arriving and departing poured up and down the broad staircase. And this solid human lava would be cut through by impatient and imperative individuals. Smolny workers, couriers, commissars, a mandate or an order lifted high in their hand, a rifle on a cord slung over their shoulder, or a portfolio under their arm.

The Military Revolutionary Committee never stopped working for an instant. It received delegates, couriers, volunteer informers, devoted friends, and scoundrels. It sent commissars to all corners of the town, set innumerable seals upon orders and commands and credentials—all this in the midst of intersecting inquiries, urgent communications, the ringing of telephone bells and the rattle of weapons. People utterly exhausted of their force, long without sleep or eating, unshaven, in dirty linen, with inflamed eyes, would shout in hoarse voices, gesticulate fantastically, and if they did not fall half dead on the floor, it seemed only thanks to the surrounding chaos which whirled them about and carried them away again on its unharnessed wings.

Adventurers, crooks, the worst off-scouring of the old régime, would sniff about and try to get a pass to Smolny. Some of them succeeded. They knew some little secret of administration: Who has the key to the diplomatic correspondence, how to write an order on the treasury, where to get gasoline or a typewriter, and especially where the best court wines are kept. They did not all find their cell or bullet immediately.

Never since the creation of the world have so many orders been issued—by word of mouth by pencil, by typewriter, by wire, one following after the other—thousands and myriads of orders, not always issued by those having the right, and rarely to those capable of carrying them out. But just here lay the miracle—that in this crazy whirlpool there turned out to be an inner meaning. People managed to understand each other. The most important and necessary things got done. Replacing the old web of administration, the first threads of the new were strung. The revolution grew in strength.

During that day, the Central Committee of the Bolsheviks was at work in Smolny. It was deciding the problem of the new government of Russia. No minutes were kept—or they have not been preserved. Nobody was bothering about future historians, although a lot of trouble was being prepared for them right there. The evening session of the Congress was to create a cabinet of ministers. M-i-n-i-s-t-e-r-s? What a sadly compromised word! It stinks of the high bureaucratic career, the crowning of some parliamentary ambition. It was decided to call the government the Soviet of People's Commissars: that at least had a fresher sound. Since the negotiations for a coalition of the "entire democracy" had come to nothing, the question of the party and personal staff of the government was simplified. The Left Social Revolutionaries minced and objected. Having just broken with the party of Kerensky, they themselves hardly knew what they wanted to do. The Central Committee adopted the motion of Lenin as the only thinkable one: to form a government of Bolsheviks only.

Martov knocked at the door of this session in the capacity of intercessor for the arrested socialist ministers. Not so long ago he had been interceding with the socialist ministers for the imprisoned Bolsheviks. The wheel had made quite a sizeable turn. Through one of its members sent out to Martov for negotiations—most probably Kamenev—the Central Committee confirmed the statement that the socialist ministers would be transferred to house arrest. Apparently they had been forgotten in the rush of business, or perhaps had themselves declined privileges, adhering even in the Trubetzkov Bastion to the principle of ministerial solidarity,

The Congress opened its session at nine o'clock in the evening. "The picture on the whole was but little different from yesterday—fewer weapons, less of a jam." Sukhanov, now no longer a delegate, was able to find himself a free seat as one of the public. This session was to decide the questions of peace, land and government. Only three questions: end the war, give the land to the people, establish a socialist dictatorship. Kamenev began with a report of the work done by the præsidium during the day: the death penalty at the front introduced by Kerensky abolished; complete freedom of agitation restored; orders given for the liberation of soldiers imprisoned for political convictions, and members of land committees; all the commissars of the Provisional Government removed from office; orders given to arrest and deliver Kerensky and Kornilov. The Congress approved and ratified these measures.

Again some remnants of remnants took the floor, to the impatient disapproval of the hall. One group announced that they were withdrawing "at the moment of the victory of the insurrection and not at the moment of its defeat." Others bragged of the fact that they had decided to remain. A representative of the Donetz miners urged immediate measures to prevent Kaledin from cutting the north off from coal. Some time must pass, however, before the revolution learns to take measures of such scope. Finally it becomes possible to take up the first point on the order of the day.

Lenin, whom the Congress has not yet seen, is given the floor for a report on peace. His appearance in the tribune evokes a tumultuous greeting. The trench delegates gaze with all their eyes at this mysterious being whom they had been taught to hate and whom they have learned without seeing him to love. "Now Lenin, gripping the edges of the reading-stand, let little winking eyes travel over the crowd as he stood there waiting, apparently oblivious to the long-rolling ovation, which lasted several minutes. When it finished, he said simply, 'We shall now proceed to construct the socialist order.' "

The minutes of the Congress are not preserved. The Parliamentary stenographers, invited in to record the debates, had abandoned Smolny along with the Mensheviks and Social Revolutionaries. That was one of the first episodes in the campaign of sabotage. The secretarial notes have been lost without a trace in the abyss of events. There remain only the hasty and tendentious newspaper reports, written to the tune of the artillery or the grinding of teeth in the political struggle. Lenin's speeches have suffered especially. Owing to his swift delivery and the complicated construction of his sentences, they are not easily recorded even in more favourable conditions. That initial statement which John Reed puts in the mouth of Lenin does not appear in any of the newspaper accounts. But it is wholly in the spirit of the orator. Reed could not have made it up. Just in that way Lenin must surely have begun his speech at the Congress of Soviets—simply, without unction, with inflexible confidence: "We shall now proceed to construct the socialist order."

But for this it was first of all necessary to end the war. From his exile in Switzerland Lenin had thrown out the slogan: Convert the imperialist war into a civil war. Now it was time to convert the victorious civil war into peace. The speaker began immediately by reading the draft of a declaration to be published by the government still to be elected. The text had not been distributed, technical equipment being still very weak. The congress drank in every word of the document as pronounced.

"The workers' and peasants' government created by the revolution of October 24–25, and resting upon the soviets of workers', soldiers' and peasants' deputies, proposes to all the warring peoples and their governments to open immediate negotiations for a just, democratic peace." Just conditions exclude annexations and indemnities. By annexations is to be understood the forceful accession of alien peoples or the retention of them against their will, either in Europe or in remote lands over the seas. "Herewith the government declares that it by no means considers the above indicated conditions of peace ultimative—that is, it agrees to examine any other conditions," demanding only the quickest possible opening of negotiations and the absence of any secrecy in their conduct. On its part the soviet government abolishes secret diplomacy and undertakes to publish the secret treaties concluded before October 25, 1917. Everything in those treaties directed toward the accruing of profit and privilege to the Russian landlords and capitalists, and the oppression of other peoples by the Great Russians, "the government declares unconditionally and immediately annulled." In order to enter upon negotiations, it is proposed to conclude an immediate armistice, for not less than three months at least. The workers' and peasants' government addresses its proposals simultaneously to "the governments and peoples of all warring countries . . . especially the conscious workers of the three most advanced countries," England, France and Germany, confident that it is they who will "help us successfully carry through the business of liberating the toilers and the exploited masses of the population from all slavery and all exploitation."

Lenin limited himself to brief comments on the text of the declaration. "We cannot ignore the governments, for then the possibility of concluding peace will be delayed . . . but we have no right not to appeal at the same time to the people. The people and the governments are everywhere at variance, and we ought to help the people interfere in the matter of war and peace." "We will, of course, defend in all possible ways our programme of peace without annexations or indemnities" but we ought not to present our conditions in the form of an ultimatum, as that will make it easier for the governments to refuse to negotiate. We will consider also every other proposal. "*Consider* does not mean that we will accept it."

The manifesto issued by the Compromisers on March 14 proposed to the workers of other countries to overthrow the bankers in the name of peace; however the Compromisers themselves not only did not demand the overthrow of their own bankers, but entered into league with them. "Now we have overthrown the government of the bankers." That gives us a right to summon the other peoples to do the same. We have every hope of victory. "It must be remembered that we live not in the depths of Africa, but in Europe where everything can become quickly known." The guarantee of victory Lenin sees, as always, in converting the national into an internatioal revolution. "The workers' movement will get the upper hand and lay down the road to peace and socialism."

The Left Social Revolutionaries sent up a representative to present their adherence to the declaration. Its "spirit and meaning are close and understandable to us." The United Internationalists were for the declaration, but only on condition that it be issued by a government of the entire democracy. Lapinsky, speaking for the Polish Left Mensheviks, welcomed "the healthy proletarian realism" of the document. Dzerzhinsky for the social democracy of Poland and Lithuania, Stuchka for the social democracy of Latvia, Kapsukass for the Lithuanian social democracy, adhered to the declaration without qualification.

The only objection was offered by the Bolshevik, Eremeev, who demanded that the peace conditions be given the character of an ultimatum—otherwise "they may think that we are weak, that we are afraid."

Lenin decisively, even fiercely, objected to the ultimative presentation of the conditions: In that way, he said, we will only "make it possible for our enemies to conceal the whole truth from the people, to hide the truth behind our irreconcilability." You say that "our not presenting an ultimatum will show our impotence." It is time to have done with bourgeois falsities in politics. "We need not be afraid of telling the truth about our weariness. . . ." The future disagreements of Brest-Litovsk gleam out for a moment already in this episode.

Kamenev asked all who were for the proclamation to raise their delegates' cards. 'One delegate," writes Reed, "dared to raise his hand against, but the sudden sharp outburst around him brought it swiftly down." The appeal to the peoples and governments was adopted unanimously. The deed was done! And it impressed all the participants by its close and immediate magnitude.

Sukhanov, an attentive although also prejudiced observer, noticed more than once at that first session the listlessness of the Congress. Undoubtedly the delegates—like all the people, indeed—were tired of meetings, congresses, speeches, resolutions, tired of the whole business of marking time. They had no confidence that this Congress would be able and know how to carry the thing through to the end. Will not the gigantic size of the task and the insuperable opposition compel them to back down this time too? An influx of confidence had come with the news of the capture of the Winter Palace, and afterward with the coming over of the bicycle men to the insurrection. But both these facts still had to do with the mechanics of insurrection. Only now was its historic meaning becoming clear in action. The victorious insurrection had built under this congress of workers and soldiers an indestructible foundation of power. The delegates were voting this time not for a resolution, not for a proclamation, but for a governmental act of immeasurable significance.

Listen, nations! The revolution offers you peace. It will be accused of violating treaties. But of this it is proud. To break up the leagues of bloody predation is the greatest historic service. The Bolsheviks have dared to do it. They alone have dared. Pride surges up of its own accord. Eyes shine. All are on their feet. No one is smoking now. It seems as though no one breathes. The præsidium, the delegates, the guests, the sentries, join in a hymn of insurrection and brotherhood. "Suddenly, by common impulse,'—the story will soon be told by John Reed, observer and participant, chronicler and poet of the insurrection—"we found ourselves on our feet, mumbling together into the smooth lifting unison of the "Internationale." A grizzled old soldier was sobbing like a child. Alexandra Kollontai rapidly winked the tears back. The immense sound rolled through the hall, burst windows and doors and soared into the quiet sky. "Did it go altogether into the sky? Did it not go also to the autumn trenches, that hatch-work upon unhappy, crucified Europe, to her devastated cities and villages, to her mothers and wives in mourning? "*Arise ye prisoners of starvation! Arise ye wretched of the earth!'* The words of the song were freed of all qualifications. They fused with the decree of the government, and hence resounded with the force of a direct act. Everyone felt greater and more important in that hour. The heart of the revolution enlarged to the width of the whole world. "We will achieve emancipation. . . ." The spirit of independence, of initiative, of daring, those joyous feelings of which the oppressed in ordinary conditions are deprived—the revolution had brought them now. ". . . with our own hand!" The omnipotent hand of those millions who had overthrown the monarchy and the bourgeoisie would now strangle the war. The Red Guard from the Vyborg district, the grey soldier with his scar, the old revolutionist who had served his years at hard labour, the young black-bearded sailor from the *Aurora*—all vowed to carry through to the end this "last and deciding fight." "We will build our own new world!" We will build! In that word eagerly spoken from the heart was included already the future years of the civil war and the coming five-year periods of labour and privation. "Who was nothing shall be all!" All! If the actualities of the past have often been turned into song, why shall not a song be turned into the actuality of the future? Those trench-coats no longer seemed the costumes of galley-slaves. The *papakhi* with their holes and torn cotton took a new aspect above those gleaming eyes. "The race of man shall rise again!" Is it possible to believe that it will not rise from the misery and humiliation, the blood and filth of this war?

"The whole præsidium, with Lenin at its head, stood and sang with excited enraptured faces and shining eyes." Thus testifies a sceptic, gazing with heavy feelings upon an alien triumph. "How much I wanted to join it," confesses Sukhanov, to fuse in one feeling and mood with that mass and its leaders! But I could not." The last sound of the anthem died away, but the Congress remained standing, a fused human mass enchanted by the greatness of that which they had experienced. And the eyes of many rested on the short, sturdy figure of the man in the tribune with his extraordinary head, his high cheekbones and simple features, altered now by the shaved beard, and with that gaze of his small, slightly Mongol eyes which looked straight through everything. For four months he had been absent. His very name had almost separated itself from any living image. But no. He was not a myth. There he stood among his own—how many now of "his own"!—holding the sheets of a message of peace to the peoples of the world in his hand. Even those nearest, those who knew well his place in the party, for the first time fully realised what he meant to the revolution, to the people, to the peoples. It was he who had taught them; it was he who had brought them up. Somebody's voice from the depth of the hall shouted a word of greeting to the leader. The hall seemed only to have awaited the signal. Long live Lenin! The anxieties endured, the doubts overcome, pride of initiative, triumph of victory, gigantic hopes—all poured out together in one volcanic eruption of gratitude and rapture. The sceptical observer dryly remarks: "Undoubted enthusiasm of mood . . . They greeted Lenin, shouted hurrah, threw their caps in the air. They sang the "Funeral March" in memory of the victims of the war—and again applause, shouts, throwing of caps in the air."

What the Congress experienced during those minutes was experienced on the next day, although less compactly, by the whole country. "It must be said," writes Stankevich, in his memoirs, "that the bold gesture of the Bolsheviks, their ability to step over the barbed-wire entanglements which had for four years divided us from the neighbouring peoples, created of itself an enormous impression." Baron Budberg expresses himself more crudely but no less succinctly in his diary: "The new government of Comrade Lenin went off with a decree for immediate peace. . . . This was now an act of genius for bringing the soldier masses to his side: I saw this in the mood of several regiments which I made the rounds of to-day; the telegram of Lenin on an immediate three months' armistice and then peace, created a colossal impression everywhere, and evoked stormy joy. We have now lost the last chance of saving the front." By saving the front which they had ruined, those men had long ceased to mean anything but saving their own social positions.

If the revolution had had the determination to step over the barbed-wire entanglements in March and April, it might still have soldered the army together for a time—provided the army was at the same time reduced to half or a third its size—and thus created for its foreign policy a position of exceptional force. But the hour of courageous action struck only in October, when to save even a part of the army for even a short period was unthinkable. The new government had to load upon itself the debt, not only for the war of czarism, but also for the spendthrift lightmindedness of the Provisional Government. In this dreadful, and for all other parties hopeless, situation, only Bolshevism could lead the country out on an open road—having uncovered through the October revolution inexhaustible resources of national energy.

Lenin is again in the tribune—this time with the little sheets of a decree on land. He begins with an indictment of the overthrown government and the compromisist parties, who by dragging out the land question have brought the country to a peasant revolt. "Their talk about pogroms and anarchy in the country rings false with cowardly deceit. Where and when have pogroms and anarchy been caused by reasonable measures?" The draft of the decree has not been multigraphed for distribution. The speaker has the sole rough draft in his hands, and it is written so badly—Sukhanov remembers—"that Lenin stumbles in the reading, gets mixed up, and finally stops entirely. Somebody from the crowd jammed around the tribune comes to his help. Lenin eagerly yields his place and the undecipherable paper." These rough spots did not, however, in the eyes of that plebeian parliament diminish by an iota the grandeur of what was taking place.

The essence of the decree is contained in two lines of the first point: "The landlord's property in the land is annulled immediately and without any indemnity whatever. The landlord, appanage, monastery and church estates with all their goods and chattels are given in charge of the town land committees and county soviets of peasant deputies until the Constituent Assembly. The confiscated property is placed as a national possession under the protection of the local soviets. The land of the rank-and-file peasants and rank-and-file Cossacks is protected against confiscation. The whole decree does not come to more than thirty lines. It smashes the Gordian knot with a hammer. To the fundamental text certain broader instructions are adjoined, borrowed wholly from the peasants themselves. In *Izvestia* of the Peasant Soviet there had been printed on August 19 a summary of 242 instructions given by the electors to their representatives at the First Congress of Peasant Deputies. Notwithstanding that it was the Social Revolutionaries who prepared these collated instructions, Lenin did not hesitate to attach the document in its entirety to his decree "for guidance in carrying out the great land transformation."

The collated instructions read: "The right to private property in the land is annulled for ever." "The right to use the land is accorded to all citizens . . . desiring to cultivate it with their own labour." "Hired labour is not permittted." "The use of the land must be equalised—that is, the land is to be divided among the toilers according to local conditions on the basis of standards either of labour or consumption."

Under a continuation of the bourgeois régime, to say nothing of a coalition with the landlords, these Social Revolutionary instructions remained a lifeless Utopia, where they did not become a conscious lie. Even under the rule of the proletariat, they did not become realisable in all their sections. But the destiny of the instructions radically changed with a change in the attitude toward them of the governmental power. The workers' state gave the peasants a period in which to try out their self-contradictory programme in action.

"The peasants want to keep their small properties," wrote Lenin in August, "standardise them on a basis of equality, and periodically re-equalise them. Let them do it. No reasonable socialist will break with the peasant poor on that ground. If the lands are confiscated, that means that the rule of the banks is undermined—if the equipment is confiscated, that means that the rule of capital is undermined. The rest . . . with a transfer of political power to the proletariat . . . will be suggested by practice."

A great many people, and not only enemies but friends, have failed to understand this far-sighted, and to a certain extent pedagogical, approach of the Bolshevik Party to the peasantry and its agrarian programme. The equal distribution of the land —objected Rosa Luxembourg for example—has nothing in common with socialism. The Bolsheviks, it goes without saying, had no illusion upon this point. On the contrary, the very construction of the decree bears witness to the critical vigilance of the legislator. Whereas the collated instructions say that all the land, both that of the landlords and the peasants, "is converted into national property," the basic decree does not commit itself at all as to the new form of property in the land. Even a none too pedantic jurist would be horrified at the fact that the nationalisation of the land, a new social principle of world-historic importance, is inaugurated in the form of a list of instructions adjoined to a basic law. But there was no reactionary slovenliness here. Lenin wanted as little as possible to tie the hands of the party and the soviet power *a priori* in a still unexplored historic realm. Here again he united unexampled audacity with the greatest caution. It still remained to determine in experience how the peasants themselves would understand the conversion of the land into "the property of the whole people." Having made so long a dash forward, it was necessary to fortify the positions also in case a retreat should become necessary. The distribution of the landlord's land among the peasants, while not in itself a guarantee against bourgeois counter-revolution, made impossible in any case a feudal-monarchic restoration.

It would be possible to speak of socialist perspectives only after the establishment and successful preservation of the proletarian power. And this power could preserve itself only by giving determined co-operation to the peasant in carrying out his revolution. If the distribution of the land would strengthen the socialist government politically, it was then wholly justified as an immediate measure. The peasant had to be taken as the revolution found him. Only a new régime could re-educate him—and not at once, but in the course of a generation, with the help of a new technique and a new organisation of industry. The decree together with the instructions meant that the dictatorship of the proletariat assumed an obligation not only to take an attentive attitude toward the interests of the land labourer, but also to be patient of his illusions as a petty proprietor. It was clear in advance that there would be a number of stages and turning-points in the agrarian revolution. The collated instructions were anything but the last word. They represented merely a starting-point which the workers agreed to occupy while helping the peasants to realise their progressive demands, and warning them against false steps.

"We must not ignore," said Lenin in his speech, "the resolutions of the lower ranks of the people, even though we are not in agreement with them. . . . We must give full freedom to the creative capacity of the popular masses. The essence of the thing is that the peasantry should have full confidence that there are no more landlords in the country, and let the peasants themselves decide all questions and build their own life." Opportunism? No, it was revolutionary realism.

Before even the applause was over, a Right Social Revolutionary, Pianykh, arrived from the Peasants' Executive Committee and took the floor with a furious protest on the subject of the socialist ministers being under arrest. "During the last days," cried the orator pounding the table as though beside himself, "a thing is on foot which has never happened in any revolution. Our comrades, members of the Executive Committee, Maslov and Salazkin, are locked up in a prison. We demand their immediate release!" "If one hair falls from their heads . . ." threatened another messenger in a military coat. To the Congress they both seemed like visitors from another world.

At the moment of the insurrection there were about 800 men in prison in Dvinsk, charged with Bolshevism, in Minsk about 6,000, in Kiev 535—for the most part soldiers. And how many members of the peasant committees were under lock and key in various parts of the country! Finally a good share of the delegates to this very Congress, beginning with the præsidium, had passed through the prisons of Kerensky since July. No wonder the indignation of the friends of the Provisional Government could not pluck at any heart-strings in this assembly. To complete their bad luck a certain delegate, unknown to anybody, a peasant from Tver, with long hair and a big sheepskin coat, rose in his place, and having bowed politely to all four points of the compass, adjured the Congress in the name of his electors not to hesitate at arresting Avksentiev's executive committee as a whole: "Those are not peasants' deputies, but Kadets. . . . Their place is in prison." So they stood facing each other, these two figures: The Social Revolutionary Pianykh, experienced parliamentarian, favourite of ministers, hater of Bolsheviks, and the nameless peasant from Tver who had brought Lenin a hearty salute from his electors. Two social strata, two revolutions: Pianykh was speaking in the name of February, the Tver peasant was fighting for October. The Congress gave the delegate in a sheepskin coat a veritable ovation. The emissaries of the Executive Committee went away swearing.

"The resolution of Lenin is greeted by the Social Revolutionary faction as a triumph of their ideas," announces Kalegaev, but in view of the extraordinary importance of the question we must take it up in caucus. A Maximalist, representative of the extreme left wing of the disintegrated Social Revolutionary party, demands an immediate vote: "We ought to give honour to a party which on the very first day and without any blabber brings such a measure to life." Lenin insisted that the intermission should be at any rate as short as possible. "News so important to Russia should be in print by morning. No filibustering!" The decree on land was not only, indeed, the foundation of the new régime, but also a weapon of the revolution, which had still to conquer the country. It is not surprising that Reed records at that moment an imperative shout breaking through the noise of the hall: "Fifteen agitators wanted in room 17 at once! To go to the front!" At one o'clock in the morning a delegate from the Russian troops in Macedonia enters a complaint that the Petersburg governments one after the other have forgotten them. Support for peace and land from the soldiers in Macedonia is assured! Here is a new test of the mood of the army—this time from a far corner of south-eastern Europe. And here Kamenev announces: The Tenth Bicycle Battalion, summoned by the government from the front, entered Petrograd this morning, and like its predecessors has adhered to the Congress of Soviets. The warm applause testifies that no amount of these confirmations of its power will seem excessive to the Congress.

After the adoption, unanimously and without debate, of a resolution declaring it an affair of honour of the local soviets not to permit Jewish or any other pogroms on the part of the criminal element, a vote is taken on the draft of the land law. With one vote opposed and eight abstaining, the congress adopts with a new burst of enthusiasm the decree putting an end to serfdom, the very foundation stone of the old Russian culture. Henceforth the agrarian revolution is legalised, and therewith the revolution of the proletariat acquires a mighty basis.

A last problem remains: the creation of a government. Kamenev reads a proposal drawn up by the Central Committee of the Bolsheviks. The management of the various branches of the state life is allotted to commissions who are to carry into action the programme announced by the Congress of Soviets "in close union with the mass organisation of working men and women, sailors, soldiers, peasants and clerical employees." The governmental power is concentrated in the hands of a collegium composed of the presidents of these commissions, to be called the Soviet of People's Commissars. Control over the activities of the government is vested in the Congress of Soviets and its Central Executive Committee.

Seven members of the Central Committee of the Bolshevik Party were nominated to the first Council of People's Commissars: Lenin as head of the government, without portfolio; Rykov as People's Commissar of the Interior; Miliutin as head of the Department of Agriculture; Nogin as chief of Commerce and Industry; Trotsky as head of the Department of Foreign Affairs; Lomov of Justice; Stalin, president of a Commission on the Affairs of the Nationalities; Military and naval affairs were allotted to a committee consisting of Antonov-Ovseënko, Krylenko and Dybenko; the head of the Commissariat of Labour is to be Shliapnikov; the chief of the Department of Education, Lunacharsky; the heavy and ungrateful task of Minister of Provisions is laid upon Theodorovich; the Posts and Telegraph upon the worker, Glebov; the position of People's Commissar of Communications is not yet allotted, the door being left open here for an agreement with the organisations of the railroad workers.

All fifteen candidates, four workers and eleven intellectuals have behind them years of imprisonment, exile and emigrant life. Five of them have been imprisoned even under the régime of the democratic republic. The future prime minister had only the day before emerged from the democratic underground. Kamenev and Zinoviev did not enter the Council of People's Commissars. The former was selected for president of the new Central Executive Committee, the latter for editor of the official organ of the soviets. "As Kamenev read the list of Commissars," writes Reed, there were "bursts of applause after each name, Lenin's and Trotsky's especially." Sukhanov adds also that of Lunacharsky.

A long speech against the proposed staff of the government was made by a representative of the United Internationalists, Avilov, once a Bolshevik, a literateur from Gorky's paper. He conscientiously enumerated the difficulties standing before the revolution in the sphere of domestic and foreign politics. We must "clearly realise . . . whither we are going. . . . Before the new government stand all the old questions: of bread and of peace. If it does not solve these problems it will be overthrown." There is little grain in the country; it is in the hands of the well-to-do peasants; there is nothing to give in exchange for grain;

industry is on the decline; fuel and raw material are lacking. To collect the grain by force is a difficult, long and dangerous task. It is necessary, therefore, to create a government which will have the sympathy not only of the poor but also of the well-to-do peasantry. For this a coalition is necessary.

"It will be still harder to obtain peace." The governments of the Entente will not answer the proposal of the congress for an immediate armistice. Even without that the Allied ambassadors are planning to leave. The new government will be isolated; its peace initiative will be left hanging in the air. The popular masses of the warring countries are still far from revolution. The consquences may be two: either extermination of the revolution by the troups of the Hohenzollern or a separate peace. The peace terms in both cases can only be the worst possible for Russia. These difficulties can be met only by "a majority of the people." The unfortunate thing is the split in the democracy: the left half wants to create a purely Bolshevik government in Smolny, and the right half is organising in the city duma a Committee of Public Safety. To save the revolution it is necessary to form a government from both groups.

A representative of the Left Social Revolutionaries, Karelin, spoke to the same effect. It is impossible to carry out the programme adopted without those parties which have withdrawn from the Congress. To be sure "the Bolsheviks are not to blame for their withdrawal." But the programme of the congress ought to unite the entire democracy. "We do not want to take the road of isolating the Bolsheviks, for we understand that with the fate of the Bolsheviks is bound up the fate of the whole revolution. Their ruin will be the ruin of the revolution. If they, the Left Social Revolutionaries, have nevertheless declined the invitation to enter the government, their purpose is a good one: to keep their hands free for mediation between the Bolsheviks and the parties which have abandoned the Congress. In such mediations . . . the Left Social Revolutionaries see their principal task at the present moment." The Left Social Revolutionaries will support the work of the new government in solving urgent problems. At the same time they vote against the proposed government.—In a word the young party has got mixed up as badly as it knows how.

"Trotsky rose to defend a government of Bolsheviks only," writes Sukhanov, himself wholly in sympathy with Avilov and having inspired Karelin behind the scenes. "He was very clear, sharp, and in much absolutely right. But he refused to understand in what consisted the centre of the argument of his opponents. . . ." The centre of the argument consisted of an ideal diagonal. In March they had tried to draw it between the bourgeoisie and the compromisist soviets. Now Sukhanov dreamed of a diagonal between the compromisist democracy and the dictatorship of the proletariat. But revolutions do not develop along diagonals.

"They have tried to frighten us more than once with a possible isolation of the Left Wing," said Trotsky. "Some days back when the question of insurrection was first openly raised, they told us that we were headed for destruction. And in reality if you judged the grouping of forces by the political press, then insurrection threatened us with inevitable ruin. Against us stood not only the counter-revolutionary bands, but also the defensists of all varieties. The Left Social Revolutionaries, only one wing of them courageously worked with us in the Military Revolutionary Committee. The rest occupied a position of watchful neutrality. And nevertheless even with these unfavourable circumstances and when it seemed that we were abandoned by all, the insurrection triumphed. . . .

"If the real forces were actually against us, how could it happen that we won the victory almost without bloodshed. No, it is not we who are isolated, but the government and the so called democrats. With their wavering, their compromising, they have erased themselves from the ranks of the authentic democracy. Our great superiority as a party lies in the fact that we have formed a coalition with the class forces, creating a union of the workers and poorest peasants.

"Political groupings disappear, but the fundamental interests of the classes remain. That party conquers which is able to feel out and satisfy the fundamental demands of a class. . . . We pride ourselves upon the coalition of our garrison, chiefly composed of peasants, with the working class. This coalition has been tried by fire. The Petrograd garrison and proletariat went hand in hand into that great struggle which is the classic example in the history of revolutions among all peoples.

"Avilov has spoken of the vast difficulties which stand before us. To remove those difficulties he proposes that we form a coalition. But he makes no attempt to lay bare his formula and tell us what coalition. A coalition of groups, or classes, or simply a coalition of newspapers? . . .

"They tell us the split in the democracy is a misunderstanding. When Kerensky is sending shock troops against us, when with the consent of the Central Executive Committee we are deprived of the telephone at the most critical moment of our struggle with the bourgeoisie, when they deal us blow after blow—is it possible to talk of misunderstanding?

"Avilov says to us: There is little bread, we must have a coalition with the defensists. Do you imagine that this coalition will increase the quantity of bread? The problem of bread is the problem of a programme of action. The struggle with economic collapse demands a definite system from below, and not political groupings on top.

"Avilov speaks of a union with the peasantry: But again of what peasantry is he talking? To-day and right here, a representative of the peasants of Tver province demanded the arrest of Avksentiev. We must choose between this Tver peasant and Avksentiev who has filled the prisons with members of the peasant committees. A coalition with the kulak elements of the peasantry we firmly reject in the name of a coalition of the working class and the poorer peasant. We are with the Tver peasants against Avksentiev. We are with them to the end and inseparably.

"Whoever now chases the shadow of coalition is totally cutting himself off from life. The Social Revolutionaries will lose support among the masses to the extent that they venture to oppose our party. Every group which opposes the party of the proletariat, with whom the village poor have united, cuts himself off from the revolution.

"Openly and before the face of the whole people we raised the banner of insurrection. The political formula of this insurrection was: All power to the soviets—through the Congress of Soviets. They tell us: You did not await the Congress with your uprising. We thought of waiting, but Kerensky would not wait. The counter-revolutionists were not dreaming. We as a party considered this our task: to make it genuinely possible for the Congress of Soviets to seize the power. If the Congress had been surrounded with junkers, how could it have seized the power? In order to achieve this task, a party was needed which would wrench the power from the hands of the counter-revolution and say to you: 'Here is the power and you've got to take it!' (Stormy and prolonged applause.)

"Notwithstanding that the defensists of all shades stopped at nothing in their struggle against us, we did not throw them out. We proposed to the Congress as a whole to take the power. How utterly you distort the perspective, when after all that has happened you talk from this tribune of our irreconcilability. When a party surrounded with a cloud of gunpowder smoke, comes up to them and says, 'Let us take the power together!' they run to the city duma and unite there with open counter-revolutionists! They are traitors to the revolution with whom we will never unite!

"For the struggle for peace", says Avilov, "we must have a coalition with the Compromisers". At the same time he acknowledges that the Allies do not want to make peace. . . . The Allied imperialists laughed, says Avilov, at the oleomargarine delegate Skobelev. Nevertheless if you form a bloc with the oleomargarine democrats, the cause of peace is assured!

"There are two roads in the struggle for peace. One road is to oppose to the Allied and enemy governments the moral and material force of revolution. The other is a bloc with Skobelev, which means a bloc with Tereshchenko and complete subjection to Allied imperialism. In our proclamation on peace we address ourselves simultaneously to the governments and the peoples. That is purely formal symmetry. Of course we do not think to influence the imperialist governments with our proclamations, although as long as they exist we cannot ignore them. We rest all our hope on the possibility that our revolution will unleash the European revolution. If the revolting peoples of Europe do not crush imperialism, then we will be crushed—that is indubitable. Either the Russian revolution will raise the whirlwind of struggle in the west, or the capitalists of all countries will crush our revolution. . . ."

"There is a third road," says a voice from the benches.

"The third road," answers Trotsky, "is the road of the Central Executive Committee—on the one hand sending delegates to the west European workers, and on the other forming a union with the Kishkins and Konovalovs. That is a road of lies and hypocrisy which we will never enter.

"Of course we do not say that only the day of insurrection of the European workers will be the day that the peace treaty is signed. This also is possible: that the bourgeoisie, frightened by an approaching insurrection of the oppressed, will hasten to make peace. The dates are not set. The concrete forms cannot be foretold. It is important and it is necessary to define the method of struggle, a method identical in principle both in foreign and domestic politics. A union of the oppressed here and everywhere—that is our road."

The delegates of the Congress, says John Reed, "greeted him

with an immense crusading acclaim, kindling to the daring of it, with the thought of championing mankind." At any rate it could not have entered the minds of any Bolshevik at that time to protest against placing the fate of the Soviet Republic, in an official speech in the name of the Bolshevik Party, in direct dependence upon the development of the international revolution.

The dramatic law of this Congress was that each significant act was concluded or even interrupted, by a short intermission during which a figure from the other camp would suddenly appear upon the stage and voice a protest, or a threat, or present an ultimatum. A representative of the Vikzhel, the executive committee of the railroad workers' union, now demanded the floor immediately and on the instant. He must needs throw a bomb into the assembly before the vote was taken on the question of power. The speaker—in whose face Reed saw implacable hostility—began with an accusation. His organisation, "the strongest in Russia," had not been invited to the congress. . . . "It was the Central Executive Committee that did not invite you," was shouted at him from all sides. But he continued: And be it known that the original decision of the Vikzhel to support the Congress of Soviets has been revoked. The speaker hastened to read an ultimatum already distributed by telegraph throughout the country: The Vikzhel condemns the seizure of power by one party; the government ought to be responsible before the "entire revolutionary democracy"; until the creation of a democratic government only the Vikzhel will control the railroad lines. The speaker adds that counter-revolutionary troops will not be admitted to Petrograd; but in general the movement of troups will henceforth take place only at the direction of the old Central Executive Committee. In case of repressions directed against the railroad workers, the Vikzhel will deprive Petrograd of food.

The Congress bristled under the blow. The chiefs of the railroad union were trying to converse with the representatives of the people as one government with another! When the workers, soldiers, and peasants take the administration of the state into their hands, the Vikzhel presumes to give commands to the workers, soldiers, and peasants! It wants to change into petty cash the overthrown system of dual power. In thus attempting to rely not upon its numbers, but upon the exceptional significance of railroads in the economy and culture of the country, these democrats of the Vikzhel exposed the whole frailty of the criterion of formal democracy upon the fundamental issues of a social struggle. Truly revolution has a genius for education!

At any rate the moment for this blow was not badly chosen by the Compromisers, The faces of the præsidium were troubled. Fortunately the Vikzhel was by no means unconditional boss on the railroads. In the local districts the railroad workers were members of the city soviets. Even here at the congress the ultimatum of the Vikzhel met resistance. "The whole mass of the railroad workers of our district," said the delegate from Tashkent, "have expressed themselves in favour of the transfer of power to the soviets." Another delegate from railroad workers declared the Vikzhel a "political corpse." That doubtless was exaggerated. Relying upon the rather numerous upper layers of railroad clerks, the Vikzhel had preserved more life force than the other higher-up organisations of the Compromisers. But it belonged indubitably to the same type as the army committees or the Central Executive Committee. Its star was swiftly falling. The workers were everywhere distinguishing themselves from the clerical employees; the lower clerks were opposing themselves to the higher. The impudent ultimatum of the Vikzhel would undoubtedly hasten these processes. No, the station masters can't hold back the locomotive of the October revolution!

"There can be no questioning the legal rights of this Congress," declared Kamenev with authority. "The quorum of the Congress was established not by us, but by the old Central Executive Committee. . . . The Congress is the highest organ of the workers and soldier masses." A simple return to the order of the day!

The Council of People's Commissars was ratified by an overwhelming majority. Avilov's resolution, according to the excessively generous estimate of Sukhanov, got 150 votes, chiefly Left Social Revolutionaries. The Congress then unanimously confirmed the membership of the new Central Executive Committee: out of 101 members—62 Bolsheviks, 29 Left Social Revolutionaries. The Central Executive Committee was to complete itself in the future with representatives of the peasant soviets and the re-elected army organisations. The factions who had abandoned the Congress were granted the right to send their delegates to the Central Executive Committee on the basis of proportional representation.

The agenda of the Congress was completed! The Soviet

government was created. It had its programme. The work could begin. And there was no lack of it. At 5.15 in the morning Kamenev closed the Constituent Congress of the Soviet régime. To the stations! Home! To the front! To the factories and barracks! To the mines and the far-off villages! In the decrees of the Soviet, the delegates will carry the leaven of the proletarian revolution to all corners of the country.

On that morning the central organ of the Bolshevik Party, again under the old name *Pravda*, wrote: "They wanted us to take the power alone, so that we alone should have to contend with the terrible difficulties confronting the country. . . . So be it! We take the power alone, relying upon the voice of the country and counting upon the friendly help of the European proletariat. But having taken the power, we will deal with the enemies of revolution and its saboteurs with an iron hand. They dreamed of a dictatorship of Kornilov. . . . We will give them the dictatorship of the proletariat. . . ."

Conclusion

A remarkable consecutiveness of stages is to be observed in the development of the Russian revolution—and this for the very reason that it was an authentic popular revolution, setting in motion tens of millions. Events succeeded each other as though obeying laws of gravitation. The correlation of forces was twice verified at every stage: first the masses would demonstrate the might of their assault, then the possessing classes, attempting revenge, would reveal their isolation the more clearly.

In February the workers and soldiers of Petrograd rose in insurrection—not only against the patriotic will of all the educated classes, but also contrary to the reckonings of the revolutionary organisations. The masses demonstrated that they were unconquerable. Had they themselves been aware of this, they would have become the government. But there was not yet a strong and authoritative revolutionary party at their head. The power fell into the hands of the petty-bourgeois democracy tinted with a protective socialist colouration. The Mensheviks and Social Revolutionaries could make no other use of the confidence of the masses but to summon to the helm the liberal bourgeoisie, who in this turn could only place the power slipped to them by the Compromisers at the service of the interests of the Entente.

In the April days the indignation of the regiments and factories again without tthe summons of any party—brought them out on the streets of Petrograd to resist the imperialist policy of the government wished on them by the Compromisers. This armed demonstration attained an appearance of success. Miliukoff, the leader of Russian imperialism, was removed from the government. The Compromisers entered the government, superficially as plenipotentiaries of the people, in reality as call-boys of the bourgeoisie.

Without having decided one of the problems which had evoked the revolution, the coalition government violated in June the *de facto* armistice that had been established on the front, throwing the troops into an offensive. By this act the February régime, already marked by the declining trust of the masses in the Compromisers, dealt itself a fatal blow. The period opened of direct preparation for the second revolution.

At the beginning of July the government, having all the possessing and educated classes behind it, was prosecuting every revolutionary manifestation whatever as treason to the fatherland and aid to the enemy. The official mass organisations—the soviets, the social-patriotic parties—were struggling against a demonstration with all their power. The Bolsheviks for tactical reasons were trying to restrain the workers and soldiers from coming into the streets. Nevertheless the masses came out. The movement proved unrestrainable and universal. The government was nowhere to be seen. The Compromisers hid. The workers and soldiers proved masters of the situation in the capital. Their offensive went to pieces, however, owing to the inadequate readiness of the provinces and the front.

At the end of August all the organs and institutions of the possessing classes stood for a counter-revolutionary overturn: the diplomats of the Entente, the banks, the leagues of landed proprietors and industrialists, the Kadet Party, the staffs, the officers, the big press. The organiser of the overturn was no other than the supreme commander-in-chief with the officer-apparatus of an army of millions to rely on. Military detachments specially selected from all fronts were thrown against Petrograd under pretence of strategic considerations and by secret agreement with the head of the government.

In the capital everything, it seemed, was prepared for the success of the enterprise: the workers had been disarmed by the authorities with the help of the Compromisers; the Bolsheviks were under a steady rain of blows; the more revolutionary regiments had been removed from the city; hundreds of specially selected officers were concentrated in shock brigades—with the officer schools and Cossack detachments they should constitute an impressive force. And what happened? The plot, patronised it would seem by the gods themselves, barely came in contact with the revolutionary people when it scattered in dust.

These two movements, at the beginning of July and the end of August, relate to each other as a theorem and its converse. The July Days demonstrated the might of the self-dependent movement of the masses. The August Days laid bare the complete impotence of the ruling groups. This correlation signalized the inevitability of a new conflict. The provinces and the front were meanwhile drawing closer to the capital. This predetermined the October victory.

"The ease with which Lenin and Trotsky overthrew the last coalition government of Kerensky," wrote the Kadet, Nabokov, "revealed its inward impotence. The degree of this impotence was an amazement at that time even to well-informed people." Nabokov himself seems hardly aware that it was a question of his impotence, that of his class, of his social structure.

Just as from the armed demonstration of July the curve rises to the October insurrection, so the movement of Kornilov seems a dress-rehearsal of the counter-revolutionary campaign undertaken by Kerensky in the last days of October. The sole military force against the Bolsheviks found at the front by the democratic commander-in-chief after his flight under cover of the little American flag, was that same Third Cavalry Corps which two months before had been designated by Kornilov for the overthrow of Kerensky himself. The commander of the corps was still the Cossack General, Krasnov, militant monarchist placed in this post by Kornilov. A more appropriate commander for the defence of democracy was not to be found.

Moreover nothing was left of the corps but its name. It had been reduced to a few Cossack squadrons, who after an unsuccessful attempt to take the offensive against the Reds near Petrograd, fraternised with the revolutionary sailors and turned Krasnov over to the Bolsheviks. Kerensky was obliged to take flight—both from the Cossacks and the sailors. Thus eight months after the overthrow of the monarchy the workers stood at the head of the country. And they stood firmly.

"Who would believe," wrote one of the Russian generals, Zalessky, expressing his indignation at this, "that the janitor or watchman of the court building would suddenly become Chief Justice of the Court of Appeals? Or the hospital orderly manager of the hospital; the barber a big functionary; yesterday's ensign the commander-in-chief; yesterday's lackey or common labourer burgomaster; yesterday's train oiler chief of division or station superintendent; yesterday's locksmith head of the factory?"

"Who would believe it?" They had to believe it. It was impossible not to believe it, when ensigns routed the generals, when burgomasters, from the ranks of common labour put down the resistance of yesterday's lords, train oilers regulated transport, and locksmiths as directors revived industry.

The chief task of a political régime, according to an English aphorism, is to put the right people in the right positions. How does the experiment of 1917 look from this point of view? During the first two months Russia was ruled, through right of monarchic succession, by a man inadequately endowed by nature who believed in saints' mummies and submitted to Rasputin. During the next eight months the liberals and democrats attempted from their governmental high places to prove to the people that the revolution had been accomplished in order that all should remain as before. No wonder those people passed over the country like wavering shadows leaving no trace. From the 25th of October the man at the head of Russia was Lenin, the greatest figure in Russian political history. He was surrounded by a staff of assistants who, as their most spiteful enemies acknowledge, knew what they wanted and how to fight for their aims. Which of these three systems, in the given concrete conditions, proved capable of putting the right people in the right positions?

The historic ascent of humanity, taken as a whole, may be summarised as a succession of victories of consciousness over blind forces—in nature, in society, in man himself. Critical and creative thought can boast of its greatest victories up to now in the struggle with nature. The physico-chemical sciences have already reached a point where man is clearly about to become master of matter. But social relations are still forming in the manner of the coral islands. Parliamentarism illumined only the surface of society, and even that with a rather artificial light. In comparison with monarchy and other heirlooms from the cannibals and cave-dwellers, democracy is of course a great conquest, but it leaves the blind play of forces in the social relations of men untouched. It was against this deeper sphere of the unconscious that the October revolution was the first to raise its hand. The Soviet system wishes to bring aim and plan into the very basis of society, where up to now only accumulated consequences have reigned.

Enemies are gleeful that fifteen years after the revolution the Soviet country is still but little like a kingdom of universal well-being. Such an argument, if not really to be explained as due to a blinding hostility, could only be dictated by an excessive worship of the magic power of socialist methods. Capitalism required a hundred years to elevate science and technique to the heights and plunge humanity into the hell of war and crisis. To socialism its enemies allow only fifteen years to create and furnish a terrestrial paradise. We took no such obligation upon ourselves. We never set these dates. The process of vast transformations must be measured by an adequate scale.

But the misfortunes which have overwhelmed living people? The fire and bloodshed of the civil war? Do the consequences of a revolution justify in general the sacrifices it involves? The question is teleological and therefore fruitless. It would be as well to ask in face of the difficulties and griefs of personal existence: Is it worth while to be born? Melancholy reflections have not so far, however, prevented people from bearing or being born. Even in the present epoch of intolerable misfortune only a small percentage of the population of our planet resorts to suicide. But the people are seeking the way out of their unbearable difficulties in revolution.

Is it not remarkable that those who talk most indignantly about the victims of social revolutions are usually the very ones who, if not directly responsible for the victims of the world war, prepared and glorified them, or at least accepted them? It is our turn to ask: Did the war justify itself? What has it given us? What has it taught?

It will hardly pay now to pause upon the assertions of injured Russian proprietors that the revolution led to the cultural decline of the country. That aristocratic culture overthrown by the October revolution was in the last analysis only a superficial imitation of higher western models. Remaining inaccessible to the Russian people, it added nothing essential to the treasure-store of humanity. The October revolution laid the foundation of a new culture taking everybody into consideration, and for that very reason immediately acquiring international significance. Even supposing for a moment that owing to unfavourable circumstances and hostile blows the Soviet régime should be temporarily overthrown, the inexpugnable impress of the October revolution would nevertheless remain upon the whole future development of mankind.

The language of the civilised nations has clearly marked off two epochs in the development of Russia. Where the aristocratic culture introduced into world parlance such barbarisms as *czar, pogrom, knout,* October has internationalised such words as *Bolshevik, soviet* and *piatiletka*. This alone justifies the proletarian revolution, if you imagine that it needs justification.

THE END

NOTE TO THE APPENDICES

Besides our historic references on the theory of permanent revolution, we have transferred into this appendix two independent chapters: "Some Legends of the Bureaucracy," and "Socialism in a Separate Country?" The chapter on "legends" is dedicated to the critical restoration of a series of facts and episodes of the October revolution distorted by the epigone historians. One of the incidental aims of this chapter is to make it impossible for lazy minds, instead of working over the factual material, to quiet themselves with the cheap *a priori* conclusion that "the truth is probably somewhere in the middle."

The chapter "Socialism in a Separate Country?" is dedicated to the most important question concerning the ideology and programme of the Bolshevik party. The question here historically illumined by us, not only still preserves all its theoretical interest, but has in recent years acquired a first-class practical importance.

We have separated these two chapters from the general text, of which they form an integral part, only for the benefit of the reader not accustomed to concern himself with secondary disputes or theoretical problems. If however a tenth, or even a hundredth, of the readers of this book take the trouble to read attentively this appendix, the author will feel abundantly rewarded for the great labour he has performed. It is through thoughtful, work-loving and critical minds that the truth in the long run makes its way to broader circles.

APPENDIX I

SUPPLEMENTARY ESSAY

Some Legends of the Bureaucracy

The conception of the October revolution developed in this book was set forth by the author more than once during the early years of the Soviet régime, although to be sure only in its general features. In order to delineate his thought more clearly he sometimes gave it a quantitative expression: the task of the overturn, he wrote, was "three-quarters if not nine-tenths" completed before the 25th of October by the method of "silent" or "dry" insurrection. If you do not give these figures more importance than figures could pretend to in such a matter, the idea itself remains absolutely unquestionable. But since the revaluation of values began, our conception has been bitterly criticised in this particular.

"If on the 9th of October a nine-tenths 'victorious' insurrection was already an accomplished fact," wrote Kamenev, "then how shall we estimate the intellectual capacities of those who were sitting in the Central Committee of the Bolsheviks, and on the 10th of October deciding in heated debates whether to make an insurrection or not, and if so when? What shall we say of the people who assembled on the 16th of October . . . and again and again estimated the chances for an insurrection? . . . Oh yes, it seems that it was already accomplished on the 9th of October 'silently' and 'legally'—so silently indeed that neither the party nor the Central Committee knew about it." This superficially so effective argument, which is canonised in the epigone literature and has politically outlived its author, is in reality an impressive piling up of mistakes.

On the 9th of October the insurrection could not possibly have been a "nine-tenths" accomplished fact, for on that day the question of the transfer of the garrison had just been raised in the Soviet and it was impossible to know how the thing would develop in the future. It was for this reason that on the next day, the 10th, when insisting on the importance of this question of the transfer of the troops, Trotsky had not yet sufficient grounds to demand that the conflict between the garrison and its command form the basis of the whole plan. Only during the next two weeks of stubborn day-by-day work did the chief task of the insurrection—the firm winning over to the people's side of the government troops—become "three-quarters if not nine-tenths" accomplished. This was not so on the 10th, nor yet even on the 16th of October, when the Central Committee took up for a second time the question of insurrection and when Krylenko did quite definitely present as a key-note the question of the garrison.

But even if the revolution had been nine-tenths victorious on the 9th—as Kamenev erroneously presents our thought—this fact could have been reliably ascertained, not by guessing, but only by action—that is, by making an insurrection. The "intellectual capacity" of the members of the Central Committee would not, even in that purely hypothetical case, have been in the least compromised by their participation in heated debates on the 10th and 16th of October. However, even supposing that the members of the Central Committee could have unquestionably assured themselves by an *a priori* calculation that the victory was actually nine-tenths won, it would still have remained necessary to accomplish the last tenth, and that would have demanded just as much attention as though it were ten-tenths. How many "almost" won battles and insurrections does history present—battles and insurrections which led to defeat only because they were not pushed through in good season to the complete defeat of the enemy! And finally—Kamenev is ingenious enough to forget this too—the sphere of activity of the Military Revolutionary Committee was Petrograd only. However important the capital may have been, the rest of the country did nevertheless exist. And from this point of view the Central Committee had sufficient ground for carefully weighing the chances of the insurrection, not only on the 10th and the 16th, but also on the 26th—that is, after the victory in Petrograd.

Kamenev, in the argument we are discussing, comes to the defence of Lenin. All the epigones defend themselves under this imposing pseudonym. How could Lenin, he asks, have fought so passionately for an insurrection, if it was already nine-tenths accomplished! But Lenin himself wrote at the beginning of October: "It is quite possible that right now we might seize the power without an insurrection." In other words, Lenin postulated that the "silent" revolution had already taken place before the 9th of October, and moreover not by nine but by ten-tenths. He understood however, that this optimistic hypothesis could only be verified in action. For that reason Lenin said in the same letter: "If we cannot seize power without an insurrection, then we must make an insurrection immediately." It was this question that was discussed on the 10th and 16th, and on other days.

The recent Soviet histories have completely erased from the October revolution the extremely important and instructive chapter about the disagreements between Lenin and the Central Committee—both upon the basic matter of principle in which Lenin was right, and also upon those particular, but very important, questions upon which the Central Committee was right. According to the new doctrine, neither Lenin nor the Central Committee could make a mistake, and consequently there could have been no conflict between them. In those cases where it becomes impossible to deny that there was a disagreement, it is, in obedience to a general prescription, laid at the door of Trotsky.

The facts speak otherwise. Lenin insisted upon raising in insurrection in the days of the Democratic Conference. Not one member of the Central Committee supported him. A week later Lenin proposed to Smilga to organise an insurrectionary headquarters in Finland, and strike a blow at the government from that point with the sailors. Again ten days later he insisted that the Northern Congress become the starting point of an insurrection. Nobody at the Congress supported this proposal. At the end of September Lenin considered the postponement of the insurrection for three weeks, until the Congress of Soviets, fatal. Nevertheless the insurrection, deferred to the eve of the Congress, was accomplished while the Congress was in session. Lenin proposed that the struggle begin in Moscow, assuming that there it would be resolved without a fight. As a matter of fact, the insurrection in Moscow, notwithstanding the preceding victory in Petrograd, lasted eight days and cost many victims.

Lenin was no automaton of infallible decisions. He was "only" a man of genius, and nothing human was alien to him, therein included the capacity to make mistakes. Lenin said this of the attitude of epigones to the great revolutionists: "After their deaths, attempts are made to convert them into harmless ikons, to canonise them, so to speak, to render a certain homage to their names . . ." in order thus the more safely to betray them in action. The present epigones demand that Lenin be acknowledged infallible in order the more easily to extend the same dogma to themselves.[1]

What characterised Lenin as a statesman was a combination of bold perspectives with a meticulous estimation of tiny facts and symptoms. Lenin's isolation did not prevent him from defining with incomparable penetration the fundamental stages and turns of the movement, but it deprived him of the possibility of making timely estimates of episodic factors and temporary changes. The political situation was in general so favourable to an insurrection as to admit several different possibilities of victory. If Lenin had been in Petrograd and had carried through at the beginning of October his

1. During the Third Congress of the Communist International in order to soften his blows at certain "ultra-Lefts," Lenin referred to the fact that he himself had made "ultra-Left" mistakes, especially while an emigré, including one during his last "emigration" in Finland in 1917, when he defended a less expedient plan of insurrection than the one actually carried out. This reference to his own mistake was made by Lenin, unless our memory deceives us, also in a letter to the commission of the congress on German affairs. Unfortunately the archives of the Communist International are not accessible to us, and the declaration of Lenin in question has evidently not been published.

decision in favour of an immediate insurrection without reference to the Congress of Soviets, he would undoubtedly have given the carrying out of his own plan a political setting which would have reduced its disadvantageous features to a minimum. But it is at least equally probable that he would himself in that case have come round to the plan actually carried out.

We have given in a separate chapter our estimate of the rôle of Lenin in the general strategy of the revolution. To point our idea in regard to Lenin's tactical proposals we will add that without Lenin's pressure, without his urgings, his suggestions, his variant plans, it would have been infinitely more difficult to get over on to the road toward insurrection. Had Lenin been in Smolny during the critical weeks, the general leadership of the insurrection—and that not only in Petrograd but Moscow—would have been on a considerably higher level. But Lenin as an "emigré" could not take the place of Lenin in Smolny.

Lenin himself felt most keenly of all the inadequacy of his tactical orientation. He wrote on September 24th in *Rabochy Put*: "The growth of a new revolution is obviously in progress—we know little unfortunately of the breadth and rapidity of this growth." These words are both a reproach to the party leaders and a complaint of his own lack of information. When recalling in his letter the most important rules of insurrection Lenin did not forget to add: "This is all approximate of course and merely for illustration." On the 8th of October, Lenin wrote to the Northern Regional Congress of Soviets: "I will try to appear with my advice from the sidelines in case the probable insurrection of the workers and soldiers of Petersburg . . . soon takes place, but it has not yet taken place." Lenin began his polemic against Zinoviev and Kamenev with these words. "A publicist set somewhat aside by the will of destiny from the main line of history constantly incurs the risk of coming in late or being uninformed, especially when his writings are delayed in publication." Here again a complaint against his isolation together with a reproach to the editors who had delayed the printing of those articles which they judged too incisive, or had thrown out the prickliest passages. A week before the insurrection Lenin wrote in a conspirative letter to the members of the party: "As to the raising of the question of insurrection now, so near to the 20th of October, I cannot judge *from a distance* just how much of the thing has been spoiled by the strike-breaking performance (of Zinoviev and Kamenev) in the non-party press." The words "from a distance" are underlined by Lenin himself.

But how does the epigone school explain the disaccord between the tactical proposals of Lenin and the actual course of the insurrection in Petrograd? It gives to the conflict an anonymous and formless character; or it passes by the disagreements altogether, declaring them unworthy of attention; or it tries to refute facts indestructibly established; or it puts the name Trotsky where Lenin was talking about the Central Committee as a whole or the opponents of insurrection within the Central Committee; or, finally, it combines all these methods, not bothering about whether they are mutually consistent or not.

"The conduct of the October insurrection," writes Stalin, "may be considered a model of (Bolshevik) strategy. To transgress this requirement (the correct choice of the moment) leads to a dangerous mistake called 'loss of tempo,' when the party falls behind the course of events or runs ahead, giving rise to a danger of failure. The attempt of one group of the comrades to begin the insurrection with the arrest of the Democratic Conference in August 1917 must be considered an example of this 'loss of tempo,' an example of how not to choose the moment of insurrection." The designation "one group of the comrades" in these lines means Lenin. Nobody but Lenin proposed that the insurrection begin with the arrest of the Democratic Conference, and nobody supported his proposal. Stalin recommends the tactical plan of Lenin as "an example of how not to choose the moment of insurrection." But the anonymous form of his account permits Stalin at the same time to deny flatly that there was any disagreement between Lenin and the Central Committee.

Yaroslavsky has a still simpler way of getting out of the difficulty. "It is not a question of particulars, of course," he writes, "it is not a question whether the insurrection began in Moscow or Petrograd." The thing is that the whole course of events demonstrated "the correctness of Lenin's line, the correctness of the line of our party." This ingenious historian simplifies his task to an extraordinary degree. That October verified the strategy of Lenin, and demonstrated in particular how important had been his April victory over the ruling stratum of "old Bolsheviks," is indubitable. But if in a general way there is no question about where to begin, when to begin, and how to begin, then, to be sure, nothing is left of the episodic disagreements with Lenin—or for that matter of tactics in general.

In John Reed's book there is a story that on the 21st of October the leaders of the Bolsheviks held a "second historic conference" at which, as Reed was told, Lenin said: "The 24th of October is too soon to act. We must have an All-Russian basis for the insurrection, and on the 24th not all the delegates will have come to the Congress. On the other hand, the 26th will be too late to act. . . . We must act on the 25th, the day of the opening of the Congress." Reed was an extraordinarily keen observer, able to transcribe upon the pages of his book the feelings and passions of the deciding days of the revolution. It was for this reason that Lenin in his day desired that the incomparable chronicle of Reed be distributed in millions of copies in all the countries of the world. But work done in the heat of events, notes made in corridors, on the streets, beside camp fires, conversations and fragmentary phrases caught on the wing, and that too with the need of a translator—all these things made particular mistakes unavoidable. This story of a session of October 21st is one of the most obvious mistakes in Reed's book. The argument about the need of an "All-Russian soviet foundation" for the insurrection could not possibly belong to Lenin, for Lenin more than once described the running after such a foundation as nothing more or less than "complete idiocy or complete betrayal." Lenin could not have said that the 24th was too early, for ever since the end of September he had considered inadmissible a postponement of the insurrection for one unnecessary day. It might come too late, he said, but "in that matter it is now impossible to be premature." However, aside from these political considerations—decisive enough in themselves—Reed's story is refuted by the simple fact that on the 21st there was no "second historic conference" of any kind. Such a conference could not fail to leave traces in the documents and memories of the other participants. There were only two conferences with Lenin present: on the 10th and the 16th. Reed could not have known this. But the documents since published leave no place for the "historic session" of October 21st. The epigone historians have not hesitated, however, to include the obviously erroneous testimony of Reed in all the official publications. By this means they have achieved a specious calendar-coincidence of Lenin's directives with the actual course of events. To be sure, in doing this the official historians put Lenin in the position of incomprehensibly and hopelessly contradicting himself. But essentially, you must understand, they are not here concerned about Lenin. The epigones have simply converted Lenin into their own historic pseudonym, and are unceremoniously making use of him in order to establish their own infallibility *ex post facto*.

But the official historians go even farther than this in the business of driving facts into the required line of march. Thus Yaroslavsky writes in his history of the party: "At the session of the Central Committee on the 24th of October, the last session before the insurrection, Lenin was present." The officially published minutes, containing a complete list of those present, testify that Lenin was absent. "Lenin and Kamenev were delegated to negotiate with the Left Social Revolutionaries," writes Yaroslavsky. The minutes say that this task was allotted to Kamenev and Berezin. But it ought to be obvious without any minutes that the Central Committee would not have put upon Lenin this secondary "diplomatic" task. That decisive session of the Central Committee took place in the morning. Lenin did not arrive at Smolny until night. A member of the Petrograd committee, Sveshnikov, relates how Lenin "went out somewhere in the evening (of the 24th) leaving a note in his room stating that he had gone at such and such a time. When we learned this we were frightened to death for Ilych." Only "late in the evening" did it become known in the district that Lenin had gone to the Military Revolutionary Committee.

Most surprising of all, however, is the fact that Yaroslavsky ignores a political and human document of first-class importance: a letter to the leaders of the districts written by Lenin during the hours when the open insurrection had already essentially begun. "Comrades! I am writing these lines on the evening of the 24th. . . . With all my power I want to convince the comrades that everything now hangs upon a thread, that questions are now in order which will not be decided by conferences, not by congresses (even though congresses of soviets) but solely by the people, by the mass, by the struggle of the armed masses. It is necessary at any possible cost this very evening, this very night, to arrest the government, disarming (vanquishing if they resist) the junkers, etc. . . ." Lenin feared to such an extent the irresolution of the Central Committee, that he was trying at the very last moment to organise a pressure on it from below. "It is necessary," he writes, "that all districts, all regiments, all forces mobilise on the instant and send delegations immediately to the Military Revolutionary Committee, to the Central Committee of the Bolsheviks, with this insistent demand: In no case leave the power in the hands of Kerensky and Co. until the 25th, not in any case—but settle the thing to-day without fail, this evening or night." While Lenin was writing these lines, the regiments and districts he was summoning to mobilise for pressure on the Military Revolutionary Committee were already mobilised by the Military Revolutionary Committee for the seizure of the city and the overthrow of the government. From this letter—every line of which quivers with anxiety and passion—it is at least evident that Lenin could not have proposed on the 21st to defer the insurrection until the 25th, nor have been present at the morning session of the 24th when it was decided to take the offensive immediately.

There is in this letter nevertheless a puzzling element. How could it happen that Lenin, in hiding in the Vyborg district, did not know until evening about a decision of such exceptional importance? From the account of Sveshnikov—as also from other sources—it is evident that communications with Lenin were kept up during that day through Stalin. It can only be assumed that, not having appeared at the morning session of the Central Committee, Stalin also did not know until evening of the decision adopted.

The immediate cause of Lenin's alarm may have been the rumours consciously and persistently circulated during that day from Smolny, that until the decision of the Congress of Soviets no decisive steps would be taken. On the evening of that day, at an emergency session of the Petrograd Soviet, Trotsky said, in his report on the activities of the Military Revolutionary Committee: "An armed conflict to-day or to-morrow is not included in our plan—on the threshold of the All-Russian Congress of Soviets. We think that the Congress will carry out our slogan with greater power and authority. But if the government wants to use that span of life which still remains to it—24, 48 or 72 hours—in order to take the offensive against us, we will answer with a counter-offensive, blow for blow, steel against iron." Such was the leit-motiv of that whole day. These defensive announcements had for their purpose to lull at the last moment before the blow the none too lively vigilance of the enemy. It was in all probability this manœuvre which gave Dan his grounds for assuring Kerensky on the night of the 25th that the Bolsheviks had no intention at all of making an immediate insurrection. But on the other hand, Lenin too, if one of these sedative declarations from Smolny happened to reach him, may, in his state of tension and distrust, have taken a military trick for good money.

Ruses form a necessary element of the art of war. It is a bad ruse, however, which may incidentally deceive one's own camp. Had it been a question of summoning masses wholesale into the streets, those words about the next "72 hours" might have proven a fatal act. But on the 24th the uprising no longer had need of any general revolutionary summons. The armed detachments designated for the seizure of the principal points of the capital were under arms and awaiting from the commanders, who were in telephone communication with the nearest revolutionary headquarters, the signal to attack. In these circumstances the double-edged ruse of the revolutionary headquarters was entirely in place.

Whenever the official investigators run into an unpleasant document they change its address. Thus Yakovlev writes: "The Bolsheviks did not surrender to 'constitutional illusions,' but rejected the proposals of Trotsky to accommodate the insurrection necessarily to the Second Congress of Soviets, and seized the power before the opening of the Congress of Soviets." Just what proposal of Trotsky is here spoken of, where and when it was considered, what Bolsheviks rejected it—of this the author has nothing to say, and not accidentally. We should search in vain among the minutes, or among any memoirs whatever, for any indication of a proposal of Trotsky to "accommodate the insurrection necessarily to the Second Congress of Soviets." The ground of this assertion of Yakovlev is a slightly conventionalised misunderstanding long ago explained away by no other than Lenin himself.

As is evident from memoirs published long ago, Trotsky had more than once since the beginning of September pointed out to those opposed to insurrection that appointing the date for the Congress of Soviets was for the Bolsheviks equivalent to appointing the insurrection. This did not mean, of course, that the uprising must not occur except upon the decision of the Congress of Soviets—there could be no talk of such childish formalism. It was a question of the outside date, of the impossibility of deferring it to an indefinite time after the congress. Through whom and in what form these disputes in the Central Committee reached Lenin, is not clear from the documents. An interview with Trotsky, who was too much in view of the enemy, would have been too great a risk for Lenin. In his attitude of caution at that time he may therefore have feared that Trotsky would place his emphasis upon the Congress and not upon the insurrection, or in any case that he would not put up the necessary resistance to the "constitutional illusions" of Zinoviev and Kamenev. Lenin may have been anxious also about the new members of the Central Committee little known to him, the former Mezhrayontsi (or fusionists), Joffé and Uritzky. There is direct evidence of this in a speech of Lenin at a session of the Petrogard committee on November 1st after the victory. "The question was raised at the session (of October 10th) about an offensive. I had fears of opportunism from the side of the internationalist-fusionists, but these were dissipated; in our party, however, (certain old) members (of the Central Committee) did not agree. This grieved me deeply." According to his own words, Lenin became convinced on the 10th that not only Trotsky, but also Joffé and Uritzky, who were under Trotsky's immediate influence, were decisively in favour of insurrection. The question of dates in general was raised for the first time at that session. When, then, and by whom, was "a proposal of Trotsky" not to begin the insurrection without a preliminary decision of the Congress of Soviets rejected? As though with a special view to enlarge still further the radius of confusion, the official investigators, with their references to an apocryphal decision of October 21st, attribute, as we have seen, exactly the same proposal to Lenin.

At this point Stalin bursts into the argument with a new version which refutes Yakovlev, but along with him also much more. It seems, according to Stalin, that the postponement of the insurrection to the day of the Congress—that is, to the 25th—met no intrinsic objection from Lenin, but the thing was spoiled by the publication in advance of the date of insurrection. Here let us give the floor, however, to Stalin himself: "The mistake of the Petrograd Soviet in openly designating and publishing abroad the date of the insurrection (October 25th) could not be corrected except by an actual insurrection before this legal date of insurrection." This assertion is disarming in its inconsistency. As though in those disputes with Lenin it was a question of choosing between the 24th and 25th of October! As a matter of fact Lenin wrote almost a month before the insurrection: "To wait for the Congress of Soviets is complete idiocy for it means letting weeks pass. But weeks and even days now decide everything." Where, and when, and from which side, did the Soviet publish abroad the date of the insurrection? It is difficult even to invent motives which might induce it to perform so nonsensical an act. In reality it was not the insurrection, but the opening of the Congress of Soviets, which was publicly and in advance set for the 25th, and this was done not by the Petrograd Soviet but by the compromisist Central Executive Committee. From this fact, and not from a pretended indiscretion of the Soviet, certain inferences were to be drawn by the enemy: The Bolsheviks, if they do not intend to retire from the scene, must attempt to seize the power at the moment of the Congress. "It flowed from the logic of things," we wrote subsequently, "that we appointed the insurrection for October 25th. The thing was so understood by the whole bourgeois press." Stalin has converted his confused recollection of this "logic of things" into an "indiscreet" publishing abroad of the day of the insurrection. It is thus that history is being written.

On the second anniversary of the revolution the author of this book, referring in the sense just explained, to the fact that "the October insurrection was, so to speak, appointed in advance for a definite date, for October 25th, and was accomplished upon exactly that date," added: We should seek in vain in history for another example of an insurrection which was accommodated in advance by the course of things to a definite date. That assertion was erroneous: The insurrection of August 10, 1792, was also appointed approximately a week in advance for a definite date, and also not through indiscretion but through the logic of events.

On August 3 the Legislative Assembly resolved that the petitions of the Paris sections demanding the overthrow of the king should be taken up on the 9th. "In thus naming the day of the debate," writes Jaurés, who has observed many things which escape the attention of the old historians, "it also named the day of the insurrection." Danton, the leader of the sections, took a defensive position: "If a revolution breaks out," he insistently declared, "it will be an answer to the treachery of the government." This handing over of the question by the sections to the consideration of the Legislative Assembly was by no means a "constitutional illusion." It was merely a method of preparing an insurrection, and therewith a legal cover for it. The sections, as is well known, rose in support of their position at the signal of the fire gong with arms in their hands.

The traits of similarity in these two revolutions separated by an interval of 125 years, are by no means accidental. Both insurrections took place not at the beginning of a revolution, but in its second stage, a fact which made them politically far more conscious and deliberate. In both cases the revolutionary crisis had reached a high stage of maturity; the masses were well aware of the irrevocableness and close approach of the uprising. The demand for unity of action forced them to concentrate their attention upon a definite "legal" date as the focus of the approaching events. The leaders subordinated themselves to this logic of the mass movement. When already in command of the political situation, with the victory already almost in their hands, they adopted what seemed to be a defensive position: Provoking a weakened enemy, they laid upon him in advance the responsibility for the approaching conflict. It is in this way that insurrection takes place at a "date appointed in advance."

These assertions of Stalin, so striking in their inappropriateness—a number of them have been cited in the preceding chapters—show how little he has thought over the events of 1917 in their inner connection, and what summary traces they have left in his memory. How shall we explain this? It is well known that people make history without understanding its laws, just as they digest food without understanding the physiology of digestion. But it would seem that this ought not to apply to political leaders—above all to leaders of a party acting on a programme grounded in science. However, it is a fact that many revolutionists, having taken part in a revolution in prominent positions, reveal very soon after an inability to comprehend the inner meaning of the thing which happened with their direct participation. The extraordinary abundant literature of epigonism gives the impression that these colossal events roll over human brains and crush them as a steam roller would crush arms and legs. To a certain degree this is true; an excessive psychical tension does quickly consume people. Another circumstance, however, is far more important. A victorious revolution radically changes the situation of yesterday's revolutionists. It lulls their scientific curiosity, reconciles them to rubber-stamp phrases, moves them to estimate past days under the influence of the new interests. Thus a web of bureaucratic legend more and more thickly obliterates the real configuration of events.

In 1924 the author of this book, in his work entitled *Lessons of October*, tried to explain why Lenin in leading the party to insurrection was compelled to struggle so violently against the right wing represented by Zinoviev and Kamenev. Stalin objected to this: "Were there disagreements at that time in our party? Yes, there were. But these were exclusively practical in character, notwithstanding the assertions of Trotsky, who is trying to discover a 'right' and 'left' wing of the party. . . ." "Trotsky asserts that in the person of Kamenev and Zinoviev we had in October a right wing of our party. . . . How did it happen that the disagreement with Kamenev and Zinoviev lasted only a few days? . . . There was no split and the disagreements lasted only a few days because, and only because, we had in the person of Kamenev and Zinoviev Leninist-Bolsheviks." Did not Stalin in exactly the same way seven years earlier—five days before the insurrection—accuse Lenin of excessive sharpness, and assert that Zinoviev and Kamenev stood upon the common ground of "Bolshevism"? Throughout all Stalin's zig-zags there is a certain thread of consistency, resulting not from a thought-out philosophy but from the general mould of his character. Seven years after the revolution, just as on the eve of the insurrection he conceives the depth of the disagreements in the party in the same vague way.

The touchstone of a revolutionary political leader is the question of the state. In their letter against the insurrection of October 11th Zinoviev and Kamenev wrote: "With correct tactics we can win a third, yes and more than a third, of the seats in the Constituent Assembly. . . . The Constituent Assembly plus the Soviet, that is the combined type of state institution toward which we are travelling." The "correct tactics" meant a renunciation of the conquest of power by the proletariat. The "combined type" of state meant a combination of the Constituent Assembly, in which the bourgeois parties would constitute two-thirds, with the soviets, where the party of the proletariat was in command. This type of combined state subsequently formed the basis of Hilferding's idea of including the soviets in the Weimar constitution. General Lisingen, commandant of the Mark of Brandenburg, in forbidding the formation of soviets on November 7, 1918, on the ground that "institutions of this kind conflict with the existing state order," showed at least a great deal more penetration than the Austro-Marxists and the German Independent Party.

Lenin gave warning in April that the Constituent Assembly would sink into a subordinate place. However, neither he himself nor the party as a whole ever during the year 1917 formally renounced the idea of democratic representation, it being impossible to declare confidently in advance how far the revolution would go. It was assumed that having seized the power, the soviets would succeed soon enough in winning the army and the peasants so that the Constituent Assembly—especially after a broadening of the electorate (Lenin proposed in particular to lower the voting age to 18)—would give a majority to the Bolsheviks, and merely supply a formal sanction to the soviet régime. In this sense Lenin sometimes spoke of a "combined type"of state—that is, of an accommodation of the Constituent Assembly to the soviet dictatorship. The thing actually developed along different lines. In spite of Lenin's insistence, the Central Committee could not make up its mind after the conquest of power to postpone for a few weeks the call for the Constituent Assembly—although without this it was impossible either to broaden the electorate or, what is most important, give the peasants a chance to re-define their relation to the Social Revolutionaries and the Bolsheviks. The Constituent Assembly came into conflict with the Soviet and was dissolved. The hostile camps represented in the Constituent Assembly entered upon a civil war which lasted for years. In the system of soviet dictatorship not even a secondary place was found for democratic representation. The question of the "combined type" was withdrawn in fact. Theoretically, however, it retained all its importance, as was subsequently proven by the experiment of the Independent Party in Germany.

In 1924 when Stalin, obedient to the demands of an inner-party struggle first attempted to make an independent appraisal of the past, he came to the defence of Zinoviev's "combined state," supporting himself in this with a reference to Lenin. "Trotsky does not understand . . . the peculiarities of Bolshevik tactics when he snorts at the theory of a combination of the Constituent Assembly with the soviets as Hilferdingism," wrote Stalin in his characteristic manner. "Zinoviev, whom Trotsky is ready to turn into a Hilferdingist, wholly and completely shares the point of view of Lenin." This means that seven years after the theoretical and political battles of 1917, Stalin had completely failed to understand that with Zinoviev as with Hilferding it was a question of bringing into accord and reconciling the powers of two classes, the bourgeoisie through the Constituent Assembly and the proletariat through the soviets, whereas with Lenin it was question of combining two institutions expressing the power of one and the same class, the proletariat. The idea of Zinoviev, as Lenin explained at the time, was opposed to the very foundation of the Marxian teaching about the state."With the power in the hands of the soviets," wrote Lenin against Zinoviev and Kamenev on October 17th, "the 'combined type' would be accepted by everybody. But to drag in under the title 'combined type' a refusal to transfer the power to the soviets . . . is it possible to find a parliamentary expression for that?" We see, then, that in order to evaluate this idea of Zinoviev, which Stalin declares to be "a peculiarity of Bolshevik tactics" supposedly not understood by Trotsky, Lenin found it difficult even to find a parliamentary expression, although he was not distinguished by an excessive squeamishness in these matters. A little over a year later Lenin wrote, applying the same thought to Germany: "The attempt to combine the dictatorship of the bourgeoisie with the dictatorship of the proletariat is a complete renunciation both of Marxism and of socialism in general." Could Lenin indeed have written otherwise?

The "combined type" of Zinoviev was essentially an attempt to eternalise the dual power—that is, a revival of the experiment completely exhausted by the Mensheviks. And if Stalin in 1924 was still standing on the same ground with Zinoviev on this question, it means that in spite of his adherence to the theses of Lenin, he has nevertheless remained at least half-way true to that philosophy of dual power which he himself developed in his report of March 29, 1917: "The rôles have been divided. The Soviet has in fact taken the initiative in the revolutionary transformation. . . . The Provisional Government has in fact taken the rôle of fortifier of the conquests of the revolutionary people." The mutual relations between the bourgeoisie and the proletariat are here defined as a simple division of labour.

During the last week before the insurrection Stalin was obviously manœuvring between Lenin, Trotsky and Sverdlov, on the one hand, and Kamenev and Zinoviev on the other. That editorial declaration of the 20th which defended the opponents of insurrection against Lenin's blows, could not—especially from the pen of Stalin—have been accidental. In questions of intra-party manœuvring he was a past master. Just as in April, after Lenin's arrival, Stalin cautiously pushed Kamenev forward, and himself waited on the sidelines in silence before again joining battle, so now on the eve of the insurrection he was obviously making ready, in case of possible failure, a retreat along the Kamenev and Zinoviev line. Stalin moved along that road up to the limit beyond which it would have entailed a break with the majority of the Central Committee. That prospect frightened him. At the session of the 21st Stalin repaired his half-destroyed bridge to the left wing of the Central Committee by moving that Lenin prepare the theses upon fundamental questions for the Congress of Soviets and that Trotsky make the political report. Both these motions were unanimously adopted. Having thus insured himself on the left, Stalin at the last moment withdrew into the shadow: he would wait. All the newest historians, beginning with Yaroslavsky, carefully steer around the fact that Stalin was not present at the session of the Central Committee in Smolny on the 24th, and did not take upon himself any function in the organisation of the insurrection! Nevertheless this fact, indisputably established by the documents, characterises better than anything else the political personality of Stalin and his methods.

Since 1924 innumerable efforts have been made to fill up the vacant space representing October in the political biography of Stalin. This has been done by means of two pseudonyms: the "Central Committee" and the "practical centre." We shall not understand either the mechanics of the October leadership, or the mechanics of the latest epigone legends, unless we now approach a little more closely the personal staff of the Central Committee of that time.

Lenin, the recognised leader, authoritative for all but, as the facts show, far from a "dictator" in the party, for a period of four months had taken no direct part in the work of the Central Committee, and upon a number of tactical questions was in sharp opposition to it. The most prominent leaders in the old Bolshevik nucleus, standing at a great distance from Lenin but also from those who came after them, were Zinoviev and Kamenev. Zinoviev was in hiding as well as Lenin. Before October Zinoviev and Kamenev had come into determined opposition to Lenin and the majority of the Central Committee. That removed them both from the ranks. Of the old Bolsheviks, Sverdlov had come swiftly to the front, but he was then still a newcomer in the Central Committee. His organising talent developed fully only later during the years of the construction of the soviet state. Dzershinsky, who had recently joined the party, was distinguished by his revolutionary temperament, but made no pretence to independent political authority. Bukharin, Rykov, and Nogin were living in Moscow. Bukharin was considered a gifted but unreliable theoretician. Rykov and Nogin were opponents of the insurrection. Lomov, Bubnov and Miliutin, were hardly counted upon by anybody in deciding big questions; moreover Lomov was working in Moscow, Miliutin was on the road. Joffé and Uritzky had been closely associated in their emigré past with Trotsky, and were working in agreement with him. The young Smilga was working in Finland. This composition and inner situation of the Central Committee sufficiently explains why until Lenin's return to direct leadership the party headquarters did not play and could not play even in the slightest degree the rôle it was to assume subsequently. The minutes show that the most important questions—that about the Congress of Soviets, the garrison, the Military Revolutionary Committee—were not discussed in advance in the Central Committee and did not issue from its initiative, but arose in Smolny out of the practical activity of the Soviet, and were worked over in the circle of soviet leaders—oftenest with the participation of Sverdlov.

Stalin, generally speaking, did not show up in Smolny. The more decisive the pressure of the revolutionary masses became and the greater the scope assumed by events, the more Stalin would keep in the background, the paler would become his political thought, the weaker his initiative. It was so in 1905; it was so in the fall of 1917. The same thing has been repeated subsequently every time great historic questions have arisen on the world arena. When it became clear that the publication of the minutes of the Central Committee for 1917 only laid bare an October gap in the biography of Stalin, the bureaucratic historians created the legend of the "practical centre." An explanation of this story—widely popularised during these last years—becomes a necessary element of any critical history of the October revolution.

At the conference of the Central Committee in Lesny on the 16th of October, one of the arguments against forcing the insurrection was to point out that "we have not yet even a centre." At Lenin's suggestion the Central Committee decided straightway, at that hasty sitting in a back corner, to make good the lack. The minutes read: "The Central Committee organises a military revolutionary centre consisting of the following members: Sverdlov, Stalin, Bubnov, Uritzky and Dzerzhinsky. This centre becomes a constituent part of the revolutionary Soviet committee." This resolution, which everybody had forgotten, was first discovered in the archives in 1924. It began to be quoted as a most important historic document. Thus Yaroslavsky wrote: "This organ (and no other) guided all the organisations which took part in the insurrection (the revolutionary military units, the Red Guard)." Those words "and no other" reveal frankly enough the goal of this whole *ex post facto* construction. But Stalin has written still more frankly: "In the staff of the practical centre summoned to lead the insurrection, Trotsky, strangely enough . . . was not included." In order to be in a position to develop this idea, Stalin was compelled to omit the second half of the resolution: "This centre becomes a constituent part of the revolutionary Soviet committee." If you bear in mind that the Military Revolutionary Committee was headed by Trotsky, it is not hard to understand why the Central Committee was content with naming the new workers who were to help those already standing in the centre of the work. Neither Stalin nor Yaroslavsky has ever explained, moreover, why the "practical centre" was first remembered in 1924.

Between the 16th and 20th of October, as we have seen, the insurrection conclusively took the soviet road. The Military Revolutionary Committee from the moment of its birth had the direct leadership not only of the garrison, but of the Red Guard, which from October 13th on was subject to the Petrograd Executive Committee. No place remained for any other directing centre. Neither in the minutes of the Central Committee, nor in any other material whatever relating to the second half of October, can you discover the slightest trace of the activity of this supposedly so important institution. Nobody makes a report of its labours; no tasks are allotted to it; its very name is never pronounced by anybody, although its members are present at sessions of the Central Committee, and take part in the decision of questions which ought to come directly within the competence of a "practical centre."

Sveshnikov, a member of the Petrograd committee of the party, who was almost continually on communication duty in Smolny during the second half of October, must at least have known where to go for practical directions upon the problems of the insurrection. Here is what he writes: "The Military Revolutionary Committee was born: from the moment of its birth the various elements of the revolutionary activity of the proletariat acquired a guiding centre." Kayurov, well known to us from the February days, tells how the Vyborg district tensely awaited the signal from Smolny: "At nightfall (of the 24th) came the answer of the Military Revolutionary Committee—prepare the Red Guard for battle." Kayurov at the moment of starting the open insurrection knew nothing of any other centre. One could cite to the same effect the memoirs of Sadovsky, Podvoisky, Antonov, Mekhonoshin, Blagonravov and other direct participants in the uprising. Not one of them remembers that "practical centre" which according to Yaroslavsky is supposed to have guided all the organisations. And finally even Yaroslavsky confines himself in his history to a bare statement of the creation of the centre: of its activity he has not a word to say. The conclusion follows of itself: A directing centre of which those who were directed know nothing, does not exist in the eyes of history.

But still more direct evidence of the fictitiousness of the "practical centre" can be adduced. At a session of the Central Committee on the 20th of October, Sverdlov read a declaration of the Military Organisation of the Bolsheviks, containing, as is evident from the debate, a demand that the leaders of the Military Organisation be brought in when questions of the insurrection were being decided. Joffé moved that this demand be rejected: "Everybody who wants to work can join the revolutionary centre under the Soviet." Trotsky offered a milder formulation of Joffé's motion: "All our organisations can join the revolutionary centre and there take up in our faction all questions interesting them." The decision, which was adopted in this form, shows that there was but one revolutionary centre, that affiliated with the Soviet—that is, the Military Revolutionary Committee. If any other centre for leading the insurrection had existed, somebody ought at least to have remembered about its existence. But nobody remembered it—not even Sverdlov, whose name stood first on the staff of the "practical centre."

The minutes of October 24th are, if possible, still more instructive upon this point. During the hours immediately preceding the seizure of the city, not only was there no talk of the "practical centre" of the insurrection, but the very resolution creating it had so completely passed into oblivion in the whirlwind of the eight days intervening, that, upon a motion of Trotsky, Sverdlov, Dzerzhinsky and Bubnov, were appointed to be "at the disposal of the Military Revolutionary Committee"—those very members of the Central Committee, who, according to the decision of October 16th, should already and without this motion have become a part of the staff of the Military Revolutionary Committee. The possibility of such a misunderstanding is explained by the fact that the Central Committee, having barely emerged from its underground existence, was still in organisation and methods far from the all-powerful, all-embracing chancellery of recent years. The main part of the equipment of the Central Committee was carried by Sverdlov in his side-pocket.

In those hot times no few episodic institutions were created during the last moments of a session and immediately drowned in oblivion. At the session of the Central Committee on October 7th there was created "a bureau of information on the struggle with the counter-revolution." That was the cipher-designation of the first organ created for working on the problems of the insurrection. As to its personnel the minutes read: "Three are elected from the Central Committee to the bureau: Trotsky, Sverdlov, Bubnov, and they are directed to create the bureau." Did this first "practical centre" of the insurrection exist? Obviously not, since it has left no traces. The political bureau created at the session of the 10th also proved unviable and revealed itself in absolutely nothing: doubtful if it met even once. In order that the Petrograd organisation of the party, the direct leader of the work in the districts, should not become separated from the Military Revolutionary Committee, Trotsky, at the suggestion of Lenin, who liked a system of double or triple insurance, was included for the critical week in the highest administrative organ of the Petrograd committee. However, this decision also remained only a paper one: never one session was held with Trotsky present. The so-called "practical centre" met the same fate. As an independent institution it was never intended to exist, but it did not exist even as an auxiliary organ.

Of the five men appointed to the staff of the "centre," Dzerzhinsky and Uritzky entered completely into the work of the Military Revolutionary Committee only after the overturn. Sverdlov played an immense rôle in connecting the Military Revolutionary Committee with the party. Stalin took no part at all in the work of the Military Revolutionary Committee and never appeared at its meetings. In the innumerable documents and testimonies of witnesses and participants, as also in the most recent memoirs, Stalin's name is not once to be met with.

In the official compendium of the history of the revolution a special volume is devoted to October, grouping, on the basis of days, all the factual information from newspapers, minutes, archives, memoirs of participants, etc. Notwithstanding that this compendium was published in 1925, when the revision of the past was already in full swing, the index at the back of the book accompanies Stalin's name with only one number, and when we open the book at the corresponding page we find again this same text of the decision of the Central Committee about the "practical centre," with the mention of Stalin as one of its five members. We should seek in vain in that volume—crowded as it is with even third-class materials—for any information as to just what work Stalin did in October, whether on the stage of the "centre" or off it.

To define the political physiogonomy of Stalin in one word, he was always a "centrist" in Bolshevism. That is, he tended organically to occupy an intermediate position between Marxism and opportunism. But this was a centrist who feared Lenin. Any fragment of Stalin's orbit up to 1924 can always be explained as a product of two forces: his own centrist character and the revolutionary pressure of Lenin. The worthlessness of centrism should reveal itself most fully under the test of great historic events. "Our situation is self-contradictory," said Stalin on October 20th in justification of Zinoviev and Kamenev. In reality the self-contradictory character of centrism made it impossible for Stalin to occupy any independent position in the revolution. On the other hand, those traits which paralysed him at the great turning point of history—watchful waiting and empirical manœuvring—must necessarily assure him a genuine ascendency when the mass movement begins to ebb and the functionary comes to the front with his zeal to consolidate what has been attained—that is, primarily to insure his own position against new disturbances. The functionary, ruling in the name of a revolution, has need of revolutionary prestige. In his capacity as an "old Bolshevik," Stalin proved the most suitable incarnation of this prestige imaginable. In crowding out the masses the collective functionary says to them: "It is we who did this for you." He begins to take a free hand not only with the present, but also with the past. The functionary-historian makes over history, repairs biographies, creates reputations. It was necessary to bureaucratise the revolution before Stalin could become its crown.

In the personal destiny of Stalin, which has outstanding interest for a Marxian analysis, we have a new refraction of the law of all revolutions: the development of a régime created by an uprising inevitably passes through periods of ebb and flow measured by years, and in this process the periods of moral reaction bring to the front those figures who by reason of all their fundamental qualities did not play, and could not play, a leading rôle in the times of the revolutionary offensive.

The bureaucratic revision of the history of the party and the revolution is taking place under Stalin's direct supervision. The sign-posts of this work clearly mark off the stages in the development of the soviet machine. On the 6th of November 1918 (new style), Stalin wrote in an anniversary article in *Pravda*: "The inspirer of the revolution from beginning to end was the Central Committee of the party headed by Comrade Lenin. Vladimir Ilych was then living in Petrograd in a conspirative apartment in the Vyborg district. On the evening of October 24th he was summoned to Smolny for the general leadership of the movement. All the work of practical organisation of the insurrection was conducted under the immediate leadership of the president of the Petrograd Soviet, Comrade Trotsky. It is possible to declare with certainty that the swift passing of the garrison to the side of the Soviet, and the skilful direction of the work of the Military Revolutionary Committee, the party owes principally and first of all to Comrade Trotsky. Comrades Antonov and Podvoisky were Comrade Trotsky's chief assistants."

Neither the author of this book nor, we must imagine, Lenin, who was recovering from a Social Revolutionary bullet, gave attention in those days to this retrospective distribution of rôles and merits. The article stood forth in a new light only some years later when it revealed the fact that Stalin had already, in those difficult autumn months of 1918, been preparing, still with extraordinary caution, a new picture of the party leadership in October. "The inspirer of the revolution from beginning to end was the Central Committee of the party headed by Comrade Lenin." That phrase is a polemic against those who considered—and quite rightly—that the real inspirer of the insurrection was Lenin, acting to a considerable degree in conflict with the Central Committee. At that period Stalin was still unable to conceal his own October waverings otherwise than under the impersonal pseudonym of the Central Committee. His two following statements—that Lenin was living in a conspirative apartment in Petrograd, and that he was called to Smolny on the evening of the 24th for the general leadership of the movement—were designed to weaken the impression prevailing in the party that the leader of the insurrection had been Trotsky. The subsequent phrases dedicated to Trotsky sound in the political acoustics of to-day like a panegyric; in reality they were the very least that Stalin could say. They were what he was compelled to say in order to disguise his polemical hints. The complex construction and careful defensive colouring of this "jubilee" article themselves convey no bad impression of the general opinion prevailing in the party at that time.

In this article, by the way, there is absolutely no mention of the practical centre. On the contrary, Stalin categorically asserts that "all the work of practical organisation of the insurrection was conducted under the immediate leadership of . . . Trotsky." But Trotsky, we recall, was not a member of the "practical centre." We have heard, however, from Yaroslavsky that it was "this organ (and no other) which guided all the organisations which took part in the insurrection." The solution of this self-contradiction is simple: In 1918 the events were still too fresh in the minds of all, and the attempt to fish up out of the minutes that resolution about a "centre" which never existed could not have been successful.

In 1924 when much was already forgotten, Stalin explained in the following manner why Trotsky was not a member of the "practical centre": "We must say that Trotsky played no special rôle in the October revolution and could not have done so." In that year Stalin flatly declared it to be the task of the historians to destroy "the legend of the special rôle of Trotsky in the October insurrection." How then does Stalin reconcile this new version with his own article of 1918? Very simply: He has forbidden anybody to quote his former article. Historians who try to steer a middle course between the Stalin of 1918 and the Stalin of 1924 are promptly expelled from the party.

There exists however more authoritative testimonies than this first anniversary article of Stalin. In the notes to the official edition of the works of Lenin, under the word *Trotsky* we read: "After the Petrograd Soviet went Bolshevik he was elected its president and in that capacity organised and led the insurrection of October 25th." Thus the "legend of the special rôle" was firmly established in the collected works of Lenin during the life of their author.

In the official reference books you can follow from year to year this process of revising the historic material. Thus in 1925, when the campaign against Trotsky was already in full swing, the official year-book, *The Communist Almanac*, could still write: "In the October revolution Trotsky took the most active and leading part. In October 1917 he was elected president of the Petrograd Revolutionary Committee which organised the armed insurrection." In the edition of 1926, in place of this there occurs a brief neutral remark: "In October 1917 was president of the Leningrad Revolutionary Committee." Since 1927 the Stalin school has put forward a brand-new story which has been incorporated in all the soviet text-books. Being an opponent of "socialism in one country," Trotsky must have been essentially an opponent of the October revolution, but by good luck there existed the "practical centre" which carried the thing through to a happy ending! The ingenious historian has only neglected to explain why the Bolshevik Soviet elected Trotsky president, and why the same Soviet, guided by the party, placed Trotsky at the head of the Military Revolutionary Committee.

Lenin was not credulous—especially in matters which involved the fate of the revolution. You could never set him at rest with verbal assurances. At a distance he was inclined to interpret every symptom in a bad sense. He finally believed that the thing was being rightly conducted when he saw it with his own eyes—that is, when he arrived in Smolny. Trotsky tells about this in his recollections published in 1924: "I remember the enormous impression it made upon Lenin when he learned that I had called out a company of the Litovsky regiment with a written order to guarantee the publication of our party and soviet papers. . . . Lenin was in rapture, and expressed his feeling in exclamations, laughter, and rubbing of his hands. Afterward he became more silent, reflected a moment and said: 'Well, well—it can be done that way too. Just take the power.' I understood that only at that moment had he finally become reconciled to the fact that we had refused to seize the power by way of a conspirative plot. Up to the last hour he was fearing that the enemy would cut off our road and catch us unaware. Only now . . . did he feel at rest and finally sanction the course which events were taking."

This story too was subsequently disputed. Nevertheless it has indestructible support in the objective situation. On the evening of the 24th Lenin experienced a last gust of alarm, which seized him with such force that he made a belated attempt to mobilise the soldiers and workers for pressure upon Smolny. How violently his mood must have changed when in Smolny a few hours later he found out the actual situation! Is it not obvious that he could not help marking the end of his anxiety, his direct and indirect reproaches addressed to Smolny, at least with a few phrases, a few words? There was no need of complicated explanations. To each of the two meeting face to face in that not altogether ordinary moment, the sources of the misunderstanding were perfectly understandable. And now they were dissolved. No use returning to them. One phrase was enough: "It can be done that way!" That meant: "Maybe I sometimes went too far in urgency and suspicion, but I guess you understand. . . ." Who wouldn't understand! Lenin was not inclined to sentimentality. One phrase from him, "It can be done that way," with a special kind of smile, was plenty enough to set aside the incidental misunderstandings of yesterday and firmly tie the knots of confidence.

Lenin's mood on the 25th reveals itself with utter clarity in the resolution introduced by him through Volodarsky, in which the insurrection is described as "in rare degree bloodless and in rare degree successful." The fact that Lenin took upon himself this appraisal of the insurrection, scanty in words as always with him, but very high in substance, was not an accident. It was just he himself, the author of "advice from the sidelines," whom he considered most free to pay a tribute not only to the heroism of the masses, but to the services of the leaders. It is hardly possible to doubt that Lenin had additional psychological motives for this. He had continually feared the too slow course taken by Smolny, and he hastened now to be the first to recognise its advantages as revealed in action.

From the moment Lenin appeared in Smolny he naturally took his place at the head of all the work, political, organisational, and technical. On the 29th an insurrection of junkers took place in Petrograd. Kerensky was moving against Petrograd at the head of a number of Cossack squadrons. The Military Revolutionary Committee was confronted with a task of defence. Lenin guided this work. In his recollections Trotsky writes: "A swift success is as disarming as a defeat. Never to lose sight of the underlying thread of events; after each success to say to yourself, 'Nothing is yet attained, nothing is yet assured'; five minutes before a decisive victory to carry on with the same vigilance, the same energy and the same high pressure, as five minutes before the beginning of an armed action; five minutes after the victory, and before the first triumphant cries have died away, to say to yourself, 'The conquest is not yet assured, we must not lose a minute'—such was the approach, such was the manner of action, such the method of Lenin, such the organic substance of his political character, his revolutionary spirit."

The above-mentioned session of the Petrograd committee on November 1st, where Lenin spoke of his unjustified fears in regard to the Mezhrayontzi, was devoted to the question of a coalition government with the Mensheviks and Social Revolutionaries. The right wing, Zinoviev, Kamenev, Rykov, Lunarcharsky, Riazanov, Miliutin and others insisted upon a coalition after the victory. Lenin and Trotsky spoke decisively against any coalition which should ex-

tend beyond the frame of the Second Congress of Soviets. "The d
agreements," declared Trotsky, "were pretty deep before th
insurrection—in the Central Committee and wide circles of ou
party. . . . The same thing was said then as now after the victorious insurrection! We will have, you see, no technical machinery. The colours were laid on thick then in order to frighten us, just as they are now, in order to prevent our making use of the victory." Hand in hand with Lenin, Trotsky waged against the partisans of coalition the same struggle which he had waged before against the opponents of insurrection. Lenin said at that same session: "An accord? I can't talk about it seriously. Trotsky long ago said that a union was impossible. Trotsky understood this, and since that time there has been no better Bolshevik."

Among the more important conditions of an accord the Social Revolutionaries and Mensheviks put forward a demand for the removal from the government of the two figures most hateful to them—"those primarily guilty of the October insurrection, Lenin and Trotsky." The attitude of the Central Committee and the party to this demand was such that Kamenev, the extreme partisan of an accord—personally ready, even for this concession—considered it necessary to declare at the session of the Central Executive Committee of November 2nd: "It is proposed to exclude Lenin and Trotsky; that proposal would behead our party, and we do not accept it."

The revolutionary point of view—for insurrection and against coalition with the Compromisers—was called in the workers' districts "the point of view of Lenin and Trotsky." These words, as documents and minutes testify, became an every day expression. At the moment of crisis within the Central Committee a large conference of women workers in Petrograd unanimously adopted a resolution hailing "the policy of the Central Committee of our party, led by Lenin and Trotsky." As early as November 1917 Baron Budberg writes in his diary of "The new duumvirs, Lenin and Trotsky." When in December a group of Social Revolutionaries decided to "cut off the head of the Bolsheviks," "it was clear to them," according to Boris Sokolov, one of the conspirators, that "the most pernicious and important Bolsheviks are Lenin and Trotsky—it is with them we must begin." During the years of the civil war those two names were always spoken inseparably, as though they were one person. Parvus, once a revolutionary Marxist and afterward a malicious enemy of the October revolution, wrote in 1919: "Lenin and Trotsky—that is a collective name for all those who out of idealism have taken the Bolshevik road. . . ." Rosa Luxemburg, who severely criticised the policy of the October revolution, applied her criticism alike to Lenin and Trotsky. She wrote: "Lenin and Trotsky with their friends were the *first* to give an example to the world proletariat. And they still remain the *only* ones who can exclaim ᵹ *I dared this!*" In October 1918 at the triumphal session ·ral Executive Committee Lenin read a quotation from ·gn bourgeois press. "The Italian workers," he said, "are ·s though they would let nobody but Lenin and Trotsky travel ·iy." Such testimonies are innumerable. They recur as a leit ·iv throughout the first years of the soviet regime and the Com- ·unist International. Participants and observers, friends and enemies, those near and those far away, have tied together the activities of Lenin and Trotsky in the October revolution with so firm a knot that the epigone historians will not succeed either in untying it or chopping it apart.

APPENDIX II

Socialism in a Separate Country?

"The industrially more developed country shows the less developed only the image of its own future." This statement of Marx which takes its departure methodologically not from world economy as a whole but from the single capitalist country as a type, has become less applicable in proportion as capitalist evolution has embraced all countries regardless of their previous fate and industrial level. England in her day revealed the future of France, considerably less of Germany, but not in the least of Russia and not of India. The Russian Mensheviks, however, took this conditional statement of Marx unconditionally. Backward Russia, they said, ought not to rush ahead, but humbly to follow the prepared models. To this kind of "Marxism" the liberals also agreed.

Another no less popular formula of Marx—"No social formation disappears before all the productive forces have developed for which it has room"—takes its departure, on the contrary, not from the country taken separately, but from the sequence of universal social structures (slavery, mediævalism, capitalism). The Mensheviks, however, taking this statement from the point of view of the single state, drew the conclusion that Russian capitalism has still a long road to travel before it will reach European or American level. But productive forces do not develop in a vacuum! You cannot talk of the possibilities of a national capitalism, and ignore on the one hand the class-struggle developing out of it, or on the other its dependence upon world conditions. The overthrow of the bourgeoisie by the proletariat grew out of actual Russian capitalism, thereby reducing to nothing its abstract economic possibilities. The structure of industry, and also the character of the class-struggle in Russia were determined to a decisive degree by international conditions. Capitalism had reached a point on the world arena where it ceased to justify its costs of production—understanding these not in the commercial but the sociological sense. Tariffs, militarism, crises, wars, diplomatic conferences and other scourges, swallow up and squander so much creative energy that in spite of all achievements in technique there remains no room for the further growth of prosperity and culture.

The superficially paradoxical fact that the first victim to suffer for the sins of the world-system was the bourgeoisie of a backward country, is in reality quite according to the laws of things. Marx had already indicated its explanation for his epoch: "Violent outbursts take place sooner in the extremities of the bourgeois organism than the heart, because here regulation is more possible." Under the monstrous burdens of imperialism that state must necessarily fall first which has not yet accumulated a large national capital, but to which world competition offers no special privileges. The collapse of Russian capitalism was a local avalanche in a universal social formation. "A correct appraisal of our revolution," said Lenin, "is possible only from an international point of view."

We have attributed the October revolution in the last analysis not to the fact of Russia's backwardness, but to the law of combined development. The historical dialectic knows neither naked backwardness nor chemically pure progressiveness. It is all a question of concrete correlations. The present-day history of mankind is full of "paradoxes," not so colossal as the arising of a proletarian dictatorship in a backward country, but of similar historic type. The fact that the students and workers of backward China are eagerly assimilating the doctrine of materialism, while the labour leaders of civilised England believe in the magic potency of churchly incantations, proves beyond a doubt that in certain spheres China has outstripped England. But the contempt of the Chinese workers for the mediæval dull-wittedness of Macdonald, does not permit the inference that in her general development China is higher than Great Britain. The economic and cultural superiority of the latter can be expressed in exact figures. The impressiveness of these figures does not however, preclude the possibility that the workers of China may win the power before the workers of Great Britain. A dictatorship of the Chinese proletariat in its turn will be far from entailing the building of socialism within the boundaries of the Great Chinese Wall. Scholastic, pedantically, single-track, or too short national criteria are no good in our epoch. World development forced Russia out of her backwardness and her Asiaticness. Outside the web of this development, her further destiny cannot be understood.

The bourgeois revolutions were directed in similar degree against feudal property relations and against the particularism of the provinces. Nationalism stood beside liberalism on their liberating banners. Western humanity long ago wore out such baby-shoes. The productive forces of our time have outgrown not only the bourgeois forms of property, but also the boundaries of national states. Liberalism and nationalism have become in like degree fetters upon world economy. The proletarian revolution is directed both against private property in the means of production and against the national splitting-up of world economy. The struggle of the eastern peoples for independence is included in this world process and will subsequently merge with it. The creation of a national socialist society, if such a goal were in a general way attainable, would mean an extreme reduction of the economic power of men. But for that very reason it is unattainable. Internationalism is not an abstract principle but the expression of an economic fact. Just as liberalism was national, so socialism is international. Starting from the world-wide division of labour, the task of socialism is to carry the international exchange of goods and services to its highest development.

No revolution has ever anywhere wholly coincided with the conceptions of it formed by its participants, nor could it do so. Nevertheless the ideas and aims of those engaged in the struggle form a very important constituent element of a revolution. This is especially true of the October revolution, for never in all the past have the conceptions of a revolution in the minds of revolutionists approached so closely to the actual essence of the events as in 1917.

A work on the October revolution would remain unfinished if it did not answer with all possible historic accuracy the question: how did the party in the very heat of the events represent to itself the further development of the revolution, and what did the party expect from it? This question acquires a greater significance, the more past days become darkened by the play of new interests. Policies are always seeking support in the past, and if they do not get it as a voluntary offering they not infrequently undertake to extract it by force. The present official policy of the Soviet Union rests upon the theory of "socialism in a separate country" as the alleged traditional viewpoint of the Bolshevik party. The younger generations, not only of the Communist International but indeed of all other parties are being brought up in the conviction that the soviet power was won in the name of the creation of an independent socialist society in Russia. Historic reality has nothing in common with this myth. Up to 1917 the party never admitted even the idea that the proletarian revolution might be achieved in Russia before it was achieved in the west. For the first time in the April conference, under pressure of circumstances then completely laid bare, the party recognised as its task the seizure of power. Although opening a new chapter in the history of Bolshevism, this recognition had nothing in common with the perspective of an independent socialist society. On the contrary, the Bolsheviks categorically rejected as a caricature the idea imputed to them by the Mensheviks of creating a "peasant socialism" in a backward country. The dictatorship of the proletariat in Russia was for the Bolsheviks a bridge to a revolution in the west. The problem of a socialist transformation of society was proclaimed to be in its very essence international.

Only in 1924 did a change occur upon this fundamental question. It was then first proclaimed that the building of socialism is wholly realisable within the limits of the Soviet Union independently of the evolution of the rest of mankind, if only the imperialists do not overthrow the soviet power by military intervention. This new theory was immediately endowed with retroactive force. If in 1917—declared the epigones—the party had not believed in the possibility of creating an independent socialist society in Russia, it would have had no right to take the power. In 1926 the Communist International officially condemned the non-acceptance of the theory of socialism in a separate country, extending this condemnation to the whole past, beginning with the year 1905.

Three series of ideas were thenceforth declared hostile to Bolshevism: (1) denial of the possibility of the Soviet Union's maintaining itself for an indefinite length of time in a capitalist environment (problem of military intervention); (2) denial of the possibility of its overcoming with its own power, and within its national boundaries, the contradiction between city and country (problem of economic backwardness and agrarian problem); (3) denial of the possibility of creating a shut-in socialist society problem of the world-wide division of labour). It will be possible, according to the new school, to defend the inviolability of the Soviet Union even without revolutions in other countries by way of the "neutralisation of the bourgeoisie." The collaboration of the peasantry in the sphere of socialist construction must be acknowledged as assured. Dependence upon world economy has been liquidated by the October revolution and the economic successes of the soviets. A refusal to accept these three propositions is "Trotskyism"—a doctrine incompatible with Bolshevism.

The task of the historian here becomes one of ideological restoration. He must dig out the genuine views and aims of the revolutionary party from under subsequent political accumulations. Despite the briefness of the periods succeeding each other, this task is very much like the deciphering of a palimpsest, for the constructions of the epigone school are by no means always superior to those theological ingenuities for whose sake the monks of the seventh and eighth centuries destroyed the parchment and papyrus of the classics.

In general, throughout this book we have avoided burdening the text with innumerable quotations, but the present essay, owing to the essence of its task, will have to supply the reader with the genuine texts, and that too, on a sufficient scale to exclude the very idea of their having been artificially selected. We must let Bolshevism speak with its own tongue. Under the régime of the Stalin bureaucracy it is deprived of this possibility.

The Bolshevik party was from the day of its birth a party of revolutionary socialism. But it necessarily saw its immediate historic task in the overthrow of czarism and the inauguration of a democratic structure. The principal content of the revolution was to be a democratic solution to the agrarian problem. The socialist revolution was pushed away into a sufficiently remote or at least indefinite future. It was considered irrefutable that this revolution might take its place practically upon the order of the day only after the victory of the proletariat in the west. This postulate, forged by Russian Marxism in its struggle with Narodnikism and anarchism, was one of the solidest possessions of the party. There followed certain hypothetical considerations: In case the democratic revolution assumes a mighty scope in Russia, it may give a direct impetus to the socialist revolution in the west, and this will enable the Russian proletariat to come to power afterward with a swifter pace. The general historic perspective remained unchanged even in this more favourable version. The course of development was only accelerated and the dates brought near.

It was in the spirit of these views that Lenin wrote in September 1905: "From the democratic revolution we will immediately begin to pass over, and in the exact measure of our strength, the strength of a conscious and organised proletariat, we will begin to pass over to the socialist revolution. We stand for a continuous revolution. We will not stop half-way." This quotation, surprising as it may be, has been employed by Stalin in order to identify the old prognosis of the party with the actual course of events in 1917. It only remains incomprehensible why the cadres of the party were taken unawares by the "April theses" of Lenin.

In reality the struggle of the proletariat for power was to develop —according to the old conception—only after the agrarian problem had been solved within the frame-work of a bourgeois-democratic revolution. The trouble was that the peasantry, satisfied in their land hunger, would have no impulse to support a new revolution. And since the Russian working class, being an obvious minority in the country, would not be able to win the power with its own forces, Lenin quite consistently considered it impossible to talk of a dictatorship of the proletariat in Russia before the victory of the proletariat in the west.

"The complete victory of the present revolution," wrote Lenin in 1905, "will be the end of the democratic overturn and the beginning of a decisive struggle for the socialist revolution. A realisation of the demands of the contemporary peasantry, the complete shattering of the reaction, the winning of a democratic republic, will be the complete end of the revolutionism of the bourgeoisie, and even of the petty bourgeoisie. It will be the beginning of the real struggle of the proletariat for socialism." By petty bourgeoisie is here meant primarily the peasantry.

Under these conditions whence arises the slogan "continuous" revolution? Lenin answers as follows: The Russian revolutionists, standing on the shoulders of a whole series of revolutionary generations in Europe have the right to "dream" that they will succeed in "achieving with a completeness never before seen the whole democratic transformation, all of our minimum programme. . . . And if that succeeds—then . . . then the revolutionary conflagration will set fire to Europe. . . . The European worker will rise in his turn and show us 'how it is done'; then the revolutionary rising of Europe will have a retroactive effect upon Russia and the epoch of several revolutionary years will become an epoch of several revolutionary decades." The independent content of the Russian revolution, even in its highest development, does not transcend the boundaries of a bourgeois-democratic revolution. Only a victorious revolution in the west can open the era of the struggle for power even for the Russian proletariat. That conception was fully in force in the party up to April 1917.

If you throw aside episodic accumulations, polemical exaggerations and individual mistakes, the essence of the dispute about the question of permanent revolution from 1905 till 1917 reduces itself, not to the question whether the Russian proletariat after winning the power could build a national socialist society—about this not one Russian Marxist ever uttered a peep until 1924—but to the question whether a bourgeois revolution really capable of solving the agrarian problem was still possible in Russia, or whether for the accomplishment of this work a dictatorship of the proletariat would be needed.

What part of his earlier views did Lenin revise in his April theses? He did not for a moment renounce either the doctrine of the international character of the socialist revolution, or the idea that the transfer to the socialist road could be realised in backward Russia only with the direct co-operation of the west. But Lenin did here for the first time declare that the Russian proletariat, owing to the very backwardness of the national conditions, might come to power before the proletariat of the advanced countries.

The February revolution proved powerless to solve either the agrarian problem or the national problem. The peasantry and the oppressed peoples of Russia in their struggle for democratic goals were obliged to support the October revolution. Only because the Russian petty-bourgeois democracy was unable to carry out that historic work performed by its older sister in the west, did the Russian proletariat gain access to the power before the western proletariat. In 1905, Bolshevism intended only after the achievement of the democratic tasks to pass over to the struggle for a dictatorship of the proletariat. In 1917 the dictatorship of the proletariat grew out of the non-achievement of the democratic tasks.

But the combined character of the Russian revolution did not stop there. The conquest of power by the working class automatically removed the dividing line between "programme-minimum" and "programme-maximum." Under the dictatorship of the proletariat—but only there!—the growing over of democratic into socialist problems became inevitable, notwithstanding that the workers of Europe had not yet succeeded in showing us "how it is done."

This change of revolutionary order between west and east, with all its importance for the fate of Russia and the whole world, has nevertheless a historically limited import. No matter how far the Russian revolution skipped ahead, its dependence upon the world revolution has not disappeared nor even decreased. The possibility of a growth of democratic into socialist reforms is directly created by a combination of domestic conditions—chief among them the interrelation of the proletariat and the peasantry. But in the last instance the limits of socialist transformation are determined by the condition of economy and politics on the world arena. No matter how great the national spurt, it does not make possible a jump over the planet.

In its condemnation of "Trotskyism," the Communist International has attacked with special force the opinion that the Russian proletariat, having come to the helm and not meeting support from the west, "will come into hostile conflicts . . . with the broad masses of the peasantry with whose co-operation it came to power. . . ." Even if you consider that the historic experiment has completely refuted this prognosis—formulated by Trotsky in 1905, when not one of his present critics even admitted the idea of a dictatorship of the proletariat in Russia—even in that case, it remains an indisputable fact that this view of the peasantry as an unreliable and treacherous ally was a common property of all Russian Marxists including Lenin. The actual tradition of Bolshevism has nothing in common with the doctrine of predetermined harmony of interest between workers and peasants. On the contrary the criticism of this petty-bourgeois theory was always a most important element in the long struggle of the Marxists with the Narodniks.

"Once the epoch of democratic revolution in Russia is past," wrote Lenin in 1905, "then it will be ridiculous even to talk of the 'united will' of proletariat and peasantry. . . ." The peasantry, as a land-owning class will play the same treacherous, unstable rôle in this struggle (for socialism) that the bourgeoisie is now playing in the struggle for democracy. To forget that is to forget socialism, to deceive oneself and others about the genuine interests and tasks of the proletariat."

In working out for his own use in 1905 a scheme of the correlaion of classes during the course of the revolution, Lenin characterised in the following words the situation which must be formed after the liquidation of landlord proprietorship: "The proletariat is already struggling to preserve the democratic conquests for the sake of the socialist revolution. This struggle would be almost hopeless for the Russian proletariat alone, and its defeat would be inevitable . . . if the European socialist proletariat did not come to the help of the Russian proletariat. . . . At that stage the liberal bourgeoisie and the well-to-do (plus a part of the middle) peasantry will organise a counter revolution. The Russian proletariat plus the European proletariat will organise the revolution. In these circumstances the Russian proletariat may win a second victory. The cause is then not lost. The second victory will be the socialist revolution in Europe. The European workers will show us 'how it is done.' "

During approximately the same days Trotsky wrote: "The contradiction in the situation of a workers' government in a backward country with the peasant population an overwhelming majority can find its solution only on an international scale, in the arena of the world revolution of the proletariat." It is these words that Stalin subsequently quoted in order to show "the vast gulf separating the Leninist theory of the dictatorship of the proletariat from the theory of Trotsky," The quotations testify however that, in spite of indubitable differences between the revolutionary conceptions of Lenin and Trotsky at that time, it was exactly upon the question of the "unstable" and "treacherous" rôle of the peasantry that their views already in those far days essentially coincided.

In February 1906 Lenin writes: "We support the peasant movement to the end, but we ought to remember that this is the movement of another class, not that class which can and will achieve the socialist revolution." "The Russian revolution," he declares in April 1906, "has enough forces of its own to conquer. But it has not enough forces to retain the fruits of its victory . . . for in a country with an enormous development of small-scale industry, the small-scale commodity producers, among them the peasants, will inevitably turn against the proletarian when he goes from freedom toward socialism. . . . In order to prevent a restoration, the Russian revolution has need, not of a Russian reserve; it has need of help from outside. Is there such a reserve in the world? There is: the socialist proletariat in the west."

In various combinations but fundamentally without change these thoughts are carried through all the years of the reaction and the war. There is no need to multiply examples. The party's conception of the revolution must have received its most finished and succinct form in the heat of the revolutionary events. If the theoreticians of Bolshevism were before the revolution already inclining towards "socialism in a separate country," this theory would necessarily have come to full bloom in the period of the direct struggle for power. Did it prove so in reality? The year 1917 will give the answer.

When departing for Russia after the February revolution, Lenin wrote in a farewell letter to the Swiss workers: "The Russian proletariat cannot with its own forces victoriously achieve the socialist revolution. But it can . . . improve the situation in which its chief, its reliable ally, the European and American socialist proletariat, will enter the decisive battle."

The resolution of Lenin ratified by the April conference reads: "The proletariat of Russia, taking action in one of the most backward countries of Europe among the masses of a petty-peasant population, cannot set itself the goal of an immediate realisation of the socialist transformation." Although in these initial lines firmly clinging to the theoretical tradition of the party, the resolution does, however, take a decisive step on a new road. It declares: The impossibility of an independent socialist transformation in peasant Russia does not in any case give us the right to renounce the conquest of power, not only for the sake of democratic tasks, but also in the name of "a series of practically ripened steps towards socialism," such as the nationalisation of land, control over the banks and so forth. Anti-capitalist measures may receive a further development thanks to the presence of "the objective premises of a socialist revolution . . . in the more highly developed of the advanced countries." This must be our starting point. "To talk only of Russian conditions," explains Lenin in his speech, "is a mistake. . . . What tasks will rise before the Russian proletariat in case the world-wide movement brings us face to face with a social revolution—that is the principal question taken up in this resolution." It is clear that the new point of departure occupied by the party in April 1917, after Lenin had won his victory over the democratic limitedness of the "old Bolsheviks," is as different from the theory of socialism in a separate country as heaven is from earth!

In all organisations of the party whatever, whether in the capital or the provinces, we meet henceforth the same formulation of the question: In the struggle for power we must remember that the further fate of the revolution as a socialist revolution will be determined by the victory of the proletariat of the advanced countries. This formula was opposed by nobody—was, on the contrary, the presupposition of all disputes as a proposition equally acknowledged by all.

At the Petrograd conference of the party on July 16th, Kharitonov, one of those Bolsheviks who had come with Lenin on the "sealed train," declared: "We are saying everywhere that if there is no revolution in the west, our cause will be lost." Kharitonov is not a theoretician; he is an average party agitator. In the minutes of that same conference we read: "Pavlov calls attention to the general proposition advanced by the Bolsheviks that the Russian revolution will flourish only when it shall be supported by the world revolution which is conceivable only as a socialist revolution." Tens and hundreds of Kharitonovs and Pavlovs were developing the fundamental idea of the April conference. It never came into the head of anybody to oppose or correct them.

The sixth Congress of the party, taking place at the end of July, defined the dictatorship of the proletariat as a conquest of power by the workers and poorest peasants. "Only these classes . . . will in reality promote the growth of the international proletariat revolution, which is to put an end not only to the war but also to capitalist slavery." The speech of Bukharin was built upon the idea that a world-wide socialist revolution is the sole way out of the existing situation. "If the revolution in Russia conquers before a revolution breaks out in the west, we will have to . . . kindle the fire of the world-wide socialist revolution." Stalin too was at that time compelled to pose the question in much the same way: "The moment will come when the workers will rise and unite round them the poor layers of the peasantry, raise the banner of the workers' revolution, and open an era of socialist revolution in the west."

A Moscow regional conference which met at the beginning of August permits us best of all to glance into the laboratory of the party thought. In the principal report, setting forth the decisions of the sixth Congress, Sokolnikov, a member of the Central Committee, said: "It is necessary to explain that the Russian revolution must take the offensive against world imperialism or be destroyed, be strangled by that same imperialism." A number of delegates expressed themselves to the same effect. Vitolin: "We must get ready for a social revolution which will be the stimulus to the development of social revolution in western Europe." Delegate Byelensky: "If you decide the question within national limits, then we have no way out. Sokolnikov has said rightly that the Russian revolution will conquer only as an international revolution. . . . In Russia the conditions are not yet ripe for socialism, but if the revolution begins in Europe then we will follow western Europe." Stukov: "The proposition that the Russian revolution will conquer only as an international revolution cannot be subject to doubt. . . . The socialist revolution is possible only on a general world scale."

All are in agreement upon three fundamental propositions: the workers' state cannot stand unless it overthrows imperialism in the west; in Russia the conditions are not yet ripe for socialism; the problem of socialist revolution is international in essence. If alongside these views, which were to be condemned in seven or eight years as heresy, there had existed in the party other views now recognised as orthodox and traditional, they would certainly have found expression in that Moscow conference, and in the congress of the party which preceded it. But neither the principal speaker nor those who took part in the debate—nor the newspaper reports—suggest by a word the presence in the party of Bolshevik views opposing these "Trotskyist" ones.

At the general city conference in Kiev preceding the party congress, the principal speaker, Gorovitz, said. "The struggle for the salvation of our revolution can be waged only on an international scale. Two prospects lie before us: If the revolution conquers, we will create the transitional state to socialism, if not, we will fall under the power of international imperialism." After the party congress, at the beginning of August, Piatakov said at a new conference in Kiev: "From the very beginning of the revolution we have asserted that the destiny of the Russian proletariat is completely dependent upon the course of the proletarian revolution in the west. . . . We are thus entering the stage of permanent revolution." Commenting on Piatakov's report, Gorovitz, already known to us, declared: "I am in complete accord with Piatakov in his definition of our revolution as permanent." Piatakov: ". . . The sole possible salvation for the Russian revolution lies in a world revolution which will lay down the foundation for the social overturn." But perhaps these two speakers represented a minority? No. Nobody opposed them upon this fundamental question. In the elections for the Kiev committee these two received the largest number of votes.

We may, then, consider it fully established that at a general party conference in April, at the congress of the party in July, and at conferences in Petrograd, Moscow and Kiev, those very views were set forth and confirmed by the voting which were later to be declared incompatible with Bolshevism. More than that: not one voice was raised in the party which might be interpreted as a presentiment of the future theory of socialism in a separate country, even to the degree that in the Psalms of King David foretastes have been discovered of the gospel of Christ.

On the 13th of August, the central organ of the party explained: "Full power to the soviets, although far from as yet meaning 'socialism,' would in any case break the resistance of the bourgeoisie and— in dependence upon the existing productive forces and the situation in the west—would guide and transform the economic life in the interests of the toiling masses. Having thrown off the fetters of capitalist government, the revolution would become permanent—that is, continuous. It would apply the state power, not in order to consolidate the régime of capitalist exploitation, but in order to overcome it. Its final success on this road would depend upon the successes of the proletariat revolution in Europe. . . . Such was and remains the sole perspective of the further development of the revolution.' The author of this article was Trotsky, who wrote it in Kresty prison. The editor of the paper that published it was Stalin. The significance of the quotation is defined already in the mere fact that the term "permanent revolution" had been used in the Bolshevik party up to 1917 exclusively to designate the point of view of Trotsky. A few years later Stalin will declare: "Lenin struggled against the theory of permanent revolution to the end of his days." Stalin himself at any rate did not struggle: the article appeared without any editorial comment whatever.

Ten days later Trotsky wrote again in the same paper: "Internationalism for us is not an abstract idea . . . but a directly guiding, deeply practical principle. A permanent decisive success is unthinkable for us outside the European revolution." Again Stalin did not object. Moreover two days later he himself repeated it: "Let them know (the workers and soldiers) that only in union with the workers of the west, only after shaking loose the foundations of capitalism in the west, can we count upon the triumph of the revolution in Russia!" By "the triumph of the revolution" is meant not the building of socialism—of that there was still no talk at all—but only the winning and holding of power.

"The bourgeoisie," wrote Lenin in September, "is shouting about the inevitable defeat of the commune in Russia—that is, the defeat of the proletariat if it wins the power." We must not be frightened by these shouts. "Having conquered the power, the proletariat of Russia has every chance of holding it and bringing Russia through to the victorious revolution in the west." The perspective of the revolution is here defined with utter clearness: to hold the power until the beginning of the socialist revolution in Europe. This formula was not hastily thrown out: Lenin repeats it from day to day. He sums up his programme article, *Will the Bolsheviks Be Able to Hold the State Power?* in these words: "There is no power on earth which can prevent the Bolsheviks, if they do not let themselves be frightened and succeed in seizing the power, from holding it until the victory of the world-wide socialist revolution."

The Right Wing of the Bolsheviks demanded a coalition with the Compromisers, citing the fact that the Bolsheviks "alone" could not hold the power. Lenin answered them on November 1—that is, after the revolution: "They say that we alone will not hold the power, etc. But we are not alone. Before us is all Europe. We must begin." In this dialogue of Lenin with the Right Wing, it becomes especially clear that the idea of the independent creation of a socialist society in Russia never even came into the head of any of the disputants.

John Reed tells how at one of the Petrograd meetings at the Obukhovsky factory a soldier from the Rumanian front shouted: "We will hold on with all our might until the peoples of the whole world rise to help us." This formula did not fall from the sky, and it was not thought of either by the nameless soldier or by Reed. It was grafted into the masses by Bolshevik agitators. The voice of the soldier from the Rumanian front was the voice of the party, the voice of the October revolution.

The "Declaration of Rights of the Toilers and the Exploited Peoples"—the fundamental state programme introduced in the name of the soviet power into the Constituent Assembly—proclaimed the task of the new structure to be "the establishment of a socialist organisation of society and the victory of socialism in all countries. . . . The soviet power will proceed resolutely along this road until the complete victory of the international workers' insurrection against the yoke of capital." This Leninist "Declaration of Rights," not formally annulled to this day, converted the permanent revolution into a fundamental law of the Soviet Republic.

If Rosa Luxemburg, who in her prison was following with passionate and jealous attention the deeds and words of the Bolsheviks, had caught in them a shadow of national socialism, she would have sounded the alarm at once. In those days she was very sternly—in the essence mistakenly—criticising the policies of the Bolsheviks. But no. Here is what she wrote about the general line of the party: "The fact that the Bolsheviks in their policy have steered their course entirely towards the world revolution of the proletariat is precisely the most brilliant testimony to their political far-sightedness, their principled firmness and the bold scope of their policy."

It is just these views, which Lenin was developing from day to day, which were preached in the central organ of the party under Stalin's editorship, which inspired the speeches of agitators great and small, which were repeated by soldiers from far-off sectors of the front, which Rosa Luxemburg considered the highest testimony to the political farsightedness of the Bolsheviks—it is just these views which the bureaucracy of the Communist International condemned in 1926. "The views of Trotsky and his followers upon the fundamental question of the character and perspectives of our revolution," says a resolution of the Seventh Plenum of the Communist International, "have nothing in common with the views of our party, with Leninism." Thus the epigones of Bolshevism have done away with their own past.

If anybody really struggled in 1917 against the theory of permanent revolution, it was the Kadets and Compromisers. Miliukov and Dan exposed the "revolutionary illusions of Trotskyism" as the chief cause of the collapse of the revolution of 1905. In his introductory speech at the Democratic Conference, Cheidze scourged the effort "to put out the fire of the capitalist war by converting the revolution into a socialist and world revolution." On the 13th of October, Kerensky said in the Pre-Parliament: "There is now no more dangerous enemy of the revolution, the democracy and all the conquests of freedom, than those who . . . under the guise of deepening the revolution and converting it into a permanent social revolution, are perverting, and it seems have already perverted, the masses." Cheidze and Kerensky were enemies of the permanent revolution for the same reason that they were enemies of the Bolsheviks.

At the second Congress of Soviets, at the moment of the seizure of power, Trotsky said: "If the people of Europe do not rise and crush imperialism, we will be crushed—that is indubitable. Either the Russian revolution will raise the whirlwind of struggle in the west, or the capitalists of all countries will strangle our revolution." "There is a third road," shouted a voice from the benches. Was this perhaps Stalin's voice? No, it was the voice of a Menshevik. It was some years before Bolsheviks discovered that "third road."

As a result of innumerable repetitions in the international Stalinist press, it is considered in a great variety of political circles almost established that two conceptions lay at the bottom of the Brest-Litovsk disagreements. One had as its point of departure the possibility not only of holding out, but of building socialism with the inner forces of Russia; the other rested its hope exclusively on an insurrection in Europe. In reality this contrast of views was created some years later, and its author did not take the trouble to bring his invention into the most superficial accord with the historic documents. To be sure, this would have been no easy task. All the Bolsheviks without a single exception were at one in the Brest period in thinking that if a revolution did not break out in Europe in the very near future, the Soviet Republic was doomed to destruction. Some counted the time in weeks, others in months: nobody counted it in years.

"From the very beginning of the Russian revolution . . .," wrote Bukharin on January 28, 1918, "the party of the revolutionary proletariat has declared: either the international revolution, unleashed by the revolution in Russia, will strangle the war and capital, or international capital will strangle the Russian revolution." But was not Bukharin, who then headed the advocates of revolutionary war with Germany, attributing the views of his faction to the whole party? However natural such a supposition may be, it is flatly contradicted by the documents.

The minutes of the Central Committee for 1917 and the beginning of 1918—published in 1929—in spite of abridgements and a tendentious editing, offer invaluable testimony upon this question too. "At the session of January 11, 1918, Comrade Sergeiev (Artem) points out that all the orators are agreed upon the fact that our socialist republic is threatened with destruction in the failure of a socialist revolution in the west." Sergeiev stood for the position of Lenin—that is, for signing the peace. Nobody contradicted Sergeiev. All three of the contending groups competed in appealing to one and the same general premise: Without a world revolution we will not pull through.

Stalin, to be sure, introduced a special note into the debate. He based the necessity of signing a separate peace upon the fact that: "There is no revolutionary movement in the west, there are no facts, there is only a potentiality, and we can't figure on potentialities." Although still far from the theory of socialism in a separate country, he nevertheless clearly revealed in these words his organic distrust of the international movement. "We cannot figure on potentialities." Lenin immediately drew aside "in certain parts" from this Stalinist support. "It is true that the revolution in the west has not yet begun," he said. "However, if in view of this we should change our tactics, then we should be traitors to international socialism." If he, Lenin, favoured an immediate separate peace, it was not because he did not believe in the revolutionary movement in the west, and still less because he believed in the viability of an isolated Russian revolution: "It is important for us to hold out until the coming of a general socialist revolution, and we can achieve this only by signing the peace." The meaning of the Brest capitulation was summed up for Lenin in the words "breathing spell."

The minutes testify that after this warning from Lenin, Stalin sought an opportunity to correct himself. "Session of February 23, 1918. Comrade Stalin: . . . We also are staking our play upon a revolution, but you are reckoning in weeks, and [we] in months." Stalin here repeats verbatim the formula of Lenin. The distance between the two wings in the Central Committee on the question of the world revolution was the distance between weeks and months.

When defending the signing of the Brest peace at the seventh Congress of the party in March 1918, Lenin said: "It is absolutely true that without a German revolution we will perish. We will perish perhaps not in Petersburg nor in Moscow, but in Vladivostok, or some other remote place whither we will have to retreat . . . but in any case, under all possible or conceivable eventualities, if the German revolution does not begin, we perish." It is not only a question of Germany, however. "International imperialism . . . which represents a gigantic actual power . . . could in no case and under no conditions live side by side with the Soviet Republic. Here a conflict would be inevitable. Here . . . is the greatest historic problem . . . the necessity of evoking an international revolution." In the secret decision adopted, we read: "The Congress sees the most reliable guarantee of the consolidation of the socialist revolution which has won the victory in Russia only in its conversion into an international workers' revolution."

Some days later Lenin made a report to the Congress of Soviets: "World-wide imperialism and the triumphal march of a social revolution cannot live side by side." On April 23 he said at a session of the Moscow soviet: "Our backwardness has pushed us forward, and we shall perish if we cannot hold out until we meet a mighty support on the port of the insurrectionary workers of other countries." "We must retreat (before imperialism) even to the Urals," he writes in May 1918, "for that is the sole chance of winning time for the maturing of the revolution in the west. . . ."

Lenin was clearly aware of the fact that the dragging out of the negotiations at Brest would make harder the conditions of peace, but he put the revolutionary international tasks higher than the "national" ones. On June 28, 1918, notwithstanding episodic disagreements with Trotsky on the subject of signing the peace, Lenin said at a Moscow conference of trade unions: "When it came to the Brest negotiations, the exposures of Comrade Trotsky came out before the whole world, and did not this policy bring it about that in the enemy-country . . . in wartime an enormous revolutionary movement broke out?" A week later in a report of the Council of People's Commissars to the fifth Congress of Soviets, he returns to the same question: "We fulfilled our duty before all the peoples . . . through our Brest delegation headed by Comrade Trotsky." A year later Lenin recalled: "In the epoch of the Brest peace . . . the Soviet power placed the world dictatorship of the proletariat and the world revolution higher than any national sacrifices, no matter how heavy they might be." "What meaning," asked Stalin, when time had erased from his memory the never very definite distinctions between ideas—"What meaning can Trotsky's assertion that revolutionary Russia could not stand in the face of a conservative Europe have? It can have only one meaning: Trotsky does not feel the inward might of our revolution."

In reality the whole party was unanimous in the conviction that "before the face of a conservative Europe" the Soviet Republic could not stand. But that was only the reverse side of a conviction that a conservative Europe could not stand before the face of revolutionary Russia. In negative form it expressed an unconquerable faith in the international power of the Russian revolution. And fundamentally the party was not mistaken. Conservative Europe did not at any rate wholly stand. The German revolution, even betrayed as it was by the social democracy, was still strong enough to trim the claws of Ludendorff and Hoffmann. Without this operation the Soviet Republic could hardly have avoided destruction.

But even after the destruction of German militarism, no change was made in the general appraisal of the international situation. "Our efforts will inevitably lead to a world-wide revolution," said Lenin at a session of the Central Executive Committee at the end of July 1918. "Things stand in such a way that, having gotten out . . . of the war with one alliance, [we] immediately experienced the assault of imperialism from the other side." In August, when civil war was spreading on the Volga with the participation of the Czecho-Slovaks, Lenin said at a meeting in Moscow: "Our revolution began as a universal revolution. . . . The proletarian masses will guarantee the Soviet Republic a victory over the Czecho-Slovaks and the possibility of holding out until the world-wide socialist revolution breaks out." To hold out until the outbreak of revolution in the west—such as before is the formula of the party.

In those same days Lenin wrote to the American workers: "We are in a besieged fortress until other armies of the international socialist revolution come to our aid." He expressed himself still more categorically in November: "The facts of world history have shown that the conversion of our Russian revolution into a socialist revolution was not an adventure but a necessity, for there was no other choice. Anglo-French and American imperialism will inevitably strangle the independence and freedom of Russia unless world-wide socialist revolution, unless world-wide Bolshevism, conquers." To repeat the words of Stalin, Lenin obviously did not feel the "inner might of our revolution."

The first anniversary of the revolution is past. The party has had time to look round. And nevertheless in his report to the eighth

Congress of the party in March 1919, Lenin again declares: "We live not only in a state but in a system of states, and the existence of the Soviet Republic side by side with imperialist states for an extended period is unthinkable. In the end either one or the other will conquer." On the third anniversary, which coincided with the rout of the Whites, Lenin recalled and generalised: "If on that night (the night of the October revolution) someone had told us that in three years . . . this would be our victory, nobody, not even the most cocksure optimist, would have believed it. We knew then that our victory would be a victory only when our cause should conquer the whole world, for we began our work counting exclusively upon world revolution." More unassailable testimony could not be asked. At the moment of the October revolution "the most cocksure optimist" not only did not dream of creating national socialism, but did not believe in the possibility of defending the revolution without direct help from outside! "We began our work counting exclusively upon world revolution." In order to guarantee the victory in a three years' fight over legions of enemies, neither the party nor the Red Army had need of the myth of socialism in a separate country.

The world situation took a more favourable form than could have been expected. The masses revealed an extraordinary capacity for sacrifices in the name of the new goals. The leaders skilfully made use of the contradictions of imperialism during the first and most difficult period. As a result the revolution revealed more stability than "the most cocksure optimist" had anticipated. But even so, the party wholly preserved its former international position.

"If it hadn't been for the war," Lenin explained in January 1918, "we would have seen a union of the capitalists of the whole world, a consolidation on the basis of the struggle against us." "Why throughout weeks and months . . . after October did we get a chance to pass so easily from triumph to triumph?" he asked at the seventh Congress of the party."Only because a specially formed international conjuncture temporarily protected us from imperialism." In April, Lenin said at a session of the Central Executive Committee: "We got a breathing spell only because the imperialist war still continued in the west, and in the Far East imperialist rivalry is raging wider and wider; this alone explains the existence of the Soviet Republic."

This exceptional combination of circumstances could not last for ever. "We have now passed from war to peace," said Lenin in 1920. "But we have not forgotten that war will come again. So long as both capitalism and socialism remain, we cannot live in peace. Either the one or the other in the long run will conquer. There will be a funeral chant either for the Soviet Republic or for world capitalism. This is a moratorium in a war."

The transformation of the original "breathing spell" into a prolonged period of unstable equilibrium was made possible not only by the struggle of capitalist groupings, but also by the international revolutionary movement. As a result of the November revolution in Germany, the German troops were compelled to abandon the Ukraine, the Baltic States and Finland. The penetration of the spirit of revolt into the armies of the Entente compelled the French, English and American governments to withdraw their troopps from the southern and northern shores of Russia. The proletarian revolution in the west was not victorious, but on its road to victory it pro tected the Soviet state for a number of years.

In July 1921, Lenin summarised the situation: "We have got a certain equilibrium, although extremely fragile, extremely unstable, nevertheless such an equilibrium that a socialist republic can exist —of course not for long—in a capitalist environment." Thus passing from weeks to months, from months to years, the party only by degrees assimilated the idea that a workers' state might for a certain time—"of course not for long"—peacefully continue to exist in a capitalist environment.

One not unimportant conclusion flows from the above data quite irrefutably: If according to the general conviction of the Bolsheviks the Soviet state could not long hold out without a victory of the proletariat in the west, then the programme of building socialism in a separate country is excluded practically by that fact alone; the very question is withdrawn, so to speak, in its preliminary consideration.

It would be, however, a complete mistake to assume as the epigone school has attempted to suggest in recent years, that the sole obstacle seen by the party on the road to a national socialist society, was the capitalist armies. The threat of armed intervention was in reality practically advanced to the front rank, but the war danger itself was merely the most acute expression of the technical and industrial predominance of the capitalist nations. In the last analysis the problem reduced itself to the isolation of the Soviet Republic and to its backwardness.

Socialism is the organisation of a planned and harmonious social production for the satisfaction of human wants. Collective ownership of the means of production is not yet socialism, but only its legal premise. The problem of a socialist society cannot be abstracted from the problem of the productive forces, which at the present stage of human development are world-wide in their very essence. The separate state, having become too narrow for capitalism, is so much the less capable of becoming the arena of a finished socialist society. The backwardness of a revolutionary country, moreover, increases for it the danger of being thrown back to capitalism. In rejecting the perspective of an isolated socialist development, the Bolsheviks had in view, not a mechanically isolated problem of intervention, but the whole complex of questions bound up with the international economic basis of socialism.

At the seventh Congress of the party, Lenin said: "If Russia passes now—and she indubitably is passing—from a 'Tilsit Peace' to a national boom . . . then the outcome of this boom is not a transition to the bourgeois state but a transition to the international socialist revolution." Such was the alternative: either an international revolution or a sliding back—to capitalism. There was no place for national socialism. "How many transitional stages there will yet be to socialism, we do not and cannot know. That depends upon when the European socialist revolution begins on a real scale."

In April of the same year, when calling for a re-formation of the ranks for practical work, Lenin wrote: "We can give serious co-operation to the socialist revolution in the west, delayed for a number of reasons, only to the degree that we succeed in solving the organisational problem which stands before us." This first approach to economic construction is immediately included in the international scheme: it is a question of "co-operation to the socialist revolution in the west," and not of creating a self-sufficient socialist kingdom in the east.

On the theme of the coming hunger, Lenin said to the Moscow workers: "In all our agitation we must . . . explain that the misfortune which has fallen upon us is an international misfortune, that there is no way out of it but the international revolution." In order to overcome the famine we must have a revolution of the world proletarit—says Lenin. In order to create a socialist society a revolution in a separate country is enough—answer the epigones. Such is the scope of the disagreement! Who is right? Let us not forget anyway that, in spite of the successes of industrialisation, hunger is not yet conquered to this day.

The Congress of the Councils of People's Economy, in December 1918, formulated the plan of socialist construction in the following words: "The dictatorship of the world-proletariat is becoming historically inevitable. . . . This is determining the development both of the whole world society and of each country in particular. The establishment of the dictatorship of the proletariat and of the soviet form of government in other countries will make possible the inauguration of the most close economic relations between countries, an international division of labour in production, and finally the organisation of international economic organs of administration." The fact that such a resolution could be adopted by a congress of the state bodies confronted with purely practical problems —coal, firewood, sugar-beets—proves better than anything else how inseparably the perspective of the permanent revolution dominated the consciousness of the party during that period.

In the *A B C of Communism*, the party text-book composed by Bukharin and Preobrazhensky, which went through a great many editions, we read: "The communist revolution can be victorious only as a world revolution. . . . In a situation where the workers have won only in a single country, economic construction becomes very difficult. . . . For the victory of communism the victory of the world revolution is necessary."

In the spirit of these same ideas Bukharin wrote in a popular brochure reprinted many times by the party and translated into foreign languages: "There rises before the Russian proletariat sharply as never before the problems of international revolution. . . . The permanent revolution in Russia grows into a European revolution of the proletariat."

In a well-known book of Stepanov-Skvortzov, entitled *Electrification*, issued under the editorship of Lenin and with an introduction by him, in a chapter which the editor recommends with special enthusiasm to the attention of the reader, it says: "The proletariat of Russia never thought of creating an isolated socialist state. A self-sufficient 'socialist' state is a petty-bourgeois ideal. A certain approach to this is thinkable with an economic and political predominance of the petty-bourgeoisie; in isolation from the outside world it seeks a means of consolidating its economic forms, which are converted by the new technique and the new economy into very unstable forms." These admirable lines, which were undoubtedly gone over by the hand of Lenin, cast a clear beam of light upon the most recent evolution of the epigones!

In his theses on the national and colonial questions at the second Congress of the Communist International, Lenin defines the general task of socialism, rising above the national stages of the struggle, as "the creation of a united world-wide economy, regulated according to a general plan by the proletariat of all nations, as a whole the tendency towards which is already revealed with complete clarity under capitalism, and undoubtedly will receive further development and full achievement under socialism." In relation to this heritable and progessive tendency, the idea of a socialist society in a separate country is reaction.

The condition for the arising of a dictatorship of the proletariat and the conditions for the creation of a socialist society are not identical, not of like nature, in certain respects even antagonistic. The circumstance that the Russian proletariat first came to power by no means implies that it will first come to socialism. That contradictory unevenness of development which led to the October revolution did not disappear with its achievement. It was laid down in the very foundation of the first workers' state.

"The more backward the country which is compelled, as a result of the zigzags of history, to begin the socialist revolution," said Lenin in March 1918, "the harder for it will be the transition from the old capitalist to the socialist relations." This idea finds its way through the speeches and articles of Lenin from year to year. "For us it is easy to begin a revolution and harder to continue it," he says in May of the same year. "In the west it is harder to begin a revolution, but it will be easier to continue." In December, Lenin developed the same thought before a peasant audience, one which finds it hardest of all to transcend national boundaries: "There (in the west) the transition to a socialist economy . . . will go faster and be achieved more easily than with us. . . . In union with the socialist proletariat of the whole world the Russian labouring peasantry . . . will overcome all handicaps." "In comparison with the advanced countries," he repeats in 1919, "it was easier for Russians to begin the great proletarian revolution, but it will be harder for them to continue it, and carry it through to decisive victory in the sense of the complete organisation of a socialist society." "For Russia," Lenin again insisted on the 27th of April, 1920, ". . . it was easy to begin the socialist revolution, whereas to continue it and carry it through to the end will be harder for Russia than for the European countries. I had to point out this circumstance at the beginning of 1918, and the two years' experience since then have fully confirmed this judgment."

The ages of history live in the form of different levels of culture. Time is needed to overcome the past—not new ages, but decades. "The coming generation, although more developed, will hardly make the complete transition to socialism," said Lenin at a session of the Central Executive Committee on April 29th, 1918. Almost two years later at a congress of Agricultural Communes he named a still more remote date: "We cannot now introduce a socialist order. God grant that in the time of our children, or perhaps our grandchildren, it will be established here." The Russian workers took the road earlier than the rest, but they will arrive later at the goal. This is not pessimism, but historic realism.

"We, the proletariat of Russia, are in advance of any England or any Germany in our political structure . . ." wrote Lenin in May 1918, "and at the same time behind the most backward of west European states . . . in the degree of our preparation for the material-productive inauguration of socialism" The same thought is expressed by him in the form of a contrast between two states: "Germany and Russia incarnated in 1918 most obviously of all the material realisation of the economic productive, socio-industrial conditions of socialism on the one side, and the political conditions on the other." The elements of the future society are split up, so to speak, among different countries. To collect and subordinate them one to another is the task of a series of national revolutions building into a world revolution.

The idea of the self-sufficient character of the soviet economy Lenin laughed out of court in advance: "While our Soviet Russia remains a solitary suburb of the whole capitalist world," he said in

December, 1920, at the eighth Congress of Soviets, "during that time to think of our complete economic independence . . . would be an utterly ridiculous fantastry and Utopianism." On the 27th of March, 1922, at the eleventh Congress of the Party, Lenin gave warning: We are confronted with "a test which is being prepared by the Russian and international market, to which we are subordinate, with which we are bound up, from which we cannot break away. This is a serious test, for here they may beat us economically and politically."

This idea of the dependence of socialist economy upon world economy, the Communist International now considers "counter-revolutionary." Socialism cannot depend upon capitalism! The Epigones have been ingenious enough to forget that capitalism, like socialism, rests upon a world-wide division of labour which is to receive its highest development under socialism. Economic construction in an isolated workers' state, however important in itself, will remain abridged, limited, contradictory: it cannot reach the heights of a new harmonious society.

"The authentic rise of a socialist economy in Russia," wrote Trotsky in 1922, "will become possible only after the victory of the proletariat in the most important countries of Europe." These words have become an indictment; nevertheless they expressed in their time the general thought of the party. "The work of construction," said Lenin in 1919, "depends entirely upon how soon the revolution is victorious in the most important countries of Europe. Only after this victory can we seriously undertake the business of construction." Those words express not a lack of confidence in the Russian revolution, but a faith in the nearness of the world revolution. But now also, after the colossal economic successes of the Union, it remains true that the "authentic rise of a socialist economy," is possible only on an international basis.

From the same point of view the party looked upon the problem of the collectivisation of agricultural industry. The proletariat cannot create a new society without bringing the peasantry to socialism through a series of transitional stages, the peasantry being a considerable—in a number of countries a predominant—part of the population, and a known majority on the earth as a whole. The solution of this most difficult of all problems depends in the last analysis upon the quantitative and qualitative correlations between industry and agriculture. The peasantry will the more voluntarily and successfully take the road of collectivisation, the more generously the town is able to fertilise their economy and their culture.

Does there exist, however, enough industry for the transformation of the country? This problem, too, Lenin carried beyond the national boundaries. "If you take the question on a world scale," he said at the ninth Congress of the Soviets, "such a flourishing large-scale industry as might supply the world with all products does exist on the earth. . . . We put that at the basis of our calculations." The correlation of industry and agriculture, incomparably less favourable in Russia than in the countries of the west, remains to this day the basis of the economic and political crises which threaten at certain moments the stability of the soviet system.

The policy of so-called "miltary communism"—as is clear from the above—was not based upon the idea of building a socialist society within the national boundaries. Only the Mensheviks, making fun of the soviet power, attributed such plans to it. For the Bolsheviks the further destinies of the Spartan régime imposed by the ruin and the civil war, stood in direct dependence upon the development of revolution in the west. In January 1919, at the height of military communism, Lenin said: "We will defend the foundations of our communist policy in production and we will carry them through unshaken to the time of the complete and world-wide victory of communism." Together with the whole party Lenin was mistaken. It became necessary to change the policy in production. At present we may consider it established that, even if the socialist revolution in Europe had taken place during the first two or three years after October, a retreat along the line of the New Economic Policy would have been inevitable just the same. But on a retrospective appraisal of the first stage of the dictatorship, it becomes especially clear to what a degree the methods of military communism and its illusions were closely interwoven with the perspective of permanent revolution.

The deep internal crisis at the end of the three years of civil war involved the threat of a direct break between the proletariat and the peasantry, between the party and the proletariat. A radical reconsideration of the methods of the soviet power became necessary. "We have to satisfy economically the middle peasant, and adopt freedom of trade," Lenin explained. "Otherwise it will be impossible to preserve the power of the proletariat in Russia in view of the delay of the international revolution." Was not the transition to the NEP accompanied, however, by a break in principle of the bond between domestic and international problems?

Lenin gave a general estimate of the new stage then opening in his theses for the third Congress of the Communist International: "From the point of view of the world-wide proletariat revolution as a single process, the significance of the epoch Russia is passing through lies in its practical experimental test of the policy in relation to the petty-bourgeois mass of a proletariat holding the state power." His very definition of the frame-work of the New Economic Policy, cleanly removes the question of socialism in one country.

No less instructive are those lines which Lenin wrote for his own use in the days when the new methods of industry were being considered and worked up: "10 to 20 years of correct relations with the peasantry and victory on a world scale is guaranteed (even with the delay of the proletarian revolutions, which are growing)."

The goal is set: to accommodate ourselves to the new, more prolonged period which may be necessary for the maturing of the revolution in the west. In this sense and only this, Lenin expressed his confidence that: "From Russia of the NEP will come a socialist Russia."

It is not enough to say that the idea of international revolution was not here revised; to a certain degree it received a deeper and more distinct expression: "In the countries of developed capitalism," said Lenin at the tenth Congress of the Party, explaining the historic position of the NEP, "there is a class of hired agricultural labourers which has been forming itself in the course of some decades. . . . Where this class is sufficiently developed, the transition from capitalism to socialism is possible. We have emphasised in a whole series of writings, in all our speeches, in all our press, the fact that in Russia the situation is not like this—that in Russia we have a minority of workers in industry and an enormous majority of petty land-owners. In such a country the social revolution could achieve its final success only on two conditions: first, on condition of its timely support by a social revolution in one or several advanced countries. . . . The other condition is an agreement between . . . the proletariat which holds the state power and the majority of the peasant population. . . . Only an agreement with the peasants can save the socialist revolution in Russia until the revolution begins in other countries." All the elements of the problem are here united in one. A union with the peasantry is necessary for the very existence of the Soviet power; but it does not replace the international revolution, which can alone create the economic basis of a socialist society.

At the same tenth Congress a special report was made on *The Soviet Republic in a Capitalist Environment*, dictated by the delay of the revolution in the west. Kamenev was put forward as spokesman for the Central Executive Committee. "We never set ourselves the task," he said, as of something unquestioned by all, "to create a communist structure in a single isolated country. We find ourselves, however, in a position where it is necessary to hold the foundation of the communist structure, the foundation of the socialist state, the soviet proletarian republic surrounded on all sides by capitalist relations. Can we fulfil this task? I think that this question is scholastic. To this question in such a situation no answer should be made. The question stands thus: How in the given relations can we hold the Soviet power, and hold it up to that moment when the proletariat in this or that country shall come to our aid?" If the idea of the spokesman, who had undoubtedly more than once gone over his outline with Lenin, was in contradiction with the tradition of Bolshevism, why did the congress not raise a protest? How did it happen that there was not one delegate to point out that on the very basic question of the revolution, Kamenev was developing views having "nothing in common" with the views of Bolshevism? How was it that nobody in the whole party noticed this heresy?

"According to Lenin," Stalin affirms, "the revolution finds its force first of all among the workers and peasants of Russia itself. Trotsky has it that the necessary forces can be found only on the arena of the world revolution of the proletariat." To this manufactured contrast, as to many another, Lenin made his answer in advance: "Not for one minute have we forgotten, nor will we forget," he said on May 14, 1918, at a session of the Central Executive Committee, "the weaknesses of the Russian working class in comparison with other detachments of the international proletariat. . . . But we must remain at our post until our ally comes, the international proletariat." On the third anniversary of the October revolution, Lenin confirmed this: "We always staked our play upon an international revolution and this was unconditionally right. . . . We always emphasised the fact that in one country it is impossible to accomplish such a work as a socialist revolution." In February 1921, Lenin declared at a congress of the workers in the needle trades: "We have always and repeatedly pointed out to the workers that the underlying chief task and basic condition of our victory is the propagation of the revolution at least to several of the more advanced countries." No. Lenin is too much compromised by his stubborn desire to find forces in the world arena: you cannot wash him white!

Just as Trotsky is placed in opposition to Lenin, so Lenin himself is placed in opposition to Marx—and with the same foundation. If Marx assumed that the proletarian revolution would begin in France but be completed only in England, this is explained, according to Stalin, by the fact that Marx did not yet know the law of uneven development. In reality the Marxist prognosis contrasting the country of revolutionary initiative with the country of socialist accomplishment, was based wholly upon the law of uneven development. In any case Lenin himself, who permitted no reticence upon big problems, never and nowhere recorded his disagreement with Marx and Engels in regard to the international character of the revolution. Exactly the opposite! If "things have turned out otherwise than Marx and Engels expected," Lenin said at the third Congress of the Soviets, it is only in relation to the historic sequence of the countries. The course of events has allotted to the Russian proletariat "the honourable rôle of vanguard of the international social revolution, and we now see clearly how the development of the revolution, will proceed further; the Russian began—the German, the Frenchmen, the Englishmen will carry it through, and socialism will conquer."

We are further admonished by an argument from the standpoint of state prestige. A denial of the theory of national socialism—according to Stalin—"leads to the uncrowning of our country." This phraseology alone, intolerable to a Marxian ear, gives away the depth of the break with Bolshevik tradition. It was not 'uncrowning" that Lenin feared but national bigotry. "We are one of the revolutionary detachments of the working class," he taught in April 1918 at a session of the Moscow Soviet, "advanced to the front not because we are better than others, but precisely because we were one of the most backward countries in the world. . . . We will arrive at complete victory only together with all the workers of other countries, the workers of the whole world."

The appeal to sober self-valuation becomes a leit-motiv in Lenin's speeches. "The Russian revolution," he says on June 4, 1918, ". . . . was due not to the special merits of the Russian proletariat, but to the course . . . of historic events, and this proletariat was placed temporarily in the first position by the will of history and made for a time the vanguard of the world revolution." "The first rôle occupied by the proletariat of Russia in the world labour movement," said Lenin at a conference of Factory Committees on July 23, 1918, "is explained not by the industrial development of the country—just the opposite, by the backwardness of Russia. . . . The Russian proletariat is clearly aware that the necessary condition and fundamental premise of its victory is the united action of the workers of the whole world, or of several countries advanced in capitalist relations." The October revolution was evoked not only by the backwardness of Russia, and this Lenin well understood. But he consciously bent the stick too far in order to straighten it.

At a congress of the Councils of People's Economy—the organs especially called to build socialism—Lenin said on May 26, 1918: "We do not shut our eyes to the fact that we alone, with our own forces, could not achieve the socialist revolution in one country, even though it were a good deal less backward than Russia." And here, anticipating the future voice of bureaucratic bigotry, he explained: "This cannot cause a drop of pessimism, because the task which we have set ourselves is a task of world-wide historic difficulty."

At the sixth Congress of the Soviets on November 8, he said: "The complete victory of the socialist revolution is unthinkable in one country, but demands the most active co-operation at least of several advanced countries, among which Russia cannot be numbered . . ." Lenin not only denies Russia the right to her own socialism, but demonstratively gives her a secondary place in the building of socialism by other countries. What a criminal "uncrowning" of our country!

In March 1919, at a Congress of the Party, Lenin pulls up on the too mettlesome: "We have a practical experience in taking the first steps in the destruction of capitalism in a country with a special relation between proletariat and peasantry. Nothing more. If we swell ourselves out like a frog, and puff and blow, this will be utterly laughable to the whole world. We shall be mere braggarts." Will anybody be offended by this? On the 19th of May, 1921, Lenin exclaimed: "Did any one of the Bolsheviks at any time ever deny that the revolution can conquer in a final form only when it comprises all or at least several of the more advanced countries!" In November 1920, at a Moscow provincial conference of the party, he again reminded his audience that the Bolsheviks had neither promised nor dreamed of "making over the whole world with the forces of Russia alone. . . . Such madness we never reached, but we always said that our revolution will conquer when the workers of all countries support it."

"We have not," he writes at the beginning of 1922, "completed even the foundation of a socialist economy. This can still be taken back by the hostile forces of a dying capitalism. We must be clearly aware of this, and openly acknowledge it. For there is nothing more dangerous than illusions and turned heads, especially in high places. And there is absolutely nothing 'terrible,' nothing offering a legitimate cause for the slightest discouragement, in recognising this bitter truth; for we always have taught and repeated this ABC truth of Marxism, that for the victory of socialism the combined efforts of the workers of several advanced countries are necessary."

A little over two years later Stalin will demand a renunciation of Marxism upon this basic question. And upon what ground? On the ground that Marx remained ignorant of the unevenness of evolution—ignorant, that is, of the most elementary law of the dialectic of nature as well as society. But what is to be said of Lenin himself, who according to Stalin is supposed to have first "discovered" this law of unevenness as a result of the experience of imperialism, and who nevertheless stubbornly held fast to the "ABC truth of Marxism?" We should seek in vain for any explanation of this.

"Trotskyism"—according to the indictment and sentence of the Communist International—"derived and continues to derive from the proposition that our revolution in and of itself (!) is not in essence socialistic, that the October revolution is only the signal, impetus and starting-point for a socialist revolution in the west." Nationalistic degeneration here masks itself with pure scholasticism. The October revolution "in and of itself" does not exist. It would have been impossible without the whole preceding history of Europe, and it would be hopeless without its continuation in Europe and the whole world. "The Russian revolution is only one link in the chain of international revolution" (Lenin). Its strength lies exactly where the Epigones see its "uncrowning." Exactly because, and only because, it is not a self-sufficient whole but a "signal," "impetus," "starting-point," "link"—exactly for that reason does it acquire a socialist character.

"Of course the final victory of socialism in one country is impossible," said Lenin at the third Congress of Soviets in January 1918, "but something else is possible: a living example, a getting to work—somewhere in one country—that is what will set fire to the toiling masses in all countries." In July at a session of the Central Executive Committee: "Our task now is . . . to hold fast . . . this torch of socialism so that it may continue to scatter as many sparks as possible to the increasing conflagration of the social revolution." A month later at a workers' meeting: "The (European) revolution is growing . . . and we must hold the Soviet power until it begins. Our mistakes must serve as a lesson to the western proletariat." A few days later at a congress of educational workers: "The Russian revolution is only an example, only a first step in a series of revolutions." In March 1919, at a congress of the party: "The Russian revolution was in essence a dress-rehearsal . . . of the world-wide proletarian revolution." Not a revolution "in and of itself" but a torch, a lesson, an example only, a first step only, only a link! Not an independent performance, but only a dress-rehearsal! What a stubborn and ruthless "uncrowning"!

But Lenin did not stop even here; "If it should happen," he said on November 8, 1918, "that we were suddenly swept away . . . we would have the right to say, without concealing our mistakes, that we used the period of time that fate gave us wholly for the socialist world revolution." How far this is, both in method of thinking and in political psychology, from the bigoted self-complacence of the Epigones, imagining themselves an eternal belly-button of the earth.

A lie upon a fundamental question, if political interest compels you to cling to it, leads to innumerable resulting mistakes and gradually revises all your thinking. "Our party has no right to deceive the working class," said Stalin at a plenary session of the Executive Committee of the Communist International in 1926. "It ought to say frankly that a lack of confidence in the possibility of building socialism in our country will lead to a renunciation of power, and the passing of our party from the position of a ruling to that of an opposition party." The Communist International has canonised this view in its resolution: "The denial of this possibility (the possibility of a socialist society in a separate country) on the part of the opposition, is nothing but a denial of the premises for a socialist revolution in Russia." The "premises" are not the general condition of world economy, not the inner contradictions of imperialism, not the correlation of classes in Russia, but a guarantee given in advance of the possibility of realising socialism in a separate country!

To this teleological argument advanced by the Epigones in the autumn of 1926, we may reply with the same considerations with which we answered the Mensheviks in the spring of 1905. "Once the objective development of the class-struggle confronts the proletariat at a certain moment of the revolution with the alternative: either take upon yourself the rights and obligations of state power or surrender your class position—the social democracy will place the conquest of state power on the order of the day. In doing this it will not in the least ignore developmental processes of a deeper kind, processes of growth and concentration of production. But it says: When the logic of the class struggle, resting in the last analysis upon the course of economic development, impels the proletariat towards dictatorship before the bourgeoisie has fulfilled its economic mission . . . this means only that history has put upon the proletariat a task colossal in its difficulty. Perhaps the proletariat will even become exhausted in the struggle and fall under its weight—perhaps. But it cannot refuse these tasks through fear of class degeneration and of plunging the whole country into barbarism." To this we could add nothing at the present time.

"It would be an irreparable mistake," wrote Lenin in May 1918, "to declare that once the lack of correspondence between our economic and our political forces is organised, 'it follows' that we should not have seized the power. . . . Only 'people in a glass case' reason that way, forgetting that there will never be a 'correspondence,' that there cannot be, either in the evolution of nature or in the evolution of society, that only by way of a whole series of attempts—each one of which taken separately will be one-sided, will suffer from a certain lack of correspondence—can complete socialism be created out of the revolutionary co-operation of the proletarians of all countries." The difficulties of the international revolution will be overcome not by passive adaptation, not by a renunciation of power, not by a national watching and waiting for the universal insurrection, but by live action, by overcoming contradictions, by the dynamic of struggle and the extending of its radius.

If you take seriously the historic philosophy of the Epigones, the Bolsheviks ought to have known in advance on the eve of October, both that they would hold out against a legion of enemies, and that they would pass over from military communism to the NEP; also that in case of need they would build their own national socialism. In a word, before seizing the power they ought to have cast their accounts accurately, and made sure of a credit balance. What happened in reality was little similar to this pious caricature.

In a report at the party congress in March 1919, Lenin said: "We often have to grope our way along; this fact becomes most obvious when we try to take in with one glance what we have been through. But that did not unnerve us a bit, even on the 10th of October, 1917, when deciding the question about the seizure of power. We had no doubt that it was up to us, according to Comrade

Trotsky's expression, to experiment—to make the trial. We undertook a job which nobody in the world had ever before undertaken on such a scale." And further: "Who could ever make a gigantic revolution, knowing in advance how to carry it through to the end? Where could you get such knowledge? It cannot be found in books. No such books exist. Our decision could only be born of the experience of the masses."

The Bolsheviks did not seek any assurance that Russia would be able to create a socialist society. They had no need of it. They had no use for it. It contradicted all that they had learned in the school of Marxism. "The tactics of the Bolsheviks," wrote Lenin against Kautsky, "were the only international tactics, for they were based not on the cowardly fear of the world revolution, not on a Philistine lack of confidence in it . . ." The Bolsheviks "contributed the maximum possible in one country to the development, support, stimulus, of revolution in all countries." With such a tactic it was impossible to mark out in advance an infallible line-of-march, and still less possible to guarantee yourself a national victory. But the Bolsheviks knew that danger was an element of revolution, as of war. They went to meet danger with open eyes.

Placing before the world proletariat as an example and a reproach the manner in which the bourgeoisie boldly risks war in the name of its interests, Lenin branded with hatred those socialists who "are afraid to begin the fight until they are 'guaranteed' an easy victory. . . . Boot-lickers of international socialism, lackeys of bourgeois morality who think this way deserve triple contempt." Lenin, as is well known, did not stop to choose his words when he was choking with indignation.

"But what shall we do," Stalin has kept on inquiring, "if the international revolution is destined to be delayed? Is there any light ahead for our revolution? Trotsky does not give any light." The Epigones demand historic privileges for the Russian proletariat: it must have a road-bed laid down for an uninterrupted movement towards socialism, regardless of what happens to the rest of humanity. History, alas, has prepared no such road-bed. "If you look at things from a world-wide historic scale," said Lenin at the seventh Congress of the Party, "there is not the slightest doubt that the ultimate victory of our revolution, if it should remain solitary . . . would be hopeless."

But even in this case it would not have been fruitless. "Even if the imperialists should overthrow the Bolshevik power to-morrow," said Lenin in May 1919, at a teachers' congress, "we would not regret for one second that we took the power. And not one of the class-conscious workers . . . would regret it, or would doubt that our revolution had nevertheless conquered." For Lenin thought of victory only in terms of an international succession of development in struggle. "The new society . . . is an abstraction which can take living body not otherwise than through a series of differing incomplete concrete attempts to create this or that socialist state." This sharp distinction, and in some sense contrast, between "socialist state" and "new society" offers a key to the innumerable abuses perpetrated by the Epigone literature upon the texts of Lenin.

Lenin explained with the utmost simplicity the meaning of the Bolshevik strategy at the end of the fifth year after the conquest of power. "When we began at the time we did the international revolution, we did this not with the conviction that we could anticipate its development, but because a whole series of circumstances impelled us to begin this revolution. Our thought was: Either the international revolution will come to our aid, and in that case our victories are wholly assured, or we will do our modest revolutionary work in the consciousness that in case of defeat we have nevertheless served the cause of the revolution, and our experiment will be of help to other revolutions. It was clear to us that without the support of the international world revolution a victory of the proletarian overturn was impossible. Even before the revolution, and likewise after it, our thought was: immediately, or at any rate very quickly, a revolution will begin in the other countries, in capitalistically more developed countries—or in the contrary case we will have to perish. In spite of this consciousness we did everything to preserve the soviet system in all circumstances and at whatever cost, since we knew that we were working not only for ourselves, but for the international revolution. We knew this, we frequently expressed this conviction before the October revolution, exactly as we did immediately after it and during the conclusion of the Brest-Litovsk Peace. And, generally speaking, this was right." The dates have shifted, the pattern of events has formed itself in many respects unexpectedly, but the fundamental orientation remains unchanged.

What can be added to these words? "We began . . . the international revolution." If a revolution in the west does not begin "immediately, or at any rate very quickly"—assumed the Bolsheviks —"we will have to perish." But in that case too, the conquest of power will have been justified: others will learn from the experience of those who perished. "We are working not only for ourselves but for the international revolution." These ideas, saturated through and through with internationalism, Lenin expounded to the Communist International. Did anybody oppose him? Did anybody offer a hint of the possibility of a national socialist society? Nobody. Not one single word!

Five years later, at the seventh Plenum of the Executive Committee of the Communist International, Stalin developed ideas exactly opposite to these. They are already known to us: If there is not "confidence in the possibility of building socialism in our country," then the party must pass over "from the position of a ruling, to that of an opposition party. . . ." We must have a preliminary guarantee of success before taking the power: it is permitted to seek this guarantee only in national conditions; we must have confidence in the possibility of building socialism in peasant Russia; then we can get along quite well without confidence in the victory of the world proletariat. Each of these links in a chain of reasoning slaps in the face the tradition of Bolshevism.

To cover up their break with the past, the Stalin school have tried to make use of certain lines of Lenin, which seem the least unsuitable. An article of 1915 on *The United States of Europe* throws out incidentally the remark that the working class in each separate country ought to win the power and enter upon the socialist construction without waiting for the others. If behind these indisputable lines there lurked a thought about a national socialist society, how could Lenin so fundamentally have forgotten it during the years following, and so stubbornly have contradicted it at every step? But there is no use resorting to oblique inferences when we have direct statements. The programme theses drafted by Lenin in the same year, 1915, answer the question accurately and directly: "The task of the proletariat of Russia is to carry through to the end the bourgeois-democratic revolution in Russia, in order to kindle the socialist revolution in Europe. This second task has now come extremely near to the first, but it remains nevertheless a special and a second task, for it is a question of different classes co-operating with the proletariat of Russia. For the first task the collaborator is the petty-bourgeois peasantry of Russia, for the second the proletariat of other countries." No greater clarity could be demanded.

The second attempt to quote Lenin is no better founded. His unfinished article about co-operation says that in the Soviet Republic we have on hand "all that is necessary and enough" in order without new revolutions to accomplish the transition to socialism. Here it is a question, as is perfectly clear from the text, of the political and legal premises of socialism. The author does not forget to remind his readers that the productive and cultural premises are inadequate. In general Lenin repeated this thought many times. "We . . . lack the civilisation to make the transition directly to socialism," he wrote in an article of the same period, the beginning of 1923, "although we have the political premises for it." In this case as in all others, Lenin started from the assumption that the proletariat of the west would come to socialism along with the Russian proletariat and ahead of it. The article on co-operation does not contain a hint to the effect that the Soviet Republic might harmoniously and by reformist measures create its own national socialism, instead of taking its place through a process of antagonistic and revolutionary development in the world socialist society. Both quotations, introduced even into the text of the programme of the Communist International, were long ago explained in our *Criticism of the Programme*, and our opponents have not once attempted to defend their distortions and mistakes. The attempt would be too hopeless.

In March 1923—in the same last period of his creative work,—Lenin wrote: "We stand . . . at the present moment before the question: shall we succeed in holding out with our petty and very petty peasant production, with our ruined condition, until the west European capitalist countries complete their development to socialism?" We see again: the dates have shifted, the web of events changed, but the international foundation of the policy remains unshaken. That faith in the international revolution—according to Stalin a "distrust in the inner forces of the Russian revolution"—went with the great internationalist to his grave. Only after pinning Lenin down under a mausoleum, were the Epigones able to nationalise his views.

From the world-wide division of labour, from the unevenness of development of different countries, from their mutual economic dependence, from the unevenness of different aspects of culture in the different countries, from the dynamic of the contemporary productive forces, it follows that the socialist structure can be built only by a system of economic spiral, only by taking the inner discords of a separate country out into a whole group of countries, only by a mutual service between different countries, and a mutual supplementation of the different branches of their industry and culture—that is, in the last analysis, only on the world arena.

The old programme of the party, adopted in 1903, begins with the words: "The development of exchange has established such close bonds between the peoples of the civilised world that the great liberating movement of the proletariat must become, and long ago has become, international. . . ." The preparation of the proletariat for the coming social revolution is defined as the task of the "international social democracy." However, "on the road to their common final goal . . . the social-democrats of various countries are obliged to set themselves dissimilar immediate tasks." In Russia the overthrow of czarism is such a task. The democratic revolution was thus regarded in advance as a national step to an international socialist revolution.

The same conception lies at the bottom of our programme adopted by the party after the conquest of power. In a preliminary discussion of the draft of this programme at the Seventh Congress, Miliutin proposed an editorial correction in the resolution of Lenin: "I propose," he said, "that we insert the words 'international socialist revolution' where it says 'the era of social revolution now begun' . . . I think it is unnecessary to argue this. . . . Our social revolution can conquer only as an international revolution. It cannot conquer in Russia alone, leaving the bourgeois structure in the surrounding countries . . . I propose that this be inserted to avoid misunderstanding." The chairman Sverdlov: "Comrade Lenin accepts this amendment, a vote is therefore unnecessary." A tiny episode of parliamentary technique ("unnecessary to argue" and "a vote is unnecessary,") refutes the false historiography of the Epigones more convincingly perhaps than the most painstaking investigation! The circumstance that Miliutin himself, like Skvortzov-Stepanov whom we quoted above, and like hundreds and thousands of others, soon after condemned his own views under the name of "Trotsky-ism," makes no change in the facts. Great historic currents are stronger than human back-bones. The flood-tide lifts up and the ebb-tide sweeps away whole political generations. Ideas, on the other hand, are able to live even after the physical and spiritual death of those who carried them. A year later, at the eighth Congress of the Party which ratified the new programme, the same question was again illumined in a sharp exchange of retorts between Lenin and Podbelsky. The Moscow delegate protested against the fact that in spite of the October overturn the programme still spoke of the social revolution in the future tense, "Podbelsky," says Lenin, "attacks the fact that in one of the paragraphs the programme speaks of the *coming* social revolution. . . . His argument is obviously inconsequent, for in our programme we are talking about the social revolution on a world scale." Truly the history of the party has not left the Epigones a single unillumined corner to hide in!

In the programme of the Communist Youth adopted in 1921, the same question is put forward in an especially popular and simple form. "Russia," says one paragraph, "although possessing enormous natural resources is nevertheless in the matter of industry a backward country in which a petty-bourgeois population predominates. It can come to socialism only through the socialist world revolution, the epoch for the development of which we have now entered." Ratified in its day by the Politburo, with the participation not only of Lenin and Trotsky but also of Stalin, this programme was in full force in the autumn of 1926 when the Executive Committee of the Communist International converted the non-acceptance of socialism in a separate country into a mortal sin.

In the two years ensuing, however, the Epigones were compelled to file away in the archives the programme documents of the Lenin epoch. Their new documents, patched together out of fragments, they called the programme of the Communist International. Whereas with Lenin in the "Russian" programme the talk is of international revolution, with the Epigones in the international programme the talk is of "Russian" socialism.

Just when and how did the break with the first openly reveal itself? The historic date is easy to indicate, since it coincides with a turning-point in the biography of Stalin. As late as April 1924, three months after the death of Lenin, Stalin was modestly expounding the traditional views of the party. "To overthrow the power of the bourgeoisie and establish the power of the proletariat in one country," he wrote in his *Problems of Leninism*, "does not mean to guarantee the complete victory of socialism. The chief task of socialism—the organisation of socialist production—lies still ahead. Can this task be accomplished? Is it possible to attain the final victory of socialism in one country, without the combined efforts of the proletarians of several advanced countries. No, it is not. The efforts of one country are enough for the overthrow of the bourgeoisie—this is what the history of our revolution tells us. For the final victory of socialism, for the organisation of socialist production, the efforts of one country, especially a peasant country like Russia, are not enough—for this we must have the efforts of the proletarians of several advanced countries." Stalin concludes his exposition of these thoughts with the words: "Such in general are the characteristic features of the Leninist theory of the proletarian revolution."

By autumn of the same year, under the influence of the struggle with Trotskyism, it was suddenly discovered that Russia is the very country, in distinction from others, which will be able to build the socialist society with her own forces, if she is not hindered by intervention. In a new edition of the same work, Stalin wrote: "Having consolidated its power, and taking the lead of the peasantry, the proletariat of the victorious country can and must build a socialist society." Can and must! Only in order "fully to guarantee the country against intervention . . . is the victory of the revolution necessary . . . at least in several countries." The proclamation of this new conception, which allots to the world proletariat the rôle of border police, ends with those same words: "Such in general are the characteristic features of the Leninist theory of the proletarian revolution." In the course of one year, Stalin has imputed to Lenin two directly opposite views upon a fundamental problem of socialism.

At a plenary session of the Central Committee in 1927, Trotsky said about these two contradictory opinions of Stalin: "You may say that Stalin made a mistake and afterward corrected himself. But how could he make *such* a mistake upon *such* a question? If it were true that Lenin already in 1915 gave out the theory of building socialism in a separate country (which is utterly untrue), if it were true that subsequently Lenin only reinforced and developed this point of view (which is utterly untrue)—then how, we must ask, could Stalin think up for himself during the life of Lenin, during the last period of his life, that opinion upon this most important question which finds its expression in the Stalinist quotation of 1924? It appears that upon this fundamental question Stalin had always been a Trotskyist, and only after 1924 ceased to be one. It would be well if Stalin could find at least one quotation from his own writings showing that before 1924 he said something about the building of socialism in one country. He will not find it!" This challenge remained unanswered.

We should not, however, exaggerate the actual depth of the change made by Stalin. Just as in the question of war, of our relation to the provisional government, or the national question, so on the general perspectives of the revolution. Stalin had two positions: one independent, organic, not always expressed, or at least never wholly expressed, and the other conditional, phraseological, borrowed from Lenin. Between two people belonging to one and the same party it would be impossible to imagine a deeper gulf than that which separated Stalin from Lenin, both upon fundamental questions of revolutionary conception and in political psychology. Stalin's opportunist character is disguised now by the fact that his power rests upon a victorious proletarian revolution. But we have seen the independent position of Stalin in March 1917. Having behind him an already accomplished bourgeois revolution, he set the party the task of "putting brakes on the splitting away" of the bourgeoisie—that is, of actually resisting the proletarian revolution. If that revolution was achieved, it is not his fault. But together with all the bureaucracy Stalin has taken his stand upon the basis of accomplished fact. Once there is a dictatorship of the proletariat, there must be socialism too. Turning inside out the argument of the Mensheviks against the proletarian revolution in Russia, Stalin, with his theory of socialism in a separate country, began to barricade himself against international revolution. And since he has never thought any question of principle through to the end, it could not but seem to him that "in essence" he always thought as he thought in the autumn of 1924. And since he moreover never got into contradiction with the prevailing opinion of the party, it could not but seem to him that the party too "in essence" thought as he did.

The initial substitution was unconscious. It was not a question of falsification, but of ideological shedding. But in proportion as the doctrine of national socialism came up against a well-armed criticism, there was need of an organised, and predominantly surgical, interference on the part of the machine. The theory of national socialism was then decreed. It was proven by the method of contraries—by the arrest of those who did not agree with it. At the same time the era was opened of systematic remaking of the party's past. The history of the party was turned into a palimpsest. This destruction of parchments still continues, and moreover with steadily increasing fury.

The decisive factor, however, was not repressions nor falsifications. The triumph of the new views corresponding to the situation and interests of the bureaucracy, has rested upon objective circumstances—temporary but extremely powerful. The possibility has opened before the Soviet Republic of playing both in foreign and domestic politics a far more significant rôle than anybody before the revolution could have estimated. The isolated worker state has not only held its own among a legion of enemies, but has elevated itself economically. This weighty fact has formed the social opinion of the younger generation, who have not yet learned to think historically—that is, to compare and foresee.

The European bourgeoisie got too badly burned in the last war to lightly undertake another. A fear of revolutionary consequences has so far paralysed the plans of military intervention. But the factor of fear is an unstable one. The threat of a revolution has never yet replaced the revolution itself. A danger which remains long unrealised loses its effect. At the same time the irreconcilable antagonism between the workers' state and the world of imperialism pushes towards the surface. Recent events have been so eloquent that the hope of a "neutralisation" of the world bourgeoisie up to the completion of the socialist structure, has been abandoned by the present ruling faction; to a certain degree it has even been converted into its opposite.

The industrial successes attained during these peaceful years are an imperishable demonstration of the incomparable advantages of a planned economy. This fact in no wise contradicts the international character of the revolution: socialism could not be realised in the world arena, were not its elements and its points of support prepared in separate countries. It is no accident that the enemies of the theory of national socialism were the very protagonists of industrialisation, of the planning principle, the Five Year Plan, and collectivisation. Rakovsky, and with him thousands of other Bolsheviks, are paying for their fight for a bold industrial initiative with years of exile and prison. But they too, on the other hand, have been the first to rise against an over-estimation of the results attained, against national complacency. On the other hand, the mistrustful and short-sighted "practicals," who formerly thought that the proletariat of backward Russia could not conquer the power, and after the conquest of power denied the possibility of broad industrialisation and collectivisation, have taken subsequently exactly the opposite position. The successes attained against their own expectations, they have simply multiplied into a whole series of Five Year Plans, substituting the multiplication table for a historic perspective. That is the theory of socialism in a separate country.

In reality the growth of the present soviet economy remains an antagonistic process. In strengthening the workers' state, the economic successes are by no means leading automatically to the creation of a harmonious society. On the contrary, they are preparing a sharpening of the contradictions of an isolated socialist structure on a higher level. Rural Russia needs, as before, a mutual industrial plan with urban Europe. The world-wide division of labour stands over the dictatorship of the proletariat in a separate country, and imperatively dictates its further road. The October revolution did not exclude Russia from the development of the rest of humanity, but on the contrary bound her more closely to it. Russia is not a ghetto of barbarism, nor yet an Arcadia of socialism. It is the most transitional country in our transitional epoch. "The Russian revolution is only one link in the chain of international revolution." The present condition of world economy makes it possible to say without hesitation: Capitalism has come far closer to the proletarian revolution than the Soviet Union to socialism. The fate of the first workers' state is inseparably bound up with the fate of the liberating movement in the west and east. But this large theme demands independent investigation. We hope to return to it.

APPENDIX III

Historic References on the Theory of "Permanent Revolution"

In the Appendix to the first volume of this history we gave extended excerpts from a series of articles written by us in March 1917 in New York, and from our more recent polemic articles against Professor Pokrovsky. In both cases the matter concerned was an analysis of the moving forces of the Russian, and partly also of the international, revolution. It was upon the basis of this problem that the fundamental principled groupings had crystallized themselves in the Russian revolutionary camp ever since the beginning of the century. In proportion as the revolutionary tide rose, they acquired more and more the character of a strategic programme, and then finally a directly tactical character. The years 1903 to 1906 were a period of intensive crystallization of political tendencies in the Russian social democracy. It was at that time that our work, *Summaries and Perspectives* was written. It was written in sections and for different purposes. An imprisonment in December 1905 permitted the author to expound more systematically than before his views on the character of the Russian revolution and its prospects. This collected work appeared as a book in the Russian language in 1906. In order that the excerpts from it given below may take a proper place in the mind of the reader, we must remind him again that in 1904–5 no one of the Russian Marxists defended, or even uttered, the thought of the possibility of building a socialist society in a single country in general, and particularly in Russia. This conception was first expressed in print only twenty years later, in the autumn of 1924. In the period of the first revolution, as also in the years between the two revolutions, the dispute concerned the dynamics of the bourgeois revolution, and not the chances and possibilities of a socialist revolution. All the present partisans of the theory of socialism in one country, without a single exception, were during that period confining the prospects of the Russian revolution to a bourgeois-democratic republic, and until April 1917 they were considering impossible not only the building of national socialism, but also the conquest of power by the proletariat of Russia before the dictatorship of the proletariat should be inaugurated in more advanced countries.

By "Trotskyism," in the period from 1905 to 1917, was meant that revolutionary conception according to which the bourgeois revolution in Russia would not be able to solve its problems without placing the proletariat in power. Only in the autumn of 1924 did

"Trotskyism" begin to mean the conception according to which the Russian proletariat, having come to power, would not be able to build a national socialist society with its own forces alone.

For the convenience of the reader we shall present the dispute schematically in the form of a dialogue in which the letter T signifies a representative of the "Trotskyist" conception, and the letter S means one of those Russian "practicals" who now stands at the head of the soviet bureaucracy.

1905–1917

T. The Russian revolution cannot solve its democratic problem, above all the agrarian problem, without placing the working class in power.

S. But does not that mean the dictatorship of the proletariat?

T. Unquestionably.

S. In backward Russia? Before it happens in the advanced capitalist countries?

T. Exactly so.

S. But you are ignoring the Russian village—that is, the backward peasantry stuck in the mud of semi-serfdom.

T. On the contrary, it is only the depth of the agrarian problem that opens the immediate prospect of a dictatorship of the proletariat in Russia.

S. You reject, then, the bourgeois revolution?

T. No, I only try to show that its dynamic leads to the dictatorship of the proletariat.

S. But that means that Russia is ripe for the building of socialism?

T. No, it does not. Historic evolution has no such planned and harmonious character. The conquest of power by the proletariat in backward Russia flows inexorably from the correlation of forces in the bourgeois revolution. What further economic prospects will be opened by the dictatorship of the proletariat depends upon the domestic and world conditions under which it is inaugurated. It goes without saying that Russia cannot arrive at socialism independently. But once having opened an era of socialist transformation, she can supply the impetus to a socialist development of Europe and thus arrive at socialism in the wake of the advanced countries

1917–1923

S. We must acknowledge that Trotsky "even before the revolution of 1905 advanced the original and now especially famous theory of Permanent Revolution, asserting that the bourgeois revolution of 1905 would go directly over into a socialist revolution and prove the first of a series of national revolutions." (The quotation is from the notes to the *Complete Works of Lenin*, published during his life.)

S. And so you deny that our revolution can arrive at socialism?

T. I think, as before, that our revolution can and should lead to socialism after having acquired an international character.

S. You do not believe, then, in the inner forces of the Russian revolution?

T. Strange that this did not prevent me from foreseeing and preaching the dictatorship of the proletariat when you rejected it as Utopian!

S. But you none the less deny the socialist revolution in Russia?

T. Until April 1917 you accused me of rejecting the bourgeois revolution. The secret of your theoretical contradictions lies in the fact that you got way behind the historic process and now you are trying to catch up and pass it. To tell the truth, this also is the secret of your industrial mistakes.

The reader should have always before him these three historic stages in the development of revolutionary conceptions in Russia, if he wishes correctly to judge the actual issues in the present struggle of factions and groups in Russian communism.

Excerpts from the Article of the Year 1905, *"Summaries and Perspectives"*

SECTION 4. *Revolution and the Proletariat*

The proletariat will grow and strengthen together with the growth of capitalism. In this sense the development of capitalism is the development of the proletariat toward dictatorship. But the day and hour when the power will pass to the hands of the working class depend directly not upon the level obtained by the productive forces, but upon relations in the class struggle, upon the international situation, and finally upon a series of subjective factors—traditions, initiatives, preparedness for fighting. . . .

In a country economically more backward the proletariat may come to power sooner than in a country capitalistically advanced. . . .

The idea of some sort of automatic dependence of the proletarian dictatorship upon the technical forces and resources of a country is a prejudice derived from an extremely over-simplified "economic" materialism. Such a view has nothing in common with Marxism.

The Russian revolution, according to our view, will create conditions in which the power may (and with the victory of the revolution must) pass to the proletariat before the politicians of bourgeois liberalism get a chance to develop their statesmanly genius to the full.

Marxism is above all a method of analysis—not analysis of texts but analysis of social relations. Is it true in regard to Russia that the weakness of capitalistic liberalism necessarily means a weakness of the labour movement?

The numbers of the industrial proletariat, their concentration, their culture, their political weight, undoubtedly depend upon the degree of development of capitalist industry. But this dependence is not direct. Between the productive forces of the country and the political force of its classes at each given moment various socio-political factors of national and international character intervene, and they displace, and even completely change the form of, the political expression of economic relations. Notwithstanding that the productive forces of industry in the United States are ten times higher than ours, the political rôle of the Russian proletariat, its influence upon the policy of the country, and the possibility of its coming influence upon world politics, is incomparably higher than the rôle and significance of the American proletariat.

SECTION 5. *The Proletariat in Power and the Peasantry.*

In the event of a decisive victory of the revolution the power will come into the hands of that class which played the leading rôle in the struggle—in other words, into the hands of the proletariat. We add at once as self-evident that this does not exclude the entry into the government or revolutionary representatives of non-proletarian social groups. . . . The whole question is, who will supply the content of the government policy? Who will consolidate in the government a homogeneous majority? It is one thing when representatives of the democratic layers of the people participate in a government which is working-class in its majority. It is another thing when representatives of the proletariat participate, in the character of more or less respected hostages, in a definitely bourgeois-democratic government.

The proletariat cannot perpetuate its power without broadening the base of the revolution. Many strata of the toiling masses, especially in the country, will be first drawn into the revolution and acquire political organisation only after the vanguard of the revolution, the city proletariat, stands at the helm of state.

. . . The character of our socio-historic relations, which throws the whole weight of the bourgeois revolution upon the shoulders of the proletariat, will not only create enormous difficulties for the workers' government, but will also, at least in the first period of its existence, give it priceless advantages. This will express itself in the relations between the proletariat and the peasantry.

The Russian revolution does not permit, and for a long time will not permit, the creation of any sort of bourgeois-constitutional order which might solve the most elementary problems of democracy. . . . In consequence of this the fate of the most elementary revolutionary interests of the peasantry—even of the entire peasantry as a caste—is bound up with the fate of the whole revolution—that is, with the fate of the proletariat. The proletariat in power will appear to the peasantry as an emancipator class.

But perhaps the peasantry itself will crowd out the proletariat and occupy its place? That is impossible. All the experience of history protests against this assumption. It shows that the peasantry is completely incapable of playing an *independent* political rôle.

The Russian bourgeoisie will surrender all revolutionary positions to the proletariat. It will have to surrender also the revolutionary leadership of the peasantry. In the situation which will be created by a transfer of power to the proletariat the peasantry will have nothing left to do but adhere to the régime of workers' democracy. Granted even that they will do this with no more consciousness than they have in adhering to the bourgeois régime! But whereas every bourgeois party after winning the votes of the peasants makes haste to use its power in order to rob them and deceive them of all their hopes and faith in promises, and then when worst comes to worst yields its place to another capitalist party, the proletariat, relying upon the peasantry, will bring all its forces into play to raise the cultural level of the village and develop in the peasantry a political consciousness.

SECTION 6. *The Proletarian Régime.*

The proletariat can come to power only while relying upon a national awakening, upon a universal popular inspiration. The proletariat will enter the government as a revolutionary representative of the nation, as the recognised leader of the people in their struggle with absolutism and feudal barbarism. But having come to power, the proletariat will open a new epoch—an epoch of revolutionary legislation, of affirmative politics—and here the preservation of its rôle as recognised spokesman of the nation is by no means guaranteed.

Each day will deepen the policy of the proletariat in power, and more and more define its class character. And therewith the revollutionary bond between the proletariat and the nation will be broken. The class dismemberment of the peasantry will appear in political form. The antagonism between its constituent parts will increase in the same degree that the policy of the workers' government defines itself and from being a general democratic policy becomes a class policy.

The destruction of feudal serfdom will have the support of the entire peasantry as a burdened caste. . . . But legislative measures in defence of the agricultural proletariat not only will win no such active sympathy from the majority, but will come up against the active resistance of the minority. The proletariat will find itself obliged to carry the class struggle into the country, and thus destroy that community of interests which is undoubtedly to be found in every peasantry, although within comparatively narrow limits. The proletariat will be obliged, in the very earliest moments of its rule, to seek support in opposing the rural poor to the rural rich, the agricultural proletariat to the peasant bourgeoisie.

Once the power is in the hands of a revolutionary government with a socialist majority, at that moment the difference between minimum and maximum programme loses both its significance in principle and its directly practical significance. A proletarian government cannot possibly restrain itself within the limits of this distinction.

Entering the government not as impotent hostages but as a ruling power, the representatives of the proletariat will by this very act destroy the boundary between minimum and maximum programme. That is, they will place collectivism on the order of the day. At what point the proletariat will be stopped in this direction depends upon the correlation of forces, but not at all upon the original intentions of the party of the proletariat.

That is why there can be no talk of any special form of proletarian dictatorship in a bourgeois revolution, namely a democratic dictatorship of the proletariat (or of the proletariat and the peasantry). The working class cannot guarantee the democratic character of its dictatorship without transgressing the limits of its democratic programme. Any illusions on this point would be absolutely ruinous.

Once the party of the proletariat takes the power, it will fight for it to the end. While one means of waging this struggle for the preservation and perpetuation of its power will be agitation and organisation, especially in the country, another means will be a collectivist policy. Collectivism will become not only an inevitable inference from the position of the party in power, but also a means of preserving its position while relying upon the proletariat.

* * *

When the idea was formulated in the socialist press of an uninterrupted revolution, linking up the liquidation of absolutism and of civil serfdom with a socialist revolution, thanks to multiplying social clashes, uprisings of new layers of the masses, unceasing attacks of the proletariat upon the political and economic privileges of the ruling classes, our "progressive" press raised a unanimous howl of indignation.

The more radical representatives of that same democracy . . . not only considered fantastic the very idea of a workers' government in Russia, but also denied the possibility of a socialist revolution in Europe in the coming historic epoch. The necessary "premises" are not yet at hand. Is this true? It is not, of course, a question of setting the date of a socialist revolution, but of giving it a place in the actual historic perspective. . . .

(Here follows an analysis of the general premises of a socialist economy and the proof that at the present time—the beginning of the 20th century—these premises, if you take the question on a European and world scale, are already at hand.)

. . . Within the closed boundaries of separate states a socialist production could not in any case be introduced—both for economic and political reasons.

SECTION 8. *A Workers' Government in Russia and Socialism.*

We have shown above that the objective premises of a socialist revolution have already been created by the economic development of the advanced capitalist countries. But what can be said in this respect about Russia? Can we expect that the transfer of power to the Russian proletariat will be the beginning of a transformation of our national economy upon socialist principles?

The Parisian workers, as Marx said, did not demand miracles of the Commune. Now, too, you cannot expect instantaneous miracles of the dictatorship of the proletariat. The state power is not omnipotent. It would be absurd to imagine that the proletariat has only to receive the power and it will replace capitalism by socialism with a few decrees. An economic structure is not a product of the activity of the state. The proletariat can only employ the state power with all its might in order to promote economic evolution in the direction of collectivism, and shorten its road.

The socialisation of production begins in those branches which offer the least difficulties. During the first period socialised production will take the form of oases united with private industrial enerprises by the laws of commodity circulation. The broader the field already seized by socialised industry the more obvious will be its advantages, the solider will the new political régime feel, and the more bold will be the further industrial undertakings of the proletariat. In these undertakings the proletariat will be able to, and will, rely not only upon the national productive forces, but also upon international technique, just as in its revolutionary politics it will rely not only upon the experience of national class relations, but also upon the whole historic experience of the international proletariat.

The proletarian régime will be compelled from the very first to undertake the solution of the agrarian problem, with which is bound up the fate of the immense mass of the population of Russia. In solving this problem, as in solving all others, the proletariat will take as its point of departure the fundamental effort of its economic policy: to conquer as large a field as possible for the organisation of socialist industry. And the forms and tempo of this policy in the agrarian problem will have to be determined both by those material resources in the command of the proletariat, and by the necessity of so deploying its activities as not to push possible allies into the ranks of the counter-revolution.

But how far can the socialist policy of the working class go in the industrial conditions of Russia? Only one thing can be said with certainty. It will run into political obstacles long before it comes up against the technical backwardness of the country. Without direct state support from the European proletariat the working class of Russia cannot remain in power and cannot convert its temporary rule into a prolonged socialist dictatorship. . . .

Political "optimism" may take two forms. It may exaggerate its own forces and the advantageous aspects of the revolutionary situation, and set itself tasks whose solution is not permitted by the given correlation of forces. But it may, on the other hand, optimistically set a bound to its revolutionary tasks beyond which the logic of the situation will inevitably push us.

We may set a bound to all the problems of the revolution by asserting that our revolution is bourgeois in its objective aims, and therefore in its inevitable result, and we may thus shut our eyes to the fact that the chief agent of this bourgeois revolution will be the proletariat, and the proletariat will be pushed toward the power by the whole course of the revolution. . . .

You may lull yourself with the thought that the social conditions of Russia are not yet ripe for a socialist economy, and therewith you may neglect to consider the fact that the proletariat, once in power, will inevitably be compelled by the whole logic of its situation to introduce an economy operated by the state.

The general sociological definition, "bourgeois revolution," does not by any means solve those politico-tactical problems, contradictions and difficulties which will be put forward by the mechanics of the given bourgeois revolution.

Within the framework of the bourgeois revolution at the end of the 18th century, whose objective task was to establish the rule of capital, a dictatorship of the Sansculottes proved possible. In a revolution at the beginning of the 20th century, which is also bourgeois in its immediate objective tasks, there appears in the near perspective the inevitability, or at the very least the probability, of a political rulership of the proletariat. That this rulership shall not prove a mere passing "episode," as certain realistic philistines hope—the proletariat itself will see to this. But it is not too early now to pose the question: Must this dictatorship of the proletariat inevitably be shattered against the boundaries of the bourgeois revolution? May it not, upon the given world-historic foundations, open before itself the prospect of a victory to be achieved after shattering these limited boundaries?

(Here follows a development of the thought that the Russian revolution may, and in all probability will, unleash a proletarian revolution in the west, which in its turn will guarantee the socialist development of Russia.)

* * *

It should be added that during the first years of the existence of the Communist International the above-quoted work was officially published in foreign languages as a theoretic interpretation of the October revolution.

INDEX

D

E

F

G

H

I

J

K

L

M

N

O

P

T

U

V

W

Y

Z